THE CHALLENGE OF ENDING RURAL POVERTY

Published for **IFAD** by

OXFORD
UNIVERSITY PRESS

OXFORD
UNIVERSITY PRESS

Great Clarendon Street, Oxford OX2 6DP

Oxford New York
Athens Auckland Bangkok Bogotá Buenos Aires Calcutta
Cape Town Chennai Dar es Salaam Delhi Florence Hong Kong Istanbul
Karachi Kuala Lumpur Madrid Melbourne Mexico City Mumbai
Nairobi Paris São Paulo Shangai Singapore Taipei Tokyo Toronto Warsaw
with associated companies in Berlin Ibadan

Oxford is a registered trade mark of Oxford University Press
in the UK and in certain other countries

Published in the United States
By Oxford University Press Inc., New York

Photographs IFAD: Giuseppe Bizzarri, viii; Robert Grossman, xii; Christine Nesbitt, xviii;
Louis Dematteis, 14; Giuseppe Bizzarri, 70; Alberto Conti, 126; Fiona McDougall, 160;
Bruno Carotenuto, 190; Radhika Chalasani, 228.

British Library Cataloguing in Publication Data
Data available

Library of Congress Cataloging in Publication Data
Data available

ISBN 0-19-924507-X

Typeset by the International Fund for Agricultural Development
Printed in Great Britain
on acid-free paper by Bath Press Ltd., Bath, Avon

FOREWORD

Poverty and chronic deprivation have long been a tragic aspect of human society. In the past this was often accepted with a sense of resignation, a sense of fatality that the poor will always be with us. Indeed poverty often served the interests of dominant social groups by assuring low-cost agriculture labourers and workers for off-farm activities as well as domestic service, to say nothing of supplying an inexhaustible and expendable source of recruits for warfare.

Compassion drove some to offer charity to the poor, particularly through religious institutions. But this was rarely enough to prevent deprivation punctuated by sharp famines.

Today perspectives on poverty have been transformed. The sheer scale of mass poverty – over 1200 million absolutely poor human beings condemned to short lives stunted by malnutrition, ill health and illiteracy – is no longer acceptable from either a moral or a realpolitik standpoint.

This new understanding is incorporated in the declaration made by world leaders at the Millennium Summit, in which for the first time in history, human society committed itself to reducing substantially – by half – the numbers in absolute poverty within a short period of time, by 2015.

I do not believe that the new consensus is merely a matter of rhetoric. In modern economies, large-scale poverty imposes an enormous economic loss, wasting the talents and energies of hundreds of millions of men and women, diverted from socially productive activities that could create wealth for society to the struggle for mere survival. Even worse, in a world of interconnection and mobility, poverty poses a growing threat to social stability and civil order and acts as a reservoir for communicable diseases and a trigger for crime and strife. Nobody, rich or poor, can remain immune from the consequences.

Moreover, with the spread of participative governance and democracy, the fate of a substantial proportion of the population who are poor, in some cases the majority, cannot be ignored by society as a whole. The poor have to be recognized as individuals with rights and as potential agents of change who can themselves play an increasing role in determining social and economic outcomes. It is not a coincidence, as Nobel Laureate A. K. Sen has emphasized, that famines occur in dictatorships, not in democracies. The latter simply cannot allow mass starvation and are under growing pressure to respond to mass poverty.

Mass poverty hurts not only the poor but claims everyone as its victim. Its continuation is in no one's interest.

Today, this recognition underpins the will and commitment to end poverty, within nations and across them, reinforced by a growing understanding that poverty is neither natural nor inevitable. The experience of the last 30 years, for example in East Asia, shows what can be done. But there remains considerable uncertainty about what are the best, most effective and rapid ways to end poverty and hunger, particularly in rural areas where the bulk of the poor live.

It is this theme that the Rural Poverty Report 2001 addresses.

The starting point is that poor groups should not be seen, as all too often they are, merely as a burden on society. Rather, the poor, especially women, are hard working and often effective microentrepreneurs, whether as smallholder farmers, herders, artisanal fishermen or in petty trades and crafts. If the conditions could be created for these small producers to become more effective in production and trade, poor groups could contribute significantly to achieving a higher and more sustainable pace of development, promoting not only economic growth but social cohesion. The empowerment of the poor is what many call this.

But such conditions will not come about easily or quickly. The legacy of history and the long marginalization of poor groups in terms of the distribution of land and other assets, in terms of institutions and of centuries of inequity in access to education, nutrition and health, create too great an obstacle.

These obstacles must be addressed and overcome if the challenging targets on poverty reduction are to be achieved. Acting directly on poverty means addressing the constraints that trap large numbers in poverty where they are, and in terms of how they earn their livelihood.

Some three quarters of the poor live in rural areas. According to projections, a majority of the poor will continue to be in rural areas well into the 21st century.

The rural poor depend primarily on agriculture and related activities for their livelihood. It would seem natural that to have a substantial effect on poverty, domestic investment and external assistance alike should focus on the rural areas where the poor live and on agriculture, the basis of their

survival. But the poor and the rural rarely have the same voice in decision-making as the better-off and the urban. Thus the proportion of official development assistance going to agriculture has fallen from about 20% in the late 1980s to about 12% today. Assistance to agriculture from international financial institutions has followed a similar path.

The declining support for agriculture is extremely damaging to efforts to reduce poverty and hunger. Food staples, cereals like wheat, rice, maize, sorghum and millet, and roots and tubers like yam and cassava are central in the rural poor's food economy and struggle for survival. Food staples provide the bulk of the output and income of the rural poor and are their main source of calorie intake. The urban poor also spend much of their incomes on purchasing food staples.

Thus, what happens to the output and yield of food staples has a large impact on poverty trends. During the 1970s and most of the 1980s, for example, food staple yields rose sharply and poverty declined rapidly. In the 1990s, on the other hand, food staple yield growth slowed down substantially, as did the rate of poverty decline. This failure to maintain the rate of growth of crop yields over the last decade is due to many causes. But certainly a major cause is the erosion of funding, for example for agricultural research, internationally at the level of the CGIAR institutions and domestically for research and extension services.

This neglect of agriculture, in terms of both international development cooperation and domestic resource allocation, must be redressed if we hope to achieve the challenging poverty targets of the Millennium Summit.

There are those who argue that what is required for poverty eradication is economic growth and that any effort to promote empowerment of the poor merely diverts energies and weakens the effort to accelerate growth. Certainly growth of production is vital. But for poverty reduction it is equally important to ask, growth in whose hands? Increases in production by commercial farmers in well-watered areas, or indeed in urban manufacturing, are certainly welcome from the point of view of national income, food availability at the national level, and exports. But such increases may do little to reduce food insecurity and poverty for the millions of smallholder farmers and herders living in resource-poor areas. A rise in production in their hands will have a significantly larger impact on poverty than a comparable increase in the incomes of better-off groups. Growth, in the current idiom, needs to be 'pro-poor'!

Moreover in many poor countries, especially in sub-Saharan Africa, up to one half of the total population live below the poverty line. In these circumstances sustained growth can be achieved only by creating conditions in which poor groups, largely poor farmers, herders and so on, can increase their productivity and output. Empowering these poor groups is not a diversion from promoting growth. On the contrary, it is an effective, and perhaps the only, way of achieving sustainable growth.

Empowerment essentially means reversing the historical legacy of marginalization that traps large numbers in chronic poverty. Key elements of this include access to economic services as well as primary health and education, and the possibility of the poor organizing themselves, especially at local community level to project their views and interests and to gain a larger voice in decision-making on local resource allocation. The empowerment of the poor and their participation in local governance would also make more accountable the use of public resources that are spent in their name but often go astray for well-known reasons. Perhaps, rather than empowerment, we might say the emancipation of poor groups from the historic constraints that bind them in poverty. 'Man is born free, and everywhere he is in chains', said a French philosopher. Our task is to help the poor remove those chains.

If empowerment is crucial for the poor, it is doubly so for poor women. Even compared to their male counterparts, poor women have significantly lower access to education and health or to economic services like credit and extension. They have often been denied the right to hold title to land and have even less voice in community decision-making. Women in many countries produce a large part of food crops and undertake most food processing and preparation in addition to their family tasks. They are the real architects of household food security and yet they suffer disproportionately from poverty and hunger. Ending hunger and poverty must begin with enhancing women's access to social and economic services and decision-making.

But empowerment will serve little purpose if the material means for increasing production and incomes are not available to the poor. The Report looks at four central factors – assets, technology, markets and institutions – and examines policies and strategies that could strengthen the position of the poor.

In terms of assets, land and water rights are obviously the most critical for the rural poor and historically among the most difficult to change. Yet in recent years new approaches have been forged for agrarian reform using collaborative, sometimes market-based, approaches that often also involve NGOs. These need to be pursued. Access to water in the coming years will be even more problematic. Indeed competition for water is already emerging as a source of tension between groups, even between nations. Greater resources and new technologies have to be mobilized, together with the direct involvement of poor farmers, to bring about more equitable and sustainable solutions to the complex issues of water use and water stress.

Human capital, and the capacity to work, are among the most important assets the poor possess. Unfortunately, past deprivation has often left them inadequately equipped in the skills required to deal with modern technologies and markets. Enhancing these skills and building the human capital of the poor is particularly important, as it would have a major impact on both their economic productivity and their human dignity, yet without affecting the assets of others, as might reforms in land and water rights.

By improving the productivity and sustainable management of land and water, technological advances offer the potential to address many of the obstacles that the lack of assets imposes on the poor. But there are two critical requirements for this. The technology must be relevant to the conditions of the poor and they must have access to it. At present neither is true in important respects.

Smallholder farmers in many parts of the world reach productivity levels that are only about one third of the potential yield under optimum conditions. Weak extension services that do not reach poor farmers, lack of competitive markets and suppliers for seeds, fertilizers and rural financial services, as well as weak output markets, limit both the possibilities of the poor in accessing better technology and their incentives for doing so. These conditions have been aggravated by the withdrawal of state-provided services, for instance for extension, under liberalization and adjustment programmes. In our own experience at IFAD, we have found that by building responsive extension services, sometimes in collaboration with the private sector and NGOs, financial services and input sources, quite remarkable increases in production and income can be achieved by poor farmers. Maize farmers in Tanzania, for example, doubled their yield by adopting better methods, seeds and fertilizers.

At the same time, the overall technological production frontier needs to be raised. Crops – and animals – which are more productive as well as pest- and drought-resistant, together with more effective land/water management methods, would transform the situation facing millions of smallholder farmers.

In this context, advances in biotechnology are extremely promising. Unfortunately, current biotechnology research, as indeed pharmaceutical research, focuses on the crops and products relevant for the better-off, especially for large farmers in temperate zones who have the purchasing power to offer profitable markets. Poor farmers in poor countries rarely offer adequate market incentives to the agribusinesses that dominate biotechnology research. And so the research tends to bypass the needs of the poor, whether for crops and animals or for medicines for diseases of the poor. Public/private partnerships combined with tax and other incentives need to be developed to change this.

Markets now play an increasing role in the livelihood systems of the poor. As countries adopt policy approaches based on market forces, as government marketing and commodity boards are abolished, and as the rules on domestic agricultural trade are made more liberal, poor farmers are more fully exposed to the demands of markets and vulnerable to their volatility.

Very often rural producers have to sell cheaply during the glut that follows harvest and buy at higher prices in the lean season, thus losing both ways. Yet, if rural producers were able to organize themselves, gain access to up-to-date market information and better rural roads to help reduce transaction costs, the market would become a powerful ally in the effort to end poverty. As the discussion in this Report shows, a number of promising initiatives have been taken by IFAD and others in order to do precisely this. Much remains to be done but the way ahead is clear.

Institutions bring us back to the relationship of society to the poor. Institutions, meaning both organizations and rules, intermediate between the competing demands of different social groups. Inevitably those who control institutions, usually the better-off, gain most in this process. Here again the issue is how to enable the poor to exercise a stronger role in both official and non-official institutions that affect their lives, especially at the local level. Progress in decentralization and devolution of authority to local institutions can sometimes be useful but only if poor groups are sufficiently organized to be able to take part effectively in such institutions.

New institutional approaches in developing financial systems for the rural poor, ranging from microfinance and village banks to reformed agricultural development banks and commercial banks, offer a wide and potentially exciting range of instruments that could open the door to saving, credit and insurance services to poor groups. Perhaps surprisingly, safe and locally accessible saving services are often considered by poor groups living in vulnerable conditions to be as valuable as credit facilities.

But decentralization and finance are just two examples of institutions relevant to the poor. Many others, including national and regional ones, also affect their lives in important ways. A wider transformation is required for the institutional framework to lead to a fairer distribution of the opportunities and benefits of economic growth. Here, NGOs and civil-society organizations could play a vital role. So far, however, only small halting steps have been taken.

The poor have long been with us. To end absolute poverty will require sustained efforts at various levels and strong partnerships among those working for this goal. The partnerships can be at the global level, as shown by the Millennium Summit Declaration, at the country level with national stakeholders and external partners acting together, and internally, with official agencies, the private sector and civil-society institutions collaborating to create conditions that emancipate poor groups from the legacy of the past and allow them to work their way out of poverty.

But the fundamental partnership, and ultimately the only one that counts, is with the poor themselves. They have the talents, the skills and the knowledge of their own environment. Moreover, the poor, especially women, have repeatedly shown the will and the capacity to grasp opportunities to better their lives and make their families and themselves less vulnerable.

Outsiders do not have to solve the problem of poverty. They only have to help remove the shackles that in the past have bound large numbers of their fellow human beings.

The Millennium Summit launched human society towards a noble and historic goal. I hope, and believe, that this Rural Poverty Report 2001 will make a significant contribution to this process, a process that will be of lasting importance to all of us in the coming decades.

Fawzi H. Al-Sultan
President of IFAD

Acknowledgements

ORGANIZATION AND MANAGEMENT

The Report has been prepared under the leadership and guidance of John Westley, Vice President of IFAD.

Preparation of the Report was managed and coordinated by Atiqur Rahman, Lead Strategist and Policy Coordinator, IFAD. He was supported by Guido Geissler, and earlier by Pietro Turilli.

The preparation of the Report was overseen by a Steering Committee consisting of Mona Bishay, Eve Crowley, Sappho Haralambous, Gary Howe, Luciano Lavizzari, Jean-Louis Lawson, Bruce Moore, Atiqur Rahman (Coordinator), Takao Shibata, Klemens van de Sand and John Westley (Chair).

PREPARATION AND FINALIZATION OF THE REPORT

The intellectual leadership in preparing the Report was provided by Michael Lipton of the Poverty Research Unit at the University of Sussex (PRUS), England.

At PRUS, Saurabh Sinha managed the work on the Report, which was written by Michael Lipton, Saurabh Sinha and Julie Litchfield. Major contributions to chapters were made by Rachel Blackman. Research assistance at different stages was provided by Joanna Church, Xavier Cirera, Reetika Khera, Jennifer Leavy, Loraine Ronchi, Kitty Stewart, Isabel Vogel and Shahin Yaqub. Data management and administrative support was provided by Rachael Straub.

Finalization of the report

The Report was finalized at IFAD through consultation between the PRUS Team, consisting of Michael Lipton and Saurabh Sinha, and an IFAD Team consisting of Uday Abhyankar, Rodney Cooke, Eve Crowley, Edward Heinamann, Gary Howe, Bruce Moore, Atiqur Rahman, Hans Dieter Seibel, Ganesh Thapa, Phrang Roy, John Westley and Doug Wholey.

Comments, reviews and inputs

Earlier drafts of the Report were reviewed both within and outside IFAD. Comments, written inputs and suggestions were provided by Uday Abhyankar, Kamaluddin Akbar, Perín Saint Ange, Ingrid Bellander, Julio A. Berdegué, Mona Bishay, Rodney Cooke, Eve Crowley, Ralph Cummings, Dana Dalrymple, Alain de Janvry, Per Eklund, Raghav Gaiha, Guido Geissler, Mohammed Hassani, Sappho Haralambous, Edward Heinemann, Gary Howe, Sean Kennedy, Aziz Khan, David Kingsbury, Luciano Lavizzari, Shantanu Mathur, John Mellor, Mike Mispelaar, Bruce Moore, Chase Palmeri, Jakob Pedersen, Raquel Peña-Montenegro, Atiqur Rahman, Thomas Rath, Phrang Roy, Nikolaus Schultze, Hans Dieter Seibel, Ahmed Sidahmed, Cristiana Sparacino, Ganesh Thapa, Phillipe Trappe, Richard Trenchard, Klemens van de Sand, John Westley, Vera Weill-Hallé, Doug Wholey and Joseph Yayock.

BACKGROUND PAPERS

Preparation of the conceptual and the issues paper: Conceptual and background papers were prepared by Ole Hansen, Patricia Parera, Siddiqur Osmani, Atiqur Rahman and Pietro Turilli. An issues paper was prepared by Michael Lipton and Saurabh Sinha for the Brainstorming Workshop held in October 1998 to define the scope of the Report. Comments on these papers were provided by Solon Baraclough, Vigdis Bröch Due, Jacques Chonchol and Oliver Saasa.

Background papers on various themes: Lawrence Haddad, Peter Hazell, John Hoddinott, Pamela Jagger, Anthony Killick, Anna Knox, Jonathan Kydd, Sanjukta Mukherjee, Siddiqur Osmani and Colin Poulton prepared background papers on the selected themes. Rudo M. Chitiga, Christina Liamzon, Bolaji Ogunseye, Lavinia D. R. Pessanha and Nader Izzat Said provided inputs from the perspective of civil-society organizations.
Within IFAD, Mona Bishay, Eve Crowley, Nikolaus Schultze and Douglas Wholey coordinated and contributed to the internal reviews of the report's background thematic papers.

Regional assessments:

Asia and the Pacific region: Pranab Bardhan, Raghav Gaiha, Jikun Huang, Govind Koirala, Gregg Morgan, K. Imai, Keijiro Otsuka, Rushidan Rahman, Phrang Roy, Bishan Singh and Ganesh Thapa.

Eastern and Southern Africa region: Marian Bradley, Daniela Capitani, Alice Carloni, Chris Cramer, Malcom Hall, Gary Howe, Jan Sligenbergh and Daphne Topuuzis.

Western and Central Africa region: Elisabetta Basile, David Kingsbury, Jaap Reijmerink, Cristiana Sparacino and Eric Tollens.

Latin America and the Caribbean region: Pilar Campaña, María Elena Cruz, Pablo Glikman, Roberto Haudry de Soucy, Alberto Hintermeister, Aníbal Monares, Raul Moreno, Raquel Peña-Montenegro, Benjamín Quijandría, Pietro Simoni, María Sisto and Carlos Trabucco.

Near East and North Africa region: Mouna Hashem, Chase Palmeri, Pietro Turilli and El Sayed Ali Ahmed Zaki.

SUPPORT

Facilitation at workshops: Peter Keller.

Editing and proof-reading: Editing by Hilary Hodgson and Michael James. Proof-reading by Tatiana Strelkoff.

Publication: María Elisa Pinzón, supported by Susan Beccio, Enza Falco, Silvia Persi, Birgit Plöckinger, David Paqui and Marie Slater.

Legal: Christian Codrai.

Secretarial and administrative: Evelyn Balde, Antonella Cordone, Jessica Lattughi and Carol Portegies.

TABLE OF CONTENTS

List of tables

Annex

List of boxes

CHAPTER 6: INSTITUTIONS AND THE RURAL POOR:

CHAPTER I
INTRODUCTION AND OVERVIEW

This Report examines the constraints faced by the extremely poor – some 1.2 billion of them – and the opportunities they have to escape from poverty in the near future.
The focus is on the rural poor, who constitute the bulk of the poor. The Report examines the potential of smallholder production and water conservation in agriculture, of existing and recent technologies, and the roles of small producers, markets and institutions in providing opportunities to the poor. It builds on the argument that, with appropriate and focused support for enhancing the productive potential of the poor in a pro-poor environment, the poor can help themselves to escape from poverty. Growth and distribution are essential for poverty reduction. But sustained poverty reduction also requires pro-poor institutions and the building of partnerships between the rural poor and other stakeholders.

Globally, 1.2 billion people are in 'extreme consumption poverty'. More than two thirds of them are in Asia; South Asia alone accounts for nearly half of them. About one fourth is in sub-Saharan Africa. Three quarters of the poor work and live in rural areas; significantly more than a half are expected to do so in 2025.

The 1995 Social Summit in Copenhagen agreed that each member should devise a programme to reduce extreme poverty, monitor and measure progress against some agreed targets and adjust policy accordingly. Subsequently, the member states in the twenty fourth special session of the General Assembly of the United Nations in June 2000 committed themselves to halve extreme poverty by 2015. This put each developing country in the 'driver's seat'. In 1996 the aid donors agreed in the Organisation of Economic Co-operation and Development (OECD) to restructure aid to sup-

port monitored progress towards poverty-reduction targets. The World Bank, the United Nations Development Programme, the Development Assistance Committee (DAC) of the OECD have all placed emphasis on taking concerted action and reducing poverty at an accelerated rate to achieve the global target of halving poverty by 2015.

Progress with poverty reduction in the last decade has been slow. The rate of poverty reduction in 1990-98 was less than one third of what is needed to halve extreme poverty during 1990-2015. It was six times less in sub-Saharan Africa. The real value of aid fell sharply between 1987-88 and 1997-98. The share of aid going to low-income or least-developed countries, which contain over 85% of the poor, stayed around 63%, and agricultural aid collapsed. The rural sector has largely remained neglected, despite its great concentration of poor people.

POVERTY AND ITS RURAL DIMENSION

The ill-being caused by poverty has many dimensions. Low consumption is only one such dimension, but it is linked to others: malnutrition, illiteracy, low life expectancy, insecurity, powerlessness and low self-esteem. Poverty is also linked to frustrated capabilities due to asset deprivation, inability to afford decent health and education and lack of power.

Poverty can co-exist with rather high levels of income, widespread infrastructure development, technological achievements and urbanization – in Latin America, the United States, and South Africa, for example. The institutional environment in which the poor derive their livelihoods, and the socio-political factors that restrict their access to resources, can influence the relationship between economic growth and the level and the extent of poverty.

Countries use different, often non-comparable, national consumption poverty lines and rural-urban borderlines. There are serious measurement problems of poverty, which has to be linked to other non-consumption-based indicators and to self-assessment to allow comparisons.

However we treat such measurement problems, the proportion of the poor making their living in rural areas has remained, and is expected to remain, strikingly high. And over half the world's extreme poor depend for their livelihoods mainly on farming or farm labour. The rural poor's welfare, of course, depends on many aspects of public action other than direct investment in support of agriculture – on schools, clinics and civil order – and on private as well as public action. Nevertheless, poverty reduction does depend, in part, on an adequate share of agricultural investment support within the portions of public spending and international aid that can be allocated among economic sectors.

Yet the absolute value of aid to agriculture fell by two thirds in 1987-98, and its share in aid that can be allocated to particular sectors halved. In key low-income countries where the poor are concentrated, agriculture's share in sectorally allocable investment, and aid, is far less than in Gross Domestic Product (GDP), let alone employment. Moreover, though price biases against agriculture have shrunk since 1980 (with ambiguous effects on the rural poor as food prices rise alongside job prospects), the slighting of agriculture and the rural sector in public investment and aid spending has increased.

Effective poverty reduction therefore requires resources to be reallocated to the rural and the

---

Box 1.1: Why focus on rural poverty?

Big rural-urban gaps in income, poverty, nutrition, health and education are not shrinking; through 2020 most of the dollar-poor will be rural.

Though rural poverty fell sharply in 1970-85, the decline has slowed; it bypassed countries, ethnic and other groups, and whole regions and agro-ecologies.

Addressing rural poverty raises food supply and may reduce migration, thus helping reduce urban poverty. Also, successful rural poverty reduction usually works by raising the productivity of the poor; but most treatments of urban poverty are welfare-oriented, often depending mainly on upgraded housing.

Poverty reduction and asset equalization, especially in rural areas, assist growth.

Ongoing big rises in worker/child ratios provide a 'window of opportunity' for poverty reduction. To that end, the rural poor need to share much more in female empowerment, and better health and education that permit fertility decline, and in research, investment and employment for the working poor.

Yet aid, even more than public investment, goes disproportionately to countries – and increasingly to non-rural sectors – where most of the poor do not live or work.

poor. But a focus on rural poverty reduction need not imply a neglect of economic growth; indeed, it can speed up economic growth (Box 1.1). It is inefficient to exclude people from schooling or managing productive assets because they are too poor to borrow; or because they are born in villages and hence lack urban facilities; or because they suffer from other forms of exclusion – upland, dryland or remote residence. Yet the rural poor suffer an inefficiently low share of schools, health care, roads, land, technology, research, and institutional and market access.

RURAL POVERTY REDUCTION:
THE CONCEPTUAL FRAMEWORK

Poverty is multidimensional; therefore, poverty reduction efforts have to be multi-targeted and are expected to show wide and diverse dimensions. The solutions have to straddle different disciplines and must encompass economic, social, political and institutional factors.

Notwithstanding such diversity, four aspects are of critical importance for understanding the challenges facing rural poverty reduction.

First, institutions, markets, technology policy and asset arrangements need to reflect the critical role of food staples in the livelihoods of the rural poor. Most rural households build up livelihoods from several sources; and some very poor rural areas grow no food staples. Yet staples provide most of the poorest with most work, income, consumption and calories. Those in extreme poverty usually get 70-80% of calories from staples, which also absorb most of their working time. While a rising proportion of the rural poor rely for income mainly on livestock, cash crops or non-farm activity, in early development staples farming or employment provides most of their income.

This is not to deny the importance of the growth of the non-staples sector for rural poverty reduction, nor to indicate only a subsistence path of development. The non-staples sector (production of cash crops and other food crops, and small-scale non-farm production) is important and will become increasingly so. In fact, widening market access and liberalization increasingly allow rural people to escape poverty through non-staples production and exchange. In this process non-farm assets and skills are critical, as are infrastructure and institutions to help small units to maintain market access during globalization.

Second, rural poverty reduction increasingly requires better allocation and distribution of water. The tightening squeeze on rural water supply demands both priority for the poor and more efficient water use. Rice and horticulture create much employment income for the poor, but are heavy users of water. Many drylands already suffer from severe water stress. Groundwater tables are falling, and surface water may become scarcer due to climate change. There is also heavy pressure to divert water to urban areas and industrial uses. Securing the more efficient water use needed to increase staples output will be difficult. Increasing the availability, quality and efficiency of farm water for the rural poor is a major challenge.

Third, feasible growth alone, even in the rural sector, will in many countries not suffice to halve dollar poverty by 2015. In some very poor countries, too many people are too deeply poor. In some middle-income countries, initial inequality is too great. In such cases, achieving the poverty target requires redistributive empowerment of the rural poor through higher shares, access and control of appropriate assets, institutions, technologies and markets. Usually that is good for growth, as well as equitable.

Fourth, particular groups – especially women – and methods – especially participatory and decentralized ones – merit special attention. Redressing disadvantage for women, ethnic minorities, hill people and semi-arid residents helps the efficient use of anti-poverty resources – schools, land, water – as well as fairness. Women especially need direct influence over resources and policies. Participatory and decentralized management, apart from securing democratic control and developing human potential, often improves the cost-effectiveness of a range of actions, from developing new seed varieties through microfinance to rural schools and public works programmes. Special measures are needed to enable the poor to participate.

Creating productive employment opportunities for the rural poor

Underlying all four themes is the fact that rural poverty reduction generally benefits from labour-intensive approaches. Labour-intensive development economizes on capital and/or land. Capital is always scarce in low-income countries, and land is scarce in more and more of them. Developing countries, with high ratios of labour to capital, also gain more from market liberalization if they encourage labour-intensive production lines – as is induced by world-market incentives. Employment-intensive policies, technologies and institutions usually help both economic growth and poverty reduction, since it is the poor who have mainly labour to supply. Thus, subsidies to labour-displacing tractors cannot normally be justified. Smaller farms and rural production tend to use more labour and less equipment than larger units.

The primacy of agriculture in development

As people become better off, their demand for food, as a proportion of income, falls, as reflected in the steady fall in the relative world price of farm products. Might this impede feasible agricultural expansion, and thus justify low public investment and aid for agriculture?

In early development, while mass poverty exists, poor and underfed smallholders (and their even poorer employees) use much of their extra income to obtain and consume their own and their neighbours' extra farm produce – provided public investment and aid supports increased food pro-

duction by the poor. Then, there is much less of a demand problem. What remains can be overcome, if, as in the Green Revolution, technical progress in seeds, infrastructure and water management on small private farms raises productivity faster than prices fall , leaving farmers, farm workers and food buyers all less poor.

In later development, extra public investment can underpin the infrastructures needed for small-scale and labour-intensive food production, partly traded and partly used to diversify and enrich the diets and employment of poor producers. In both phases rural non-farm growth contributes a rising share of rural incomes, but depends substantially on consumer demand based on smallholder prosperity.

Four themes

This Report explores four themes: access to assets (physical and financial), technology and natural resources for rural poverty reduction, markets for the rural poor, and institutions for the rural poor. This does not mean that other issues, such as the security and vulnerability, and the ownership and agency, of the poor are less important. These issues have been discussed in depth in various forums in recent months. Rather, this Report focuses on aspects of poverty reduction that are critical but often neglected. It concentrates very heavily on concrete production and income issues, and on agriculture. But the answer to rural poverty is not just agriculture, although this is a big part of the story. Agricultural change can work to reduce poverty, but only when linked to social changes that give the poor greater power over the social factors that shape, and far too often circumscribe, the horizons of their possibilities, including their agricultural options and assets.

ASSETS AND RURAL POVERTY REDUCTION

Assets empower the rural poor by increasing their incomes, reserves against shocks, and choices to escape from harsh or exploitative conditions ('exit options'). The poor can directly control assets by ownership, rent or communal tenure, or indirectly gain from assets, whoever controls them: through employment, for example. Urban-rural and rich-poor gaps in asset ownership exceed greatly the corresponding gaps in income and consumption, making the rural poor especially dependent on their labour-power. Assets most help rural poverty reduction when they are employment-intensive, divisible into small low-cost units, and low-risk.

For many important assets, gender bias doubly harms the poor: as a source of injustice to children and women, and as a source of inefficiency and slow growth. Feasible remedies are indicated.

There are strong complementarities among asset types. The poor (and economic growth) do better with some improvement in health, nutrition and schooling than with a lot of one and none of the others. Such human assets do more for a poor person if he/she also has some farm or non-farm assets and his/her productivity is rising. Previous education helps a poor person to get better returns from irrigation.

Land reform: back on the agenda

An important element in the quest for greater access to assets is land redistribution. Extreme land inequality is bad for growth, and steers its benefits away from the rural poor. Most of the rural poor depend on farm income, yet usually control little farmland. Land reform to create small, not-too-unequal family farms is often cost-effective in reducing beneficiary poverty. It also helps hired farmworkers; small farms employ more people per hectare than do large farms, and small farmers and their employees spend more of their incomes on employment-intensive rural non-farm products.

To escape poverty sustainably, post-reform farmers need appropriate infrastructure and serv-

ices; these needs are likely to change with liberalization and globalization. It is important to draw distinctions between confiscatory, statist or top-down approaches and the 'new-wave land reform': decentralized, market-friendly, with support from and involvement of civil-society action and with consensus.

Imposition of modes of tenure can 'go against the grain' of preference or efficiency. Both communal land tenure and private tenancy can be pro-poor; restricting them is usually counterproductive. Furthermore, exclusive emphasis on land asset control by households misses the problem that many households, laws and customs discriminate against women, thus damaging efficiency, equity, child health and poverty reduction.

Poverty reduction among the rural poor would require increased support, from governments and aid agencies, for farmland redistribution to poor communities, households and women. Extreme land inequality appears to 'fix' social relationships: its impact on overall inequality does not appear to diminish, even after agriculture's role does. Hence land redistribution remains cost-effective against poverty in Latin America and Southern Africa, where some ethnic groups remain in rural poverty, largely due to exceptional inequality of farmland as well as education.

Access to water

Some control by the poor over water is essential if they are to realise the full benefits from farmland. East and South Asia's fast poverty reduction and farm growth owe much to the 30-35% of irrigated cropland – and the persistence of rural poverty and agricultural stagnation in most of sub-Saharan Africa to its mere 1-5%. Water control is also vital for adequate and healthy drinking water and sanitation. Yet the rural and the poor have even less access to water-yielding assets, and hence water control, than to land. Worse, climatic and economic developments threaten many rural people – especially the poor – and their food production with growing water stress. Improving this depends partly on redistributing water-yielding assets, and partly on incentives for asset types that save water by using labour. Small, divisible, farmer-controlled water supply systems benefit the poor most, but in some conditions, and with environmental caution, large systems remain essential. In either case, user participation in design, management and maintenance are proven keys to asset efficiency, yet are usually absent.

Special attention to women's water rights is needed. Women and children are also the main losers from distant, inadequate and unhealthy drinking water. Modest but enforced water charges (payable as maintenance labour), complementary water improvement and health care, and managed credit to acquire water-yielding assets are keys to pro-poor and efficient use of increasingly scarce rural water for production or consumption.

Access to other assets and non-farm activities
Livestock in a few areas, and small stock in many, are more than proportionately controlled by the poor. Improving returns from such stock through better marketing, extension, and research, and supporting institutions for small or joint herd control, are necessary.

Rural non-farm activity provides 25-40% of rural income – sometimes more for the poor, sometimes less – and is growing faster than farm income. But its dynamism usually depends on demand from a growing, fairly equal farm sector. So neglecting poor farmers and farmworkers in order to free resources for the non-farm poor is often self-defeating. Further, usually some rural non-farm activities (trade, transport, construction) are dynamic, but other activities (traditional services and crafts) contract as the rural economy develops; the poor are helped much more by skills and infrastructure for the former than for the latter.

Usually, poor people, who are primarily rural, are deprived of 'human assets' – health, child nutrition, education, skills – and are especially prone to gender biases in their allocation. In the medium term, extra human assets are the most effective, just and growth-inducing ways to advance the rural poor – provided there are also natural or physical assets, or work, yielding more to the educated, in a growing economy.

More (and better) health, education and nutrition normally stimulate each other, are complementary and, if acquired by parents, especially mothers, also benefit children. Usually, provision and quality discriminate heavily – and inefficiently – against rural areas, remote places, ethnic minorities and (in education) women. Such discrimination is most severe among the poor.

Most human assets, notably primary schooling and health care for the poor, must be financed mainly by the public sector. Financial viability and participatory management are real problems. But user fees in primary health and education are not the answer. They have proved almost impossible to target correctly; have saved little public money; and have discouraged use of services by the rural poor and hence growth of their incomes. Other ways to financial viability and participation for human asset provision are feasible.

TECHNOLOGY, NATURAL RESOURCES AND RURAL POVERTY REDUCTION
The importance of technology for rural poverty reduction and recent trends
Technology is central in reducing rural poverty.

In 1965-85, rice, wheat and maize, in much of Asia and Central America, experienced a big technology shift, the 'Green Revolution', that increased yields, enhanced employment and brought about a rapid fall in poverty. But these effects have since slowed.

Technical progress has by-passed hundreds of millions of poor people – many of the remaining hard-core poor – in specific regions (including most of Africa), agro-ecologies (dryland, upland), and products (sorghum, yams, cassava, smallstock).

Water resources in many areas, and land in some areas, face serious threats of depletion and pollution, which appropriate technical change can reduce or reverse.

Recent scientific advances bring new prospects for reigniting and spreading to laggard areas and crops the technical progress that can reduce poverty and conserve resources.

Bio-agricultural technology: old and new

In bio-agricultural research, the goals must be enhanced yield potential (and yield growth) in 'lead' areas and spreading progress to neglected regions and main staples. Both require a sharp reversal of the long fall in levels (and security) of funds for public-sector agricultural research – and of the growing diffusion of such research systems, often at the behest of donors, into matters other than yield enhancement, stabilization and sustainability. Also needed is much more public-sector research into transgenic food staples, with traits selected by labour-intensive smallholders. This requires different incentives for scientists – and research – now increasingly locked into a few large science-based companies and directed towards traits, crops, and farmers of little interest to the poor.

The priority for bio-agricultural research is employment-intensive but sustainable yield growth, in a context of improved transformation and recycling of water and nutrients. Land/water technology should aim at outcomes attractive to farmers by links with varieties fertilized for sustainably higher and more profitable yields – not, in most cases, with 'low-external-input' farming, which usually raises the dilemma of whether the land should be used for low outputs or soil mining.

Transgenic crops and animals have triggered justified public demand for open, participatory systems, involving farmers and consumers in scientific decision-procedures that effectively regulate food safety and the environmental impact of introduced varieties, species and foods. To realize the huge potential of transgenics, especially for areas hitherto little affected by research, requires big changes in the criteria and incentives now guiding the allocation, use, and civil-society overview of scientific resources. Public/private, and donor-agency/civil-society, partnership action is urgent, especially for those developing counties that have limited scientific capacity yet are heavily dependent on food staples yield growth. Inaction in agricultural and water technology could undermine all other efforts for rural poverty reduction in coming decades.

Often, especially in West Africa, chemical fertilizers, better germplasm and humus enrichment by natural manures, though presented as rivals, are complements in sustainable small farming. Participatory methods are allies of, not populist alternatives to, formal research, including early-generation plant breeding and even biotechnology.

Pro-poor, sustainable technical progress should seek robustness, stability, yield enhancement and labour-intensity. In moving from such principles to selecting product and method priorities in technology policy, complementarity is desirable, and hence cooperation between research groups and types, including groups of farmers. So is allowing for time-lags: the conditions prevailing when research is planned often differ greatly from those when farmers adopt the resulting innovations – worker/land ratios may be sharply higher, or water-tables lower, for example.

Existing technologies: write them off?

It is certainly premature to write off existing technologies. In many cases, their potential has not been exhausted and needs to be explored further. In many cases, their potential in breaking the barrier of higher yield and sustainable development is constrained by institutional factors: lack of water and extension and of adequate support services. New technologies are not panaceas for such problems. On the contrary, they remain issues for all forms of technical progress at the small-farm level.

Technologies for land and water management

Improved land management technology is historically slow to spread, or to improve farm income. It is often inadequately integrated with bio-agricultural research, yet is vital to reduce land depletion. To attract poor farmers, such technology needs to show production returns (such as vegetative erosion barriers usable for fodder, rather than stone bunds), and should employ labour (preferably slack-season) rather than equipment. For these purposes, some forms of conservation tillage and land reclamation have proved far better than others.

Technical choices are crucial to solving the water crisis that increasingly threatens many rural poor people. Agriculture is being pressed in most developing countries to 'use' less water. But 'using' need not mean 'using up'. With appropriate drainage and recycling, significant water saving can be achieved. Employment-intensive ways to improve conveyance and use efficiency of water have proved feasible with proper incentives and user institutions. However, the justified emphasis on farmers' methods of water control and irrigation should not be allowed to distract attention from the need for faster progress in this area with formal, 'frontier' invention and innovation suitable for smallholders.

Despite justified pressure for water economy, in many places more irrigation is needed. Africa's slow progress in agriculture and reducing rural poverty, compared with Asia's, has much to do with lack of water control. Successful adoption of farmer-controlled, very small-scale irrigation has

shown that it can benefit the poor. This should be built on, and progress accelerated. Larger irrigation schemes in Africa have a mixed and often weak record, but some of the difficulties have abated. Major improvement in water availability, timing and management is essential for rapid continent-wide progress against rural poverty. That may require advances in water research and some major irrigation.

Reviving pro-poor technologies

However, reviving pro-poor, resource-conserving agro-technical progress faces problems. The central issue is how the poor can benefit more from recent technological progress. What conditions, circumstances and policies make this possible? How far does the concentration of recent technical progress in private firms, as opposed to the public sector during the Green Revolution, make such technologies less pro-poor? How much progress in land and water management technologies needs to be achieved to complement the progress in new crop varieties? To what extent does current research consider the priorities of the poor, the demands of the complex, diverse, risk-prone dry and hilly farm systems?

Fortunately there is evidence that economic returns on crop research are now higher in some neglected areas than elsewhere. New resources for the public sector, and institutions to shift incentives for the private sector, are crucial, as is participatory priority-setting by and with the rural poor.

MARKETS FOR THE RURAL POOR: EXPOSURE TO THE WINDOWS OF OPPORTUNITY

Most of the rural poor are already substantially involved in markets for labour, food, farm and non-farm inputs, and credit. But poor people and remote places often face very high physical and transactions costs of marketing per kilometre-tonne, which restrict trade, specialization and growth.

The market access problems of particular groups (such as the illiterate) are different from the problems of remote areas. In each case, problems of physical access (e.g. bad or no roads) are distinct from, but often compounded by, the transactions costs of, or bias in, institutional market access (e.g. trader or marketing-board monopsony). Problems interact: women, and indigenous ethnic minorities in both Asia and Africa, are more likely to be remote dwellers; bad roads are linked to trader monopsony power. But resources can be saved by deciding at the start which problems are tackled most cost-effectively, so as to achieve a given poverty reduction through better rural market access.

Almost everywhere, remote and ill-connected rural people are poorer. If they have potential tradable surpluses, then realizing these, usually through better farm technology, is a precondition for generating exchange and cutting poverty through better roads. If an area feeds itself adequately but lacks transport links, these are usually needed to make yield-enhancing staples technology attractive. For cash crops or non-farm products, better roads are usually needed to permit expansion, marketing and growth through specialization. There are many cases of poor non-remote people – separated by terrain, not distance, from nearby markets – whose welfare increases greatly when improved access to such markets allows trade and exchange.

Beyond physical access to markets

Physical access is not just about access to roads. Even if the rural poor or the remote have roads, their lack of choice over modes of transportation and other forms of market access can expose them to large transactions costs or institutional costs. Private monopoly traders and parastatal marketing boards expose the poor to market power, while the non-poor can more readily find alternatives. Yet withdrawal of parastatals or monopsony traders following liberalization often leaves the rural poor

stranded altogether. Marketing cooperatives, to bulk up for purchase or sale, are a decentralized solution, depending for success on acceptance as 'institutions of trust' or so-called 'social capital'. Regulation to control adulteration, weights and market-rigging can be useful; improving market institutions is often a necessary complement to liberalization, if the effect of better prices on poor rural people is not to be swamped by marketing costs.

Commercialization usually improves the welfare of the poor. Being intelligently risk-averse, they usually avoid premature commitment to all the risks of commercialization, e.g. keeping part of their land for self-provisioning. Indeed, cash-crop income is often used to acquire improved staples technology. Crop diversification is another way of diffusing risk, but rapid change is often not practicable: for example, tree crops require several years growth before a crop can be harvested.

Access to input markets and technology

Access to transparent input markets is crucial for the poor. Land tenure reform is a poor substitute for land asset distribution. Water markets, while providing fewer benefits for the poor than ownership of water-yielding assets, are almost always more pro-poor than non-price water rationing and subsidy, which benefit mostly the non-poor and leave the poor with the distortion costs. Hence rural user charges for water are usually pro-poor. In many regions, too, the tightening rural water squeeze makes some form of water pricing essential on efficiency grounds.

New farm technology is sometimes embodied in costly capital confined to the better-off (e.g. deep tubewells or tractors, whose services can of course be marketed), but has often been distributed free, as information – sometimes alongside free or subsidized seed or seed-fertilizer packages – through agricultural extension. Returns have often been high and in Asia remain so; but in Africa most public extension services are in disarray, and unresponsive to the demands of the rural poor while in Latin America extension, like research, is increasingly privatized, even for the poor. New market routes or other mechanisms to reduce the time-lag before the poor adopt better technologies are badly needed if the poor are not to miss out on new opportunities.

Access to labour market

Labour markets affect the main income source of the poor. Discrimination against indigenous and ethnic minorities and women, though prohibited by law, is common in practice, but it works less through specific wage rates than through exclusion from high-productivity tasks or places: through lack of education and skills needed to upgrade tasks; through women's domestic 'duties' that restrict tasks; and through remoteness and language for ethnic rural minorities. Rural public works can powerfully enhance access to labour markets.

The poor are restricted by asymmetric information and high unit costs from most formal credit, and, given the co-variance of local loans, by lack of collateral from much money-lender lending. Efforts to reach the rural poor through directed, subsidized state-backed credit have largely failed. The current approach is to generate unsubsidized, but non-exploitative, microfinance markets through local peer-monitored intermediation. This has had considerable success, but outreach to the very poor may conflict with financial sustainability at least until the difficult problem of the interface between informal and formal institutions has been solved.

Trade liberalization, globalization and the rural poor

Markets for the rural poor are being restructured by trade liberalization and globalization. This removes biases against farm prices, thus raising food production and employment but also food prices, with ambiguous effects on the poor.

Economic growth should normally benefit them in the long run, as should labour-intensive specialization. However, such gains can be destroyed by bad market transmission and functioning. Remote areas, benefiting despite gross inefficiencies from pan-territorial pricing, have lost out where subsidies have been removed, and where the parastatal has been withdrawn and not replaced by competing private buyers.

Though the poor on the whole gain from liberalization, substantial and disparate groups often lose, and need compensation. People with little education, few roads or contacts, or not speaking a majority language, are especially likely to be 'stuck' as immobile losers. Conversely, reasonably equal access to markets and to asset control greatly help the poor to gain quickly from liberalization; great rural inequalities, conversely, ensure that higher food prices penalize many of the rural poor as net food buyers, rather than benefiting them through extra farm income. Moreover, liberalization probably increases income fluctuations, especially though exposure to changes in export crop prices. Access to quasi-insurance or safety-nets therefore becomes important if the poor are to realize secure gains from trade.

Finally, though small farms are generally efficient and employment-intensive, globalization brings new strains – and prospects. It links product sales – especially in the booming horticultural sector, in principle ideal for small labour-intensive farms – increasingly to exports to rich countries and to supermarkets, abroad and (especially in Latin America) at home. This exposes farmers to a range of requirements, from uniform product appearance through pesticide rules to restrictions on child labour. The cost per unit of output, both of meeting these requirements for farmers and of supervising them for buyers, is initially much higher on small farms. Such agricultural globalization can undermine their economic advantages. Stimulating and supporting institutional remedies may be vital to a pro-poor trajectory. It can be done: such solutions are emerging; no trend to larger farm size has appeared in most of Asia, nor has one been well documented in Africa or Latin America, despite globalization.

INSTITUTIONS AND THE RURAL POOR

The distribution of benefits between rich and poor, urban and rural, men and women, depends on institutions: organizations such as banks, and rules (customary or legal) such as those affecting division of inherited land or the shares of landlord and tenant in a sharecropping arrangement.

Some acceptance of institutionally mediated outcomes is essential if transactions are not to be impossibly costly and unreliable; but, unless institutions can change under pressure, a society's outcomes are 'frozen' in the interests of the existing controllers of the institutions. This favours the rural poor only if they control the institutions, or at least can compel attention to their needs from those who do.

All efforts to benefit the poor through institutional reform face a serious problem. Institutions are usually created and run in the interests of the powerful. That rural big men run local institutions in their interests is the problem for current modes of top-down institutional devolution, decentralization and participation. Governance is not only a macro issue.

Decentralization and devolution

Decentralized institutions for natural resources management and financial services rarely help the rural poorest 'directly' but often reach the moderately poor and help all through increased efficiency and sustainability, as the locally powerful are driven to recognize their shared interests with the poor in these. We review striking examples – all in more or less open societies – of the rural poor's 'learning by doing' to enhance their political power, influence and agility in the 'civic culture'.

The case for decentralization arose partly from increasing consensus that the state needed to retreat from many formerly centralized areas of production, regulation and provision, whereas in developing countries most central governments, even if motivated to perform well, lacked information to do so. While some such areas could be privatized, in others – including the management of common-property natural resources and the provision of financial services to the poor – that policy was, for various reasons, seldom considered sufficient. Various forms of decentralized control by common rural groups have therefore been tried, often with NGO facilitation and sometimes with government support for administration.

State attempts to manage formerly common property in grazing land, forests, or water-bodies generally failed; centralized exclusion of outsiders, and rationing among insiders, could be enforced, but not without tyranny or profligacy, and seldom without corruption. Privatization too proved inefficient and unequal. The third way – participatory decentralization – has become a growing trend with potential for better conservation and efficiency. What are the necessary preconditions for improving the record of conservation and efficiency and ensuring a better share for the poor? What methods are needed, what processes need to be built in to enlist the poor in natural-resources conservation? And how can women benefit from this devolution of natural resources management?

Financial institutions: making them work for the poor

State credit subsidies, credit labelled 'for the rural poor', usually benefited mainly the rich (and 'gatekeepers' in banks or bureaucracies), permitted low-yielding investment, and drove out competitive financial institutions. Untrammelled markets, too, did not adequately reach even the creditworthy poor. Hence microfinancing agencies were widely attempted, usually lending without subsidy to small groups of borrowers with joint liability, and often providing deposit and other financial services. They were often supported by NGOs and often targeted on women and on non-farm lending. In respect of sustainability, repayment, and outreach to the moderately poor, microfinance greatly improves on most previous public and private rural credit; yet it, too, seldom reaches the poorest. Their risk-proneness and complex, fluctuating household economies require a wider range of financial services, often at high unit cost, and centering on insurance (and occasional consumer credit) rather than microenterprise support.

This experience of improved sustainability and efficiency, but limited outreach to the poorest, is thus shared by two of the most important types of decentralized rural institutions. To the extent that they participated, the poor did so by sharing in gains, not by raising their share: by coalition, not redistribution. This can achieve something, but seldom for the poorest, and seldom fast. With regard to the poorest, the microfinance and decentralization 'revolutions' are very far from complete.

More generally, development programmes can be captured by elites or vested interests, or can give rise to broad coalitions which share the gains. The rich may get the lion's share, or may find that it pays them to do with less, especially if the poor have political voice or can organize themselves into counter-coalitions with other persons of power. There are several examples of successful actions by women's and poor people's groups. But they need options and voice; hence the impor-

tance of a reserve of land, even if tiny, and of literacy and political openness.

Partnership and participation
Finally, the dilemma of 'willing participation into being from above' is increasingly softened, if not solved, by partnerships involving donors, governments and NGOs. But these partnerships will have an impact only if they are directed to where it really matters for the rural poor. Poverty is not an intrinsic attribute of people, but a product of livelihood systems and the socio-political and economic forces that shape them. Concretely, most rural people, and especially the rural poor, make their living in and around agriculture. Thus, for sustainable poverty reduction, the problems of smallholder agriculture must be addressed directly and effectively. This involves change in material factors – land, water and infrastructure – and in technology and knowledge for, and in the hands of, the poor. But it also means change in social and economic relations, usually involving institutional change that gives the poor more control over their own environment. Many of the policy changes in the developing world have the potential to benefit the poor. But globalization and decentralization will work for them only if broad partnerships are mobilized to solve the challenges they confront: equitable and efficient market-mediated relations, and accountable social and political institutions. Economic empowerment is creating an institutional framework in which the poor can put assets, both public and private, to work on their own behalf.

CHAPTER 2
THE RURAL POOR

The majority of the world's poor are rural, and will remain so for several decades. Poverty reduction programmes must therefore be refocused on rural people if they are to succeed. Poverty is not gender-neutral: women enjoy less access to, and control over, land, credit, technology, education, health care and skilled work.

GETTING THE PRIORITIES RIGHT

Most of the poor are rural and will be so for several decades. Their income, spending and employment usually concentrate on staple food. They have little land, schooling or other assets, and face many interlocking barriers to progress. Poverty and hunger have fallen massively, mainly due to rural and agricultural development, especially during 1975-90. Yet this improvement, and parallel progress in agricultural production, have stalled during the last decade, and many rural regions have been excluded. Rural-urban poverty gaps have not declined globally. The share of international aid and attention devoted to agriculture, rural development and the rural poor has been small and falling. The sustainable reduction of poverty and reaching the poor through development efforts, investment and aid still remain a major challenge for the development community.

Rural poverty reduction deserves much greater emphasis. The demographic window of opportunity which has transformed the prospects for progress in East Asia in the past 30 years can do so in other developing countries in the next 30, but only if benefits target the rural poor. Some rural poverty is transient; this can be reduced by attacking the causes of rural vulnerability.

Donors recognize the need to reverse the decline in progress in the effort against poverty, but may not be aware of the need to concentrate on rural poverty. Yet, the poor are mainly rural; they, and their civil societies and governments, can be empowered to participate in development only if they have the resources to do so.

RURAL POVERTY?

Some 1.2 billion people worldwide consume less than a 'standard' dollar-a-day; they are in dollar poverty.[1] Forty-four per cent are in South Asia, about 24% each in sub-Saharan Africa and East Asia, and 6.5% in Latin America and the Caribbean.[2] Seventy-five per cent of the dollar-poor work and live in rural areas; projections suggest that over 60% will continue to do so in 2025[3] (Chart 2.1).

These are good reasons to emphasize rural poverty reduction, and to redirect attention and expenditure towards agricultural development

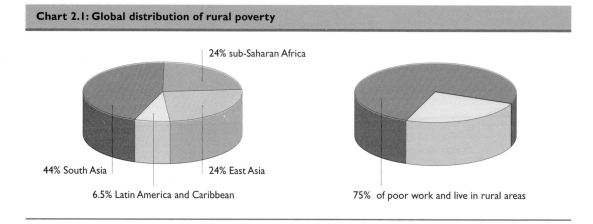

Chart 2.1: Global distribution of rural poverty

24% sub-Saharan Africa

44% South Asia

24% East Asia

6.5% Latin America and Caribbean

75% of poor work and live in rural areas

that generates employment. Moreover, official data overestimate the shift of the poor from the countryside to cities, further strengthening the case for greater emphasis on rural poverty.

There would be less need to emphasize the importance of reducing rural poverty if
• public action were more cost-effective in reducing urban poverty;
• the rural poor gained far more from urban poverty reduction than vice versa;
• rural anti-poverty spending discouraged the poor from migrating; or
• rural poverty reduction promoted less economic growth than urban poverty reduction.
None of these is usually the case.

Cost-effectiveness
Where resources have to be divided between rural and urban spending on, for instance, health and education, outlay per head is normally less in reaching rural areas, even though rural people have lower initial health and literacy. So higher spending in rural areas should normally improve outcome more than higher spending in urban areas.

Rural anti-poverty policy is focused on increasing the productivity of the poor, often with success. But much urban anti-poverty policy concentrates on improving the shelter and sanitation of the poor rather than their opportunity to earn.

Public spending in rural areas is also likely to be more effective in reducing poverty than spending in urban areas where the costs in infrastructure and direct investment to create work are higher.

Within agriculture, the main rural activity, there are few economies of scale. Small, labour-intensive rural units are more likely to be efficient in rural areas than in urban industry and modern services.

However, the dispersion of rural public action, and consequent high management costs, could offset the advantages of rural public spending.

Rural-urban interactions
Urban work encourages migration from the countryside to the city. Creating work in the cities might well attract more people seeking work from rural areas. This could well leave urban unemployment rates unchanged.[4] Urban-oriented policies alone may fail to reduce urban poverty: they may make urban living more attractive, but congestion costs would rise and the wages of the urban poor would fall.

If staples prices fall, but non-labour costs of staples cultivation on smallholdings fall faster, then poor small farmers, farm workers and urban food buyers, who spend most of their incomes on food staples, can all benefit. Evidence from the Green Revolution shows that this can be achieved. There is no corresponding urban output that, by being expanded or made cheaper, enriches the rural poor: the most cost-effective way to reduce urban poverty may be to reduce rural poverty.

Rural-to-urban migration

This migration is partly a way of sharing risk by[5] families which maintain rural and urban households, often shifting members between them.[6] But there are risks and costs in rural-to-urban migration which the poorest can rarely bear. 'Unequal', rather than low-income, villages seem to have high rates of rural-to-urban migration, with moderately poor people pushed out and moderately well-off people pulled out. But the poorest are not likely to stay in the city permanently.[7] Reduction in rural poverty probably reduces short-term migration to towns, too, but raises the medium-term mobility of the near-poor, as many South and East Asian experiences show.

Growth effects of rural and urban poverty reduction

Countries with very unequal assets and (perhaps) income usually experience slower economic growth.[8] This matters for the choice between rural and urban poverty reduction in two ways. First, some inequality of reward seems necessary to create incentives for effort, achievement, or meeting effective demand. But inequality that reflects ascribed position, status or inheritance reduces earned incomes, and creates barriers to the advancement of capable persons. This happens when more or better schools, clinics, prices, or research inputs are assigned to people just because they are born in towns. So, severe rural-urban inequality probably retards growth. Second, concentrating resources in large units of production is usually bad for equality, but can be good for growth if, and only if, there are economies of scale. Agriculture generally lacks these; many urban activities feature them. Concentrating anti-poverty resources on the rural poor is consistent with small-scale (and labour-intensive) production, and this is likely to promote both efficiency and equality.

The apparently higher returns which expenditure brings to reducing rural, rather than urban, poverty justifies that commitment, particularly given the greater incidence and depth of rural poverty (Annex Table 2.1)

DEFINITIONS OF 'RURAL'

There are two main rural characteristics. First, rural people usually live in a farmstead or in groups of houses containing perhaps 5 000-10 000 persons, separated by farmland, pasture, trees or scrubland. Second, most rural people spend most of their working time on farms.

National distinctions between rural and urban are arbitrary and varied. The most common definition of the borderline is 5 000 persons, as in India; often it is 2 500 persons or fewer, as in Mexico, or 10 000 or more, as in Nigeria. Other countries, including Brazil and China, do not specify a population size but use various characteristics, from typical metropolitan facilities to legal or political status.[9] The lower the rural-urban borderline is set, the fewer people are classified as rural. Legislative and political borderlines are even harder to interpret. This requires caution in inter-

---

Box 2.1: Why does it matter how different countries define 'rural'?

Suppose that Country A (Gabon) sets the rural-urban borderline at 2 000 persons, and Country B (Nigeria) at 20 000 persons. A much higher proportion of the population – and of the consumption-poor, with less than, say, USD 1 a day – will be counted as rural in B than in A, even if the actual distribution of the population among different sizes of place within A and B is identical. In that case, the proportion of public outlay on health, education, or food relief in rural areas, as officially defined, ought to be far higher in B than in A. And any migration from rural to urban areas will normally seem greater in A than B owing to the definition of 'urban', even if events on the ground in A and B are identical.

preting, evaluating and comparing facts about the rural poor, and policies affecting them (Box 2.1).

The rural-urban borderline in a country is seldom changed. It is more reliable to compare rural and urban shares of the population and of the poor, and disparities among them (mean income, dollar-poverty incidence, doctor/patient ratios, or illiteracy) in the same country over time than to compare countries. We can track what is happening to rural population shares and disadvantages in a country; but caution is needed, even here.

Borderline problems lead to serious overestimates of the urban population and poor (Box 2.2). Annual population growth in most developing countries has been 2-3%, sometimes more. That makes many places grow across the rural-urban borderline between surveys, or decennial censuses: in India, where the borderline is 5 000 persons, most villages of 4 250 persons in the census of 1961, 1971 or 1981 would expect to count as towns ten years later. Since many of these villages and people hardly change their lifestyles during reclassification, this means that between censuses and surveys, the rise in the proportion of genuinely urban persons, including the proportion of poor persons, is systematically overstated.[10] This over-statement of urbanization is increased when nearby villages join up between censuses, so that their joint population crosses the urban-rural borderline; and when municipalities legislate or lobby for expanded boundaries, swallowing villages in the process. Many people are affected; some may change their characteristics but many do not. Often, rural-to-urban migration is overstated for the same reasons. Moreover, many such migrants are transient, and many more return home in old age. Many others, typically 8-10% of urban workforces, and even more of urban women and the urban poor, are mainly engaged in agriculture, even in big cities, especially in Africa.

It is often claimed that urbanization of people and of poverty renders rural poverty less important. Even in official data, over 70% of the world's poor are now rural, and over 60% is likely to be rural in 2025. These measurement issues imply that the proportion of the poor in places with genuinely rural characteristics (whether or not arbitrarily reclassified) is even higher, and its decline slower.

WHAT IS POVERTY?

Poverty can be seen as broad, multidimensional, partly subjective, variable over time, comprising

---

Box 2.2: Can we have a common definition of 'rural'?

'National statistical offices are in the best position to distinguish between urban and rural-type areas in their own countries' (UN/ECOSOC 1998: 31). Nevertheless, it is important to have a constant, if incomplete, definition of rurality, so that comparisons are feasible. The *UN Demographic Yearbook* classifies populations periodically into size-groups of locality, but only for a minority of nations and usually only down to 20 000. One possibility, requiring urgent review, is that the UN system might:

(a) assist countries to produce standardized international data sets that show changing proportions of persons living in places of different sizes;

(b) publish census information on places below a common international rural-urban cut-off, say 5 000 persons, for use in analytical work;

(c) publish and track shares of population, women, children, the poor, the illiterate living not only in places of different sizes, but in places above the rural-urban cut-off population only at the earlier date of an intercensal period. Genuine rises in the urban population share could then be separated from boundary effects; and

(d) reorganize the data on dollar poverty held by the World Bank to permit valid international and intertemporal comparisons of rural and urban population shares (defined at the 5 000 cut-off) of the poor, and their characteristics.

Box 2.3: What does poverty mean?

Poverty has both physical and psychological dimensions. Poor people themselves strongly emphasize violence and crime, discrimination, insecurity and political repression, biased or brutal policing, and victimization by rude, neglectful or corrupt public agencies (Narayan *et al.* 2000). Some may feel poor or be regarded as poor if they cannot afford the sorts of things available to other people in their community. A review of 43 participatory poverty assessments from four continents concluded that poor people report their condition largely in terms of material deprivation: not enough money, employment, food, clothing and housing, combined with inadequate access to health services and clean water; but they are also liable to give weight to such non-material factors as security, peace and power over decisions affecting their lives (Robb, 1999).

---

capabilities as well as welfare, and in part relative to local norms, comparisons and expectations (Box 2.3). In practice, most poverty measurement focuses on private consumption below an objective poverty line that is both fixed over time and defined in terms of an absolute norm for a narrow aspect of welfare: for example, defining poverty as deprivation of sufficient consumption to afford enough calories, or as dollar poverty.[11] Most studies settle for an over-simple poverty measure because it can be compared among persons, groups, places and times in a testable way. This is important in evaluating poverty-reducing policies. This report, too, follows this route, but also looks at the characteristics and descriptions of the poor themselves.

What definition of poverty should we use?

Individuals are often classified as poor on some definitions but not on others (women in Guinea are more likely than men to be poor on assessments that focus on self-esteem, but not on dollar-poverty measures).[12] In Côte d'Ivoire, varying definitions, confined to material and other objective indicators, identified substantially different people as 'poor'.[13] In Chile, income proved to be an unreliable guide to nutrition and education.[14] In two Indian villages, people whose real incomes had actually declined over 20 years reported their situation as having improved, citing decreased dependence on low-status jobs, patrons and landlords, improved mobility, and better consumption patterns.[15]

Yet groups or communities that are poor in terms of income and consumption tend to be poor in other respects. Those below the World Bank dollar-a-day poverty line (see Box 2.4) typically spend at least 70-80% of all income on food, most of it basic food staples, and are at risk of consuming too few calories for health and efficiency. People this poor are usually unable to afford the cash or time for adequate clothing, housing, schooling and health care. Bad education and health, common among the children of poor parents, restrict earning potential. Income poverty largely explains inter-country variations in health outcomes. Paradoxically, the poor report sickness less often than the rich, because they cannot afford sickness.[16] The poor need to hold on to liquid assets as a hedge against shocks, rather than investing for high yields and escaping poverty.[17]

How can we measure poverty?

We must be able to measure poverty consistently if we are to make comparisons. Measuring poverty helps policy-makers target resources to reduce poverty and helps them, and others, to assess progress in reducing poverty.

Poverty can be measured in three ways: a scalar approach using a single indicator such as income or consumption, a multidimensional-indexed approach where several indicators are combined in a single index of poverty (Box 2.5), and a vector multi-dimension where several indicators are used to classify people as poor on each indicator (for example, income poor but health non-poor).

Box 2.4: Measuring consumption poverty: identification and aggregation

Step 1: Identify the poor

Five techniques are in widespread use for setting the poverty line.

1. The food energy method (FEM) estimates a food-energy minimum required to satisfy dietary energy (caloric) requirements and then determines the level of income/consumption at which this minimum is typically met.

2. The cost-of-basic-needs (CBN) method sets the poverty line as the level just sufficient to buy an exogenously set low-cost adequate diet plus other cheap basic requirements.

3. The food-share method (FSM) estimates the minimum cost of a food basket that satisfies the food energy minimum and multiplies this by the share of non-food expenditure in total consumption of a sub-group defined as poor.

4. The international poverty line method is described in endnote 1.

5. The relative consumption method sets the poverty line at a percentage of national mean or median consumption, often half or one third.

Often a set of poverty lines is used, ranging from extreme poverty to moderate poverty.

Step 2. Add the numbers up

Once a poverty line is set, poverty below the line can be added up. There are many ways of doing this, each telling us something different about the extent and nature of poverty. The three most widely used measures of poverty are as follows.

1. The headcount ratio measures the incidence of poverty (P0) and is simply the number of poor people divided by the total population. But this fails to show how poor the poor are. Two countries may have the same headcount ratio but the poor in one country may be much poorer than the poor in the other country.

2. The poverty gap (P1) index gets over this problem by incorporating the depth of poverty. Each poor person is weighted by his/her proportionate shortfall below the poverty line, indicating how poor he/she is. But neither P1 nor P0 allows for inequality amongst the poor: if a poor person consumes ten rupees a day more but an even poorer person ten rupees fewer, neither P1 nor P0 rises, yet most of us would agree that poverty has got worse.

3. The poverty severity (P2) measure solves this by weighting each poor person by the square of his/her proportionate shortfall below the poverty line. The P2 measure is the most comprehensive because it increases when the number of poor people increases, or the poor get poorer, or the poorest get poorer compared with other poor people.

All of these poverty measures express values between zero and one, with numbers close to zero indicating little poverty and numbers closer to one suggesting substantial poverty.

The scalar approach identifies who is poor and then aggregates the information into a scalar measure or index. This requires choosing the indicator of poverty, setting a threshold in this indicator below which lie the poor, and adding up the numbers. This can be done in different ways (Box 2.4). We use absolute poverty lines fixed over time, and indicate where we use lines (such as the Purchasing Power Poverty [PPP] dollar-a-day measure) that are the same for all countries, as against national lines.

WHO ARE THE POOR?

Knowing and understanding the poor is as important as understanding poverty. Three quarters of the world's poor people, amounting to 0.9 billion, live in rural areas. Who are they, and where do they live? How do they get and use income? What are the barriers to their progress, especially in terms of inadequate health, schooling, land and other assets? In each case we ask how these characteristics differ across regions, and whether they help us resolve an issue crucial for policy: are these characteristics causes or effects of poverty? IFAD's categorization of the rural poor in its regions of operation provides an overview of the location and the types of poor people (Table 2.1).[18]

Wage labourers, especially landless or casually employed farm-workers, are almost everywhere

---

Box 2.5: The human development and human poverty indexes

The evolving concepts of the human development index (HDI) and human poverty index (HPI), defined in successive issues of UNDP's *Human Development Report*, are multidimensional-indexed basic needs measures. The HDI is a weighted index of: life expectancy at birth; a weighted average of over-15 literacy and primary, secondary and tertiary enrolment rates; and per capita purchasing-power-parity GDP. A country with imposed maximum values of, respectively, 85 years, 100%, 100% and USD 40 000 scores the best feasible HDI, while a country with 25 years, 0%, 0% and USD 100 scores zero. The HPI is measured in developing countries by the average of (a) percentage of persons not expected to survive to 40, (b) percentage of adults illiterate, and (c) the average of percentage without access to safe water, percentage without access to health services and percentage of under-fives moderately or severely underweight.

Weightings within the HDI and HPI are somewhat arbitrary. A bigger problem with a single misery indicator, combining consumption poverty with health and education deprivation, is that it loses information compared with separate measures. For instance, identifying which groups escape consumption poverty, or achieve high literacy and low mortality, helps to unravel the linked disadvantages of the rural poor — who tend to show worse mortality, under-education and gender discrimination, for example, than do the urban poor.

---

among those most likely to be poor, though in Africa smallholders are the largest poor group. Poverty incidence among children is everywhere much higher than among adults. Female-headed households are more often found in Latin America and the Caribbean, West and Central Africa and East and Southern Africa than in Asia and the Pacific; but in most of West and Central Africa and East and Southern Africa they are not much more likely to be consumption-poor than male-headed households. In Near East and North Africa, a high proportion of the rural poor are women, children and the elderly due to high out-migration of prime-age males in the region.

Where do the poor live?

National surveys often show that poverty incidence and numbers concentrate in rural parts of a few geographic areas, for example, North-Western China, East-Central India, North-East Brazil and North-Western Mozambique. The incidence and severity of rural poverty almost everywhere exceed urban poverty, though in Latin America high levels of urbanization mean that most of the poor live in urban areas.[19]

People in irrigated zones within rural areas face much lower poverty risk.[20] Many poor people live in marginal and degraded areas; vulnerability, and probably poverty incidence and intensity, are much greater there. One study found that 634 million rural poor, of whom 375 million are in Asia, live in marginal lands.[21]

Generally, the poorest of the rural poor live in remote areas, even in East and Southern Africa, where most of them live in densely populated areas, particularly near capital cities. Smallholders tend to live in dryland areas in West and Central Africa, Asia and the Pacific and Latin America and the Caribbean. Poor farmers in former East and Southern African colonies are found in areas of low agricultural potential, but elsewhere in the region the poor are in areas of moderate to high agricultural potential, often unrealized, because of barriers to progress. Geographic concentrations of poverty may be intensified by further discrimination or exclusion: for instance, high-poverty areas will fall even further behind if banks refuse them credit.

Poverty in Latin America is highest in some of the more remote, less densely populated areas: the rural sierra and selva of Peru, southern states of Mexico, the Andean highlands and northern lowlands of Bolivia, the semi-arid Norte Chico of Chile and the rural Oriente of Ecuador. Many of the poorest regions in Latin America are located at high altitudes or have low levels of rainfall.

Table 2.1: Who are the poor? by region

Region	Rainfed farmers	Smallholder Farmers	Pastoralists	Artisanal fishermen	Wage labourers/ landless	Indigenous people; scheduled castes/tribes	Female-headed households	Displaced people
WCA		✓						
ESA		✓		✓	✓			
AP		✓	✓	✓	✓	✓	✓	✓
LAC	✓	✓	✓	✓	✓	✓	✓	✓
NENA	✓			✓	✓	✓	✓	✓

WCA: West and Central Africa; ESA: East and Southern Africa; AP: Asia and the Pacific; LAC: Latin America and the Caribbean; NENA: Near East and North Africa

Source: IFAD 1999 a, b, c, d, e, i.

Pastoralists in Near East and North Africa tend to be transhumants, but are generally found in the steppe regions. In Asia and the Pacific and Latin America and the Caribbean, pastoralists are found on high mountain slopes and on plateaux, remote areas with harsh climates. In Near East and North Africa and Latin America and the Caribbean, in contrast with other groups, wage earners are located in lowland and more densely populated areas, where work opportunities exist. Indigenous groups are the most isolated, living in the highlands and rainforests of Latin America and the Caribbean and mountainous areas of Near East and North Africa and Asia and the Pacific.

How do the poor get income and how do they use it?
Most poor rural households diversify their sources of income. Smallholder households in all regions often combine traditional or cash-crop cultivation with raising small livestock. For instance, in Near East and North Africa, households with livestock grow food crops to supplement their incomes. Own-farm income is often only a small proportion of total household income. In Near East and North Africa, West and Central Africa, Asia and the Pacific and East and Southern Africa, off-farm income is often the poor smallholder's main source of cash income, although this is often from low-return activities. In Near East and North

Africa, farmers dependent on rain might migrate to irrigated areas.

Artisanal fishermen diversify their incomes in a number of ways. In East and Southern Africa, they supplement their low fishing incomes by growing cassava in the hinterland. In Near East and North Africa, fishermen engage in crop or livestock production.

The landless in Near East and North Africa and Latin America and the Caribbean are permanently or seasonally involved in daily farm or off-farm work. In Latin America and the Caribbean the landless might be involved in small enterprises or food processing, but often control enough land to produce food for home consumption. In contrast, the landless in Asia and the Pacific are mostly agricultural wage labourers.

Indigenous people tend to be less socially and economically integrated. In Asia and the Pacific they rely on gathering and animal husbandry; in Latin America and the Caribbean they earn a living from river fishing and making handicrafts for local markets.

Poor people typically save in good seasons but run down their reserves in lean times; overall, their consumption is seldom much below their income. Of their consumption, typically 45-60% is on food staples – cereals, roots and tubers, and pulses – and a further 15-20% on other foods. In developing countries in 1996-98, 55% of calories came from cereals (51% from rice, wheat and maize alone), and a further 7% from roots, tubers and pulses.

The proportions are considerably higher for lower-income countries – in 1996-98, 78% of calories were derived from staples in Mozambique, 72% in China, 69% in India and Nigeria, and 49% in Bolivia – and, within such countries, for poor people, as many household surveys confirm. Among the rural poor, the proportion is highest; in Asia and Africa over three quarters of calories come from staple foods. For the poorest 10-20%, at serious risk of nutritional harm, the share of consumption of food, and of calories from staples, both usually exceed 75% in rural areas. Rice and wheat are prominent in the diets of the Asian poor, and to a lesser extent the Latin American poor; maize, millet, sorghum, yams and cassava are typical in sub-Saharan Africa.[22]

The importance of staples in the lives of the poor is enhanced by three facts: agriculture provides about 60-75% of rural work; staples cover about 62% of arable area; and the rural poor are relatively more likely to grow staples. In poorer countries these proportions tend to be higher. For example, of arable area harvested in 1966-68, staples covered 97% in Mozambique, 90% in Nigeria, 78% in China and 74% in India, but only 46% in Bolivia, 44% in the Russian Federation and 38% in Brazil. For low-income countries as a whole, staples provide over two thirds of farm income from employment and self-employment; poor people deriving part of their income from cash crops are likely to grow staples as well. In remote areas with high transport costs, staples probably dominate the income and employment of most of the rural poor. They are also a major source of non-farm income: in Bangladesh over a quarter of value added in rice, the main crop, is derived from post-harvest rice processing.[23]

Cash crops and livestock are important for the survival of some very poor people; staples are not necessarily better for them than cash crops. In much of Near East and North Africa, and in arid areas elsewhere, pastoralism and cash crops are the only available source of income and employment. Groups such as migrant cocoa farmers in Southern Ghana and coffee smallholders in Costa Rica have escaped poverty through cash-cropping. But usually for very poor rural people livestock and cash-crops are not the main source of income and employment, but supplement and contribute to growing staples. Indeed, rapid growth in yields of staples has contributed most to the reduction of poverty in recent decades, and has released land and labour for further poverty reduction based on cash crops, livestock and non-farm activity.

What access do the rural poor have to assets?
In all regions, the rural poor lack the important asset of good quality land. Land size is often too small to ensure the nutritional well-being of the household. Indigenous groups in Latin America and the Caribbean face particular problems in gaining access to land. Many have lost land owing to abuse, discrimination and poor information about property rights.

Access to other productive assets is also lower among the rural poor. In Near East and North Africa lack of access to water is a particular concern. In Asia and the Pacific, East and Southern Africa and Near East and North Africa, lack of draught power severely handicaps poor farmers, as does lack of access to credit, agricultural inputs and technology. Women find such assets particularly difficult to obtain in Asia and the Pacific and Near East and North Africa, where lack of male labour in female-headed households is an important constraint. In Latin America, the higher poverty rates in rural and remote areas stem partly from the concentration of indigenous people in these areas. Poverty rates among the indigenous populations in Mexico, Peru and Bolivia are much higher than among other racial groups. Indigenous people elsewhere, for example in Brazil and Colombia, also have higher poverty rates than others. Human capital levels are lower for these groups in Latin America but, even after taking low access to education into account, they are more likely to be poor. Only half the rural poor in Nicaragua possess legal title to housing, and they have much more restricted access to services.[24]

The rural poor also lack human capital in all regions. In West and Central Africa, Latin America and the Caribbean, and East and Southern Africa the public provision of health services, education, water and sanitation is strongly biased towards urban areas. In East and Southern Africa, households led by people who have little education are poorer than those with some education. In Near East and North Africa and Asia and the Pacific, female-headed households have particularly low levels of education and literacy, health and nutrition. Indigenous groups located in remote areas are excluded from education and health services in Near East and North Africa. Whenever possible, the poor make social investments, such as education, for the future of the family.

Social support networks are important assets for the rural poor in two regions. In Near East and North Africa displaced people are particularly vulnerable because their traditional connections have broken down. In Latin America and the Caribbean, where the poor are geographically isolated, reciprocity networks are important for economic and social survival.

Lack of boats and equipment severely handicaps poor artisanal fishermen in East and Southern Africa. In Asia and the Pacific, tribal people suffer from a particularly serious lack of infrastructure.

What are the barriers to progress for the rural poor? Rural people are poorer partly because they are likelier to live in remote areas, to be unhealthy and illiterate, to have higher child/adult ratios, and to work in insecure and low-productivity occupations. They may also experience discrimination as members of ethnic minorities. These disadvantages, which form an interlocking logjam,[25]

- *overlap*: the gender gap in literacy is larger in rural areas; illiterate people are more likely to be poor; rural, illiterate women and children are more likely to come from ethnic minorities; gaps between ethnic groups are greater among illiterates and in rural and remote areas;
- *cumulate* to reduce the prospect of escape from poverty; and
- *multitarget*, affecting access to production-based food entitlements (work, land, other assets); use of pro-poor techniques of production; and mobility towards better prospects for production, consumption and hence out of poverty.

The logjams are evident from the profiles of the rural poor (Box 2.6).

The rural poor, especially women, normally have higher age-specific mortality rates than the non-poor (Table 2.2). The proportion of malnourished children in the bottom quintile is typically twice that in the top quintile.[26] Girls aged 2-4 suffer serious disadvantages in access to health care compared with boys, and hence worse malnutrition, in Bangladesh, Pakistan, North India, parts of China

---

Box 2.6: Interlocking log-jams and lagging groups in Nepal

In Nepal, gross primary school enrolment rates in 1984-85 varied from 14% for girls from poor households in the rural terai (plains) to 83% for boys from non-poor households in towns in the hills. Invariably, lagging groups did worse than otherwise comparable groups: for example, poor girls in rural hill areas had worse enrolment chances than poor boys in the same areas. Poor Nepalese children, at ages 6-9 and even more at 10-14, in each location (e. g. urban terai, rural hills), spent much more time than non-poor children in domestic and economic work.

Source: de Haan and Lipton, 1999.

Table 2.2: Poor/non-poor mortality ratios

	Adults (15-59)		Children (0-5)	
	Male	Female	Male	Female
West and Central Africa				
Côte d'Ivoire	1.5	1.5	2.4	3.3
Guinea	2.1	3.5	3.7	5.6
Guinea-Bissau	1.7	2.1	2.2	3.0
Mauritania	1.9	3.4	3.0	3.7
Niger	1.9	3.5	3.4	4.8
Nigeria	1.8	2.8	3.1	3.7
Senegal	2.2	3.8	4.0	4.9
East and Southern Africa				
Botswana	2.3	4.0	4.9	4.8
Ethiopia	2.2	3.6	3.0	4.0
Kenya	2.1	3.8	3.7	3.8
Lesotho	2.6	5.4	3.9	5.2
Madagascar	2.0	3.4	3.8	4.1
Rwanda	1.2	1.0	2.7	4.2
South Africa	1.7	3.6	4.7	5.3
Tanzania	2.1	3.3	5.6	5.0
Uganda	1.4	1.4	2.1	2.5
Zambia	2.5	3.6	3.5	3.9
Zimbabwe	2.1	2.3	4.1	5.0
Latin America and Caribbean				
Brazil	2.4	7.9	6.5	5.0
Chile	3.7	12.3	7.1	8.3
Colombia	2.1	5.2	5.6	6.8
Costa Rica	5.5	10.6	5.5	5.1
Dominican Rep	3.4	9.7	6.5	6.5
Ecuador	2.7	4.4	4.2	4.9
Guatemala	1.9	3.5	3.5	3.3
Honduras	2.0	4.0	3.2	3.2
Jamaica	3.4	7.2	7.5	10.0
Mexico	2.9	8.6	7.6	7.8
Nicaragua	2.1	5.6	3.8	4.0
Panama	3.7	7.7	6.2	5.8
Peru	1.7	3.6	3.6	3.7
Venezuela	3.0	7.6	8.9	10.8
Asia and Pacific				
China	3.4	11.0	5.9	6.6
India	2.1	3.7	4.5	4.3
Indonesia	2.3	3.1	4.1	4.1
Malaysia	3.1	5.1	13.7	15.0
Nepal	2.2	3.8	4.0	4.6
Pakistan	2.8	4.4	2.7	2.8
Philippines	2.9	6.1	5.8	5.9
Sri Lanka	2.7	5.7	10.8	8.7
Near East and North Africa Former Soviet Union				
Egypt	2.5	4.1	3.2	3.5
Kyrgyz Republic	2.1	8.0	5.7	6.1
Romania	2.3	8.4	9.9	9.2
Tunisia	2.2	3.8	3.8	3.7

Source: WHO 1999.

and Near East and North Africa;[27] gender disadvantage does most harm to poor girls, because the average level is already so low.

Education illustrates this problem of interlocking disadvantage well. The rural poor have few human assets; the household head is likely to be illiterate; and high dependency ratios, correlated with poverty, independently reduce access to schooling. It is especially among the poor that girls have worse chances of education than boys. Educational enrolment is uniformly lower among the poor, and access is conditioned by location. Rural enrolment ratios are especially low; rural girls, unlike equally poor urban girls, have few prospects of escaping from poverty. In many developing countries the second or third poorest urban decile gets more education than the second or third richest rural decile.[28] Poor rural children are likely to become poor adults.

Land ownership is a key determinant of poverty: most of the rural poor are landless, or small farmers. Increasing land pressure from population growth impedes rural farmers' ability to expand production beyond the subsistence level in East and Southern Africa. If the poor own land, the farms are typically very small, dryland or in low-fertility regions. In Near East and North Africa, landholding size is declining owing to inheritance laws.

In East and Southern Africa (as suggested by evidence from Kenya, Madagascar and Uganda), most of the rural poor are smallholders, mainly growing subsistence crops and augmenting their incomes with small ruminants or poultry. There, as in Latin America and the Caribbean, Asia and the Pacific and West and Central Africa, marketing problems are a particular barrier to the advancement of the rural poor. This reflects a lack of physical assets such as production inputs and infrastructure in East and Southern Africa. In Asia and the Pacific, smallholders' distance from markets results in high transportation costs for acquiring inputs and selling produce. In East and Southern Africa and Latin America and the Caribbean, smallholders often lack capacity to establish reasonable terms of trade; in Latin America and the Caribbean, they have no political lobby to fend off competition from large enterprises. In Latin America and the Caribbean and West and Central Africa, smallholders adopt risk-avoidance strategies, preferring productive stability to increased productivity. Until measures are taken to decrease hazards of smallholder cultivation in these regions, the poor find it harder to pull themselves over the poverty line.

The rural landless are most likely to be poor in many situations. The diversification of household income and prospects for the landless are held back in East and Southern Africa by limited off-farm opportunities. Here, poverty interacts with high vulnerability. In Near East and North Africa, low health and education endowments result in low remuneration levels for the landless.

Landless agricultural workers, and smallholders, are vulnerable to seasonal unemployment. In bad harvests, landless and near-landless hired workers are the first to become unemployed, before farm self-employment is cut. The landless are more likely than farmers, even small ones, to die in famines.[29]

Interlocking barriers can also be socio-political. For example, indigenous people often face discrimination in the intense competition for scarce rural employment. Political instability makes it harder for the rural poor to move above the poverty line. Parts of East and Southern Africa and Near East and North Africa have suffered from civil conflict in recent years, which has adversely affected male labour supply. Some isolated areas of Latin America and the Caribbean are affected by guerrillas and drug trafficking, which displaces populations to marginal land or urban areas. Upland areas of Asia and the Pacific are also experiencing rising violence and political instability, which intimidates the rural poor and increases the risks to agricultural production.

Pastoralists are also over-represented among the rural poor in parts of Africa, and Near East and North Africa especially. More than 10% of Africa's rural population is pastoralist. They are especially likely to lack schools and clinics. Because of their high mobility, as well as official neglect, they are often omitted from income and expenditure surveys, as in Mauritania, despite being a significant part of the population.[30] Their grazing land is likely to be encroached upon by settled farming communities, partly because of degradation caused by over-grazing and drought.

Government interference in traditional livestock management practices threatens the livelihood of pastoralists in Near East and North Africa. In Latin America and the Caribbean, as in East and Southern Africa, overgrazing of pasture, which causes soil erosion and reduces cropping, poses an environmental problem.

Artisanal fishermen in Near East and North Africa suffer owing to the highly perishable nature of their product. Lack of refrigeration and access to markets limits the time available for sale. The prospects for their families are affected by very low provision of social services, including health and education. In Asia and the Pacific, fishermen are at risk from natural disasters and competition from commercial fishing enterprises.

In most regions, poverty incidence is highest in marginal areas at risk from poor soils, low rainfall and adverse climatic change, though poverty is much less the cause than the consequence of environmental degradation.[31] Soil erosion leads to a vicious circle of falling yields, increased exploitation, and further erosion. However, given the right conditions, such as access to capital, poor people have proved capable of improving their environments; intensified land use can be accompanied by environmental improvement rather than degradation.[32]

Drought affects much of East and Southern Africa and some of West and Central Africa every few years with devastating consequences for smallholders and local economies. Water is scarce in Near East and North Africa and increasingly in other drylands. The poor, lacking irrigation technologies, are particularly vulnerable to climatic change. Low investments in rainfed technology exacerbate the problem. Limited water supply and short growing seasons in mountain terrain restrict cropping patterns.

Indigenous populations face barriers to progress owing to both discrimination and their geographical location. In Near East and North Africa, they have little voice in government affairs. In Latin America, they are more likely to be poor, especially if they lack literacy in Spanish (or Portuguese); 85% of households headed by Aymara speakers in the rural sierra of Peru are poor.[33] Poverty overlaps with location (the Sierra and the Amazonian region in Ecuador; the North, North-West and South-West regions of Guatemala; the Chiapas region in Mexico; and the northern and the Segovias regions in Nicaragua). Such people tend to be excluded from education, employment and health care. The steady exclusion of indigenous minorities from good land is also associated with persistent rural poverty in parts of Asia.

Barriers to progress often form a vicious circle. (a) Many remote rural populations lack social services, which in turn affects their productive ability. (b) Physical (remoteness) and social barriers to markets interact similarly. (c) Remoteness and low population density result in inadequate infrastructure provision in East and Southern Africa, Asia and the Pacific and Near East and North Africa. This affects not only productivity but also access to social services, making the rural poor more vulnerable to famine and disease, and prolonging sickness. (d) Poor access to health facilities, sanitation and immunization impairs the productivity, income and nutritional status of the poor in all regions, in turn making them less able to escape poverty or seek out health care. (e) Poverty increases exposure to short-term migration and hence Acquired Immunodeficiency Syndrome (AIDS), which in parts of Africa has terribly impaired the working capacity of the poor. (f) Lack of education for poor rural women keeps fertility high in Asia and the Pacific, and large family size impedes female education and the escape from poverty.

In spite of this, the last 50 years have seen unprecedented progress in reducing global poverty. This has been possible despite interlocking constraints. Key constraints vary across countries and regions. Removing a critical constraint – sometimes land maldistribution, sometimes low-yielding seed varieties or lack of schooling – often enables rural people to overcome others themselves. A simultaneous attack on many fronts can sometimes work well; in 1977-85, rural poverty in China plummeted with the combined impact of egalitarian distribution of communal lands, better seeds, more irrigation and less repression of farm prices. In general, rural poverty reduction requires correct identification of key constraints, and correct sequencing of actions to relieve them.

The linked disadvantages of poverty and gender
Poverty is not gender-neutral. Women have less access to, and control of, land, credit, technology, education and health, and skilled work. Women also suffer discrimination in pay and in access to land, legacies and credit. Though the evidence (in most countries) does not suggest that women are more consumption-poor than men, their control over income is certainly less. It is based on more menial and less self-directed work accompanied by the 'double day' of care for home and children, frequent pregnancies and frequent child deaths.[34]

Women's disadvantages, even in terms of survival chances, are not always a matter of poverty: the sex ratio is most adverse in the two Indian States with lowest poverty incidence, Haryana and Punjab.[35] Female participation in the rural labour force varied by region: in 1981, from 2.6% in India's Punjab to 47% in Andhra Pradesh.[36] In districts with low female participation in the workforce, girls are seen as a burden and their survival prospects are worse than those of boys.[37] Women's relative survival prospects are generally brightest in countries where their workforce share is largest (around 35% for Hong Kong, China, Korea and Singapore; and over 40% for the People's Republic of China, Mongolia, Thailand and Vietnam). Discrimination in nutrition is marked in Pakistan, where the share of the female workforce is only 13%.

Rural women in India in 1983 were 12% more likely to be poor than rural men,[38] though this is offset by the excess of men among the poorest urban adults. In most Asian countries women, and female-headed households, are only slightly more likely to be poor than men and in female-headed rather than male-headed households.[39] In rural Thailand and Cambodia, female-headed households are less likely to be poor than male-headed households.[40] In Indonesia, the Philippines, Viet Nam, and to a small extent Kyrgyz Republic, rural households headed by women were more likely to be poor than male-headed households, but the opposite is the case in cities.[41]

Female-headed households have less access to productive assets and social services in all regions. This affects not only their current productive ability and the well-being of the household but also the intra-household allocation of resources such as food and education, which could result in intergenerational transfer of poverty. Discrimination also plays a part in Near East and North Africa where women suffer from cultural limitations on their mobility. Gender bias in customary laws is common in Latin America and the Caribbean. But in the highlands of Asia and the Pacific, where traditional society is still strong, women suffer less discrimination than do those in the rest of the region.

Discrimination in education early on in life affects the economic, social and political position of women later on. In West and Central Africa, although female-headed households are not necessarily poorer than other households, the impact of poverty is harder on women in both types of household because of the time spent on household chores and farmwork; the type of work they do is limited by their low education levels and lack of decision-making authority within the household. Exclusion from decision-making at local and national levels is also an important yet neglected female deficiency. This is sometimes not only a female phenomenon. In West and Central Africa and Near East and North Africa, the lack of effective institutions excludes the rural poor from services and prevents their voices being heard. In Latin America and the Caribbean, female-headed households are sometimes, but not generally, poorer than male-headed households, possibly because of better developed social security systems, education opportunities and employment prospects for women (such as in export agriculture) than in other regions. However, in Bolivia female-headed households are associated with a reduction of 37% of household per capita income in urban areas and 45% in rural areas, even after allowing for differences in education, household size and age.[42] The most vulnerable group in Guatemala is female-headed indigenous households self-employed in agriculture.[43]

Even when they are not on average poorer than men, women are more vulnerable. Women have less chance to escape poverty than men. Seventy per cent of poor women in India remain illiterate.[44] Poor rural women are almost uniformly illiterate in Bihar, Madhya Pradesh, Orissa, and Rajasthan.[45] In much of South Asia and more remote areas of the People's Republic of China the lack of education discourages women from moving to towns. Those who do move often have much lower employment rates than in rural areas.[46]

Even at East Asian growth levels and in female-employing sectors such as textiles, leather, or light electronics, alleviating this gender disparity depends in part on the spread of female education. As in the case of the textile industry in Bangladesh, women usually need at least a little education to gain from expanded employment in modern manufacturing.

Cultural and policy factors impinge on gender disadvantage in poverty, as upon urban and regional bias: Laos, Sri Lanka and Viet Nam show much less female disadvantage than would be expected at their income levels. The disadvantages of female-headed households in Asia tend to be not so much lower income or higher poverty as less leisure, fewer opportunities, greater vulnerability, worse health, or less education.

The removal of gender inequities in the face of poverty has been as much a cause as an effect of growth: depriving a good farmer of land, or a bright child of schooling, because she is female, is not only unfair, it is also a barrier to growth. Gender inequality in education and employment in sub-Saharan Africa reduced per capita growth during 1960-92 by 0.8% a year.[47] In Burkina Faso, inefficient factor allocation within the household results in an estimated 6% loss in output.[48] In Zambia, if women were to have the same degree of capital investment in agricultural inputs as men, output would increase by up to 15%.[49]

Female farmers are at least as efficient as men when individual characteristics and input levels are accounted for.[50] In Burkina Faso, if they have the same education, women use land somewhat more productively than men. Education is the key. For maize in Kenya, primary education has a positive and significant impact on yields only on female-managed farms, perhaps because women are much less likely than men to receive agricultural extension (a good substitute for education as a source of farm knowledge). Furthermore, it has been estimated that if female maize farmers are given sample mean characteristics and input levels, their yield increases by 7%. If given the same characteristics and inputs as men, their yield would increase by 9%. Giving women one year of education can lead to an estimated 24% increase in yields. Removal of gender discrimination is both intrinsically right and has beneficial effects.

VULNERABILITY

Rural areas are more at risk from large falls in employment induced by climate; from droughts and floods; from illness and high mortality; and often from war, cattle raiding, or civil disturbance. The poor are especially vulnerable to most such risks. They are also less resilient: a 5% fall in income, or an illness involving lost work and costs of treatment, is more threatening for those with little or no savings, insurance or access to credit. Rural people, especially in remote areas, also have weaker access to governmental, financial, or insurance support. On the other hand, rural people in emergency situations are usually supported by closer links to community or kin, and are less vulnerable than townspeople to macroeconomic phenomena such as cyclical unemployment or inflation,[51] though not to market collapses affecting particular products.

The rural and the poor are, in general, much more vulnerable to fluctuations in well-being than the urban and the non-poor: the fluctuations are larger and resilience is less. But this is not true of some of the rural and the poor; their main problem in irrigated areas with adequate primary health provision is low average well-being, not sharp downward shocks. It is an empirical matter whether the poor's vulnerability is better attacked by reducing their downward fluctuation or by raising their average incomes – a vital issue in many irrigation systems. Like ill-health and illiteracy, vulnerability is a characteristic often linked to poverty, especially rural consumption poverty, but it is not the same as poverty, or part of it.[52]

Poor people, especially in rural areas, are particularly likely to be vulnerable to the consequences of two patterns of events. The first involves a high rate of child deaths, linked to many and closely spaced births, and large, chronically poor families. The second pattern involves sharp income reductions in bad times, inability to build up or keep assets (including skills), reliance on unskilled and often casual labour for income, residence in unreliably watered rural areas and transient but frequent and severe poverty. The current rapid transition from higher to lower fertility is transforming both these patterns of events. Deaths (outside the worst AIDS-hit areas) and births that push people into, or deeper into, transient poverty are getting rarer and, with delayed marriages, later. The fertility transition also alters the dynamics of chronic poverty by inducing large rises in the proportion of people who are of working age.

The rural and the poor are usually late in acquiring the changes in provisions and incentives that reduce fertility: better prospects for child survival, girls' education and women's work. So the gains from fertility transition – sharply rising worker/dependant ratios in the long run, fewer poverty-increasing deaths and births in the short run – arrive later among the rural and the poor, unless policy speeds them up.

Demographics: delayed transitions, windows of opportunity, and the shadow of AIDS[53]

In much of Asia and Africa 50 years ago – and still often among the rural poor in many areas, notably of West and Central Africa – 20 to 30% of newborns died before the age of five. Parents insure against high death rates with even higher birth rates. Poorer families usually have higher ratios of dependent children to adults: Pakistan's 1984-85 household survey showed that the poorest quintile of households averaged 4.3 children and the richest 1.5.[54] Poorer families in this position are more likely to stay poor and assetless. Large family sizes and high dependency ratios are associated in many empirical studies with under-nutrition, ill-health, discrimination against girl siblings and low education, as well as with poverty itself: such households are often unable to feed children adequately, or to release working children for school.[55] Women who are pressed to marry young and produce many children can seldom develop their capabilities when preoccupied with pregnancy, often risky childbirth, and lactation. Their low-skill status reduces women's earning prospects – increasing men's insistence that they produce more children instead.

This situation is being transformed by the impact on rural poverty of falling child mortality, followed 10-25 years later by falling fertility. At first this makes child/adult ratios even higher, as more new-borns survive. Later, as they grow into adulthood and as fertility falls, child/adult ratios fall sharply. Both phases affect dependency ratios (the ratio of the number of people aged 0-15 or over 60 to the number aged 15-60) dramatically: in China the ratio fell from 154 in 1950 to 115 in 1970, then rose to 133 in 1980 and 186 in 2000.

Adults aged 15-60 are most likely to work and save; this factor is estimated to account for 1.7% per year of East Asia's growth of real GDP per person in 1970-90.[56] This helps the poor; each percentage point of growth normally produces at least a comparable fall in the incidence and severity of extreme poverty. Fertility decline also reduces poverty almost as much through improved income distribution (typically with a time-lag), perhaps by moderating the supply of labour and the demand for food. The gains for the poor are highest where initial poverty and fertility are highest.[57]

Fertility has been declining, since the 1980s at least, throughout most of the developing world, including Africa.[58] The dramatic effects on worker/dependant ratios, following earlier rises as child mortality fell, can be seen in Annex Table 2.3. The rising proportion of working-age persons in 2000-15 affects almost all the developing world. Even the damage from AIDS in Africa will not radically change this.

Will this huge demographic boom in workers and savers be enough to reduce most rural poverty, as it has helped to do in much of East and South-East Asia? The answer depends mainly on whether the fertility transition quickly reaches the rural poor and on whether extra workers and savings are matched by extra and attractive chances for productive work and investment. Both depend mainly on the use of assets, including health and education as well as land, technology, institutions and markets – in particular their capacity to enhance staples food production, water availability and distributive empowerment.

In other words, realizing the potential for reducing poverty, especially rural poverty, in the ongoing demographic revolution is a matter of policy: it is not automatic. Success in making it possible and attractive for the rural poor to cut their dependency ratios, and to translate that into escape from poverty, requires careful actions by civil society, governments and the international system to steer more, and better managed, resources to rural and poor agents.

The rural and the poor have come later than others to benefit from the decline in child mortality and other incentives to later marriage and lower marital fertility. Rural women in developing countries tend to have between one and three more children than urban women. For the rural poor the gap is bigger.

The outcome of this demographic change, and of rural-to-urban migration, is summarized in Table 2.3 for all four developing countries with more than one year of data for rural (and also urban) age structures. Typically 4-8% more of rural than of urban populations is aged under 15, and the gap is increasing. Despite lower rural life expectancy, the rural proportions aged over 60 are also usually higher, because many rural-to-urban

Table 2.3: Trends in prime-age dependency ratios, rural and urban

| Country | Year | Persons aged 15-59 per hundred people aged 0-14 or 60+ | |
		Urban	Rural
Brazil	1960	125	99
	1991	148	111
China	1982	195	132
	1990	228	161
Egypt	1960	105	104
	1985	135	104
India	1961	127	111
	1995	172	133

Source: UN, Demographic Yearbooks, 1979: 240-66; 1979 (special Issue): 288-372; 1985: 210-45; 1996: 218-61.

migrants return to rural areas in later life. The advantage of urban over rural areas in workforce/dependant ratios was already pronounced in the earlier years, and around 1990 the urban-rural gaps had become wide.

All four countries have already benefited from part of their fertility transition. Early rural gains tend to be smaller than urban gains and offset by adult urbanization and may even, as in Egypt, be non-existent. Rural areas eventually catch up, but if the potentially higher worker/dependant ratios in rural areas are to be realized, the fall in the death rate has to be accelerated by redressing urban bias in health assets and creating other incentives to fertility decline.[59] This suggests policies to empower rural people to choose rapid mortality and fertility transitions: better child health and nutritional care, readier access to contraception, improved work and school chances for women. Policy and institutional structures must become more pro-rural and pro-poor if the rural poor are to experience the huge overall rises in worker/dependant ratios as personal paths out of poverty.

Casting a shadow over this demographic potential is the threat of HIV/AIDS. Some 34 million are now infected, about two thirds of them in Africa. Initially a problem of the urban non-poor, HIV/AIDS in the developing world increasingly affects the rural poor. For them especially, its demographic effects are crucial and little appreciated. In Africa, deaths particularly affect women aged 15-30: women's chances of contracting HIV/AIDS are about double that of men's. This has led to a large fall in the female/male ratio; a big rise in the numbers of motherless children; and special difficulties in hoe agricultures, often reliant by culture and tradition on women's work. And this has also led to an initial fall in the proportion of workers under 30 at the start of an epidemic, sharply reversed as age cohorts mature, so that from the mid-1990s, 15 years into the epidemic, the proportion of economically active persons aged 15-30 has been much higher than before, especially for women.[60] Yet despite the devastating impact of HIV/AIDS, and the great importance of active policy to contain it if rural poverty is to fall, its effect on the medium-term demographic transition is small. It hardly alters the major projected rises in the adult/child and worker/dependant ratios, even in badly AIDS-damaged countries such as Kenya (Annex Table 2.3).

In India, where over 70% of the population is rural, HIV is spreading faster in some rural areas than in urban ones. In many countries in Africa, urban and rural HIV/AIDS prevalence rates are similar. Particularly vulnerable are rural areas along truck routes, sources of migrant labour to urban areas, nomadic pastoralists, and women remaining on farms with seasonal migrant husbands.[61]

Now that HIV/AIDS can no longer be seen as mainly a disease of the urban non-poor, the special problems of the rural and the poor – in exposure to infection, risk of transmission and hence infection once exposed, and impact once infected – become alarmingly clear.[62] Exposure originates substantially from male migration and female prostitution. Risk of infection, given exposure, rises with female gender, female circumcision, lesions due to prior untreated venereal disease, non-use of barrier contraceptives, and probably impaired immune response due, for example, to earlier severe undernutrition before or soon after birth. Impact, given infection, worsens with lack of medical care, urgent seasonal work needs, large dependent families, and absence of savings, reserves and therefore resilience.

Countries with the highest HIV/AIDS incidence are mostly in Southern Africa, with massive, selectively male, rural-to-urban migration to seek employment in mines. This is much increased by rural inequality[63] and probably also by rural stagnation; policies to tackle these will also reduce the damage from HIV/AIDS. Gender roles matter too: if women can insist on condoms, refuse intercourse to men with HIV/AIDS, and obtain sufficient equality to reduce polygamy, new infections will decline. However, the main short-run remedies for HIV/AIDS are medical: free, widely distributed condoms; the registration of sex-workers and requiring them to supply condoms and checking that they comply; and regular health checks on prostitute and migrant communities. These policies must be based on government awareness and public frankness about HIV/AIDS and on consent and good practice in civil society, including the rural and the poor. HIV/AIDS will spread without health care and information, alternatives to migration (and in extreme cases to prostitution), and reduced gender biases. Appropriate interventions have greatly reduced new infections, and hence incidence, in Brazil, Senegal, Thailand and Uganda.

HIV/AIDS probably reduces fertility substantially in the short term, as sexual behaviour changes.[64] Yet this fertility decline will not accelerate the long-run gains to the poor from fertility transition. First, such gains arise largely from higher adult/child ratios; but these are not projected to fall much as a result of AIDS. Second, even if they do, any macro-level benefits to growth, and hence to poverty reduction, arise through improved personal capacity to save, work and pay taxes, and reduced personal needs for public outlay on education; but these are swamped as AIDS imposes new health costs, reduces tax-paying capacity, and erodes the ability of victims and carers to save and work, with worst effects on the rural and the poor. Third, household gains from normal fertility transition are swamped in the wake of AIDS by household losses from disease and suffering; from death of breadwinners and mothers; and from extra care for the sick and orphaned. Finally, despite the pressures towards condom use or abstinence during AIDS epidemics, AIDS-affected African countries have only recently emerged from a high-fertility, high-mortality regime. Where AIDS has sharply raised under-five mortality, people may later revert to high-fertility behaviour, at least among uninfected couples.

The AIDS tragedy consumes lives and resources both nationally and at household level. It also diverts labour and health-care resources, sabotaging poverty reduction and development. Increasingly it attacks the medically underprivileged, the rural and the poor. Preventive remedies are known, and used in several countries. But vast as it is, the AIDS tragedy is unlikely to remove the opportunities for human advance, including rural poverty reduction, through demographic transition, and rising ratios of workers and savers to dependants.

Transience and vulnerability: short-run dynamics

Some of the poor are not poor all the time. In South and East Asia, for instance, the International Crops Research Institute for the Semi-Arid Tropics' (ICRISAT) work in six southern Indian villages shows that around a quarter of consumption-poor households had not been poor in the previous year, and a similar proportion would not be poor in the succeeding year.[65] Similar results have been observed in four villages in rural Pakistan,[66] in four provinces in rural China,[67] and in a subsample of the All India National Household Sample Survey.[68] The situation is shown clearly by an overview of panel data based on year-to-year observations (Table 2.4).

The dynamic nature of poverty means that the policies for reducing transitory poverty may be quite different from those needed to combat chronic poverty. This distinction between chronic and transitory[69] has particular implications for rural poverty:

- a stronger emphasis on indicators which determine long-run welfare, such as land ownership;
- comparison using panel data as well as non-panel time-series,[70] as rural poverty may fluctuate more than urban poverty (given the former's dependence on agriculture and the weather);
- analysis of migration, remittances and seasonality, which ideally should be analysed within poverty dynamics; and
- policy to address targeting, consumption smoothing and insurance, and to assess who exactly within the household bears the brunt of welfare swings, and how.

Several recent panel surveys trace short-run changes in the fortunes of the rural poor and near-

Table 2.4: Extent of transient and chronic poverty

| | Study dates | Number of observations in panel | Proportion of households | | |
			Always poor	Sometimes poor	Never poor
West and Central Africa					
Côte d'Ivoire	1985-86	2	14.5	20.2	65.3
Côte d'Ivoire	1986-87	2	13.0	22.9	64.1
Côte d'Ivoire	1987-88	2	25.0	22.0	53.0
East and Southern Africa					
Ethiopia	1994-95	2	24.8	30.1	45.1
South Africa	1993-98	2	22.7	31.5	45.8
Zimbabwe	1992/93-1995/96	4	10.6	59.6	29.8
Latin America and the Caribbean					
Chile	1967/68-1985/86	2	54.1	31.5	14.4
East Asia and thePacific					
China	1985-90	6	6.2	47.8	46.0
India	1968/69-1970/71	3	33.3	36.7	30.0
India	1975/76-1983/84	9	21.8	65.8	12.4
Pakistan	1986-91	5	3.0	55.3	41.7

Note: The surveys use national poverty lines and different lengths of panel and are therefore comparable, if at all, only with great caution and to a modest extent.

Source: Baulch and Hoddinott 1999.

poor (Annex Table 2.4).[71] Three emerging issues are relevant for anti-poverty policy.[72]

Identifying the poor

For many people, whether they are identified as poor depends on the year of survey. So at any time, many more people in developing countries are vulnerable to poverty than are actually in poverty, and many of those actually in poverty are usually not. Table 2.4 shows that generally between about one quarter and one third of households move in and out of poverty in the survey year.

The proportion of poor who are transient is much higher in rural than in urban areas, and highest in rural places with unreliable water supply. Estimates of the incidence of chronic poverty range from 3% of households (Pakistan, 1985-90) to 54% (Chile, 1967-85). Incidence of transient poverty, on the other hand, ranges from 20-22% (Côte d'Ivoire, 1985-88) to nearly 66% (India, 1975-83). It is important to note that estimates of chronic and transitory poverty vary with the choice of poverty line since mobility is unlikely to be uniform throughout the distribution.

Experience of poverty

Poverty varies over time in other ways. (a) Depth of even chronic poverty varies among years. (b) Absolute poverty may be more likely to be transient than relative poverty, i.e. being poorest may be more persistent than being absolutely poor. (c) Some who make the transition out of poverty fall back: how much transient poverty reflects people who repeatedly move above and below the poverty line; how much of poverty is just a one-off incident; or do the same unfortunate people suffer many incidents?

All this matters, because various sorts of chronic and transient poverty may demand different remedies. Knowledge of factors associated with movements in and out of poverty allows us to target anti-poverty policies to particular vulnerable groups. For

example, people who typically sink into poverty after loss of employment or changes in family status (in particular childbirth, divorce or widowhood) need employment guarantee schemes combined with support for mothers and female-headed households. We can intervene more effectively if we know the frequency and duration of poverty spells for different categories of households. Numerous short, recurring spells of poverty demand measures such as safety nets, credit and insurance schemes for vulnerable households, or in some cases more child nutrition support, or more robust plant or animal varieties. Extended spells of poverty call for policies that improve the assets and entitlements of the poor, such as education, land reform, or improved disability and old-age pensions. Further, victims of mainly transient or mainly chronic poverty, whether adults or children, or workers on irrigated or dryland farms, may differ in resilience, or otherwise benefit from distinct policies geared to the interaction of poverty, duration and type of person.

Furthermore, transient poverty may often deepen and evolve into chronic poverty through repeated poverty triggers. Policy-makers need to know what these triggers are in each region, and to interact sensibly with poor people's own attempts to anticipate or cope with them.[73]

Explanations of poverty

The emerging, though tentative and largely country-specific, explanations of poverty shown in panel data are summarized in Annex Table 2.4.

RECENT HISTORY OF RURAL POVERTY AND DONOR RESPONSE

Rural welfare indicators have improved, but rural-urban gaps are high and not shrinking

Rural areas generally have less access than urban areas to safe water, adequate sanitation and some health services (Table 2.5). The data are very approximate, but differences are generally larger in West and Central Africa than elsewhere. In

Table 2.5: Access to health and sanitation

	Adequate sanitation (1990-97)[a]		Safe drinking water (1995)[b]		Health services (1985-95)[c]	
	Urban	Rural	Urban	Rural	Urban	Rural
West and Central Africa						
Burkina Faso	41	33	n.a.	n.a.	100	89
Cameroon	64	36	n.a.	30	44	39
Chad	n.a.	n.a	48	17	64	n.a.
Ghana	62	44	88	52	92	45
Guinea-Bissau	n.a	n.a	38	57	n.a.	n.a.
Mauritania	44	19	87	41	72	33
Niger	79	5	70	44	99	30
Nigeria	50	32	80	39	85	62
Senegal	71	15	90	44	n.a.	n.a.
Sierra Leone	17	8	58	21	90	20
East and Southern Africa						
Ethiopia	97	7	n.a.	n.a.	n.a.	n.a.
Kenya	69	81	n.a.	n.a.	n.a.	40
Lesotho	56	35	64	60	n.a.	n.a.
Madagascar	68	30	n.a.	n.a.	65	65
Uganda	75	55	60	36	99	42
Zambia	94	57	66	37	100	50
Zimbabwe	96	32	n.a.	n.a.	96	80
Asia and the Pacific						
Bangladesh	83	38	49	n.a.	n.a.	n.a.
Cambodia	n.a.	9	20	12	80	50
China	74	7	n.a.	n.a.	100	89
India	70	14	n.a.	82	100	80
Indonesia	77	49	87	57	n.a.	n.a.
Kazakhstan	100	98	n.a.	n.a.	n.a.	n.a.
Malaysia	94	94	100	86	n.a.	n.a.
Mongolia	99	74	100	68	n.a.	n.a.
Nepal	28	14	61	59	n.a.	n.a.
Pakistan	93	39	85	56	99	35
Philippines	89	63	91	81	77	74
Sri Lanka	68	62	88	65	n.a.	n.a.
Thailand	97	94	94	88	90	90
Viet Nam	43	15	n.a.	n.a.	100	80
Latin America and the Caribbean						
Bolivia	74	37	88	43	77	52
Brazil	80	30	80	28	n.a.	n.a.
Chile	90		99	47	n.a.	n.a.
Colombia	97	56	90	32	n.a.	n.a.
Costa Rica	95	70	100	99	100	63
Dominican Republic	76	83	88	55	84	67
Ecuador	95	49	81	10	70	20
Guatemala	95	74	97	48	47	25
Honduras	n.a.	57	91	66	80	56
Nicaragua	34	35	93	28	100	60
Panama	n.a.	n.a.	99	73	95	64
Paraguay	65	14	70	6	90	38
Peru	89	37	91	31	n.a.	n.a.
Trinidad and Tobago	99	98	100	88	100	99
Venezuela	64	30	79	79	n.a.	n.a.
Near East and North Africa						
Algeria	99	80	n.a.	n.a.	100	95
Morocco	94	24	97	20	100	50
Tunisia	96	52	100	76	100	80

a/ UNICEF 1999. b/ World Bank 1999b. c/ UNICEF 1996.

n.a. data not available

Ethiopia, Niger and Sierra Leone, less than 10% of rural people had access to adequate sanitation in 1990-97.

Illiteracy among over-15s has considerably declined in almost all countries with both rural and urban data for at least two years since 1950 (Table 2.6). Yet over half the rural over-15s were illiterate in large countries of Asia and Near East and North Africa during 1987-95. Despite much greater initial lack of rural schooling, the disparity has been widening. The odds ratio of rural-to-urban illiteracy risk rose between the 1970s and the 1990s for all eight countries in Asia with available data, for women, men and all adults; for almost all cases in Latin

Table 2.6: Illiteracy rates

| | Year | Over 15s illiterate, percentage of population | | | | | |
| | | Total | | Male | | Female | |
		Urban	Rural	Urban	Rural	Urban	Rural
East and South Asia							
Bangladesh	1961	62.5	84.9	53.6	77.2	75.2	93.0
	1974	51.9	76.6	37.5	65.4	66.9	87.9
	1981	51.9	74.6	42.0	64.6	65.9	84.7
	1991	37.7	69.6	27.3	57.9	47.5	80.0
China	1982	17.6	37.8	9.5	23.1	26.4	53.2
	1990	12.0	26.2	6.1	15.7	18.4	37.1
India	1971	40.1	73.6	27.9	60.4	55.1	87.5
	1991 a/	26.7	55.3	18.9	42.1	35.9	69.4
Nepal	1981	52.6	81.3	40.3	70.4	67.0	92.4
	1995 b/	35.8	64.2	22.7	49.9	49.5	77.6
Pakistan	1961	63.3	84.2	52.6	74.7	78.9	94.6
	1981	52.6	83.2	43.1	73.9	64.1	93.4
	1994 c/	43.0	n.a.	n.a.	72.5	n.a.	n.a.
Philippines	1970 c/	7.2	21.3	6.0	19.8	8.2	22.8
	1990	2.7	10.3	2.4	9.6	3.0	11.0
Sri Lanka	1971	14.1	25.0	9.4	15.5	19.7	34.9
	1981	6.6	15.2	4.4	10.0	8.9	20.5
Thailand	1970	12.3	22.9	6.3	13.9	18.1	31.6
	1990	3.3	7.5	1.9	5.0	4.5	9.9
Latin America and the Caribbean							
Bolivia	1976	16.0	55.3	6.6	37.7	24.3	67.8
	1992	8.9	36.1	3.7	23.0	13.5	49.4
Brazil	1976	14.4	40.6	12.0	39.4	16.6	41.9
	1991	10.7	31.1	n.a.	n.a.	n.a.	n.a.
Costa Rica	1950	8.1	27.9	6.1	26.7	9.7	29.3
	1973	4.9	17.0	4.0	16.6	5.7	17.5
Guatemala	1973	28.2	68.6	20.0	59.9	35.5	77.6
	1994	16.8	47.8	11.2	38.5	21.6	56.9
Near East and North Africa							
Algeria	1971	58.8	81.1	42.0	66.5	74.2	94.0
	1987	42.9	71.2	29.5	55.8	56.2	87.2
Morocco	1971	61.3	88.5	45.6	78.1	75.8	98.7
	1994	41.1	79.3	27.7	65.5	53.8	92.3
Tunisia	1975	49.5	75.4	36.9	61.9	62.1	89.2
	1989	31.9	60.0	21.9	44.9	42.4	75.1

a/ over 7s. b/ over 6s. c/ over 10s. n.a. data not available.

Source: UNESCO Statistical Yearbooks, various years.

America; and for a substantial majority of cases in the three Near East and North Africa countries.[74] Comparable health data are few but, for 12 developing countries with available data, the ratio of rural to urban mortality among under-fives grew from 1.4:1 in the mid-1970s to 1.6:1 in the mid-1980s.[75]

The uneven decline in rural poverty

Rural and urban areas differ in poverty levels as well (Annex Table 2.1). Comparisons are difficult because national poverty lines are used, and because of difficulties in setting urban and rural poverty lines and different definitions of 'urban'. But urban poverty is clearly lower than rural poverty. So is average depth of poverty.[76] Most country data use national poverty lines and are based on nationally determined nutritional requirements, with an assumption made about the share of non-food expenditure in the minimum necessary budget. Annex Table 2.2 summarizes the trends in rural-urban poverty, growth and income and sectoral distribution for countries for which such data is available. Here we present some broad conclusions (Table 2.7 provides a summary).

- Rural-urban poverty gaps remain wide in Latin America, in spite of much higher mean incomes than in Africa or South Asia, and some falls in rural and urban poverty. This is due partly to the choice of high national poverty lines but also to higher inequality.[77]
- Faster falls in rural and urban poverty occurred in Asia, especially but not only East Asia, but region-wide ratios of rural to urban poverty have risen since 1985, especially in China.
- Most of Africa (except Ethiopia and Uganda) has seen little poverty reduction since the late 1970s but a fall in the exceptionally high ratios of rural to urban poverty.
- Rates of poverty reduction, and its responsiveness to faster economic growth, have been substantially lower since the late 1980s than in 1975-88.

- Sharp rises in poverty, especially in farming areas, have occurred in ten transitional countries since the late 1980s.[78] This reflects collapsing safety nets and a failure either to maintain subsidies to the poor within unreformed agriculture or to undertake egalitarian land reforms except in Albania, Armenia, Romania and Viet Nam.

These broad findings mask many regional variations in poverty trends. For instance, even though rural poverty has appreciably declined in China, parts of the north-west are still very poor. Overall there has been no global correction since the late 1970s of the urban biases that sentence rural people to more widespread and deeper poverty, illiteracy and ill-health. Only in sub-Saharan Africa, where the biases were greatest and then only for consumption poverty, have the disparities systematically lessened. Since the suppression of farm prices has declined with liberalization and globalization, it follows that other factors have turned against the rural poor.

Poverty, including rural poverty, fell sharply around 1975-88 and continues to fall, even if more slowly, for rural and urban people in much of Asia and some other areas. But the rural-urban gaps, which appear inefficient as well as inequitable, and which penalize rural areas where most of the poor still live, are not shrinking in most developing countries.

A relevant issue is how to reduce poverty by incorporating the rural and urban poor in manufacturing and services. Indonesia and China, like several smaller East Asian countries, have had some success, with poverty reduction continuing well after the agricultural workforce started to fall. The future of rural poverty, and of rural-urban disparity, is bound up with the capacity to educate and otherwise equip the children of the poor to make this enriching transition. Where this is neglected, long-term prospects for rural poverty and the rural-urban poverty disparity are

Table 2.7: Country classification of rural poverty trends

Rural poverty trend (1980-99)*	WCA	ESA	EAP	LAC	NENA	EE&FSU
No appreciable decline	Burkina Faso	Kenya	Bangladesh Cambodia Philippines	Peru		
Decline but still high	Mauritania	Zambia	Pakistan	Colombia Ecuador Guatemala Honduras		
Initial decline but running out of steam			India			
Appreciable decline		Ethiopia Uganda	China Indonesia Malaysia Sri Lanka		Morocco Tunisia	
Increase		Zimbabwe	Dominican Republic		Algeria	Kyrgyz Republic Romania
No clear trend	Nigeria					

* This is the broad period for which data is available. For individual countries, the period may vary.
Sources: See Annex Table 2.2.

bleak. For many Asian countries this is increasingly a problem of islands of regional poverty.

International aid and the rural poor

Aid[79] can reduce poverty in several ways. It can go to countries or to sectors, especially rural and agricultural, where poverty is widespread and severe. (This reaches the poor only to the extent that such aid is not fungible, i.e. that it does not mean less of other poverty-reducing resources, such as efforts by governments or private citizens, or flows of foreign investment.) Aid can be cost-effective against poverty within countries and sectors. And, even with weak sector and country allocation and cost-effectiveness, aid volume can be high enough to reduce poverty substantially.

Aid volume and poverty volume

Between 1987-88 and 1998 net aid disbursed in real terms fell from 0.33% to 0.24% of sharply rising OECD Gross Domestic Product (GDP), the lowest proportion ever,[80] as against an agreed target of 0.7%. For low-income countries, net aid comprised only 1.4% of GNP, or USD 6.90 per person per year (down from 2.7% in 1992) per year. Aid is nevertheless very important for many countries with substantial poverty. In 1998, for sub-Saharan Africa (excluding South Africa and Nigeria), net aid disbursed was 8.6% of GNP, and for Latin America and the Caribbean 7.3% – respectively, about half and about a third of gross domestic investment. Yet South and East Asia,[81] together containing two thirds of the world's dollar-poor, received only 25% of net aid disbursements, less than 1% of GNP and below one twentieth of gross domestic investment.[82] By the late 1990s real net aid flows, especially to low-income countries in Asia, had fallen far below the volumes required to make major dents in poverty, despite donor commitments at the 1995 UN Social

Summit and in the Development Assistance Committee of the OECD in 1996 to manage aid around anti-poverty partnerships led by each developing country.

Yet in another sense aid is substantial relative to extreme poverty. We compared dollar poverty in the 47 countries with reliable surveys for various years around 1995, with net aid disbursed in the survey year.[83] In this sample, extra consumption needed to remove poverty for those consuming below PPP USD 1 a day was USD 106 billion a year. The total aid disbursements in the survey years to these same countries were USD 339.5 billion. With perfect targeting by donors to recipient countries, and by each country on its poor, aid disbursements would have covered 37% of the global dollar poverty gap.

Why then is aid at such levels too small to make a major poverty impact in many countries? Mainly because aid leaks into regions, countries and sectors with low poverty and/or little cost-effectiveness in reaching the poor.

Country aid allocation and poverty

The politics of country targeting undermines the impact of aid on poverty.[84] Bilateral aid is influenced by commercial interests,[85] focuses still upon ex-colonies,[86] and hugely disfavours large countries even if they have massive poverty. Table 2.8 shows the weak congruence of aid with poverty at regional level.

Much aid goes to regions of quite high average real GDP and quite low poverty incidence. In both 1992 and 1998, 39% of net aid went to middle-income countries, the rest to low-income countries. South Asia and China receive a far lower proportion of aid than their low mean income and high share of world poverty would suggest; Latin America, the Confederation of Independent States, and the Near East and North Africa receive a far higher, and sub-Saharan Africa a somewhat higher, proportion.

This mismatch with poverty does not prove that aid is misallocated. Moderately poor countries or regions receiving large amounts of aid might be better at using aid to remove residual poverty than are worse-off and less-aided places. However, the low shares of world aid, and low aid per person, in 1998 in India (3.9% and USD 1.80) and China (5.7% and USD 1.90) are striking in view of their large shares of the world's extreme poor (over 400 and over 200 million, respectively, out

Table 2.8: Aid and extreme consumption poverty by main regions, 1998

Region	Persons consuming below 1993 PPP USD 1/day			Net aid disbursements				GNP/person
	No in mns	% of all dollar poor	Incidence of poverty in the region	USD mn	% of global	% of GNP	USD/person	
All rcpt countries	1198.9	100.0	–	41102	100.0	2.9	8.3	–
All dvpg countries	>1188.9	>99.0	24.0	34449	83.8	3.2	7.5	1250
E/SE Asia, Pacific*	278.3	23.2	15.3	7794	18.9	0.7	3.0	1138
E Eur/Cent Asia	24.0	2.0	5.1	5565	13.5	0.7	14.0	2110
LAC	78.2	6.5	15.6	4388	10.7	7.3	8.8	3830
S Asia	552.0	43.6	40.0	5034	12.2	0.8	3.8	490
SS Africa	290.9	24.2	46.3	12580	30.6	4.4	21.4	530
Middle East/ North Africa**	5.5	0.5	1.9	4607	11.2	0.9	18.1	2220

Notes: * World Bank category. In the UNDP Human Development Report categories, of this, East Asia (including China) received USD 2678m. aid (0.2% of GNP, USD 1.9 per person); SE Asia and the Pacific received USD 5516m. (1.1%, USD 10.0). **World Development Report category; 'Arab States receiving aid' (in UNHDR categorization) corresponds very closely.

Source: World Bank 2000a: Fig. 1 and table 1.1; UNDP, 2000: 205, 222.

of 1.2 billion)[87] together with their relatively good reputations for using aid to reduce poverty.

Focusing aid on poorer countries also means focusing it on countries with higher proportions of rural people and of the rural poor. In 2000, the proportion of persons mainly engaged in agriculture was 64% in sub-Saharan Africa and 55% in South Asia, but 41% in East and South-East Asia and only 21% in Latin America and the Caribbean.[88]

Consistent with this, in our 47-country sample aid is very badly targeted on countries with high extreme-poverty gaps: a recipient country's proportion of gross aid disbursements bears almost no relation to its proportion of the world's 'dollar poverty gap' of around USD 106 billion in 1995. However, aid is somewhat less badly targeted on countries with a high proportion of the world's dollar-poor. The distinction between the two indicators lies in the depth of poverty. Country aid allocation appears to take some slight account of poverty numbers, but none of poverty depth. For example, Morocco, The Gambia and Algeria have roughly the same share of the world's poor people, but on average the poor in The Gambia are about 46 times poorer than the poor in Algeria and Morocco. Yet current allocations give far less aid to The Gambia than to Algeria and Morocco.

It is sometimes claimed that the high proportion of aid allocated to low-poverty countries matters little, in the sense that public spending falls to offset aid increases. It is odd to dismiss aid because its impact is felt partly in increased private, rather than public, spending. The evidence from a 38-country sample is that an extra dollar of aid increases public spending by 33 cents in the average case;[89] the increase, of course, would be far more in highly-aided and very poor countries such as Malawi, Mozambique or Nicaragua, where aid is about 30% of GNP and covers almost all public expenditure.

Sector allocation and poverty

The much lower cost per workplace in agriculture, and its tendency to employ the poor and increase the reliability of their food, suggest that giving aid to agriculture and rural development is good for the poor if it raises output. Indian evidence that only agricultural growth is associated with substantial poverty reduction supports this.[90]

The proportion of sectorally allocable aid reaching agriculture, forestry and fisheries, which fell sharply from the mid-1970s to only 20.2% in 1987-89, plummeted further to 12.5% in 1996-98 (Annex Table 2.5), in contrast to the 52% of workforce (and presumably over two thirds of the poor) mainly dependent on agriculture for livelihoods. The real value of net aid disbursed to agriculture in the late 1990s was only 35% of its level in the late 1980s.

Aid is often fungible and hence bad at promoting particular economic policies even with alleged conditionality, though it is good at supporting countries that already have policies conducive to achieving good returns on aid.[95] These findings have coincided with an agreement among OECD donors to coordinate and subordinate their aid to monitored poverty targets, that is, halving dollar poverty in 1995-2015, and relevant funding gaps, identified by each developing country. Five years after this agreement, no such aid partnerships existed. In 2000 several have at last begun to take shape, principally under the aegis of World Bank/International Monetary Fund (IMF) Poverty Reduction Strategy Papers and the eight country strategies for halving poverty by the Asian Development Bank (ADB). This can contribute substantially to the ambitious targets of halving poverty in 1995-2015 only if aid concentrates much more on reducing rural poverty through stimulating agricultural growth and especially food production, yield and employment. It is on this that the poor depend for their work, income, health and poverty reduction; and it is here that dramatic progress has been possible. However, progress has stalled and is in dire need of revival.

Annex

Table 2.1: Rural–urban differences in poverty (country-specific poverty lines)

	Poverty Head Count Index			Poverty Gap Index	
	Rural	Urban	Rural–urban Ratio	Rural	Urban
West and Central Africa					
Burkina Faso 1994 [a/]	51.1	10.4	4.91		
Burkina Faso 1998	50.7	15.8	3.21		
Cameroon 1984 [b/]	32.4	44.4	0.73		
Chad 1985-6 [b/]	67.0	63.0	1.06		
Ghana 1987-8 [c/]	41.9	27.4	1.53		
Ghana 1991-2	33.9	26.5	1.28		
Guinea-Bissau 1991 [b/]	60.9	24.1	2.53		
Mauritania 1987 [a/]	72.1	43.5	1.66		
Mauritania 1996	58.9	19.0	3.10		
Niger 1989-93 [b/]	66.0	52.0	1.27		
Nigeria 1985 [a/]	45.1	29.6	1.52		
Nigeria 1992	67.8	57.5	1.18		
Nigeria 1985 [b/]	49.5	31.7	1.56		
Nigeria 1992	36.4	30.4	1.20		
Nigeria 1985 [c/]	16.1	4.9	3.29		
Nigeria 1992	15.4	10.9	1.41		
Senegal 1991 [b/]	40.4	16.4	2.46		
Sierra Leone 1989 [b/]	76.0	53.0	1.43		
East and Southern Africa					
Ethiopia 1989-95 [a/]	61.3	40.9	1.50		
Ethiopia 1994-7	45.9	38.7	1.19		
Kenya 1992 [b/]	46.4	29.3	1.58		
Kenya 1992 [c/]	46.3	29.3	1.59		
Kenya 1994	46.7	28.9	1.62		
Lesotho 1993 [a/]	53.9	27.8	1.94		
Madagascar 1993-4 [b/]	77.0	47.0	1.64		
Uganda 1992 [a/]	59.4	29.4	2.02		
Uganda 1997	48.2	16.3	2.96		
Zambia 1991 [b/]	88.0	46.0	1.91		
Zambia 1991 [c/]	79.1	27.2	2.91	50.1	9.5
Zambia 1996	74.9	34.0	2.20	37.8	11.4
Zimbabwe 1991 [a/]	51.5	6.2	8.31		
Zimbabwe 1996	62.8	14.9	4.21		
Zimbabwe 1990-1 [b/]	31.0	10.0	3.10		
East and South Asia					
Bangladesh 1983-4 [c/]	53.8	40.9	1.32	15.0	11.4
Bangladesh 1991-92	52.9	33.6	1.57	14.6	8.4
Bangladesh 1991-92 [b/]	46.0	23.3	1.97		
Bangladesh 1995-96	39.8	14.3	2.78		
Cambodia 1993-4 [b/]	43.1	24.8	1.74		
Cambodia 1997	40.1	21.1	1.90		
China 1978 [c/]	33.0	4.4	7.50		
China 1990	11.5	0.4	28.7		

(cont'd)

	Poverty Head Count Index			Poverty Gap Index	
	Rural	Urban	Rural–urban Ratio	Rural	Urban
China 1994[b/]	11.8	<2			
China 1996	7.9	<2			
China 1998	4.6	<2			
China 1988[f/]	22.6	2.7	8.37	7.2	0.4
China 1995	17.4	4.1	4.24	4.6	0.9
India 1992[b/]	43.5	33.7	1.29		
India 1994	36.7	30.5	1.20		
India 1957-8[g/]	55.2	47.8	1.15	19.0	16.0
India 1977-8	50.6	40.5	1.25	15.0	11.7
India 1987-8	38.9	35.6	1.09	10.0	9.3
India 1990-1	36.4	32.8	1.11	8.6	8.5
India 1994-5	34.2	28.4	1.20	8.7	7.1
India 1995-6	35.4	27.3	1.30	8.3	6.9
India 1997	34.2	27.9	1.23	8.1	7.2
Indonesia 1987[b/]	16.4	20.1	0.81		
Indonesia 1990	14.3	16.8	0.85	2.1	3.2
Indonesia 1996	12.3	9.7	1.27		
Indonesia 1998	22.0	17.8	1.24		
Indonesia 1984[c/]	45.7	15.9	3.87	12.8	3.5
Indonesia 1990	26.6	11.2	2.37	5.3	1.8
Lao PDR 1993[b/]	53.0	24.0	2.21		
Malaysia 1973[c/]	55.3	44.8	1.23		
Malaysia 1989	19.3	14.3	1.35		
Malaysia 1987[d/]	24.7	7.3	3.39		
Mongolia 1995[b/]	33.1	38.5	0.86		
Nepal 1995-6[b/]	44.0	23.0	1.91		
Pakistan 1991[b/]	36.9	28.0	1.32		
Pakistan 1984-5[d/]	49.3	38.2	1.29		
Pakistan 1990-1	36.9	28.0	1.32	7.8	5.7
Philippines 1961[c/]	64.0	51.0	1.25	19.0	13.9
Philippines 1988	53.0	23.0	2.30		
Philippines 1994[b/]	53.1	28.0	1.90		
Philippines 1997	51.2	22.5	2.28		
Papua New Guinea 1996[d/]	39.4	13.5	2.92	12.8	3.4
Sri Lanka 1985-6[b/]	45.5	26.8	1.70	18.0	21.8
Sri Lanka 1990-1	38.1	28.4	1.34		
Sri Lanka 1985-6[c/]	31.7	16.4	1.93	7.7	3.5
Sri Lanka 1990-1	24.4	18.3	1.33	5.3	4.1
Thailand 1992[b/]	15.5	10.2	1.52		
Viet Nam 1993[b/]	57.2	25.9	2.11		
Latin America and the Caribbean					
Bolivia 1996[e/]	81.7	33.8	2.42	56.7	12.7
Brazil 1990[b/]	32.6	13.1	2.49		
Brazil 1995[e/]	41.5	13.2	3.14	20.0	6.5

(cont'd)

Rural–urban differences in poverty (country-specific poverty lines) (cont'd)

	Poverty Head Count Index			Poverty Gap Index	
	Rural	Urban	Rural–urban Ratio	Rural	Urban
Chile 1995 [e/]	14.7	5.6	2.63	4.3	2.1
Colombia 1978 [e/]	38.4	12.1	3.17	16.6	4.6
Colombia 1992	31.2	8.0	3.90	13.5	2.4
Dominican Republic 1989 [b/]	27.4	23.3	1.18		
Dominican Republic 1992	29.8	10.9	2.73		
Ecuador 1990 [c/]	85.0	47.7	1.78		
Ecuador 1994	47.0	25.0	1.88		
Guatemala 1980 [c/]	83.7	47.0	1.78		
Guatemala 1986-7	79.7	60.3	1.32		
Guatemala 1989 [b/]	71.9	33.7	2.13		
Honduras 1989 [c/]	58.0	51.0	1.14		
Honduras 1993	51.0	57.0	0.72		
Nicaragua 1993 [b/]	76.1	31.9	2.39		
Panama 1997 [b/]	64.9	15.3	4.24		
Paraguay 1991 [b/]	28.5	19.7	1.45		
Paraguay 1995 [e/]	45.3	7.5	6.04	21.5	3.0
Peru 1994 [b/]	67.0	46.1	1.45		
Peru 1997	64.7	40.4	1.60		
Trinidad and Tobago 1992 [b/]	20.0	24.0	0.83		
Venezuela 1995 [e/]	73.1	45.8	1.60	34.6	19.9
Near East and North Africa					
Algeria 1988 [b/]	16.6	7.3	2.27		
Algeria 1995	30.3	14.7	2.06		
Morocco 1984-5 [b/]	32.6	17.3	1.88		
Morocco 1990-1	18.0	7.6	2.37		
Tunisia 1985 [b/]	29.2	12.0	2.43		
Tunisia 1990	21.6	8.9	2.43		
Yemen 1992 [b/]	19.2	18.6	1.03		
Eastern Europe and Former Soviet Union					
Estonia 1994 [b/]	14.7	6.8	2.16		
Georgia 1997 [b/]	9.9	12.1	0.82		
Kazakhstan 1996 [b/]	39.0	30.0	1.30		
Kyrgyz Republic 1993 [b/]	48.1	28.7	1.68		
Kyrgyz Republic 1997	64.5	28.5	2.26		
Romania 1989 [b/]	5.9	1.2	4.92		
Romania 1993	23.4	17.0	1.38		

Sources:

a/ Demery 1999; data given in World Bank 2000a.

b/ World Bank 2000b.

c/ Lipton and Eastwood 1999: Table III.1 – see below for original sources.

d/ de Haan and Lipton 1999: Table 4 – see below for original sources.

e/ Wodon 1999: Table 1.9, World Bank staff estimates.

f/ Khan 1998: Tables 6 and 10.

g/ Jha 1999: Table 4.

Lipton and Eastwood 1999, original sources:

Ghana: World Bank 1995e: 27.

Nigeria: World Bank 1996a: 22-6.

Kenya: Ayako and Katumanga 1997: 7.

Zambia: McCulloch and Baulch 1999.

Bangladesh: Jayarajah et al. 1996: 60.

China: World Bank 1992b: ix, 23, 146-7.

Indonesia: Jayarajah et al. 1996: 60.

Malaysia: de Haan and Lipton 1999 and Shari 1992 (NB: data not the same as in Lipton and Eastwood).

Philippines: World Bank 1995f: 3.

Sri Lanka: World Bank 1995g: 7.

Colombia: World Bank 1994b: 6.

Ecuador: World Bank 1995h, Vol. 2: 7.

Guatemala: World Bank 1995b, Annex 2: Table 1, data originally from CEPAL.

Honduras: World Bank 1994c, Appendix: Table C12.

de Haan and Lipton 1999 - original sources:

Malaysia: Ahuja et al. 1997: 14-15.

Pakistan: World Bank 1995i. 52.

Papua New Guinea: Ahuja et al. 1997: 14-15.

Notes:

(1) The poverty line

All data from Demery (1999), Wodon (1999), Khan (1998) and Jha (1999) are for national poverty lines. These are based on nationally determined nutritional requirements, with an assumption made about the share of non-food expenditure in the minimum necessary budget. This is also true of all data from Lipton and Eastwood (1999) and de Haan and Lipton (1999) with the following exceptions: for Nigeria, the poverty line is set at one third of mean per capita household expenditure; for Ghana, the poverty line is two thirds of mean per capita expenditure in the first year of the survey 1987-8; for Indonesia, the poverty line is USD 30 a day adjusted to PPP; for Guatemala and Malaysia, the nature of the poverty line is not given in the source.

Data from the World Bank (2000b) are for a national poverty line, but it is not clear how this is calculated in each case.

Malaysia data given in Lipton and Eastwood (1999) appear to be for poverty incidence of households, rather than a headcount. In all other cases the data are headcount data.

(2) Income or expenditure?

Poverty rates presented are based on income with the following exceptions:

Wodon (1999) and Jha (1999) are based on expenditure.

From Lipton and Eastwood (1999), data for Ghana, Nigeria, Kenya and Sri Lanka are based on expenditure. Ecuador data are based on income for 1990 and expenditure for 1994.

From de Haan and Lipton (1999), data for Pakistan and Papua New Guinea are based on consumption.

In a number of other cases, including all data from the World Bank (2000b), and data for Indonesia and Bangladesh in Lipton and Eastwood (1999), it is not clear whether income or expenditure is taken as the measure of household living standards.

(3) Definitions of urban and rural

The definitions of urban and rural used in each source are not clear. Almost all sources use a different poverty line for urban and rural areas, reflecting both different nutritional requirements and differences in the cost of living. Ghana is an exception.

It follows for the above that data cannot be compared across sources. However, the aim has been to provide more than one data point from a single source. Exceptions: data for Ecuador are from two different studies and use different measures of household living standards in each case.

Table 2.2: Poverty trends and profiles, with growth and redistribution

ASIA AND THE PACIFIC (AP)

Country	Period	Poverty Trends [1]	Growth Performance [2]
Bangladesh	1984-96	Sharp decline in rural Head Count Index (HCI); urban HCI fell faster so increase in rural-urban ratios.	Increase in output rates in 1980s and 1990s, but below target rate of 7% recommended for sustainable poverty reduction.
Cambodia	1993-4 to 1997	Decline in both urban and rural poverty. Slightly increased rural-urban HCI ratio.	Despite an increase in industrial output and tourism, agriculture is key to growth. But it is vulnerable to bad weather such as floods in 1996 which slowed growth.
China	1978-95	Decline in both rural and urban poverty in 1977-84, though urban poverty fell faster. Nearly fourfold increase in rural-urban HCI ratio in 1978-90. Rural poverty increased in 1985-9 and then decreased from 1990.	Economic reform resulted in high rates of growth, enabling large investments in social welfare.
India	1970-89	Faster decline in rural HCI than urban leading to a decline in rural-urban Poverty Gap Index (PGI) ratio.	Whereas the Green Revolution resulted in growth of agricultural output, manufacturing output suffered a bottleneck in the 1970s and 1980s.
Indonesia	1976-95	Fast falls, especially in rural poverty, led to a decline in rural-urban PGI ratio (1984-90).	Agriculture gained importance after the oil crisis in 1973; manufacturing suffered in the 1970s but has since achieved higher growth rates than agriculture.
Kazakhstan	1996	Trend data not available. Rural HCI higher than urban HCI.	Output stabilized in 1996 for the first time since independence. Good outlook as industry geared towards developing the natural resource base [World Bank [3]].
Kyrgyz Republic	1993-7	Increase in rural poverty, but decrease in urban poverty leading to an increase in rural-urban HCI ratio.	Data not available for this period.
Lao PDR	1993	Trend data not available. In 1993 rural HCI more than twice that of urban HCI.	Primarily a subsistence economy with slow growth.
Malaysia	1970-90	Both rural and urban poverty declined but at varying rates so poverty indicators diverged (1973-89).	Varied growth performance – a general slump in the early 1980s, but agricultural growth in 1976-87. Significant growth since 1987.

Redistribution	Poverty Profile[3/]
Increase in rural-urban, intra-sectoral and overall inequality.	In spite of decline in both, rural poverty incidence still higher than urban. Large variations in poverty rate by geographical area. Landlessness the foremost determinant of rural poverty.
Sharp fall in urban-rural inequality from 1978-83 with quasi-privatization of farmland. Moderate fall in urban inequality as well. Substantial rises in total, intra- and intersectoral inequalities in 1983-95 as the focus of reform shifted to the urban sector.	Rising rural-urban poverty ratios reinforced by rising intra-rural inequality after 1983 as township & village enterprises replaced agriculture as engine of rural growth.
Little change in urban-rural inequality; small rise in urban inequality; small decline in rural inequality.	Poverty is mainly rural. Gender, literacy, land ownership, employment status, caste and location closely associated with poverty.
Rises in rural, urban and rural-urban inequalities in 1976-78; A steady fall in the rural Gini but a U-shaped pattern for urban and overall Ginis since 1978.	Poverty is mainly rural but with large regional disparities.
	Poverty concentrated in the south of the country, in large households and among the unemployed and pensioners.
	Poverty fundamentally a rural phenomenon. Nearly 80% of the poor live in rural areas and the gap between urban and rural areas is growing.
	Large urban-rural differential in poverty. Poverty is higher in the South, coincident with unfavourable nutrition and health indicators.
Falling total, inter-sectoral and urban inequalities; small rise in total inequality in the 1970s associated with a temporary rise in rural inequality.	

(cont'd)

ASIA AND THE PACIFIC (AP) (cont'd)

Country	Period	Poverty Trends[1]	Growth Performance[2]
Mongolia	1995	Trend data not available. In 1995 urban HCI was slightly higher than that of rural HCI.	Liberalization boosted small-scale agricultural output and industry recovered after a decline in the early 1990s. Growth since 1994.
Nepal	1995-6	Trend data not available. In 1995/6 rural HCI was nearly twice that of urban HCI.	Good, stable GDP growth, but contribution of agriculture is declining due to weather and increasing importance of non-agricultural sectors.
Pakistan	1979-91	Rate of reduction of urban HCI no faster than rural HCI in 1984/5-1990/1.	Good growth performance resulting in food grain self-sufficiency and increased government development expenditure.
Papua New Guinea	1996	Trend data not available. Rural HCI nearly three times that of urban HCI in 1996.	Disappointing economic performance due to dependency on minerals sector and agriculture vulnerable to weather conditions such as *El Niño*.
Philippines	1957-91	Rural-urban ratios of both HCI and PGI increased as urban poverty fell faster (1961-88).	Industrialization in the 1980s, but more recently the agricultural sector has received more attention to improve output.
Sri Lanka	1970-91	Decline in rural HCI and PGI, but urban indices increased in 1985/6-1990/1	Liberalization in the late 1970s led to increased public investment in agricultural development, irrigation, etc.
Thailand	1962-92	Trend data not available. In 1992 rural HCI was higher than urban HCI with rural-urban HCI ratio of 1.52.	Rapid industrial growth since the 1960s, but agriculture is still important in GDP growth.
Viet Nam	1993	Trend data not available. Rural HCI more than twice as large as urban HCI.	Survived economic transition well, with rapid economic growth. Industrial growth above target, but declining agricultural sector, despite its high employment.

Redistribution	Poverty Profile [3/]
	Incidence and depth of poverty, along with social indicators, worse in rural than in urban areas; in remote than in more inaccessible rural areas; for women, and for people belonging to certain occupational castes.
Insignificant changes in overall, intra-rural and rural-urban inequality in 1979-85/6. Substantial annual fall in rural-urban inequality in 1985-6 to 1990-1 partly offset by rises in urban and rural Ginis leading to a sharp rise in overall Gini, despite rural-urban equalization.	Rural areas have higher poverty and worse human development indicators than urban areas. Among regions, rural South Punjab and Baluchistan poor relative to other provinces.
An inverted U-pattern for rural, urban and total inequality during the mid-1950s to mid-1980s. Sharp narrowing of the urban-rural gap during the mid-1960s to the mid-1970s. All components of inequality turned upwards since then.	Mainly rural. Most of the poor are engaged in the agriculture, fisheries and forestry sectors.
Fall in urban-rural and rural inequalities; urban inequality unchanged.	Poverty is mainly rural. Individuals are more likely to be poor if working members of the household are employed in agriculture.
A large rise in urban-rural inequality (73%) in 1981-92.	Most of the poor lived in the northeast and the north and the bulk of the poor are concentrated in rural areas. Poor households are mainly involved in agriculture.
	A large majority of the poor, concentrated in rural areas, are farmers. The highest incidence of poverty is found in the North Central Coast. Ethnic minorities have a higher incidence of poverty than the national average.

Poverty trends and profiles, with growth and redistribution

WEST AND CENTRAL AFRICA (WCA)

Country	Period	Poverty Trends[1]	Growth Performance[2]
Burkina Faso	1994-8	Decline in rural poverty, increase in urban leading to a decrease in the rural-urban HCI ratio.	Year-to-year fluctuations due to rain-fed agriculture. Limited manufacturing growth because of lack of raw materials and the need to import fuel.
Cameroon	1984	Trend data not available. Higher urban HCI than rural HCI.	Good growth until 1985 when oil, coffee and cocoa prices declined.
Chad	1985-6	Trend data not available. Rural and urban HCI roughly equal.	An agrarian economy reliant on rains, which has stunted economic growth.
Ghana	1988-92	Big fall in the ratio of rural-urban poverty.	Growth low but constant; growth in output of food crops despite drought.
Guinea-Bissau	1991	Trend data not available. Rural HCI over twice as high as urban HCI.	Fluctuating growth due to reliance on agricultural sector.
Mauritania	1987-96	Both urban and rural poverty has declined, but urban poverty has fallen faster, resulting in a doubling of rural-urban HCI ratio.	Dual economy with a small modern sector and a traditional subsistence sector vulnerable to climate change. Growth has slowed.
Niger	1989-93	Trend data not available. Rural HCI slightly higher than urban HCI.	Good rains in 1988 and 1990 led to good growth; mineral sector suffered when world uranium prices depressed.
Nigeria	1985-92	Fall in rural poverty, increase in urban poverty leading to a decrease in rural-urban HCI ratios.	Steady increase in GDP due to recovery of oil prices and economic reform in the agricultural sector. Heavily dependent on oil prices.
Senegal	1991	Trend data not available. Rural HCI more than twice as high as urban HCI.	Economy recovered in 1990 after a poor farming season in 1988-9. Affected by poor groundnut harvest in 1990-91.
Sierra Leone	1989	Trend data not available. Higher rural than urban HCI.	Negative growth due to a large agricultural subsistence sector and decline of the mineral sector.

Redistribution	Poverty Profile [3/]
	The poor are concentrated in rural areas. Geographic location is a strong indicator of poverty.
	More than four fifths of the population and an even larger proportion of the poor live in rural areas.
Rise in urban inequality offset by falls in rural and rural-urban inequality.	Poverty is mainly rural but the gap with urban poverty is narrowing. Whole communities in the northern areas of Ghana are poor while poverty is lowest in the capital, Accra. Gender is an important dimension of poverty in Ghana, especially in the Northern Region.
	Poverty is an overwhelmingly rural problem, with most of the poor living in the regions of Rural Norte, Rural Leste and Rural Sul.
	Poverty appears more severe in rural areas (particularly in the east and the Senegal River Valley) than in urban areas. Nearly 30% of Mauritanian households are headed by women, partly explained by high divorce rates and increasing long-term migration.
	Because of the population weighting, rural areas contribute more than urban areas to total poverty.
	Mainly rural, but the share of urban poverty is increasing. The largest number of poor people is concentrated in northern regions.
	Poverty in Senegal essentially a rural phenomenon, with over 80% of poor households living in rural areas.
	Sierra Leone is one of the poorest countries in the world. In 1992, it had a per capita income of only USD 170. The great majority of the poor live in rural areas. Social indicators are among the worst in the world. Life expectancy is only 42 years, the second lowest in the world.

Poverty trends and profiles, with growth and redistribution

EAST AND SOUTHERN AFRICA (ESA)

Country	Period	Poverty Trends[1]	Growth Performance[2]
Ethiopia	1989-95 to 1994-7	Greater decline in rural than urban poverty leading to decline in rural-urban HCI.	Largely an agricultural economy, growth dependent on rainfall. High output in 1992, a wet year, but since then low growth due to civil war.
Kenya	1992-4	Fall in the ratio of rural-urban HCI.	Negligible growth due to lack of rainfall, political disorder and foreign exchange crisis. Export smallholders successful, but high inequality of landholding has worsened conditions for the poor.
Lesotho	1993	Trend data not available. Rural HCI almost twice as high as urban HCI.	Manufacturing output strong. Reliant on remittances from migrant miners. Declining agricultural yields due to soil erosion and poor farming practices.
Madagascar	1993-4	Trend data not available. Rural HCI much higher than urban HCI.	Slow recovery after sluggish growth in the 1980s. Agriculture's share of GDP declining.
Uganda	1992-97	Greater decline in urban than rural poverty, resulting in an increase in rural-urban HCI.	Good growth performance due to improved security, but agricultural output strongly affected by drought.
Zambia	1991-6	Rural poverty fell while urban poverty increased; small decline in rural-urban HCI, larger fall in PGI.	Liberalization, investment in industry has been low resulting in negative growth rates.
Zimbabwe	1991-6	Increase in both urban and rural poverty, but urban most significant, resulting in halving of rural-urban HCI ratio.	Erratic growth pattern due to droughts affecting agriculture, but industrial growth significant and constant.

Redistribution	Poverty Profile [3/]
	Landless, refugees, those displaced due to war and demobilized soldiers are an important component of the poor in Ethiopia. Poverty is mainly rural.
	The majority of the poor in rural areas are food and subsistence farmers and those who derive the bulk of their income from the informal sector. About one third of rural poor households are headed by widowed, divorced, or separated women with children.
	Poverty mainly a rural phenomenon and the incidence is disproportionately high among households engaged in agriculture, informal business or casual labour. Boys suffer more than girls from higher malnutrition rate and lower school enrollment ratios.
	Poverty is deeper in rural than in urban areas. Farmers (especially smallholders) are the poorest group in the country. Most of the poor are seven to 20 years old who do not attend school.
	Rural poverty incidence and severity higher than in urban areas. Correlates of poverty (such as household size, dependency ratio and illiteracy) are higher for rural Uganda. Poor households tend to have older, less educated and (more likely) a woman as head of the household.
Rises in intra-rural equality	Rural poverty more prevalent, deeper and more severe than urban poverty. Increased likelihood of poverty in remote provinces and especially severe in remote districts.
	Overwhelming majority of the poor live in rural areas. Poverty is most common and deepest in the low rainfall areas of Matabeleland South, Masvingo and Matabeleland North provinces.

Poverty trends and profiles, with growth and redistribution

LATIN AMERICA AND THE CARIBBEAN (LAC)

Country	Period	Poverty Trends[1]	Growth Performance[2]
Bolivia	1996	Trend data not available. Rural HCI more than twice that of urban HCI.	Agriculture a major engine of growth. Economic output increasing, but below target of 5.6% recommended for meaningful reduction in poverty.
Brazil	1981-95	Increases in rural and urban poverty (1990-95); greater increase in rural areas leading to an increase in rural-urban PGI ratio (1990-95).	Negative growth in early 1980s. Revival of growth by 1984, but recession once again in early 1990s. Agricultural sector largely neglected.
Chile	1987-94	Trend data not available. In 1995 rural HCI was almost three times higher than urban HCI.	High rates of growth in late 1980s, but slowed in 1990 due to anti-inflationary measures.
Colombia	1978-92	Decline in rural and urban poverty, but an increase in rural-urban HCI.	Stable growth. Agricultural growth has been negligible, with a poor performance in the 1990s due to trade liberalization.
Dominican Republic	1989-92	Increase in rural poverty, but sharp decline in urban poverty; twofold increase in rural-urban HCI.	Erratic growth with construction, tourism and communications being important engines.
Ecuador	1990-94	Sharp decline in both urban and rural poverty with a negligible increase in rural-urban HCI.	Trade liberalization caused tough competition for local manufacturers.
Guatemala	1980-1986/7	Decrease in rural poverty, increase in urban poverty.	Stagnation in early 1980s due to a drop in export prices and left-wing insurgency. Agriculture worse hit than industry.
Honduras	1989-93	Decline in rural poverty, increase in urban poverty leading to a decline in rural-urban PGI ratio.	Steady growth in output; manufacturing performance weaker than agricultural.
Nicaragua	1993	Trend data not available. Rural HCI more than twice that of urban HCI.	Agriculture recovered better than industry in the early 1990s after economic decline in the 1980s.

Redistribution	Poverty Profile[3/]
	Poverty associated with a low level of education and more common among the indigenous population. In rural areas the poor are generally agricultural labourers or wage-earners with limited landholdings and no access to credit and basic infrastructure.
Rising inequality in 1981-90. Sharp decline in rural-urban inequality, though no change in rural inequality in 1990-95. Overall rise in inequality 10-20% in urban and rural sectors.	More than half of all poor Brazilians live in the northeast. In spite of urbanization, rural and urban areas contribute equally to national poverty. Poverty disproportionately affects the young and a quarter of children under the age of five suffer from chronic malnutrition.
Inequality trend similar to Brazil. Sharp fall in urban sector inequality, large enough to swamp rising rural inequality.	
	More than three out of four poor people live in rural areas. The rural poor are poorer than the urban poor. Important regional differences.
	In 1992, rural poverty was almost three times urban poverty, and more than one in four children lived in poverty.
	Poverty is higher in rural areas and among the indigenous people, especially those who live in the rural highlands (Sierra) and the Amazon region, than for the non-indigenous population.
	Poverty is especially prevalent in rural areas in the north, northwest and southwest and occurs primarily among the poorly educated and indigenous members of the population. More than 90% indigenous population is poor.
Rise in both urban and rural inequality. Decline in inter-sector inequality.	Poverty is mainly rural.
	Poverty is mainly concentrated in rural areas and the northern regions (Jinotega and Matagalpa) and the Segovias (Esteli, Madriz, and Nueva Segovia).

(cont'd)

LATIN AMERICA AND THE CARIBBEAN (LAC) (cont'd)

Country	Period	Poverty Trends[1/]	Growth Performance[2/]
Panama	1997	Trend data not available. Rural HCI more than four times greater than urban HCI.	Growth due to exports and service sectors. Agriculture and manufacturing slow to adjust to international competition. Agriculture affected by El Nino.
Paraguay	1991-5	Massive increase in rural HCI, decrease in urban HCI leading to a fourfold increase in rural-urban HCI ratio.	Positive growth, but heavily dependent on agriculture, vulnerable to weather conditions and international commodity market [World Bank[3/]].
Peru	1994-7	Decline in poverty greater in urban than rural areas leading to a slight increase in rural-urban HCI.	Strong investment-led economic recovery in mid 1990s. Boom 1993-5 due to dismantling of guerrilla groups and increased mining revenue, but agriculture hit by El Nino in 1997.
Trinidad and Tobago	1992	Trend data not available. Urban HCI slightly higher than rural HCI.	Recession in 1992-3 due to falling oil production.
Venezuela	1995	Trend data not available. Higher rural HCI than urban HCI.	Dependent on oil prices, manufacturing important. Agricultural decline since 1950s when oil extraction started.

Redistribution	Poverty Profile [3/]
	Poverty concentrated in rural areas, especially in indigenous areas.
	Poverty relatively more prevalent in small cities and in rural areas, and associated with low education levels, female-headed households, language (monolingual Guarani speakers) and migration.
	Poverty particularly high among the indigenous population. The poor are found largely among two occupational groups – the self-employed and private sector workers. Working in agriculture positively associated with poverty.
	Poverty is evenly divided between urban and rural areas, though the severity of poverty is worse in urban areas, with high criminality.

Poverty trends and profiles, with growth and redistribution

NEAR EAST AND NORTH AFRICA (NENA)

Country	Period	Poverty Trends [1]	Growth Performance [2]
Algeria	1988-95	A doubling of both urban and rural poverty.	Negative growth due to collapse in oil prices in 1985. Improvement since 1995.
Estonia	1994	Trend data not available. Rural HCI more than twice as high as urban HCI.	Economic recovery began in 1994 after independence in 1991.
Georgia	1997	Trend data not available. Urban HCI higher than rural HCI.	Decline in GDP growth in early 1990s, but picked up again in 1994-7 with small-scale privatization, and a law on the ownership of agricultural land, and the freeing of bread prices stimulating wheat production [IFAD 1999c].
Jordan	1984-5 to 1990-91	Increases in both urban and rural poverty; greater increase in rural areas 1986-92.	Massive decline in output over this period, worsened by the Gulf Crisis.
Morocco	1984-5 to 1990-91	Decline in both urban and rural poverty, but urban poverty fell faster leading to an increase in rural-urban HCI ratio.	Improvements in growth performance when five year drought ended in 1985; but being an agricultural economy, growth erratic due to susceptibility to drought.
Romania	1989-93	Rapid increases in urban and rural poverty; urban poverty worse than rural, hence a reduction in rural-urban HCI ratio.	Negative growth after 1989 revolution. Macroeconomic programme in 1993 caused positive growth thereafter [IFAD 1999c].
Tunisia	1985-90	Decline in both urban and rural poverty. No change in rural-urban HCI ratio.	Growth in manufacturing sector, but 1986 drought, locusts and regional tensions cause problems for agriculture and tourism.
Yemen	1992	Trend data not available. Rural HCI slightly higher than urban HCI.	Data not available.

Note: HCI refers to headcount index or the incidence of poverty which is the number of poor people divided by the population.

Sources: 1) Refer to Annex Table 1.1.

2) Growth performance are taken from Economist Intelligence Unit Country Profiles unless otherwise stated.

3) World Bank website http://www.worldbank.org/html/extdr/regions.htm

Redistribution	Poverty Profile [3/]
	Most of the poor live in rural areas, but the share of the urban poor has increased.
	Rural poverty tends to be more severe than urban poverty. Rural poor households have little or no formal income, i.e. those with unemployed and underemployed members.
	Urban poverty is more widespread, deeper and more severe than rural poverty, concentrated in some regions and among those unable to work (the inactive, elderly or disabled) or the unemployed.
Sharp rises in rural and urban inequalities.	High inequality of access by gender to economic opportunities. The incidence of poverty is higher in rural areas but only one third of the poor live in rural areas.
Overall flat inequality with a slight fall in urban inequality.	Poverty is primarily a rural phenomenon.
	Nearly half of the poor live with wage earners and the unemployed, while the rest reside in farm and pensioner households. Highest incidence of poverty among households headed by the unemployed and by farmers.
	Poverty remains primarily a rural phenomenon. There is a marked disparity in poverty among regions: the north-west and the centre-west have the highest incidence of poverty.
	Rural and urban HCI are roughly equal.

Table 2.3: Age-structure and ratio of persons aged 15-59 to others, 1959-2030

	1950 <15	1950 60+	1950 R	1960 <15	1960 60+	1960 R	1970 <15	1970 60+	1970 R	1980 <15	1980 60+	1980 R
WCA												
DR Congo	43.6	5.6	1.03	44.0	4.7	1.05	44.3	4.5	1.05	45.1	4.6	1.01
Ghana	45.1	4.1	1.03	45.5	4.2	1.01	45.5	4.4	1.00	44.9	4.5	1.03
Nigeria	45.7	4.0	1.01	42.9	4.1	1.13	44.4	0.98	1.06	46.2	4.3	0.97
ESA												
Ethiopia	44.2	4.6	1.05	44.5	4.1	1.06	45.0	4.3	1.03	46.6	4.8	0.95
Kenya	39.8	6.3	1.17	45.6	6.4	0.92	48.1	5.9	0.85	50.1	5.0	0.81
Tanzania	46.0	3.8	1.01	47.9	3.8	0.93	46.8	4.0	0.97	47.6	3.8	0.95
AP												
Bangladesh	37.6	6.2	1.28	40.9	6.2	1.12	45.4	6.1	0.95	46.7	5.3	0.92
China	32.5	7.5	1.54	38.9	7.2	1.17	39.7	6.8	1.15	35.5	7.4	1.33
India	38.9	5.6	1.22	39.8	5.7	1.22	40,6	6.0	1.15	38.5	6.5	1.22
Indonesia	38.7	6.2	1.23	40.1	5.2	1.21	42.2	5.2	1.09	40.8	5.3	1.17
Malaysia	40.9	7.3	1.07	44.3	5.3	1.01	44.6	5.5	1.00	39.6	5.7	1.21
Myanmar	37.8	5.5	1.31	41.1	5.6	1.14	41.2	6.1	1.11	39.6	6.4	1.17
Pakistan	37.8	8.2	1.20	41.9	8.3	0.99	46.3	5.0	0.95	44.4	4.6	1.04
Philippines	43.6	5.6	1.03	46.7	4.9	0.94	45.4	4.3	1.01	41.9	4.5	1.15
LAC												
Brazil	41.7	4.9	1.15	43.2	5.3	1.06	42.3	5.7	1.05	38.1	6.2	1.26
Colombia	42.6	5.0	1.10	46.4	5.0	0.95	45.8	5.4	0.95	42.7	5.7	1.07
Mexico	42.0	7.1	1.04	45.0	8.9	0.86	46.5	6.1	0.91	45.0	5.4	0.98
NENA												
Iran	39.1	8.3	1.11	44.8	6.3	1.11	45.7	5.4	0.96	44.9	5.1	1.06
Iraq	44.8	4.3	1.04	46.1	4.0	1.00	46.6	4.0	0.98	46.0	4.3	0.99

Notes: <15: percentage of population aged 0 to 14. 60+: percentage of population aged 60 or over. R: persons aged 15-59 as a proportion of persons aged below 15 or over 60 (prime-age dependency ratio) R stops falling and starts rising – due to ageing of 'cohorts' saved from child mortality, and to falling fertility - between 1970 and 1980 in Brazil, China, Colombia, India, Indonesia, Kenya, Malaysia, Myanmar, Pakistan and the Philippines; between 1980 and 1990 in Bangladesh, Iraq, Kenya and Tanzania; 1990-2000 in Ghana, Iran and Nigeria; and 2000-2015 in DR Congo and Ethiopia. R stops rising and starts falling (due to the impact of the rising proportion of over-60s) only in some countries before 2030, and there not before 2015: Brazil, China, Colombia, India, Indonesia, Iran, Malaysia, Mexico, and Myanmar.

Source: UN (1999) Data from 2000 are medium projections.

1990			2000			2015			2030		
<15	60+	R	<15	60+	R	<15	60+	R	<15	60+	R
47.3	4.6	0.93	48.3	4.4	0.88	44.3	4.3	1.06	39.1	4.9	1.27
45.3	4.6	1.00	43.1	5.1	1.07	38.5	5.8	1.25	32.0	7.6	1.53
46.4	4.5	0.96	45.1	5.0	1.00	39.2	5.0	1.26	32.5	6.5	1.56
45.4	4.7	1.00	46.2	4.5	0.97	43.7	4.2	1.09	37.7	4.9	1.35
49.2	4.5	0.86	43.0	4.3	1.11	35.8	3.9	1.52	26.6	6.0	2.07
46.5	4.1	0.98	45.4	4.1	1.02	41.3	4.0	1.21	34.1	5.0	1.56
44.3	4.9	1.03	35.1	5.1	1.49	28.1	6.9	1.86	23.0	6.7	2.36
27.4	8.1	1.82	24.9	10.1	1.86	19.6	14.7	1.92	17.1	23.2	1.73
33.4	6.9	1.48	33.3	7.6	1.44	25.7	11.1	1.72	22.2	14.2	1.73
38.7	6.3	1.22	30.7	7.5	1.62	24.6	8.7	2.02	22.0	14.9	1.71
36.5	5.8	1.36	34.0	6.6	1.46	25.4	10.1	1.82	22.8	15.2	1.56
35.6	6.4	1.38	31.7	7.6	1.54	24.0	9.4	1.99	20.8	15.9	1.72
43.1	4.7	1.09	41.8	4.9	1.14	35.2	6.3	1.41	26.4	4.9	1.76
41.4	5.3	1.13	36.7	5.7	1.36	32.0	6.9	1.57	23.5	8.4	2.13
34.8	6.7	1.41	28.8	7.8	1.73	24.3	11.1	1.82	21.6	16.8	1.60
36.0	6.3	1.36	32.7	6.9	1.52	27.0	8.9	1.79	22.7	15.8	1.60
38.6	5.9	1.26	36.2	6.9	1.43	26.1	10.9	1.77	22.1	15.9	1.63
45.5	5.7	0.95	36.1	6.3	1.36	26.7	7.5	1.92	22.9	12.0	1.87
44.2	4.5	1.05	41.3	4.9	1.16	36.8	6.1	1.33	27.8	8.8	1.73

Table 2.4: Summary of research on poverty dynamics and main findings

Country	Dataset(s)	Sample size	Time span of panel(s)	No. of waves in panel(s)
Burkina Faso[1]	Rural Burkina Faso – ICRISAT	150 households	1983-4 to 1984-5	2
Chile[2]	Rural Chile – authors	146 households	1968-86	2
China[3]	South-West Rural China – State Statistical Bureau	38 000 individuals	1985-90	6
Côte d'Ivore[4]	Cote d'Ivoire Living Standards Measurements Surveys – World Bank	700 households	1985-6, 1986-7 and 1987-8	2
Ethiopia[5]	Rural Ethiopia – Universities of Addis Ababa and Oxford	1411 households	1994-5	3
Hungary[6]	Various[a]	1 744-5 945 households	1992-6 and 1987-9	2, 5
India[7]	Various[b]	100-4 118 households	1957-8 to 1984	3,4,8,9
Indonesia[8]	Indonesia – RAND Corp., Univerity of California, Los Angeles and University of Indonesia	30 000 individuals	1993-94 to 1998	3[c]
Pakistan[9]	Rural Pakistan – International Food Policy Research Institute (IFPRI)	686-727 households	1986-89, 1986-91	12, 5

Form(s) of study	Welfare indicator(s)	Main findings
Impact of agro-climatic shocks on poverty dynamics	Income	Off-farm income increases inequality after a severe drought.
Mobility across poverty classes, trends in inequality	Income	More households moved out of poverty than into it. Chronic poverty strongly associated with residence in semi-arid region, being an ethnic minority, losing livestock and living in a large household. Upwards income inequality is greater the poorer the household. Inequality declined due to increased coverage of targeted public transfers.
Estimating, targeting and determinants of transient and chronic poverty	Consumption	Consumption variability accounts for a large share of poverty. Anti-poverty policies need greater emphasis on transient poverty.
Mobility across poverty classes; determinants of changes in household per capita expenditure levels	Expenditure	Very few, even the poorest, improved their standard of living amid general decline. In some socio-economic groups, the poor had a greater chance of escaping poverty. In rural areas, physical capital significant in affecting welfare changes.
Poverty and nutrition dynamics	Consumption and indices of adult body mass	Large seasonal variations in consumption and body mass index. One third to half of households moved out of poverty. Households do not smooth consumption much, but boost nutrition in favourable times.
Mobility across income deciles and relative poverty classes; impact of public transfers on poverty dynamics	Income, consumption	Growing inequality over time coupled with declining real income. Poverty persistence affects children more than the elderly. Cash benefits protected many, but promoted few out of poverty.
Methodological issues in targeting the chronically poor, economic and social intra- and inter-generational mobility, extent of mobility across deciles and poverty classes, estimate and characteristics of chronically poor, distributional dynamics	Income, consumption, food consumption, food share in household budget, access to land, occupation	Current consumption is not always a better indicator of chronic poverty than current income, but both perform much better than other common indicators such as food share and access to land. Agricultural labourers are at severe risk of poverty and their mobility out of agricultural labour is low. Despite greater upward relative mobility amongst poorer deciles, few escaped absolute poverty. The chronically poor are not necessarily the poorest. Land distribution and irrigation adoption affected income distribution, whereas Green Revolution technical change did not.
Impact of macro-shocks on welfare	Expenditure, employment, earnings, education, health care	Health and education investments in children have been hit, particularly amongst the poorest households.
Determinants of inequality and mobility across poverty classes, targeting chronically and transitorily poor using household characteristics	Income and expenditure	Non-farm income accounts for one third to one half (poorest quintile) of total income and, with livestock income, decreases overall inequality. Majority of poverty is transitory.

(cont'd)

Summary of research on poverty dynamics and main findings (cont'd)

Country	Dataset(s)	Sample size	Time span of panel(s)	No. of waves in panel(s)
Peru[10]	Peru LSMS – World Bank and Cuánto	676 households	1991-1996	3
Philippines[11]	Rural Philippines – collected by IFPRI et al.	448 households	1984-92	5[d]
Russia[12]	Russia Longitudinal Monitoring Survey I – University of North California	6 300 dwellings	1992-94	4
Rwanda[13]	Rural Rwanda – Government of Rwanda	270 households	1982-83	4
South Africa[14]	Kwazulu-Natal Income Dynamics Survey – University of Cape Town, Natal, Wisconsin, and IFPRI	1 400 households	1993-98	2
Zimbabwe[15]	Rural Zimbabwe – Kinsey	385 households	1982-3 to 1997-8	10

Source: adapted from Yaqub 2000.

Notes:

1/ Reardon and Taylor 1996.

2/ Scott 1999; Scott and Litchfield 1994.

3/ Jalan and Ravallion 1998; 1999.

4/ Grootaert and Kanbur 1995; Grootaert *et al.* 1997.

5/ Dercon and Krishnan 1999

6/ Galasi 1998; Ravallion *et al.* 1995.

7/ Chaudhuri and Ravallion 1994; Dreze *et al.* 1992; Gaiha 1988; Gaiha 1989; Lanjouw and Stern 1991; Lanjouw and Stern 1993.

8/ Frankenberg *et al.* 1999.

9/ Adams and He 1995; Baulch and McCulloch 1998; 1999.

10/ Cumpa and Webb 1999.

11/ Bouis *et al.*1998.

12/ Mroz and Popkin 1995.

13/ Muller 1997.

14/ Maluccio *et al.* 1999a.

15/ Gunning *et al.* 1999.

a/ Hungarian Household Panel Survey: collected by Tarki; Hungarian Household Budget Survey: collected by the Central Statistical Office. Source: Yaqub 2000.

b/ Rural Maharashtra and Andhra Pradesh, India: collected by ICRISAT; Palanpur village in Uttar Pradesh: collected by the authors; Rural India: collected by the National Council of Applied Economic Research.

c/ Third wave covered only 25% sub-sample.

d/ Four of the five waves were in 1984-5.

Form(s) of study	Welfare indicator(s)	Main findings
Mobility across poverty classes	Expenditure	More households were upwardly mobile than downwardly mobile.
Intra-household resource allocations and contributions	Income, food intakes, education and health	Adolescents make major contributions to family welfare.
Poverty and occupational mobility	Income	Over half the dwellings moved out of income poverty and only one quarter of the very poor remained very poor.
Methodology, estimates and determinants of transient and chronic seasonal poverty	Consumption	Worst poverty crises are after dry season. Transient seasonal poverty important for households around the poverty line, but of little importance to the poorest of the chronically poor.
Social dynamics and poverty	Expenditure	Education and social capital yielded substantial household returns in 1998 due to a more efficient economy. The effect of social capital is significant, but smaller than that of education.
Income dynamics	Income	Households resettled on white farms have increased returns to their accumulated assets. Income increases are greatest amongst those with the lowest incomes at the beginning of the survey.

Table 2.5: Aid to agriculture, forestry, fisheries (percentage of sectorally allocable aid)

	1987-9	1990-2	1993-5	1996-8
Multilateral	24.0	15.9	15.2*	n.a.
DAC Countries	16.1	13.7	11.6	11.9
EU Members, Total	15.4	12.5	12.3	11.0
ALL Donors, Total	20.2	15.3	12.1	12.5

*1993 and 1995 average; multilaterals not available separately for 1994 and 1996-8.

Source: OECD/DAC (2000).

Table 2.6: Agriculture/forestry/fisheries: percentage of total technical cooperation

	1993	1994	1995	1996	1997	1998
North Africa						
DAC Countries	22.8	17.8	13.7	13.2	12.2	12.0
EU Members	26.3	17.9	9.4	10.7	9.6	16.4
Sub-Saharan Africa						
DAC Countries	21.7	18.5	16.6	16.2	15.5	12.2
EU Members	21.7	12.3	14.7	14.9	13.8	11.5
Americas						
DAC Countries	18.9	24.5	17.5	15.3	15.7	12.1
EU Members	18.6	19.8	14.5	12.1	12.1	15.5
Asia						
DAC Countries	13.0	14.3	11.9	11.2	12.1	9.2
EU Members	11.8	13.3	12.2	9.8	11.6	9.2
Middle East						
DAC Countries	7.8	4.7	6.9	3.8	6.7	6.1
EU Members	4.9	1.7	5.0	1.4	5.5	4.6

Total Technical cooperation as % of aid to developing and transition countries

	1993	1994	1995	1996	1997	1998
EU members	22.2	21.8	25.0	24.8	25.6	24.1
DAC countries	23.2	21.9	24.7	25.5	26.7	25.1

Source: OECD/DAC (2000).

Endnotes

1   Commonly used for international comparisons, this poverty line adjusts for differences across countries and times in PPP. At this line, a person obtains a 'global consumption bundle' worth USD 1 per person per day in constant purchasing power of 1993.

2   World Bank 2000b.

3   Ravallion 2000.

4   Harris and Todaro 1970.

5   Stark 1991.

6   Epstein 1973.

7   Connell et al. 1976.

8   Birdsall et al. 1995; Clarke 1995; Kanbur and Lustig 1999.

9   UN 1998: 31, 38.

10 Lipton 1977; 1982.

11 See note 1.

12 Shaffer 1999.

13 Glewwe and van der Gaag 1990.

14 Laderchi 1997.

15 Jodha 1988.

16 Sinha and Lipton 1999.

17 See Dercon 1998 for a discussion of cattle in Western Tanzania.

18 However, the poor in each grouping (a) are heterogeneous and (b) frequently draw livelihoods from several sources, especially where farmwork is highly seasonal or uncertain.

19 There are exceptions even here. In Guatemala, nearly three quarters of the poor live in rural areas, and in Nicaragua over two thirds (World Bank 1995b, 1995c).

20 Rao et al. 1988.

21 Nelson et al. 1997.

22 FAO Food Balance Sheets; Lipton 1983b.

23 FAOSTAT 2000; FAO Food Balance Sheets; Barrett 1994; Greeley 1987.

24 World Bank 1995c.

25 de Haan and Lipton 1999.

26 Sahn et al. 1999.

27 But not usually in sub-Saharan Africa, South India or Latin America: Harriss 1986; Lipton 1983a; Svedberg 1989.

28 On Asia see Lipton and Osmani 1997.

29 Sen 1981; Mitra 1978.

30 World Bank 2000e.

31 Vosti et al. 1991.

32 Tiffen et al. 1994.

33 World Bank 1993.

34 Lipton 1999.

35 Arunachal Pradesh, Nagaland and Uttar Pradesh have fewer than 900 women per 1000 men. By contrast, in China there is a bias against girls in allocation of health goods in a poorer province (Sichuan) but not in a richer province (Jiangsu) (Ahuja et al. 1997).

36 The differences (also the lowness of female participation rates in rural areas of some Muslim countries) are exaggerated by inaccurate reporting but are real, although less than official data suggest.

37 Rosenzweig and Schultz 1982.

38 Dev et al. 1991.

39 Lipton 1983a; Visaria 1980.

40 Krongkaew et al. 1994; Prescott and Pradhan 1997.

41 World Bank 1995d; Firdausy 1994; Balisacan 1994.

42 Wodon 1999.

43 World Bank 1995b.

44 Dev et al. 1991.

45 World Bank 1989.

46 Lipton 1983a.

47 World Bank 1999c.

48 Udry 1996.

49 Saito et al. 1994.

50 Quisumbing 1994.

51 This is clear for small farmers largely subsisting on their own food production, but less so for the rural poorest. These increasingly rely mainly on wage income, which normally lags behind price rises during inflation (Mellor and Desai 1985).

52 Sinha and Lipton 1999.

53 To avoid a hail of statistics, we give only fragmentary evidence for many points in this section. References (and much more evidence) are in Livi-Bacci and de Santis 1999 and Lipton 1983.

54 Allison et al. 1989.

55 These associations, which also apply in many countries alleged to be exceptions (e.g. in West Africa), show that the poverty/household-size link is not much offset by 'economies of scale in consumption' in big households. Such economies could hardly apply to the dollar-poor, over 70% of whose consumption is normally on food, where scale economies are infeasible (Livi-Bacci and de Santis 1999: 34-41).

56 Bloom and Williamson 1997.

57 The median developing country in 1980 had dollar poverty incidence of 18.9%; the sample median fall in fertility through the 1980s of four per 1000, if achieved in 1980 and sustained, would have cut this to 13.9% by 1990, with growth and distribution effects about equally responsible (Lipton and Eastwood 1999).

58 In countries with 'fair' data, 'moderate to large' falls in total fertility rates (TFR) of 1.5-2 or more happened since 1980 in Kenya, Rwanda, Zimbabwe, Botswana, South Africa, Côte d'Ivoire and Senegal, with 'smaller' falls of 0.5-1.5 in Malawi, Tanzania, Zambia, Cameroon, Burkina Faso, Ghana and Benin (Cohen 1998: 1431-5). Demographic and Health Survey (DHS) data, usually good, imply 'smaller' but clear falls in Northern Sudan (Cleland *et al.* 1994), and for women aged 15-34 in Namibia, Niger, Madagascar and Uganda (Kirk and Pillett 1998: 5). On weaker data, Ethiopia and Swaziland also show moderate to large falls and Eritrea, Lesotho, The Gambia and Mauritania smaller falls. Mali seems the only African country with 'fair' data with no perceptible TFR fall.

59 Rural disadvantage can also be addressed through heavy urbanization by persons of working age who can remit or bring home resources to their rural families. This is consistent with big, growing urban-rural gaps in the dependency ratio (Table 2.3). But, to the extent that it is happening, it is not permitting rural people to achieve parity with their urban neighbours in income, security from poverty, or access to health or education.

60 Gregson *et al.* 1994.

61 FAO/UNAIDS 2000.

62 Basu 1999.

63 Connell *et al.* 1976.

64 Gregson 1994.

65 Walker and Ryan 1990.

66 Adams and He 1995.

67 Ravallion and Jalan 1996.

68 Gaiha 1989.

69 A household is deemed to be chronically poor if its mean income is below the poverty line, while a household is transitorily poor if its mean income is above the poverty line but its annual income falls below the poverty line at least once during the period of analysis. The chronically poor may also be defined as those who have been poor for more than a certain number of periods and the transitorily poor as those who have been poor for fewer periods. Gaiha and Deolalikar (1993) apply the latter definition in their analysis of the Indian data.

70 Panel data involve the same households in each survey, tracking numbers and characteristics of people who move in and out (or further in and out) of poverty. Non-panel time-series involve random samples of households and track true trends in poverty incidence and characteristics. The two are not substitutes.

71 At the moment it is not possible to generalize the evidence in the poverty dynamics literature because studies vary too widely in terms of interests, methods and data. The range of interests across studies includes: relative versus absolute mobility; transient versus chronic poverty; changes in welfare levels associated with socio-economic characteristics of households versus changes associated with socio-economic 'shocks'; poverty dynamics over seasons versus dynamics over longer-run time frames; and targeting and other public policy issues.

72 Yaqub 2000.

73 See for example Walker and Ryan 1990; Reardon and Taylor 1996; Dercon and Krishnan 1999.

74 No time-series for urban and rural literacy separately are available anywhere in sub-Saharan Africa. See UNESCO Statistical Yearbooks 1965, 1970, 1980, 1990, 1994, 1998.

75 Sastry 1997.

76 The subsequent regional and country analyses draw upon the results presented in Annex Table 2.1.

77 Deininger and Squire 1998.

78 Milanovic 1998.

79 Aid is overseas development assistance to developing and transitional countries, either in grant form or as loans with an over 25% grant element. Net aid is gross aid minus capital repayments of past loan aid. Disbursements are aid paid by donors (as against 'commitments').

80 Randel *et al.* 2000.

81 Excluding South-East Asia but including China.

82 UNDP (2000): 218-222; World Bank 2000a: Ch. 11.

83 The 47 countries contained 4.2 billion people, of whom 1 billion consumed less than PPP USD 1-a-day.

84 Burnside and Dollar 1998.

85 White 1996.

86 Alesina and Dollar 1998.

87 UNDP 2000: 224-5, 170; World Bank 2000a: Table 1.1.

88 FAO State of Food and Agriculture 2000: 226.

89 Beynon 1999.

90 Datt and Ravallion 1996.

91 Beynon 1999.

92 Collier and Dollar 1999.

93 Beynon 1999.

94 Collier and Dollar 1999.

95 Dollar and Pritchett 1998.

CHAPTER 3
ASSETS AND THE RURAL POOR

The key to sustainable rural development is legally-secure entitlement to assets – land, water, credit, information and technology – on the part of the poor. Without secure property rights, farmers lack the incentive to invest in land management.

ASSET POVERTY: SCOPE FOR RURAL POVERTY REDUCTION THROUGH POLICY CHANGES

This chapter deals with various strategies to improve the asset holdings of the rural poor. In most cases, if the poor get a bigger share of asset control or benefits, efficiency and economic growth also improve. For many types of asset, reducing inequality between rural and urban areas slows down out-migration to the cities, and increases rural farm and non-farm income-earning opportunities.[1]

Well-targeted policies can reduce poverty by increasing the opportunities for poor people to gain and maintain secure access to productive assets, especially land, water and other natural resources, together with social assets such as extension services, education and basic health care. The nature of their tenure over productive assets and related factor markets has a direct bearing on the extent of lasting benefit and opportunity for the rural poor to improve their livelihoods.

Assets take various forms and can be owned in various ways. Since this diversity has implications for the way assets are acquired and used sustainably, it is important to define the various meanings of 'asset' in the context of the rural poor (Box 3.1).

Lack of assets is an effect as well as a cause of poverty in terms of income opportunities, consumption and capability-building of people and their own institutions.

The term 'asset poverty' indicates a vicious circle.[2] People without assets tend to be consumption-poor because they rely mainly on selling their labour in poorly paid markets or to the landed class, have nothing to sell or mortgage in hard times, and are economically dependent and politically weak. Apart from the link between lack of assets and consumption poverty, asset disparities are huge.

Rural rich-poor total asset disparity. In rural India in 1971-72, the average household in the top decile owned 294 times as many natural, physical and net financial assets as those in the bottom decile.[3] The average *person* in the top rural decile owned almost 400 times as much assets as a person in the poorest: over eight times the disparity in income.[4]

Rich-poor specific disparities. In the median country of 41 developing countries with appropriate surveys, below half the children aged 6-11 from the poorest fifth of households were in school, as against over 90% in the richest fifth.[5] In Ghana, in the richest quintile, two households in three have electricity, as against one in six in the poorest quintile.

Urban-rural asset disparities. The ratio of rural to urban illiteracy among persons over 15 in the early 1970s ranged from 1.4 to 2 in North Africa and Asia, and 2 to 3.5 in Latin America. In the following 10-20 years the disparity increased in all 24 cases (male, female and total, for eight countries with data) in Asia; in 15 of the 16 cases in Latin America; and in ten of the 15 cases in Africa.[6]

Complementarity and sequencing in assets reform are crucial to maximize benefits to the poor. For instance, their nutrition is usually advanced more cost-effectively by combining efforts on nutrition, health, water and education than by concentrating on only one asset.

Efficiency is improved by the participation of beneficiaries, including poor ones, in the 'project cycles' where specific activities focus on building up their asset base. The inclusion of women in civil society, encouraging their training in health issues, and participation in education and financial decisions can only improve efficiency. However, the goal must be to progress from participation to empowerment, so that the rural poor become effective interlocutors with their governments and local authorities in decision-making that affects their resource entitlements and livelihoods.

Improving the assets of the rural poor has multiplier effects on the rate of economic growth.[7] The rural poor have frequently been excluded from access to land and other resources owing to the

---

Box 3.1: Assets: definition; ownership, control and benefit; gain and loss; and outcomes for the rural and the poor

Definition: An asset (also called 'capital', 'stock', or 'endowment') is anything that can be used, without being used up, to increase regular returns above receipts from labour, whether hired or self-employed, and thus enhance producers' income or consumers' welfare. Typical assets are land, wells, cattle, tools, houses, shares, skills, health and roads.

Access, ownership, benefit: Assets can be owned individually, by a group (such as the common grazing land of a village), by the state, or on an open-access basis where there are institutional understandings governing use but no one institution has control over access. People can control assets (by rent, hire, or influence in family, village or polity) without ownership, and can benefit even from assets controlled by others (when using a road, or earning at a sugar-mill).

Gain, loss: People **gain** assets by: diverting income from buying food to saving for a plough; diverting effort, for example, from growing rice to digging wells or attending school; theft or fraud; or luck – often inheritance, or an appreciation in the value of what one already owns. One **loses** assets by physical depreciation (through non-maintenance of assets), environmental depletion or pollution; obsolescence; theft or fraud; or sale or mortgage.

The poor's assets: (a) The poor are hard pressed to gain assets. Much income and work are committed to basic consumer needs (and social obligations). Inheritances are small and rare. (b) The poor readily lose assets. In hard times they must often sell or mortgage them, to avoid even deeper transient poverty. (c) Indeed, if the poor do save, their vulnerability often leads them to put their savings into assets that, though low-yielding, are readily sold in crisis; or into other safe but low-yielding production assets; or even into zero-yielding stocks of food grains against a shortage.

Rural people's assets: Rural people have more 'rural-specific' assets (farmland, livestock, irrigation) per person than urban people, but fewer human, infrastructural or total land assets, and fewer assets overall. Often the consumption-poorest urban quintile is healthier and better educated than the middle rural quintile. Further, the agriculture-based rural poor are especially vulnerable to climatic stress and hence make forced sales of land or animals; they concentrate where land and water are environmentally vulnerable.

Upshot for the rural poor: Characteristics of the rural poor include low levels of assets, especially land, labour and human assets such as health, education and nutrition. Though countries differ greatly, urban-rural disparities in asset and consumption ownership and poverty globally have not shrunk since the 1970s. For the rural poor, consumption poverty and asset poverty help to cause and perpetuate each other.

Sources: Haddad *et al.* 2000; World Bank 2000a; Eastwood and Lipton 2000.

power of vested elites and poor rural services, including education, extension services, health care, or institutions and departments that do not engage with local people in decisions on resource allocations. Opportunities for rural economic development are, in many places, complicated further by historic urban biases in the allocation of public services.

Policy can improve the poverty impact of assets by increasing the extent to which such assets:

- use family labour and generate additional labour requirements in asset-building, maintenance and use (production);
- link to on-the-job training that upgrades the skills of smallholder farmers and agricultural workers;
- provide safe, healthy and non-degrading work;
- provide equal access to work and promotion for women and minorities;
- lower or reduce risk and seasonal variation, especially of employment;
- lessen exposure to sudden physical disuse, obsolescence, environmental or market non-sustainability;
- produce items that loom largest in the consumption of the poor and make them available on a reliable and affordable basis;
- produce goods or services in price-elastic demand; and
- experience rapidly growing demand for their products.

The key to sustainable rural development is legally secure access to assets by the land poor. When property rights are lacking or insecure, farmers cannot be sure they will benefit from their efforts and therefore lack the incentive to invest in sustainable practices of land management. The resulting land degradation and soil loss threaten the livelihoods of millions of people as well as future food security, with implications also for water resources and the conservation of biodiversity. This vicious circle linking poverty to the degradation of natural resources can be broken,

however, by ensuring that the rural poor gain secure access to land, water, credit, information and technology.

It is not easy to correct asset inequalities. Asset redistribution can disrupt the economy: deterring saving, inducing capital flight and impeding growth, especially in increasingly open world markets. But while this might sometimes be a risk, the risk of neglecting the rural poor can be even greater: rural conflict, environmental deterioration and expanding mega-cities. The methods of redistribution must take into account the transition costs from land-ownership patterns of high concentration by the few to smallholdings that may improve the livelihoods of the many. It is in this context that the evidence on the higher productivity of smaller farms shows that redistribution can often improve aggregate production while also redressing the problems of inequitable access.

Experience suggests that pro-poor asset policy should concentrate on three main types of asset.

First, land redistribution is a powerful weapon against poverty, essential for fast progress in very unequal rural areas with limited options. Small, fairly equal farms are good for employment, efficiency and growth. Yet land – often the main rural asset – is often locked into unequal, and socially and economically inefficient, farms. Although land reform has achieved much, in its conventional, centralized and imposed form it has run into problems resulting in concentration once again in the hands of the more powerful. But new methods of land reform have shown promising results. The nature of the approach must be location-specific since important opportunities exist in different contexts, amongst others, for civil society-based reform, resettlement schemes, restitution, negotiated or market-assisted land reform, land leasing and sharecropping.

Second, policies should raise poor people's control over water-yielding assets so they can improve their returns from land, meet family needs for drinking water, reduce female drudgery and reduce the incidence of debilitating water-borne diseases. Such policies are urgent given the economic and climatic pressure to cut overall rural water use. Water reform involves techniques, participatory institutions, asset types and better water pricing.

Third, redistribution of chances to improve key human assets – including health, education, information and communication skills – should favour rural people, with particular attention to the poorest, women and girls, indigenous people and excluded minorities.

FARMLAND ASSETS AND THE RURAL POOR

Owner-occupied farming is one source of livelihood for rural people, especially the poor. Hired agricultural labour and non-farm activity are increasingly important. Yet policy helps the rural poor mainly by raising their income from farming. In this respect, the redistribution of rights in land to poor individuals has achieved much more than is commonly realized. It is economically sound, since in poor regions smaller, labour-intensive farms normally favour efficiency and growth.

Sustainable development is about improving the livelihood opportunities for the poor. For the rural poor, secure access to land is not just about farming; it is about asset formation. Land is a convertible asset that can be used to leverage credit or sold to finance the start-up costs of other income-earning businesses. Opening these wider opportunities provides families with the security that currently eludes the landless.

Hired farmwork and non-farm activity are significant and growing sources of rural income. But their growth usually depends on rapid, widely shared growth of incomes in local farming.[8] Also, some 70% of rural household income in Asia comes from farming and farm labour, and about 60% in Africa and Latin America. Even by 2010, at

least two thirds of rural people – and 47% of all people – in developing countries will depend on agriculture.[9] In the poorest regions, the rural dollar-poor are more dependent on agriculture in Africa than are other rural groups, though the evidence in Asia is mixed.[10] The poor's other main source of rural income – non-farm activity – depends largely on local spending by the farming poor.

This enquiry into farmland assets produces seven conclusions.

1. Control of farmland is crucial for overcoming rural poverty, which, if it remains widespread in middle-income areas, is closely linked to extreme land inequality. In low-income areas rural labour income alone seldom suffices to avoid poverty, so most landless or near-landless rural people stay poor. Even the landless fare better where land is more equally distributed among small family farms. Small farms employ more people per hectare than large farms and generate income more likely to be spent locally on employment-intensive rural non-farm products, thereby stimulating overall economic development in the rural sector.

2. Land redistribution has been substantial and successful in many areas; the process is continuing and is usually equitable and efficient: small farms remain usually at least as productive as large farms.

3. To sustain their escape from poverty, post-reform farmers need appropriate infrastructures and services – more so if they are to compete as technology, information and farm-to-market systems adapt to urbanization and globalization.

4. Economic liberalization is gradually removing incentives and reforming macroeconomic policies that have favoured large-holder agriculture and the interests of the landed classes. In many cases, these changes make large-scale agriculture less profitable, and therefore indicate that more land may come onto local markets. This can potentially benefit the rural poor if the

valuation, financial and legal/judiciary systems are appropriate.

5. Previous land reform programmes have often been unduly confiscatory, statist or top-down. 'New wave' land reform, which is decentralized, market-friendly and involves civil society action or consensus is sometimes feasible and consistent with just and durable property rights.

6. Land reform processes need to be inclusive of both the intended beneficiaries and other parties with legitimate interests. Collective or state farming is seldom chosen voluntarily, seldom works well, and in some cases has worsened poverty. Both communal land tenure and private tenancy can be pro-poor; restricting them is counter-productive.

7. In supporting the processes to help the poor gain and maintain their access to land and other assets, reform agencies need to press for women to have equal entitlements and inheritance with their male counterparts. Women's control of land helps efficiency, equity, child health and poverty reduction.

Control of the farmland asset is crucial for reducing rural poverty

Poverty incidence usually rises as the amount of land owned or operated by poor rural households declines. The land the poor do control is usually of low quality, with less water control, and less secure rights, so villages with higher land inequality, other things being equal, have more poverty.[11]

The poor's gains from land distribution have several sources.

- If the poor operate land, they can combine it with labour, skills, management and purchased inputs, eating or selling the product and reaping a higher share of net income, even if output does not change.
- Furthermore, output often rises: yield and total factor productivity tend to be greater on smaller and more equal operated farms.[12]

- Low-income people with secure land access usually find it easier to graze animals.
- Land in smallholdings tends to be managed more labour-intensively, raising demand for labour and increasing the wages and/or employment of low-income workers, even if they do not control any land.
- All these forms of control of land and hence income, if more equal, raise local spending on rural non-farm products, and hence employment in it.[13]

Tenancy arrangements such as leaseholds can reduce poverty by transferring farm-management responsibilities, and thus income, from owners to tenants.[14] However, inequalities in land ownership, operation, access, management and control usually go hand-in-hand. Where ownership holdings are highly unequal, great land inequality usually persists even for operated farmland, that is, after tenancies are allowed for; the management of larger operated holdings usually provides fewer jobs per hectare.

With such extreme inequality, widespread poverty can persist despite quite high average rural income. Rich landed classes pass on to succeeding generations not only land and power but lasting protection against progress and mobility by the land-poor. This 'frozen history' stems from inheritance, across many generations, of land enclosed by colonial or national elites. The disadvantaged groups, often ethnic minorities, become landless and are forced by coercion or hunger to work for the elites, or escape (or are pushed) into areas that the elites do not covet: ill-watered, hilly, remote, or otherwise marginal lands.[15]

This process, and concentration of inherited rural disadvantage, make it hard to relieve rural poverty. Where this has produced extreme land inequality with few options for the rural poor – in Kenya, South Africa, Zimbabwe, North-East Brazil, Bihar in India, parts of the Philippines – land distribution must be addressed for rural poverty to fall rapidly.

Table 3.1: Poverty profile by landholding class, rural Bangladesh, 1988-89

Landholding class (acres of owned land)	Per cent of population	Head count index of poverty (%)
Landless (0-0.04)	13.9	61.4
Near landless (0.05-0.49)	31.5	53.9
Marginal (0.50-1.49)	19.2	43.4
Small (1.50-2.49)	11.3	34.2
Medium (2.5-7.49)	18.8	26.6
Large (7.50+)	5.3	10.1
Rural Bangladesh	100.0	47.5

Source: Bangladesh Bureau of Statistics in Ravallion and Sen 1994.

IFAD's regional poverty assessments confirm that in most of the developing world lack of access to land is associated with low incomes and rural poverty. Landlessness and poverty risk go together also in Ethiopia, Chile, China, Côte d'Ivoire, Kenya, India, the Philippines, Tanzania and Zimbabwe. In El Salvador, a 10% rise in land ownership boosts income per person by 4%. Even tiny holdings of decent, adequately watered land reduce poverty: in rural Bangladesh, a rural household with below 0.2 ha of land consumed 7% more per person and, with over 1 ha, 43% more than a landless household.[16] Thus even among those controlling land, poverty is correlated with the amount of land a household controls (see Table 3.1 for Bangladesh). Rural poor landowners suffer from high inequality in distribution of land in much of the developing world. Box 3.2 shows evidence of landholding inequality in selected countries.

Greater farmland equality helps to reduce poverty in the larger economy also; even as agriculture's share of output falls in developing countries, 'agrarian structure does not wither away' as an explanation of national inequality and therefore poverty.[17] Moreover, land equality is associated with faster overall growth.[18] It is also complementary to market-oriented growth in reducing poverty: for example, when liberalization reduces farm price repression, lower-income people are much more likely to benefit if they have enough land to be net sellers of food, not net buyers.

Land distribution also alleviates the poor's vulnerability. In an emergency, the landless have no land to sell or mortgage. Their infant mortality is much higher than among the landed.[19] Landless labourers are much more likely than farmers to die in famines.[20] During harvest shortfalls, farm families do more of their own work and eat more of their own product, so that they hire fewer, or no, harvest labourers.

Land reform has demonstrably reduced poverty. This was notable in Taiwan. In India the States with faster falls in poverty in 1958-92 are those that have implemented more land reform, other things being roughly equal. Beneficiaries of land resettlement in Zimbabwe saw their real incomes quadruple in 15 years. Quite modest land reform in Kerala, India, produced sharp poverty reduction (despite sluggish output) due, in part, to the complementary public investments in education and healthcare plus overseas family remittances.[21] Most strikingly, the shift of Chinese farmland in 1977-85 from larger-scale brigade management to a highly egalitarian household responsibility system accompanied unprecedented and sustained growth in staples and other farm output; in this brief period more than one in 20 of the world's rural population moved out of food poverty.

Thus, with appropriate policy, land redistribution tends to raise both employment and income. It can be community-driven and may take various forms tailored to local conditions. It can also build

---

Box 3.2: Inequality of land distribution in selected countries

Guatemala: In 1979, 2.5% of farms (with an average farm size of 200 ha) controlled 65% of agricultural land, while 16% of the land was cultivated by 88% of farms (average farm size 1.5 ha).

Bolivia: In 1989, landholdings larger than 2 500 ha (0.6% of all landholdings) occupied 66.4% of the land, while landholdings smaller than 3 ha (52.5% of all landholdings) occupied only 0.8% of the land.

Chile: In the early 1990s, commercial farmers cultivated 61% of the farm area, while the poorest farmers (*minifundistas*), who were three times more numerous, cultivated only 2% of farm area.

India: In 1961-2, 60.6% of rural households were marginal farmers (farming an area less than 2.5 acres) who owned 7.3% of the land, while large farmers (owning more than 25 acres), who represented 3.1% of households, owned 30.3% of the land. By 1991-2, these disparities had eased, with marginal farmers and large farmers controlling roughly equal areas of land (around 15% each).

Pakistan: In 1960 landholdings of less than five acres were held by 19% of farms and covered 3% of farm area, while landholdings greater than 150 acres (representing 0.5% of farms) controlled 11.5% of farm area. By 1991, 47.5% of farms controlled less than five acres and covered 11.3% of farm area, but 0.3% of farms with more than 150 acres of land controlled 10.1% of farm area.

Sources in country order: World Bank 1995a; World Bank 1996c; World Bank 1995k; NSS data in Pal and Mondal 1994, Sarvekshana 1997; Mahmood 1993.

---

on existing communal or tenancy systems as long as these systems do not present equitable opportunities by all sub-groups including men and women. Even so, some cautions are needed.

(a) Land distribution shifts many resources to poorer people only where land inequality is initially large per person. In a Punjabi case, land inequality per person was only half as much per person as per household.

(b) The national scope for redistribution is limited where large holdings are commonest in regions with inferior land. Such land is less valuable to recipients and cannot readily be assigned to the land-poor far away. However, the local scope for land redistribution is increased because farmers with more land tend to have better land and more access to major irrigation.

(c) Occasionally those with little land are as prone to poverty as those with none, for example in Burkina Faso, Mali, Western Kenya and some other areas of Africa; this is most common where land quality is very poor or where the landless have more non-farm income.

(d) Not only household access to land, but also women's access within the household, affect poverty.[22]

The successes of previous land reforms: the efficiency and equity case for persisting

Latin America

Latin America has the world's most unequal farmland, and hence much more poverty than would be predicted from income per person. Yet there has been massive land reform. The pace slowed after 1985, partly because so much had been done (Box 3.3); partly because severe land inequality persisted even after reform; and partly because some land reforms had imposed collectivism, with bad economic outcomes, retrieved by egalitarian privatizations only after a costly and disruptive detour.[23]

South Asia

In the 1950s, India reallocated most northern intermediary *zamindari* (tax-farmed) colonial land to working middle farmers. But the second phase of land reform – redistribution of land rights and improvement in terms of tenancy, within a largely

---

Box 3.3: Experience of land reform in Latin America

In **Mexico** intermittent but at times truly revolutionary reforms in 1918-68 redistributed 64 million ha, yet left huge inequalities and masses of near-landless farm workers, largely indigenous 'Indians' whose alienation has precipitated violent disturbances in Chiapas since 1994.

In **Ecuador** in 1964, 83.9% of all agricultural land, about 809 000 ha, was distributed to about 15% of farm families: about 86 000, plus 48 000 settled on colonized land. There was no clear tendency towards large or reconcentrated units in the reform sector.

In **El Salvador** after 1980, about 80% of 100 000 intended households obtained direct access to lands expropriated from holdings above 100-250 ha.

In the **Dominican Republic** by 1961, 83 000 ha were distributed as 32 275 private parcels (13% of peasant holdings), plus 30 000 ha as collectives.

In **Peru** 8.6 million ha, 40-50% of agricultural and grazing land, were expropriated in 1969-80 to 375 000 direct beneficiaries, or 24% of the rural economically active population. The initial cooperatives and associative enterprises proved unstable and were later largely privatized.

In **Chile** the reform sector, by July 1972, comprised 35% of agricultural land (in quality-adjusted units, basic irrigated hectares). Over two thirds of these 900 000 basic irrigated hectares remained reformed (or public) in 1986 after Pinochet's major counter-reforms – though much land did revert to the original owners, or (as forests) to large and multinational enterprises.

Other Latin American countries had major reforms, but with exceptions. **Colombia** illustrates aborted reform. In **Argentina** and **Brazil** most land is unreformed, but the reform process in Brazil, initiated in 1998 by President Cardoso, has distributed over 2 million ha of land with very encouraging lessons emerging from the Negotiated Land Reform programme under way in the north and north-east.

Sources in country order: King 1977: 93; Carter and Mesbah 1993: 291 and Zevallos 1989: 50-2; Strasma 1989: 409-12; Stanfield, 1989: 319-23; Carter and Mesbah 1993: 288-9; Thome 1989: 204 and Jarvis 1989: 245; de Janvry 1981.

---

intermediary-free system – was largely frustrated as large landholders used the law, political manoeuvring and corruption, and *mala fide* (bad-faith) land transfers to supposedly powerless poor relations and clients, to avoid loss of land under ceilings legislation. In India by 1990 'only' 2.9 million hectares had been declared surplus, 2.4 million possessed and 1.8 million distributed to 4.1 million persons. As with the further 0.9 million hectares distributed in 1952-54 in the *Bhoodan* movement, the land was mostly low-grade, and the scale of the distribution was modest, though some 12-18 million, mostly poor and often members of scheduled castes and tribes, gained from it. In Pakistan, evasion of land reform was even greater.[24]

The South Asian experience, however, shows that even modest 'official' reforms can lead to considerable indirect land redistribution.

- Beneficiaries of *mala fide* sales and transfers began to insist on their rights.
- To escape ceilings, big farmers sold land to poor relations and clients.
- Even in remote villages of recalcitrant States, land ceilings changed the atmosphere: despite personal risks, a few very poor people insisted on making their claims and a few exceptional officials on enforcing them.
- Political activism prevented the avoidance of tenancy reforms for the poor through evictions in at least two Indian States, namely, Kerala and West Bengal. In some other States, such as Karnataka and Maharashtra, populist politics led to successive land reforms that benefited castes comprising mainly poor tenants.[25]

India has redistributed less than 2% of total operated farmland. Yet the rise in the proportion of land in smallholdings suggests indirect land gains for the poor, caused by sales to escape ceilings legislation. Operated area per marginal holding probably rose in 1961-81. India is among several countries where inheritance among growing farm families, alongside a threat of ceilings implementation, outweighed pressures towards larger farm size: both owned and operated holdings became less unequal. This pattern was confined to countries with land reforms, including several, such as Pakistan and Sri Lanka, where evasion was widespread.[26]

Sub-Saharan Africa

For several reasons, many African countries have not attempted land redistribution. First, land is widely believed not to be scarce and hence not to require distribution. Second, some consider land redistribution as irrelevant to communal tenure systems. Third, it is often wrongly alleged that African small farms are less efficient than large ones (Box 3.4). Yet the future of conventional land reform lies, in part, in sub-Saharan Africa. Ethiopia transformed one of the world's most feudal land systems, through a terrible collectivist detour in the

---

Box 3.4: The efficiency of small farms: some evidence

Allowing for land quality, 'land productivity of smaller farms is usually at least twice that of the largest ones ... in Colombia ... in NE Brazil in most of the six zones; in India [and in the Muda Valley], Malaysia'. This is confirmed by farm-level data in 12 of 15 'countries [and] in a study of Indian villages, where a 20% decline in [gross output per hectare] was associated with a doubling of farm size'. Though this effect was not confirmed in Peru, it was strong in Mexico and Barbados, and confirmed for Brazil, through many studies. There is strong evidence in the same direction for the Philippines, Bangladesh, the Dominican Republic, Madagascar and Kenya. In Malawi, 'evidence ... on domestic resource costs [per unit of tobacco output] reveals that the smallholder sector holds the productivity edge' despite massive discrimination against it. For rice in West Africa, small farmers with traditional systems – not big mechanized farmers with subsidized irrigation – are competitive and efficient at world prices.

Output per hectare in north-east Brazil in 1973 was 5.6 times higher on farms of 10-50 ha than on farms above 100 ha; in the Pakistan Punjab, 2.7 times higher on farms of 5.1-10.1 ha than on farms above 20 ha in 1968-9; and among double-cropped farms in Muda, Malaysia, 1.5 times higher on farms of 0.7-1 ha than on farms of 5.7-11.3 ha in 1972-3. These comparisons understate the apparent output gains from shifting land from the very largest units into small ones. In Brazil in 1980, receipts per hectare of agricultural land in the smallest farm size (below 1 ha) were 100 times those in the largest (above 10 000 ha); per hectare of cropland, three times larger; per unit of capital, five times larger – and per unit of labour 20 times smaller. Some of these gaps may be due to land quality; mostly, they show how much small farmers' higher employment-intensity leads to higher land productivity.

Usually, small farmers' advantages are due less to higher yields of the same crop than to a higher-value crop-mix, more double cropping and intercropping, and less fallowing. All this carries environmental risks and benefits, which need careful review before land reform.

Poorer farmers also support local food security by concentrating their higher labour-per-hectare on raising yields in staples, and by putting more of their land into them. Aversion to purchase price risk stimulates staples production for net buyers (normally poorer), but aversion to sales price risk deters staples production for net sellers. This was confirmed in Mozambique.

Sources in order: Colombia, North-East Brazil, Muda: Berry 1984. Indian villages: FAO 1991. Peru, Mexico, Barbados: Cornia 1985.
Mexico, Brazil: Thiesenhuesen 1989: 20. Brazil: Kutcher and Scandizzo 1981; Thiesenhuesen and Melmed-Sanjak 1990.
Then in country/region order: Hayami *et al.* 1990; Boyce 1987; Stanfield 1989; Barrett 1994a; Hunt 1984: 254-62; Sahn and Arulpragasam 1990;
and on West Africa, Pearson *et al.* 1981. On Brazil, Pakistan Punjab and Muda, Binswanger et al. 1995, analysing Berry and Cline 1979.
On Brazil 1980, Thiesenhuesen and Melmed-Sanjak 1990; then in country order Barrett 1994a; Bharadwaj 1974; Boyce 1987, for Bangladesh.
Finkelstein and Chalfant 1991, and Fafchamps 1992, on farm size and response to price risk; and Barrett 1994a, on Mozambique.

1970s, to something approaching, in many areas, not-too-unequal family farming. Over a million hectares in Kenya were distributed, much of them to the rural poor, in the 1960s, but Kenya (like Malawi, Zimbabwe and South Africa) remains an extreme case of post-colonial land inequality. In Zimbabwe, it is estimated that some 4 500 largely white commercial farmers own over 11 million hectares of mainly high-quality agricultural land, while over 1.2 million poor black households are confined to low-quality communal areas covering a little over 16 million hectares. Zimbabwe and South Africa have embarked on reform: the former with long delay (only 70 000 ha between independence and 1998) and much disruption; the latter very tentatively; both under growing pressures to transfer reform lands to the non-poor. African land reform will need to spread, but even within Southern and Eastern Africa, IFAD identifies three distinct situations (Box 3.5). Much land legislation is under way in sub-Saharan Africa, which in many areas is emphasizing the strengthening of rights and security in an attempt to accommodate the divide between statutory and traditional tenure regimes. Redistributive reform is occurring on a smaller scale, however.

In all these cases, it is hard to envisage affordable employment prospects for the rising poor workforce without smallholder-based agricultural growth. Yet the rising workforce means that area expansion takes place into steadily more remote or low-quality land, even in most of West Africa. Especially if yield expansion continues to be disappointing, IFAD's conclusion that 'many smallholders do not have access to sufficient land to [anticipate] significant reductions in poverty through agricultural development' means that rural poverty reduction in much of Africa requires land redistribution to smaller and more equal holdings. Efficiency requires the same: even in an apparently favourable case, Malawi, growth based on large farms, that is, without land reform, is increasingly unviable as land scarcity and labour-surplus become the norm. In many other African countries, not only poverty reduction but also efficient rural growth require redistribution of emerging modern land-rights to the poor, away from absentee yeoman politicians and their clients.[27]

Transitional Economies

Box 3.6 outlines experience of land reform in ex-Communist countries in the 1990s. There is a striking contrast with China in 1977-85, where egalitarian distribution of formerly state or collective land-rights induced massive poverty reduction alongside efficiency gains. Most of the former Soviet Union lost this opportunity, leaving land

---

Box 3.5: Land reform in Southern and Eastern Africa: three situations

'In ... Zimbabwe, Lesotho, Malawi, South Africa, and to some extent Namibia ... [very unequal] access to land under conditions of limited agricultural potential ... [is] the result of historical circumstances [rather than] population pressure ... it is difficult to see how smallholder agriculture can contribute to a significant reduction in rural poverty without revision of the distribution of land' – as in much of Kenya, Eastern Zambia and parts of Uganda.

In a second set of areas, 'particularly in montane zones (Rwanda, Burundi and Southwest Uganda) land availability is limited and smallholding is the dominant system of land use'; here, the scope for land redistribution may be less, but can be ascertained only by careful enquiry into the actual inequality of control over land (in quality-units per person).

In 'parts of Tanzania, Mozambique, Angola and Zambia, unused good land is relatively abundant and there are real prospects for area expansion by smallholder producers (particularly [with] mechanical or animal traction)'; but incentives – and institutions of land allocation – do not now favour small-farm or employment-intensive development of such areas.

Source: IFAD 1999f.

locked into inefficient modes of ownership; but some land reform has taken place.

Reform experience confirms the greater efficiency of small farms (Box 3.4). Redistributing farmland control to poor families (a) relieves poverty because their income from farming rises, and because they hire more labour per hectare from other poor families; (b) gives the poor property rights incentives to investment and management; and (c) increases yields (and often total factor productivity) by shifting land to people with lower transaction costs in screening, applying and supervising both family and hired labour.

Thus, well-conducted land redistribution can both favour efficiency and reduce rural poverty. Lieten[28] argues that land reform in West Bengal triggered faster growth and poverty reduction, from 52% in 1978 to 28% in 1988; improved efficiency of irrigation required prior equalization in the agrarian system. Besley and Burgess[29] show that Indian States with more land reform also later achieved faster poverty reduction. Tyler *et al.*[30] show that countries with more equal land

enjoyed faster agricultural growth. We have seen that economic growth tends to be sluggish in very unequal countries, probably mainly because excluding large proportions of people from access to land and human capital is inefficient.

Today, land reform has returned to national and international agendas, as seen in the international summits and agreements of the 1990s. Land reform is a central pillar of, amongst others, the UN Commission on Sustainable Development, the World Food Summit, the Convention to Combat Desertification and the Convention on Biological Diversity. Each of these events has been informed by the challenges and difficulties experienced in the past ranging from (a) redistributed land to the non-poor; (b) failure to identify, train or support beneficiaries committed to farming; (c) lack of mechanisms to resolve conflicts and address complex situations such as civil strife and land invasions; (d) confiscation without compensation; (e) top-down state-led reform; or (f) forced collectivization.

The 1980s saw progress in Iran, Nicaragua and El Salvador. In the 1990s reform moved on to the

---

Box 3.6: Land reform in ex-Communist countries

Countries like **Poland**, have little to reform. They avoided wholesale collectivization, preserving small-scale family farming throughout the Communist period, and still do so. But they face acutely the problems of keeping poverty falling after land reform, discussed below.

Some, like the former **Czechoslovakia** and **East Germany**, have undertaken 'restitution', not land reform. Former state and collective land is being restored to those, mostly large, farmers from whom it had been confiscated.

Other countries, such as the **Ukraine** and **Russia**, have allowed some collectives to privatize, but most farmland remains in state farms or top-down collectives. Yet there has been a big rise, from a tiny base, in the highly productive areas in auxiliary household plots; this has limited the impact of rural and urban poverty during the severe stresses of the 1990s. Even as privatization advances, it is doubtful whether vast, flat, combine-harvested wheatlands can return to small-scale farming. Elsewhere in Russian farming, land reform will remain a live issue, not only to reduce rural poverty and inequality, but because labour absorption is politically and socially urgent.

Viet Nam, notably, followed **China's** 1978-84 lead in land reform. Both have privatized, to fairly equal family farms, much ex-collective farmland. In **Romania** in 1991-2, about 80% of collectivized farmland was redistributed, largely as small, family-size farms. Reform in **Armenia** and **Albania** was also egalitarian, and drastic, and showed that family farmland assets can reduce suffering even during violent disruption. However, these situations reveal that the impact on poverty depends on ensuring adequate training in farming skills, access to related resources and capital and the degree of land fragmentation.

Source: Ukraine: Csaki and Lerman 1997; Russia: Brooks *et al.* 1996; China and Viet Nam: Kerkvliet 1998 and Albania: Kodderitzsch 1999, IFAD 2000.

agenda in Brazil, Colombia, Ethiopia, Honduras, South Africa and Zimbabwe. While the extent of reform varies from country to country, there was a shift – notably in Indonesia, Thailand, Tunisia, Morocco and Algeria – from redistribution of private lands to settlement schemes, market-assisted reforms and, in several transitional economies, smallholderization of state lands.[31] The conclusion for Latin America has resonance for the world's poor: 'reports of land reform's death are . . . greatly exaggerated'.[32]

Finding new paths to reform and fostering multi-stakeholder alliances is essential, since the experience of agriculture-sector reform has shown that civil-society movements lacking the necessary institutional and public support, and government-led reforms lacking the support of civil society, have both failed. What are needed are revitalized alliances between governments and civil-society organizations, coupled with the moral and financial persuasion of the international community.

Revitalizing support for land reform and improving the access by the rural poor to productive assets was stimulated within and between countries by the IFAD-sponsored 1995 Conference on Hunger and Poverty, which resulted in the for-

mation of the Popular Coalition to Eradicate Hunger and Poverty. This global consortium of intergovernmental, civil-society and bilateral organizations is working towards the empowerment of the rural poor by increasing their access to productive assets, especially land, water and common property resources, and by increasing their direct participation in decision-making processes at local, national, regional and international levels.

Many land reforms have achieved much. The critics are disappointed because they expected even more (Box 3.7).

Keeping poverty falling after land reform: services, inputs, markets
Complementary service provision must be within the cost capacity of small farmers' needs, or else cooperatively or publicly supported. The lack of access to inputs and services can deny land recipients the benefits from reform. In Nicaragua and the Philippines, restricted access to credit, together with poorly defined property rights, led land reform beneficiaries to sell their land. In the 1980s, under the West Behiera Settlement Project, IFAD helped the Egyptian Government to

---

Box 3.7: Four land reforms: high expectations, deep disappointment, medium achievement

In **Ecuador**, some claim that neither the 1964 nor the 1970 reform 'brought about a major redistribution of land'. Yet in 1964-83 9% of all agricultural land . . . had been adjudicated to . . . 15% of the country's farm families'; in 1954-74 land in holdings above 1 000 ha fell from 37.4% to 22.1%.

In **Peru**'s early reforms (1964-68) 384 254 ha were distributed to 14 345 peasants, yet these acconted for 'only 4% of the land that could have been distributed with the legal instruments available and less than 2% of the peasants in need of land'.

In **El Salvador**, some complain that 'a much-vaunted smallholders' reform has accomplished only half its goals . . . 40% or more of the rural population [the landless] are not statutorily included in the reform'. Yet 22.7% of rural families benefited – not bad, even 'as against a goal of 60%'.

In **Iran**, the lands in 16.5% of villages had been purchased and distributed to 710 000 families in Stage 1 of the reforms, and in a further 4% of villages to 7% of rural families in the second stage, by October 1972. In all three stages (1962-75), lands in 53% of villages were redistributed and 1.9 million families, 92% of those eligible, benefited. Yet critics stress that the landlords kept the best land; that most peasants received (as owners) small plots, 'probably less than the holdings they used to cultivate' as pre-reform tenants; and that though 'land reform [gave land] to a large majority of the eligible peasants . . . most of the remainder lost their rights and joined the landless'.

Sources in country order: Carter and Alvarez 1989: 23-43; Lastarria-Cornhiel 1989: 138; Diskin 1989: 429, 435, 443; Amid 1990: 93-9, 102-3.

rehabilitate the West Behiera State Farm's irrigation and drainage infrastructure and to then privatize it by distributing the land to smallholders. To ensure higher agricultural production and incomes, the project also provided adaptive research, extension and poverty-oriented credit services to small farmers. In the reclaimed desert areas of the West Delta, the Newlands Agricultural Services Project is providing post-settlement support services in technology generation and transfer, improved on-farm water management, access to institutional credit and marketing services in order to assist the landless settled on 2 ha plots to establish sustainable and profitable farming systems.

However, if governments wait until all input supply conditions are ideal, they will never enact land reform. Markets, not governments, supply most farm inputs and services to farmers, whatever their size. The problem arises when inputs and services are mainly geared to demand from the large and/or capital-intensive farm sector. Governments should avoid subsidizing such private services, but should create incentives to realign them to meet small-farm needs. Large farmers, with big surpluses, can overcome remoteness directly – marketing crops, or trucking in fertilizers in lorryloads – whereas smallholders need appropriate access, via competitive traders, to services, inputs and markets. Also, large farmers' information often allows them to rely on private research; whereas small farmers need public research, as well as competitive, logistically available inputs from the market.[33]

Small farms face four threats to efficiency gains after they receive land assets, but these can usually be managed at costs far less than those of the huge efficiency dispersion (and poverty) associated with a very unequal land asset.

1. Wealthy farmers often gain most from public provision or subsidy for credit, services, information, irrigation and farm research. Often a tiny proportion of these inputs reaches small farmers, especially remote-area and drylands farmers and women. While small farms are thus made artificially uncompetitive with big ones, their yields – and interest in farming – will disappoint. Removing price distortions that selectively harm small farms may induce rich farmers to sell land to poor farmers, and is anyway a desirable complement to land reform. In the case of some inputs, like pesticides and water, subsidies can also be environmentally harmful.

2. Some crops, such as rubber, sugar, some beverage crops, tobacco, soft fruits and vegetables need timely, coordinated collection and processing. This favours large farms unless institutions to service small ones are in place. But such services are often provided cooperatively by small farmers, or privately by processors, traders, or contract farmers.

3. The potential for large farmers to shift from their role in commercial production to a new role as the provider of services to smallholders can often be easily realized. As large holders they frequently engage in processing, marketing, finance and extension. In some cases there may be mutual benefits if they take on this new role. This is harder if land reform, even with fair compensation, is often conflictual. Also, there is a risk that the rural poor will remain dependent on the former landowner in their new role as sole provider of factor markets.

Such intermediation, by pre-reform large farmers turned service managers, is one way for small farmers and land reform beneficiaries, provided they do not face new monopolies of power and control or gain benefits from the knowledge of former landowners on how to function in a world of market integration and globalization. To benefit they must adapt, combine and bargain. Public policy would be needed to moderate potentially exploitative practices that could easily become monopolistic unless governments stimulate expansion in the number of competitive service providers.

'New wave' community-based land reform

Many of the rural rich are experienced, hard-working farmers, not personally guilty of past land theft. How can they be fairly accommodated or compensated in situations where avoiding land reform will doom to failure efforts to overcome hunger? Experience suggests that new methods for negotiating land reform need to recognize both the legitimate needs of the landed class and the resource entitlements of the landless and near landless. Unless there is greater transparency in the negotiations between the poor and government officials on the methods of land transfer, the poor are likely to find themselves excluded. But community-based land reform puts the poor at the centre of the process.

The government must show sensitivity in handling the conflict of interest between landowners and the rural poor, those who now possess and those who stand to gain access to public land. The unique nature of each situation requires a specific local model tailored to each case. Such efforts include negotiated land reforms in Colombia and Brazil. Governments provide an appropriate legal framework, and some or all of: credit; some subsidy, perhaps as a land voucher, with an upper limit (in South Africa in 1995-99 some USD 2 000) to target help to the poor; smallholder-geared support services; and tax or other incentives for land to move towards smallholders. Potential buyers organize themselves, identify land for purchase and draw up plans for its productive use.

Beneficiary selection may be based on self-selection or social criteria. Such schemes encourage potential buyers to seek out run-down or under-utilized farms as these are less costly to purchase. The need to develop careful farm-planning models induces beneficiaries to consider how they will develop the land and identify problems, before resettlement. Thorough planning enables greater intensity of land use, reducing the amount of land area required. 'Farm plans also serve as a first step towards the identification and prioritization of investment needs, and to provide justification for guiding the allocation of public funds to the most productive use.'[34]

Land reform today has new institutional requirements: group formation, land search and valuation, negotiation, bidding, farm planning, and training and service support for several planting seasons while beneficiaries learn the skills and develop the market linkages to become profitable smallholder farmers. Guidance is often required by outside organizations; it has often come in the past from an NGO or civil-society group which has supported the community during the period of acquiring the land. Conversely, the support has often come from multilateral or international financial institutions, such as IFAD, that support land management projects. An example is IFAD's Sustainable Development Project for Agrarian Reform Settlements in the Semi-Arid North-East in Brazil, which is to provide smallholder support services based on the concept of community-based land reform.

Land reform can be supply-led and push up the net supply of land from sub-dividing government-held public lands and large-scale farms for sale in small units to the landless or near landless. Or reform can be demand-led: pushing up net demand for land by land-poor households. Demand-led methods, with farmland increasingly scarce, induces large land-price rises for only small rises in the quantity of land supplied from rich to poor. Even announcing pure willing-seller/willing-buyer concepts, in a context of purely demand-led reform, can push land prices up. Such reform is expensive, raising problems about what the taxpayer is able and willing to afford. It is likely to transfer land exclusively to the poor when land prices are relatively low, for example when the rich are facing mortgage foreclosure, natural disaster, collapsing product markets, or fear of land seizures or invasions.

Supply-led reform is more promising. The *Bhoodan*, or land-gift, movement in India in the 1950s appealed to rich people's sense of moral and religious duty, and released substantial areas of land, but mostly bad land, which did not always pass to the poor quickly, or at all. In Taiwan in the 1950s, the government could induce higher land supply by offering landlords compensation in the form of shares in seized Japanese urban assets. In much of Southern Africa, colonial laws against subdivision remain; scrapping them would raise land supply from rich to poor. Where there are well-recorded individual land rights, even quite modest rates of progressive land tax can both raise land supply and steer it towards small sales, helping poorer buyers. In north-east Brazil's decentralized reforms, local authorities secured consensus by offering large landowners access to new irrigation on their retained land, in return for giving up some land cheaply to the reform;[35] but this requires the taxpayer to pay (helped in this case by a World Bank loan).

Where the land needs of the rural poor are suppressed over long periods, as in many countries, conflicts will arise in various forms. Land invasions are regarded by some as illegal acts, whereas others argue that in the absence of any stable way to feed the families, which are the victims of intergenerational poverty, land invasions are understandably a last resort for desperate people. To fail to redress land inequality merely postpones civil conflict, like that in Central America from the 1970s to the 1990s. While land invasions (as in Zimbabwe in 2000) can involve violence, destroy farm assets and alienate big farmers, they should be seen as a symptom, not the cause, of the land problem.[36]

Even with suitable incentives, very unequal farmland control – unlike the mode of that control through tenancy, sharecropping, communal lands, or otherwise – may persist even if it is inefficient, because it enhances the power or security of the rich. That makes a strong efficiency and equity case for reducing extreme inequality in farmland control. But, given the distribution of farmland control, there is no obvious case for restructuring tenurial and managerial forms; with correct incentives they reform themselves. Most attempts to replace land redistribution by imposing changes in tenurial and managerial forms, but without consensus, including the poor, or moves towards more equal rights in land, have been unsuccessful, often counter-productive, and sometimes disastrous (see Annex 3.1).

Women, land and poverty

Reducing the barriers to women's control of rural assets, especially land, is crucial for policy against poverty.

- The barriers against women's possession and control of land cause poverty through discrimination within households that do not pool income from assets, or do not distribute that income equally. 'The risk of poverty and the physical well-being of a woman and her children could [depend on whether] she has direct access to . . . land, and not just access mediated through . . . male family members, [especially] for female-headed households with no adult male support.'[37]

- Denying efficient managers access to assets because they are women is expensive. In Burkina Faso, household output could be increased by 10-20% by reallocating currently used agricultural inputs more evenly between men and women. The same household income, if it comes from women's asset holdings, improves child health, nutrition and education in Bangladesh, Ethiopia and South Africa; assets in the hands of women significantly raise the share of household expenditures on education. Extra income, including asset income, accruing to women rather than men is in several countries linked to more outlay on, and gains in, child nutrition.[38]

• Denying women assets is unjust.

Few traditional or reformed land allocation systems have significantly raised women's control over land, though most Latin American countries have revised their land reform title laws to obtain gender equity. Many societies have shifted education, health, non-farm assets and access to assets through credit towards women; but large shifts of farmland towards women are far rarer. Giving women rights to land also gives them power, helping them to take more control in existing relations, not least by improving women's reservation wage, and hence their role and bargaining strength within marriage. Such empowerment reduces their vulnerability within the household; in Bihar, India, allocation of title to men but not women led to increased drunkenness and domestic violence. Similarly in the Mwea irrigation scheme, Kenya, failure to guarantee women's rights to land led to a reduction in their well-being. If a woman

has the 'reservation option' to work and earn on her own land, it also gives her power in social and economic relations, and makes participation in local political institutions more likely.[39]

Legal and even constitutional rights notwithstanding, both inheritance and purchase of land by women face severe customary obstacles. The varying effect on farmland access and poverty is summarized in Box 3.8.

There are other ways besides giving women access to land to bring gender concerns into the foreground: via other assets, notably education; via microfinance, as in many IFAD-supported activities; and via technology, for example, of rice production in IFAD's experience in The Gambia. Agarwal argues for concentrating on the land asset because of the 'feminization of agriculture': the movement out of agriculture has been faster for men.[40] Hence, female-headed households in rural India increased from 20% to 35% in 1970-96. So it is increasingly inefficient and unjust if land law, custom or practice deny women effective control over farmland. In much of Asia, and increasingly other developing regions, too, little public land is

---

Box 3.8: Obstacles to the purchase of land by women

In **South Asia**, most daughters in all Indian States do not inherit land, though legally eligible. Some tribals customarily give unmarried daughters usufruct rights; in Bihar, India, some Ho women remain unmarried to keep this access. In Rajasthan, a survey of three villages found that, of the 36 women with land in their names, 34 were widows; for 27, the land was registered with their sons. Most areas of matrilineal inheritance (much of Kerala, and many tribal land systems) show less gender-biased land control than areas of patrilineal inheritance. In Bangladesh, increasing numbers of women are making claims on their share of land. However, in Pakistan, little has changed.

In parts of **North Africa**, competition for access to land and historical customs can work against women even in situations where women have legal rights of access or inheritance rights to land.

In **East and Southern Africa**, poverty is explained much less by gender bias than by policy and institutional bias against all smallholders (men and women). In Ethiopia, there is no legal discrimination by gender. In Southern Africa, women can usually inherit land; male migration has left many rural women heads of household; female land control is common.

In **West and Central Africa**, poverty alleviation is closely linked to intra-household distribution of, and control over, resources and incomes. In Imo and Abia States, Nigeria, the average household farms 9.8 ha, but only 2.4 ha are allocated to women and then not as a claim on land but through lease, from their husbands, for a farming season. Even widows do not have land as it is kept in trust by their husbands' family for the children.

Sources in order of regions: Agarwal 1994; UN 1991; IFAD 1999a: 57 and UN 1991; IFAD 1999b: 47 and Odii 1997.

left. Unlike Latin America, land ceilings would not greatly increase the amount of land available (in 1996 in India, the surplus area above the ceiling was only 1.6% of arable land). Better access for women to private land is the only option.

The two routes are inheritance and purchase. Apart from customary and social obstacles to ownership by women (Box 3.8), even the wife's ownership (or, as in much of West Africa, day-to-day management and retention of usufruct) of particular plots often leaves the husband in control, because of social impositions on women: less school access and hence higher illiteracy; restrictions on mobility (and interaction with markets and public extension services) such as *purdah*; taboos against female farm tasks, for instance, ploughing or (in Southern Africa) cattle management. Perhaps, especially where fertility remains very high, women's family and household tasks militate against hands-on farm management in peak-season; yet women's farm productivity is usually at least as high as men's, so that their relative exclusion from land asset control is due partly to the structure of rural power, not only to physical realities or to women's own preferences.

The strength of custom and of male power make it difficult to identify practical changes to land systems that will improve women's land rights. In Mashonaland, communal land is allocated only to married men, and inherited only by sons; in Swaziland, land is acquired through inheritance or application to the local chief, but women very rarely get land in this way. As for distributive land reform, in four of 13 Latin American countries which desegregated gender data on reforms in the 1960s and 1970s, women formed only 4-25% of beneficiaries, as land titles were given mainly to household heads. In India, though West Bengal's 1970s Operation Barga covered female-headed households, few received land in practice. In Midnapur, of 107 000 ha, 98% was distributed to men; even in 90% of female-headed households which

received land, it was only for sons. Of 18 single women, only eight were given land. No married women were given joint title with their husbands.[41]

Thus, neither traditional nor reformed landholding systems have much increased women's share of farmland. Though more women than men depend on agriculture, many fewer own land. Where they do, their ability to use it to its full potential is usually limited by inferior access to inputs, credit and extension, and by low mobility. Where women gain land-use rights through male kin, men may still control key aspects of land use; women's rights often end with divorce (or even the death of the husband), forcing women to return to the natal home, often with no access to land. Massive reforms of women's legal rights, such as inheritance, even embodied in constitutions, though desirable (and quite widespread), have usually proved slow and ineffective in getting land assets to rural women, especially the poor, in face of male dominance and religious and customary law and practice. In spite of Agarwal's interesting small-scale examples of successful collective action by women to secure individual control of land,[42] the issue has so far proved largely intractable by markets, reforms and laws – and even by selective male movement from villages to cities. More thought, and more carefully selected actions, are needed to address female disadvantage in land access effectively.

The rural poor and the land asset: conclusions, donor implications

More widespread access to farmland assets remains central to rural poverty reduction. The poor acquire land directly. Indirectly, smaller and more equal holdings lead to increased employment and more demand for rural non-farm products. Supposed substitute reforms (assaults on tenancy or communal tenure; enforced state or collective farming) have failed. Much redistributive reform into family farms has taken place, with generally good outcomes, but the classical land reform

---

Box 3.9: Partnerships and actions that contribute to successful agrarian reform

Where it is possible to merge the interests of civil society, intergovernmental organizations and governments into a common effort, the synergistic effect on rural reform can be promising. The Popular Coalition to Eradicate Hunger and Poverty suggests the following plan:

1. Supporting alliances among sectors

- Build broad-based political and economic support for land-tenure reform, access to farm inputs (including credit and technology), and protection of the natural resource base.
- Inform the general public, through educational programmes, that smallholder farms are potentially more productive and environmentally sustainable than large-scale commercial agriculture.
- Establish coalitions of urban and rural peoples around such common concerns as the effects of the rural exodus on rural economies and urban poverty.
- Promote innovative opportunities for public debate on citizen resource rights and the role of sustainable agriculture in improving rural livelihood systems.
- Strengthen the collection, analysis and sharing of knowledge of the innovative approaches to land reform that can overcome the constraints experienced in earlier models of agriculture-sector reform.

2. Assisting governments

- Establish appropriate legal, regulatory and judicial frameworks that can register and protect people's resource rights.
- Promote the 'ratification and application of existing international conventions relevant to indigenous people and their communities and promote the adoption by the General Assembly of a declaration on indigenous rights'.[1]
- Establish independent and accountable land commissions, with adequate participation by potential beneficiaries.
- Ensure that women's names appear on land records, that their rights be enshrined in communal property systems, and that the inheritance rights of widows and daughters be established and protected, and promote representation by women in local decision-making bodies and on land commissions.
- Halt the expansion of the agricultural frontier on to fragile lands.
- Remove the subsidies and tax provisions that provide distorting privileges to large-scale farmers.
- Establish land-tax systems, especially for under-utilized land and land held for speculative purposes.
- Develop methods for increasing finance for land reform and post-land acquisition services, including land banks, land-for-debt schemes and land for taxes.
- Strengthen land registries, cadastral systems and land-survey methods.
- Develop human capital by investing in rural schools, health facilities and extension services.
- Establish mechanisms for the speedy settlement of land disputes.

---

process has often been slow, statist and inadequately pro-poor. Also, post-reform family farms need appropriate infrastructures, especially for farm products requiring swift and coordinated collection and processing, or connected to liberalized or global market systems. New approaches to land redistribution address these problems, often with decentralized, consensual, or citizen-driven reform processes.

The importance of land redistribution for poverty reduction is increased by:
- continuing growth of the workforce in rural areas;
- declining short-run prospects to raise employment by the growth in the yield of food staples;
- increasing awareness of the high, rising cost per job of employing the poor off-farm;
- exhaustion in many areas of the scope for increasing farmed areas sustainably, given the

3. Strengthening rural people's organizations

- Support consciousness-raising among landless and near-landless people regarding their rights and the opportunities for change.
- Strengthen rural worker and peasant organizations, ensuring that they include female-headed households, widows, indigenous peoples, lower castes and other marginalized groups.
- Foster the organization of communities into units of sufficient scale for viable credit and marketing systems that will be of interest to commercial service providers.
- Protect indigenous people's knowledge and strengthen the efficiency of their resource-management systems.[2]
- Demarcate and protect traditional forms of land tenure with, for example, the registration of common property and pastoral areas.
- Promote improved land-management and soil-conservation practices.
- Ensure beneficiary participation in land-valuation processes and in determining repayment terms based on available labour, production skills, the productive capacity of the land, available technology and projected profitability.
- Ensure the cost-effective provision of rural services by using community-based organizations to deliver government programmes.

4. Working in partnership with international organizations

- Leverage the moral persuasion and financial conditionality of international organizations in order to place issues of land and resource rights on national agendas.
- Elaborate participatory methods to assist governments and civil society in monitoring progress towards secure access to land and other productive assets in the context of the World Food Summit and the Commission on Sustainable Development.

1. UNCED. (1992), Chapter 26.4
2. UNCED, (1992), Chapter 26.5

loss of farmland to degradation and urban expansion; and
- the especially limited and low-quality land rights of many ethnic minorities and many women.

Some of the costs of consensual land distribution can be borne by beneficiaries through long-term credit, but too much of this creates a debt trap and may force land disposals in bad times. And even partial compensation of losers in consensual land redistribution is expensive. So are complementary public (or in some cases NGO) infrastructures to facilitate private and competitive provision, often via former large farmers, of smallholder-friendly, competitive transport, input and output marketing, finance, research and extension, and credit.

Successful land reform can benefit from the lessons of the past. These point to a number of practical actions involving rural peoples' organizations, governments and international organizations. These actions have been consolidated from lessons gathered from around the world by the Popular Coalition to Eradicate Hunger and Poverty (Box 3.9).

WATER-YIELDING ASSETS AND POLICIES AGAINST RURAL POVERTY

Assets, water, and water crisis: selecting responses that do not harm the rural poor

Water is vital to most production. One third of cropland is irrigated in Asia (growing about two thirds of its crops by value), but less than 5% in sub-Saharan Africa. This partly explains Africa's generally lower yields, cropping intensity and food security. Water is also vital to consumption. Low-quantity and -quality drinking water in most developing countries harms health, and indirectly productivity, above all among poor rural households. These have least water security in production and consumption, partly for want of water-yielding assets (taps, wells). Hence they have less, worse or more unreliable farm water than others, and must divert calories and earning-power – almost always mainly female – to fetch water for many hours each week.

Remedies face several obstacles. First, water is becoming scarcer and less reliable in much of the world. With increasing populations and farm use, groundwater tables are falling; many major dams increasingly face management problems and are perceived as environmental threats; declining real prices of farm products, too, have undermined arguments for irrigation construction and maintenance. Second, pervasive water subsidies encourage waste, and are steered to the rich, who control most water-yielding assets. Third, there are strong and understandable pressures to divert commercial water offtake in low-income countries away from agriculture – now using over 75-90% and paying far below market rates – towards thirsty townspeople who are willing to pay. Given the importance of water resources and control for the rural poor, how can the amount, efficiency and poverty impact of water and water-yielding assets be enhanced?

Water can be stocked in tanks or rivers, but outflows deplete the stock. Someone who controls water has a once-for-all source of value, which can be consumed or sold, but not an asset, like farmland or housing, which yields repeated returns. However, the controller of a water-yielding asset can often generate sustainable returns, as with farmland.

The water crisis and poverty

This raises two issues.

1. Given the amount, distribution and control of water-yielding assets, can the amount and use-efficiency of water, and benefits from it – and the poor's sustainable access to such benefits – be improved for life, health, comfort and escape from poverty?

2. What shifts, in the amount, distribution or control of water-yielding assets, might improve the amount, sustainability, or poverty impact of water benefits flowing from them?

Scarce and low-quality water in many developing countries, most critically in Near East and North Africa,[43] already restricts development, health and poverty reduction. In the next two decades the water constraint will tighten, and affect more countries, due to population growth, urbanization and probably climate change. Further, many aspects of water use threaten sustainability. In most developing countries, heavy subsidies and other public policy towards water use – and current allocations within agriculture – are unsustainable.

Yet rural water need is a generally underemphasized, rural contribution to water inefficiency and environmental harm is overemphasized, and the case for shifting water from farms to cities is overstated. So steps to meet the crisis may further harm the rural poor by steering water away from them. Though subsidies to water use, rural or urban, are inefficient, many proposals to axe water use for farms overestimate how much water farms 'use up' (as opposed to 'use') and the ease of transferring it cheaply to urban domestic use. Sustainable, poverty-reducing farming in many low-income areas, especially in Africa, will need more irrigation, not less. As water gets scarcer and subsidies fall, expensively irrigated areas will rightly shift from staple foods to high-value products such as horticulture; but, correspondingly, many rainfed areas will require supplementary low-cost irrigation for higher-yielding cereals.

The World Water Council[44] gives pride of place, in slashing water waste, to (a) water pricing and (b) water users' associations. These matter, but so also do (c) drainage, (d) more incentive and technology for adequate, non-polluted re-use of water, after initial use, and (e) breeding water-economizing crop varieties. Focusing water benefits on the rural poor further involves (f) getting water-yielding assets to them, and (g) saving water by asset choices that use labour (especially in slack seasons) rather than capital – cross-bunding rather than centre-pivot irrigation. Water scarcity and movability are regional and watershed-specific; in many areas (such as the Eastern Cape in South Africa) there is spare water, which could be cost-effectively used to provide irrigation to poor smallholders. In general, priority recipients of more, cleaner water are often rural.

Water, rurality and poverty: facts and implications
The facts about water are striking.

- *Scarcity*: by 1992, 8% of people in sub-Saharan Africa and 53% in Near East and North Africa lived in countries with water resources below 1 000 m^3 per head a year, defined as severe constraint.
- *Deterioration*: 50 countries suffer severe constraint or are water-stressed (1 000-1 600 m^3 per head a year) in 2000 – as against 40 countries in 1990.

- *Quantity and quality* create separate health problems: adequate water availability alone would cut child diarrhoea morbidity by 25%; adequate quality alone by 16%.
- *The poor suffer more*: the richest income quintile in Peru, the Dominican Republic and Ghana is, respectively, three, six and 12 times more likely to have a house water connection than the poorest.
- *Rural quality is worse*: in developing countries, 30% of rural and 18% of urban people lacked safe water; respectively, 82% and 37% lacked adequate sanitation. (Bad maintenance, especially in rural areas, makes matters worse than these official estimates.)
- *The rural poor are worst hit*, being more reliant on unprotected shallow wells and less able to adopt preventive measures such as boiling water.
- *Agriculture is the main water user*: it consumes 88-95% of annual water withdrawals (from rivers and aquifers) in China, India, other low-income countries, and sub-Saharan Africa overall; 69% in middle-income countries; and 39% in high-income countries.
- *Farm water subsidies remain huge*, though less than in the early 1990s (when farm water users seldom paid more than 10% of operating costs, and hardly any costs of capital or maintenance). IFAD project work confirms that such subsidies make for water waste, impede maintenance and seldom help the poorest.[45]

These facts – together with the impact on domestic water supplies as farmers exploit ever depleting groundwater supplies and pollute water with agrochemicals – suggest policy measures to shift water and/or water-yielding assets from farmers (who are heavily subsidized) to domestic users (who are willing to pay market prices). Water policy is doing this in many countries; in South Africa the target is to reduce agriculture's share of water offtake from its present 70% to 50% in 10-15 years. Apart from the undoubted need to slash subsidies to water, water-yielding assets and water use (with appropriate safety nets for the poor), we suggest important caveats and more disaggregation and caution about any universal thrust to divert water from farming, given the impact of that thrust on the efficiency and equity of the rural-urban, rich-poor, and farm-non farm water splits.

- Municipal and industrial water withdrawal is often already increasing much faster than withdrawal by agriculture. For example, the presence of 31 textile firms in the Ciwalengke irrigation system, West Java, has reduced available water for irrigation, fishing and domestic use.[46]

- Using water need not mean using it up. Much farm water is recycled through surface or underground transfer downstream; the most efficient policy may well be incentives, institutions, or interventions to improve the quality of recycled water (by substituting better crop varieties for some agrochemicals) or its quantity (through less evaporation or better drainage). Industry and mining seem more likely to use water up than agriculture. Many processes add chemicals that render the water unsuitable for re-use. Much industry is near coasts, so that used water runs into the sea.

- Substantial local irrigation expansion, especially of minor schemes with run-off or recharge usable elsewhere, is often consistent with national emphasis on industrial or domestic needs.

- The rural poor, already hardest hit by water scarcity, are likely to be increasingly exposed if global warming brings higher evaporation rates and less reliable rainfall – and are the least able to buy their way out of damage. They need safety-nets in the event of policies to desubsidize water use, as is often indicated on efficiency grounds.

- Agriculture often pays higher implicit taxes than other activities (for example, through trade policies); cuts in farm water subsidy should not be delayed on these grounds, but should be at least matched by reductions in such 'taxes'.

- Complementary policies should aim to save farm water by labour-using methods, and to shift control over water and water-yielding assets to the rural poor.

Farm production, water, and water-yielding assets for the rural poor

Irrigation has induced huge rises in farm yields, cropping intensity, and thus both smallholder and employee incomes, taking hundreds of millions out of poverty and reducing their vulnerability to poor rains. The Green Revolution of 1965-85, which induced huge falls in rural and urban poverty, has had much more impact on production and poverty in irrigated areas than elsewhere. Despite the need to refocus new farm technology on rainfed areas, reversal of past progress with irrigation, or failure to spread it where suitable, especially in Africa, would be a tragedy for the poor, and for world soils; if the poor cannot get enough work and food from well-watered lands, they and their suppliers will be driven to overfarm fragile drylands. Farmer-controlled or improved traditional microirrigation has been unduly neglected in favour of uneconomic modern schemes, notably in West Africa.[47] But the accumulating problems of large dams must also be addressed; larger-scale irrigation remains essential to the environmentally sustainable food and jobs needed to fight rural poverty.

Irrigation can both improve yields and reduce rural poverty. The IFAD-supported Southwest Rural Development Project in Bangladesh installed tubewells and provided input credits to the poor; after five years, net returns to a typical small (one-acre) farm rose by over 50%. But do the poor obtain the water-yielding assets? Though at national level in India small farms are more likely to be irrigated than big ones, this is mainly because in ill-watered lands more area is needed even to survive. Irrigated parts of India have far less poverty and variability. Within most

Indian States, large farm size tends to accompany access to irrigation and hence multiple cropping. And locally the non-poor usually have more or better irrigated land than the poor. In Andhra Pradesh, India, large farms are concentrated at the head end of the Tungabhadra Left Bank Canal and smaller farms in the tail-end reaches; the poor thus obtain farm water later and less reliably. Water access is often also conditional on access to other resources (such as credit) and to political representation. In South India 'organizational connection' is an important influence on water distribution. Irrigation bureaucracies are often biased towards the more (financially) powerful in the setting of rosters for water distribution.[48]

For women, access to irrigation assets is especially challenging. In Kenya, since claims on water are allocated within the community through contribution to maintenance (carried out by men), women cannot obtain water-yielding assets directly. They must pay men for irrigation water; some widows have had to give up irrigated farming. In Burkina Faso, some women are lent irrigated land in the dry season in order to grow vegetables; in Ecuador, women are heavily reliant on social networks. In such cases women obtain water rights annually and *ad hoc*, rather than secure claims on water-yielding assets. Access is unsure and conditional, partly because it is linked to women's limited rights to land. Unfortunately projects that address this problem by providing irrigation for a crop traditionally farmed by women, without a change in power-structures, incentives or social norms, may cause the crop to become a 'man's crop' alongside control over the water-yielding asset, as with rice irrigation in an IFAD project in The Gambia.[49]

Even such partial participation in irrigation projects may be in women's interest. Women's consumption improved in the case of The Gambia, though their status and asset control did not. Also,

they may be able to use the water for domestic needs. But public, non-government organizations (NGOs) and donor stakeholders can facilitate irrigation incentives, rules of participation and management, and organizational forms that allow for women's and female-headed households' farming and other needs. A large Bangladesh NGO, Proshika, has financed and trained mainly women's groups to control water-yielding assets and sell the water mainly to male farmers.[50]

Given total water supply to agriculture, the poor can gain more from water or water-yielding assets by either redistribution or improved efficiency. Can the two go hand-in-hand? How will the poor's share of water-yielding assets affect water efficiency, which includes sustainability? Land usually yields at least as much in small farms as in large, but what about water? There is little evidence, but the same principle probably applies to water. Large, rich farmers would find it paid to save water (like land) by using capital; small farmers by using or hiring labour. Overall, economic efficiency of water use in agriculture is low; it would pay society (if not always the individual farmer) if more were spent on reducing, among other things, spillage, leakage, infiltration, evaporation, clogging of water with weeds, failures of drainage, diversion of water to drown weeds (as on the IFAD-supported Kirindi Oya Irrigation and Settlement Project in Sri Lanka), and impediments to river and aquifer recharge through mistimed or mislocated irrigation or drainage. What can be done?

- Public works with slack-season labour, as in the Food-for-Work Programme in Bangladesh and the Employment Guarantee Scheme (EGS) in Maharashtra, India, can help with irrigation and drainage maintenance.
- Reducing or removing water subsidies normally increases incentives to avoid waste.
- So does reduced prestige (and sometimes corruption) for the construction and water-delivery

aspects of big dams, and more for the vital but unfashionable maintenance side.

- Economic efficiency in water use, and hence more water for the poor, could also be advanced by better integration between water and crop research, extension and delivery systems.

What sorts of irrigation-yielding assets benefit the poor most?

Small-scale, farmer-managed irrigation schemes include small tanks and non-grid shallow wells, mainly in Asia; and, mainly in Africa, valley-bottom irrigation (*fadama*) as in Nigeria, minor stream diversions (*molapo*) as in much of Southern Africa, sandriver diversion, and rainwater catchment schemes. Such schemes can be low-cost alternatives to large irrigation projects, easier to manage bottom-up, rooted in locally relevant traditional knowledge, yet often with good rates of return due to associated enhanced crop and water management. Moreover, they often provide the very poor with access to water for irrigation. In India small individual wells were the form of irrigation asset most associated with smaller farms in the late 1970s, followed by tanks, with formal dam systems and tubewells – requiring purchased or negotiated access to substantial assets – far behind. In Latin America, most irrigated rice lands are minor schemes developed by farmers diverting water from streams, rivers and wells. In the Philippines, almost half the irrigated land is watered by such small schemes, involving local associations. Box 3.10 shows the role of *dambos* in Southern Africa.[51]

Small-scale irrigation schemes can have clearer rules about distribution and maintenance. Members can be few, close and homogeneous; institutional arrangements can be local and quick; and women may be able to participate more. However, there are limitations on small-scale, member-controlled schemes. There is no outside agency to bear the risk; lack of financial or bor-rowing capacity can retard uptake and investment, damaging growth and equity. Small schemes tend not to cover entire watersheds or aquifers, increasing the downstream problems; these require negotiation if inequity is to be avoided.[52] Above all, the design and management of irrigation is often uneconomic, or even infeasible, at levels too small to allow for the borders, slopes, flows, water resources and channels of large and integrated watersheds, or even river-basin systems.

For such reasons, and to exploit some underused African lakes and rivers efficiently and sustainably, large-scale projects, often with dams, will continue to be needed. They can indeed concentrate water on elites and head-enders; link them to the leaderships of sometimes corrupt irrigation bureaucracies, raising water uncertainty for tail-enders and the poor; weaken overview and participation in maintenance,[53] resulting in long, frequent breakdowns which harm poorer farmers most, as they cannot afford alternative, private access to water; and risk passing 'thresholds' of environmental damage, leading especially to salinity and waterlogging as in parts of Pakistan. But such problems often have been overcome as water markets spread. The poor may not own a share of any major system, but they can buy water. So must better-off head-enders, who then often switch to groundwater systems, leaving the surface water to be bought and controlled in part by the poor.

Groundwater pricing has complex effects. It is surprisingly popular: farmers may neglect subsidized (but frequently inefficient) public tubewell or borehole supplies and pay high prices for reliable private supply, as in Northern India. However, as more and more tubewells are sunk and used, the water-table falls, damaging the (usually poorer) farmers and householders with shallow dug wells or tubewells. However, water markets can provide access for the poor, even if they own neither pumps nor deep wells; in Mexico, poorer *ejido* farmers have good access to surface irrigation, because less-poor private farmers have sunk tubewells to water their high-value crops. In Bangladesh, small farmers benefit more from deep tubewells than large farmers; as they are more likely to grow high-yielding varieties, it pays them to irrigate a larger percentage of land.[54]

The poor are well placed to benefit from shallow wells as long as they are not fighting a losing battle with deeper wells for groundwater. In one area of Bangladesh, access to shallow wells benefited the poorest more than deep tubewells or land; landless households bought very low-capacity

pumps, designed for drinking-water use, and moved them around farms, pumping water day and night for sale to farmers in peak seasons – a labour-intensive and uncomfortable activity unlikely to attract the rich, but a lifeline to the poorest. The capital costs per unit of water delivered are lower (but the labour costs higher) than for those of deep tubewells, making shallow tubewells more accessible and attractive for the poor. Also, handpumps need not require large outlays for fuel. For example, the treadle pump, pioneered in Bangladesh, can be used on shallow wells,

---

Box 3.10: Farmer-run *dambos* in Zimbabwe

Why is less than 15% of sub-Saharan Africa's irrigation potential exploited, far less than elsewhere?

- Partly due to reliance on foreign consultants/contractors with market power, extra full-control medium/large irrigation is more costly per hectare: USD 8 300 (1995 dollars) as against USD 6 800 in North Africa and USD 2 500 in South Asia. Adding indirect costs for social infrastructure, development costs in Africa approach USD 18 300 per hectare. Small-scale irrigation with full water control is no cheaper if farmers' labour and survey costs are fully costed.

- Many past irrigation investments did badly. In the 1980s, of 15 projects with World Bank funding, five showed returns above 10%, but six had negative returns. Matters improved in the late 1980s and 1990s (with more normal climate and less anti-agricultural price bias): average return on 11 gravity projects was 9%, for seven pump projects 13%, and for five mixed projects 14%.

- Many projects are not financially or environmentally sustainable, and managerial capacity is often lacking. Government-controlled small-scale schemes did no better than large-scale schemes, despite greater promise.

Can small-scale, farmer-controlled irrigation expansion help? In Zimbabwe, irrigated gardens in *dambo* wetlands illustrate low-cost indigenous water management. Control by local communities, allocating land for garden cultivation, is an advantage over many formal irrigation systems, allowing flexible water management.

Dambo farmers fence a plot and dig water channels between beds, often adding a shallow well. Water reaches the plants mostly through sub-irrigation in the root zone. Investment is below USD 500 per hectare, making *dambos* more affordable for the poor than standard irrigation (USD 2 000-USD 10 000 per hectare); farmers bear the costs. *Dambos* yield about twice the return to land and water of standard irrigation; flexible water management lets farmers diversify into high-value horticultural crops.

Despite their potential, new *dambos* have been banned in Zimbabwe since 1975 to prevent erosion and protect downstream flows. Yet, if indigenous management practices are used without deep drains or mechanized pumping, *dambos* need not be erosive, and the water not used by the crops still flows downstream. Since *dambos* are far more productive than dryland farming and are the main source of production for smallholders in communal areas (and cause less soil and water erosion), they can relieve pressure on upland resources. At present there are about 15-20 000 ha of *dambos* in Zimbabwe, compared with 150 000 ha of formal irrigation, of which a much smaller proportion is controlled by the poor, and with potential to develop another 60 000 ha. *Dambos* are also extensive in many other parts of Southern and Western Africa, particularly Malawi and South Africa. *Dambo* cultivation seems especially promising for the rural poor; most *dambos* are located where most of them live; they support labour-intensive horticultural crops, yet give a decent return per man-day. But expansion requires legal acceptance, improved marketing, and institutions to prevent over-exploitation of water.

Sources: Rosegrant and Perez 1997; Jones 1995; Rukuni *et al.* 1994; Meinzen-Dick and Makombe 1999; Hazell *et al.* 2000.

requires low capital investment and uses human energy; in 1989 most users were very poor and there was high social acceptance. Although such schemes cannot serve many farmers or large areas – the wells are shallow or produce only small amounts of water at a time – there is much potential for individual smallholders.[55]

Productive water and water-yielding assets:
raising the poor's access and gains

With appropriate policies including safety-nets, desubsidization and water market access can greatly help the rural poor to control water. However, control over a water-yielding asset provides more water security. How can water-yielding assets for the rural poor be increased, or made more productive?

- Well and pump permits can regulate pumping of groundwater resources, with fines or shutdown for over-pumping. This could benefit poorer farmers who use shallow wells. Despite serious risks of rent-seeking and corruption by regulators (harming the poor), the downstream and distributional effects of unrestricted private pumping are so significant that regulation is becoming almost universal.

- Irrigation technologies need to respond to the needs of the user. For poor farmers this often means building on traditional methods such as *dambos* (Box 3.10), or introducing low-cost technology that is easy to operate and maintain. Yet large systems, with top-down water management, provide many poor people with water, work and food; though serious sustainability and management problems have usually developed, they can be corrected with more participatory management and appropriate new technologies such as rotational irrigation and cross-bunding.

- The poor can be helped to invest in their own wells, pumps and so on, with credit, technical assistance, input distribution, extension and the provision of hydrological data. Ownership of irrigation equipment can be feasible even for the landless.

- Water asset acquisition illustrates how the poor can be helped by appropriate management of – and, even more, civil-society influence by the poor upon – the current shift in the role of stakeholders. In that shift, governments reduce their role in production and subsidy, and create incentives which encourage competitive private provision for the poor. However, experience with water, with its many externalities and long-term effects, shows that for a pro-poor government creating an enabling environment for the private sector through law enforcement, mass education and information is necessary but not enough to benefit the poor. Government needs to target benefits to them, in its role as facilitator, provider of safety-nets and regulator of external and hidden impacts, and farmers and labourers need to control more water-yielding assets. Since the poor use their labour to save water, this should increase efficiency in water provision and use.

Water user associations can help keep water-yielding assets, especially degraded large-scale public irrigation systems, well-managed, responsive to users and sustainable. But even on small-scale irrigation projects in West and Central Africa, the poor have barely participated in them.[56] Labour contributions to a system should be recognized as a substitute for financial contributions, so the poor can legitimately and easily gain access to water for irrigation. Water user associations can also help ensure that those at the head-end and tail-end benefit equally, as efficient and equitable irrigation performance depends on cooperation of all affected by an irrigation system. With adequate planning where farmers know the schedule for the canal and are active in decision-making about the distribution method,[57] more equitable access to irrigation should result.

Access for the rural poor to water and water-yielding assets for consumption

In consumption, too, water waste and wrong price incentives go alongside worsening global shortage and severe local scarcities, yet are addressed through policy priorities reflecting the power and interests of the urban rich. For example, urban health damage is rightly addressed by public measures to improve water supply and sanitation; yet much less, per resident, is spent to address graver rural problems.

In many developing areas, scarcity, remoteness and pollution of water for consumption impose heavy collection costs and damage health, particularly of children.[58] The burden is heaviest for the rural poor. Better domestic water would also raise their returns from other assets such as land. Educational asset-building also suffers when girls must carry water, or children miss school because they are ill with water-borne diseases.

Yet, to have the best impact on health, clean rural water requires complementary sanitation and hygiene education. In Imo State, Nigeria, water at the borehole was clean, but became contaminated in transportation, storage and contact with users' hands. Even a bundle of health-related water policies – clean supply, sanitation, education – may be much less cost-effective in reducing mortality among the rural poor than similar outlays divided between such policies and measures to improve child nutrition directly, as in Narangwal (in the Indian Punjab) in the 1970s. Nevertheless, a comprehensive review of over 100 studies of the effects of feasible water and sanitation improvements in developing countries in 1990 suggested that they would reduce deaths from diarrhoea among under-fives by two million a year, one fifth of such deaths from all causes.[59] The incidence of disease, and the potential benefit from water improvement, are greatest for the rural poor; so is the difficulty of maintaining and sustaining equipment to improve water quality, and of recruiting support for the costs from influential people exposed to infection.[60]

Health damage from dirty water apart, poor rural women and children now incur much time, effort, calorie loss and exposure to insect vectors while collecting water, especially in remote drylands. A village handpump or standpipe reduces the burden of water transport over long distances, reduces water losses, needs and contamination, and brings further gains to health.[61] In a Mozambican village with a standpipe in the square, women spent only 25 minutes a day collecting water, as against 131 in a village where access to water meant a two-hour round trip; in the standpipe village the average woman enjoyed 433 minutes of rest daily (compared with 385) and more water was used.

How to increase access to consumption water, and to related assets, for the rural poor

The International Water Decade launched by the UN General Assembly in 1980 sought 'water and sanitation for all'. Thousands of water supply systems were installed, but fewer were maintained. In rural areas, dispersion of settlements impedes water provision and maintenance. Also, population growth masks the gains. By 1994, 800-850 million rural dwellers still lacked 'formal' water supplies.[62] Many villages lack even communal handpumps and use river water, springs, tanks or hand-dug wells with a rope and bucket, raising transaction costs and harming health. Some rural people get water from vendors, but often at a high price. In El Nahud, Sudan, some poor families spend up to half their cash income on drinking water.[63]

Slow progress is partly due to lack of funds, but more to the types of technology and lack of effective incentives, information and institutions for poor users to manage and maintain these systems. In the 1970s, at least 70% of handpump projects were not sustainable.[64] Technologies, and systems and incentives to maintain them, need to be appropriate to rural realities. This often means 'non-grid' water-yielding assets, each controlled by one poor household (or a few closely linked).

Wider-scale community approaches require shared, and policeable, community interests and contributions. Village Level Operation and Maintenance (VLOM) was introduced in the 1970s to give the community control over their water supply, minimizing pump downtime through simple community maintenance and quick response to breakdown. This requires an easily maintainable handpump, locally available spare parts, a paid, trained villager responsible for maintenance and repair, and therefore regular payments into a village fund. Although sometimes effective, VLOM has shown serious weaknesses. Donors overlooked many local technologies. Hardware was emphasized (and often complicated by variations among donors) at the expense of local training, maintenance and management. Social acceptance or appropriateness was often not realized, and a reliance on imported parts limited opportunities for communities to take control of their water supply. Users often thought that the institution that installed the handpump had ownership, and were thus reluctant to take responsibility for operation and maintenance. One IFAD drinking water rehabilitation project experienced badly organized villager participation in management, compounded by reliance on outsiders for spare parts and fuel, harming sustainability.[65]

Funds and organization to provide training and incentives to individual or group maintainers are crucial to success in rural community water supply. In India, as part of the United Nations Children's Fund (UNICEF) water supply projects, women, the main managers and users of the water, were trained in pump maintenance and repair. In one State, a cooperative of women mechanics was later contracted by the State government for rural pump maintenance and repair. In another, landless men demanded training, too, since there is

much scope for income generation if these skills can be learned.[66]

To retain the desirable aspects of VLOM while avoiding the top-down choice of assets and technology that damaged much of it, the World Bank promoted the Demand Responsive Approach to Water (DRAW). Communities start this process, making informed choices about their project and how to fund it. This move away from supply-led water systems could increase coverage, reduce waste, enhance community participation and improve maintenance and sustainability through a sense of ownership. Under DRAW, water is seen as an economic good, and in all countries studied (Benin, Bolivia, Honduras, Indonesia, Pakistan, Uganda) the rural poor proved willing and able to pay the recurrent (and some capital) cost of supplying water, if it is clean and reliable.[67]

However, even modest water charges could exclude the very poorest. Moreover, if they do buy the water, they have even less to spend on basic food. This makes a case for contribution in the form of labour. In the Swajal project in India, poor communities in the hills contribute only labour to the capital cost of the water-supply system. A water institution should also build on communities' altruism; many will, at the extreme, share their well with those who cannot contribute; in others, subsidies are arranged internally. In a village in Swajal, the community undertook a wealth-ranking exercise and asked the poorest to contribute less. In Tanzania, widows were exempt from handpump maintenance funding. Systems such as DRAW require not only community/group financial or labour contribution but often also a shift by the state from provider to facilitator and water-quality regulator (though the World Water Commission rightly stresses the state's welfare role as at very least the water provider of last resort) and an increased role for NGOs (to facilitate demand) and the private sector (providing pumps and spare parts). It is crucial that incentives and institutions are appropriate to induce the stake-holders to undertake their new roles.[68]

The key points for sustainable rural water supply systems to reach the poor are:

- response to demand, expressed through willing-ness to pay or to contribute labour;
- user financing of at least the recurrent costs;
- technology appropriate to the service level demanded by a community, and practicable to operate, maintain and repair, with affordable and locally available energy and spares;
- water groups, from a few households to commu-nity committees, to administer financing and to operate, maintain and repair their own part of the water supply system; such groups to include the working poor, especially women, in ways that do not overburden them;
- complementary hygiene education, sanitation and nutrition support for growth-faltering under-fives and pregnant women, to achieve the most cost-effective impact on health;
- subsidies targeted effectively, so government budgets are released for increased coverage, while taking account of the willingness of some com-munities to cross-subsidize; and
- appropriate institutions and incentives for all stakeholders, including the state 'water safety-net', to act properly.

LIVESTOCK ASSETS AND THE RURAL POOR

Benefits to the poor of controlling livestock assets

In many poor regions[69] the rural poor depend heavily on income from livestock production, but can seldom afford to eat animal products; they must usually trade them for staples with lower costs per calorie. Yet paradoxically the poor (a) depend most on livestock income, not where trade is easy and cheap, but in sparsely populated drylands where trade involves high transaction costs, and (b) control relatively few large stock, that is, the livestock with more regularly and read-ily traded products (such as cattle, water buffalo,

camels). Explaining this paradox suggests the live-stock products, assets and policies that can improve the livelihoods of the poor.

In arid areas, extensive or transhumant large stock-grazing is the only way to support many peo-ple from land use. In semi-arid areas, large stock supplement coarse staples (maize, millet, sorghum, roots and tubers) as a source of income. In Asian and some African semi-arid regions, livestock are integrated into smallholder and labourer livelihoods through mixed farming systems, providing draught power and manure for cropping, and living off crop residues as well as grazing. Large stock enhance land and labour productivity through draught power in large areas with physical or economic conditions intermediate between those suitable for tractor and for hoe cultivation.[70] The poor can benefit from livestock asset control, especially in areas of newly settled or expansible land frontiers, but only with appropriate institutions for acquisition, man-agement and trade. IFAD's Smallholder Cattle Development Project in Sumatra provided trans-migrants with draught animals, to be paid for in kind by returning two offspring within five years. This increased average cultivated area from 1.4 ha to 2.3 ha, doubling incomes.[71]

Livestock produce several benefits for the poor:

- They provide food direct; the poor consume a little of this but sell more for cash, which is then used to buy staples.
- Livestock manure can be used as fertilizer or fuel.
- Livestock 'embody' saving in a pro-poor way, with yield extracted largely by labour (for example, milking).
- In bad times animals are sold, and many are kept with this in mind.[72] However, when hardship, such as drought, strikes almost everyone in an area, many seek to sell stock and buy grain – and the value of stock decreases as the grain becomes dearer. This cuts the food-security value of the poor's 'livestock savings', especially if, as in much

of Africa, livestock are very unequally distributed, with few potential buyers who have market power.

• Sale of livestock in hard times also acts as a buffer against loss of other assets. In Northern Nigeria, those without livestock at the beginning of a survey had 12% less land four years later; those with livestock retained the same acreage.[73]

Given asset value, a mix of livestock and cropland often brings more income than either type alone because of close links between crop and livestock production, the flexibility each provides for the other (like choice of ploughing and manuring times), and difficulties with animal-hire markets. Zimbabwean smallholders who combine livestock and crop production have incomes twice as high as those with only crops.[74] However, in marginal arid-to-semi-arid lands, livestock alone can be the only sustainable land use. In less extreme cases, drought risk to crops can exceed even the risk to cattle, especially for poor farmers with less prospect of water access in crisis.

Livestock bring new risks: illness, death, theft. Nonetheless, 'since crop income is risky, [a few] assets in the form of cattle [and] small livestock [are carried, to increase] risk-bearing capacity . . . even at the cost of lower levels of income'.[75] It may reduce risk to spread one's portfolio even into risky assets, if some of the risks are weakly correlated (drought threatens both crops and livestock, but pests, theft and flood usually affect one much more than the other). Apart from often reducing total risk, livestock help in managing risk if they can be sold in bad times.

There are far fewer transaction costs of large stock if the controller also controls land; many of the poor do not. However, this can be overcome, enabling even landless households to keep livestock assets. Quasi-cooperative service arrangements, such as those pioneered in Gujerat, India, and now widespread under the National Dairy Development Board, collect milk daily from many owners (sometimes landless) of just one cow or water buffalo, and sometimes provide small feed packages. Many communities have common grazing. Others practise transhumance, helping to move cattle away from drought areas, as with the Fulani in Nigeria (though the poorest often lack access to trek routes, or food for the journey). Even when land scarcity erodes such options, stall-feeding (zero grazing) increasingly allows the poor to substitute labour for land. Small stock, especially poultry, often have minimal land requirements.

Though the rural poor benefit from livestock asset control, it is often skewed against them. In Botswana, though most farm income is from cattle, the poorest 40% of farm households owned none. However, as in much of Africa, they could often exchange labour for some control of cattle owned by others, being rewarded for cattle-care with the rights to animal products, fallen animals and some calves (the *mafisa* system). In Bayan Tsgaan village, Mongolia, the poorest quartile of households had only 5% of privately owned livestock. However, in Madhya Pradesh, India, livestock ownership was less unequal than ownership of land,[76] as in parts of rural North India, where livestock income is over a quarter of the total, and more for the poor. In a village in Pakistan small farms obtain over half of their farm income from livestock, as against 30% on larger farms.[77]

So the extent to which livestock are the focus for livelihoods among the rural poor varies greatly. How, if at all, asset policy should concentrate on getting livestock to the poor depends on the specifics. However, in Asia, Latin America, Near East and North Africa and parts of sub-Saharan Africa the 'livestock revolution'[78] is sharply raising the share of farm resources going to livestock, and the share of grain consumed by animals rather than humans. From such changes in asset structure and use, the rural poor – who still derive most calories, and employment incomes, from staples – are not, in most cases, well placed to benefit. Can they be helped to do so?

The poor, types of livestock assets and livestock asset policies

Poor farmers are less likely than others to own several species of animals, but more likely to own poultry, sheep and goats rather than large stock. Small animals are also much more often controlled by children and women (who in Senegal own 60% of sheep and goats). Effective pro-poor policies for animal assets need to recognize why poor households tend to own smaller animals – whether to support them in this, or to relieve constraints to their profitable and safe control of large stock. A number of reasons can be suggested:

- Small animals require less cash, capital and loans, relative to labour, to buy and maintain.
- Given herd value, more and smaller animals simplify distress sales and make death of an animal less risky.
- Small animals grow and breed faster, reducing pay-back period (the poor pay higher interest and have greater time-preference), diffusing risks from disease, and permitting mixed-age herds (even small ones have some animals mature and food-yielding at most times).
- Goats and sheep can thrive on harsher terrain and vegetation than large stock (benefiting poor farmers on marginal land) and contrary to conventional wisdom tend to do less harm in ecologically fragile zones than larger animals.[79]

This suggests two ways to reduce poverty. Larger proportions of livestock extension, public-goods provision and research should aim at improving the labour-intensive management of small herds of small stock, for example, by better management of infectious diseases. Second, artificial or non-economic barriers to control of large stock assets by the poor should be removed through better access to small dispersed livestock auctions, as is attempted in Botswana, or through cooperative arrangements for rapid collection and processing of small amounts of milk.

Provision or subsidization of ranches, a popular livestock policy in Eastern and Southern Africa until well into the 1990s,[80] has proved counterproductive for the poor. Enclosing common land for ranching deprives their small stock (and their few cattle) of grazing; ranchers replace cattle guards with fences, cutting demand for the labour of the poor.

Control over livestock assets can help the poor even without ownership. However, the crucial savings/sale function of livestock is available only to owners; and large herd-owners are much more likely than small ones to displace employment with equipment. Nevertheless, livestock costs and benefits can be shared in ways helpful to the poor, as with *mafisa* in Botswana, or as in Nepal, where households owning more than five buffalo often lend one to poorer households and share the profits.[81]

Just as larger farmers of tobacco or cotton can become contractors for inputs and services, with the poor taking over the farming in small units and gains for all, so larger herd-owners may be well placed to switch to management, finance and sales of processing products (hides and skins, tanning, dairy processing). This creates new employment, often for women, while leaving the control of cattle increasingly to smaller herders. It is important and feasible for policy to encourage such shifts.

OTHER PHYSICAL ASSETS AND RURAL POVERTY REDUCTION

The rural non-farm sector

Poor households typically have diverse sources of livelihood, both to reduce risk and to provide income in slack farming seasons and bad times. While farming and hired farm labour usually predominate, the rural non-farm sector (RNFS) is becoming increasingly important as a source of income and employment for the poor. The RNFS now accounts for some 44% of rural employment in Asia, and is growing over twice as fast as farm employment in India. The RNFS share of rural employment has increased rapidly in Latin America; in Brazil and Ecuador it reached at least 30% in the early 1990s. The proportion of rural incomes earned from RNFS has also increased in most cases, averaging 45% in 25 African country case-studies; in India the range is 25-35%. The proportion is higher for poor than non-poor households in many places (India, Pakistan, Mexico) but in Africa the RNFS share in non-poor incomes may be twice that of the poor.[82]

The growth of RNFS is more labour-intensive, lower-skilled, stable, and thus pro-poor than urban non-farm growth. But the sorts of RNFS growth that reduce poverty usually work best where farm income, and thus local consumer demand, grows too. RNFS often comprises 'distress diversification' into otherwise declining crafts, because farming is doing badly. This can sometimes revive rural incomes; Botswana craft baskets are a striking example. However, almost all studies indicate that RNFS growth based on growth linkages to successful farmers and their employees, who demand booming services (construction, trade, transport), has a better chance to cut poverty. Most traditional RNFS participation, reflecting family skills, land shortage, or the need to diversify against seasonal unemployment or annual drought risk, is linked to poverty, so should not be neglected; but modern, linkage-based RNFS is a more promising way out of poverty.[83]

Usually, poverty-reducing growth of the modern RNFS is more likely to arise from widely shared agricultural growth (leading to rising demand for local RNFS activity), and from interventions to provide the poor with appropriate skills, education and competitive nearby credit,[84] rather than with physical non-farm assets. Unlike agriculture, where one can identify public goods for farming, and public strategies for private asset support likely to reach the poor, RNFS is diverse in assets

required; the history of asset subsidization in the RNFS suggests that centralized intervention seldom picks winning techniques, sub-sectors, or potential entrepreneurs, or targets gains on the poor. Rural 'industrial estates' have a long history of failure and mistargeting, often subsidizing medium entrepreneurs against tiny, poor competitors. An IFAD report on microenterprise in West and Central Africa shows that most RNFS asset support leaked to the non-poor, partly because of the lower fixed costs of administering larger transactions: the mean loan size for the Alliance de Crédit et d'Epargne pour la Production in Senegal was USD 1 500.[85] India's Integrated Rural Development Programme (IRDP), intended to direct grants and subsidized loans to the poor for non-farm asset formation, had mixed results but is widely agreed to have been ill-targeted and cost-ineffective.

In remote areas, high transport costs can provide natural protection for RNFS, making it potentially profitable. Also, RNFS income can be a source of savings for farm investment. Yet RNFS itself seems often to need outside credit as a catalyst, more than does farm investment: Indian districts with good branch bank networks show faster growth in RNFS, not in agriculture. Often RNFS profit levels are dependent on local farm production: forward and backward linkages to agro-industry, and especially 'consumption linkages' to higher incomes, locally spent, for smallholders and farmworkers. Roads and communications, as well as bank infrastructure, often affect inputs and marketing more for RNFS than for farms.[86]

Where land is scarce yet farm yields cannot keep up with the growth of rural working population, RNFS growth is needed to reduce excess pressure on natural resources, as well as to provide workplaces and keep poverty falling. Yet the modern, dynamic, RNFS sub-sectors, such as construction, transport and shops, seldom prosper where agriculture is stagnant. Traditional crafts and services are most likely to engage large proportions of the rural poor, keeping them alive if not lifting them out of poverty. Policy should avoid undermining these sectors, for example, by supporting otherwise unviable medium-scale rural brickworks in 'industrial estates'. Conversely, artificial support for RNFS sectors associated with distress diversification, such as household-based craft products, is doomed, especially as competition from modern urban sectors and imports is liberalized. The best prospect is offered by appropriate regulatory and credit frameworks, public support for training, and other measures to revitalize RNFS by upgrading assets in very small units for the rural poor.

Such policies should be directed at a number of areas.

- *Public goods and facilitation of agriculture-RNFS linkages.* In North Arcot, India, a 1% increase in agricultural output is associated with a 0.9% increase in non-farm employment.[87] RNFS should therefore not become the focus of rural policy at the expense of agriculture. Policy should increase positive intersectoral linkages.

- *Support for RNFS activities induce the most and fastest poverty reduction.* Where growth is rapid in RNFS sub-sectors, entry barriers faced by the poor should be publicly identified and, where cost-effective, addressed. They include lack of finance; information about technology and markets; skills; and infrastructure.

- *Appropriate government regulation* (of construction or transport, for example) should avoid arbitrary imitation of Western or urban density or other aesthetic norms, and emphasize essentials for health, safety and competition. Implementation should be open, bound by simple published rules, concentrated on important cases, and enforced through civil-society pressures and light but applied laws.

- *Appropriate credit support.* Although many microfinance institutions, like India's IRDP or Bangladesh's Grameen Bank, target the RNFS, access for the poorest is very limited.

- *Human capital provision to give the poor the capacity to enter RNFS.* This need not consist of formal primary education. There is plenty of scope for basic literacy, numeracy and bookkeeping classes which could improve the position of the poor within the rural off-farm labour market, if not enable them to set up their own profitable enterprises. Indeed, the ageing workforces of Asia and Africa mean that most of the working poor in 2020 have already completed formal education; in RNFS and elsewhere, it is too late to meet their skill needs that way.

Housing

The house often comprises the poor's main physical asset by value. For consumption purposes rural houses of mud or sticks are often worse than urban slums; the average rural standard of drainage, power supply and sanitation is far worse. As for production, whereas most urban people live and work in different places, rural people often obtain much of their livelihood in or near the home. The rural poor can benefit from 'fungibility' by adapting the use of space within the house between production and consumption, spare rooms and workrooms, and supportive labour between child care and outwork such as lacemaking.[88]

Despite the importance of housing for the rural poor, housing and support policy have been overwhelmingly urban. The main thrust of urban anti-poverty policy, in sharp contrast to rural concerns, remains upgrading slums and improving shelter and supportive infrastructure. This has encouraged migration to cities, which has raised housing costs, reduced quality for the poor, and enlarged squatter settlements, with serious health hazards and congestion problems. This urban focus neglects rural areas where even worse housing (and other) conditions encourage urbanization.

A poverty-oriented policy for rural housing assets would first confront the problems of seasonal intra-rural migrants, mostly for farmwork or construction (such as the *Torrontes* in parts of Latin America). Lack of dwellings have worse effects in rural areas than in cities on untreated illness, unprovided education, and unpoliced crime and violence against women. Second, public research is needed on (a) improving access for the poor to traditional housing materials (for example, thatching grasses), which have great advantages but are becoming scarcer or more distant because of deforestation and new land uses; (b) economizing on such materials by enhancing their durability; and (c) controlling pests, and instability during rainy seasons. In India more than half of the rural housing substantially uses mud bound with cow-dung.[89] Third, large local employment programmes in Bangladesh, Bolivia and India might test improved designs, based on local materials, to help with off-season house construction, maintenance and repair,[90] normally using small construction firms, not undercutting them with subsidies.

Apart from stimulating supply, policy can support rural housing by redistribution and service support. Land reform in Kerala concentrated more on house-plots and surrounding home gardens than on farms.[91] Normally, the redistribution of house space must be consensual: the supply of inexpensive housing to the poor is reduced by rent controls, but increased by making rental markets better informed and less restricted. Also, there may be scope for rural site-and-service programmes in areas of severe housing deficiency. Where house waste-water can be safely applied, a garden used for home consumption or marketed vegetables often greatly enhances the housing of the rural poor, especially women.

Transport, communications and infrastructure assets
Rural roads in India and elsewhere deliver high rates of return. Bad roads in Africa make marketing margins – the gaps between farm and market

prices – far higher than in Asia; so rural people, especially remote and poor ones, can therefore benefit less from improved incentives and liberalization. In areas such as Wollaito, Ethiopia, off-take of fertilizers, and of higher-yielding maize and other crops, is limited by the huge costs of marketing over long distances along terrible roads. However, paving Africa is not a simple solution to rural poverty. In many drylands, returns to roads are depressed by sparse and dispersed population, low value added per square mile and per person, and small exchangeable economic surplus. In such regions the cost of building roads to many dispersed villages is prohibitive. Imaginative solutions are needed to reduce costs of transport grids, or to find affordable alternatives. One approach is through the size and location of stores. Another is to divert some resources from long and usually expensive rural-to-urban highways to short inter-rural roads, permitting specialization and exchange. A third option is labour-intensive maintenance (and some local contribution) to all-weather roads through rural areas. A fourth is migrating nearer water sources and outwork. A fifth is consolidating farm fragments (not farms) to save travel.

The gains of the rural poor from improved transport go far beyond market access. Apart from easier trips for schools, clinics, extension and so on, on-farm transport can relieve drudgery and save time. For the rural poor, most travel occurs within the village, mostly for subsistence tasks; transport improvements here could especially benefit women and children. In a Kenyan study, only 22% of journeys were for exchange; half were for farm work and housekeeping. In a Tanzanian village, 75% of transport time and 80% of tonne-km. involved women. In Ghana and Tanzania most movement around the village is on foot. Although the terrain and lack of storage capacity sometimes dictate head-loading for water collection, new forms of transport could help in collecting firewood.[92]

Though roads normally raise output, choice and income for most people, the poor may gain little, because they seldom control the means of transport. Non-motorized vehicles, like bicycles or donkeys, can often meet the poor's needs relatively cheaply and reliably. In Uganda, of 715 journeys a day recorded at 55 points on rural roads, 75% were on foot, 22% by bicycle and only 2% motorized. In rural India, bicycle ownership was far higher among the poorer households. Credit-insurance schemes might help more poor people to acquire bicycles. Where households are not too dispersed an animal cart or bicycle trailer might be feasible; a trailer can quintuple a bicycle's load capacity.[93]

At times modern communications can substitute for some transport. However, there is no content to most speculation about the Internet as a remedy for the transport and communication problems of the rural poor.[94]

HUMAN ASSETS

Why shift human asset-building towards the rural poor?

Human assets, which capital 'embodied' in people, are in most ways like other assets. They are built up by sacrificing current consumption or leisure. They depreciate unless maintained. They help people controlling them, both by providing a cushion against bad times and by increasing income, welfare or capabilities above what can be achieved with heavy labour power. In this respect, human assets are becoming much more important, relative to physical assets, due to global acceleration of information, technical knowledge and mobility. Yet the share of human assets enjoyed by rural people, the poor, and above all poor rural girls and women, is arbitrarily low (and has not been rising globally), though their private and social return on such assets is high. Especially where the rural poor are a large proportion of the population, that is inefficient, as well as unjust – ever more so as the relative role of human assets increases. Policy must focus on human asset acquisition for rural poor people, especially women and girls; otherwise their disadvantage will become increasingly stubborn.

Human assets are conventionally classified as nutritional status, health and education, but their nature is changing radically. Education increasingly involves lifetime skill acquisition for management and for acquiring and processing information, in a context of more rapid and frequent changes of work and residence. Health and nutrition needs are being transformed alongside demographics (especially age-structure), work, and medical threats, knowledge and technology.

Human assets have intrinsic value in raising capabilities and/or happiness, and instrumental value in raising income – and thus access to further capabilities and happiness. These values can be realized directly, by applying improved skill or health to initial leisure, labour and natural and physical assets; and indirectly, by using improved health, education and nutrition to control more assets that raise consumption, leisure or earned income: to obtain information and to implement choices, especially through mobility.

Most extra instrumental benefit from human assets depends on combining them with extra natural or physical assets (land, a workshop) or with new or better work. Skills and good health raise income by increasing productivity of labour and/or natural or physical capital, and hence encouraging people (or their employers) to use more of them. Extra human assets and other inputs are complements. Conversely, the poverty impact of skills and health is less if there are few profitable outlets for labour or for physical or natural capital. In rural Pakistan the extra income obtainable from education is substantial in the green-revolutionary province of Punjab, but small and unattractive in the more sluggish rural Sind.[95]

In Eastern and Southern Africa, 'as long as small-holder agriculture remains the principal economic activity of the rural poor' – although better health and education retain intrinsic value – their instrumental 'impact . . . will be limited until the major institutional and resource constraints facing smallholder producers are reduced'.[96] Income gains, often attributed to better rural nutrition, health and education, are seldom achievable unless it pays those who acquire them to obtain more, or more productive, complementary work or natural or physical assets.

Educational provision and outcomes have been improving globally, though unevenly; so had nutrition outside Africa, and also health provision and outcomes, until the terrible reversals of the 1990s due to AIDS, tuberculosis and malaria. But the rural and the poor remain far behind and the gaps have not narrowed: the rural poor still have worse health, education and nutrition outcomes and worse provision than others. So for the rural poor, a little extra – a dozen more clinics, a hundred calories a day, an extra year of adequate schooling – enhances welfare, capabilities and income more than for urban or rich people. Further, that little extra normally costs less: since the rural poor, especially the remote and minorities, have least provision, educational and health options with high returns are most likely to have been overlooked; an extra year of education, for example, is likely to mean costly tertiary education for the richest urban children, but primary education for the rural poorest.

Human capital assets of the rural poor

Access to educational assets differs sharply between rich and poor, and between urban and rural people; since the rich can seek out urban schools, rich-poor differences are greatest in rural areas.

Rich and poor. In Bangladesh, Pakistan, Malawi, Mozambique and Egypt the richest income quintile enjoyed, on average, twice as many years of education as the poorest, in addition to huge quality advantages. Moreover, the spread of school access (by region, gender, and so on) is much bigger among the poor. It follows that the median poor child is particularly disadvantaged educationally compared with the median rich child, above all in the poorest developing countries. In the 1990s in India, the median 15-19-year-old from the best-off quintile of households had completed school grade 10; but the equivalent person from the poorest two quintiles had zero schooling.[97] In Indonesia the respective grades were 9 and 6. Education greatly reduces risk of subsequent chronic poverty in rural China and rural and urban Egypt; chronic and transitory poverty in rural Pakistan; and total poverty in rural and urban South Africa.

Rural and urban. There is no overall evidence of a fall in the huge rural-urban differences, identified in the 1970s, in educational provision and access. As for outcomes, the latest reported rural and urban illiteracy rates were: China 26% and 12%; India, 55% and 27%; Egypt, 67% and 40%; Brazil, 31% and 11%. This is not just because rural households are poorer: in India in 1986-87 the literacy rate in the poorest quintile of urban households (50%) was above that of the second richest rural quintile (48%). Globally, these gaps have widened. The typical rural adult, surveyed in the 1960s or 1970s, had 1.4-2 times the urban adult illiteracy risk in the countries of North Africa and Asia; the ratio was 2-3.5 in Latin America.[98]

On the health of the poor, poor people are less likely to report sick, because they expect to feel unwell, and anyway can seldom afford time off or health care. Objectively the poorest quintile have higher infant mortality rates where inequality is great and medical care mainly for those who pay. Recent infant mortality rates in the poorest (richest) quintile of households by consumption per equivalent adult were about 70 (25) per 1 000 in

Brazil, 100 (40) in Nicaragua, 97 (52) in South Africa and 107 (62) in Côte d'Ivoire, but the gap was far smaller (though absolute rates were high) in Pakistan and Ghana. The disparities in child mortality rates were greater, for example 116 (11) in Brazil and 155 (71) in South Africa.[99]

As for rural and urban health, in 12 developing countries, the ratio of rural to urban mortality from birth to age five rose from an average of 1.4 in the mid-1970s to 1.6 in the mid-1980s. As for the infant mortality rate (IMR), in most developing countries with good data, while both urban and rural IMRs were declining, the ratio of rural to urban risk was, until the late 1980s, high and stable or widening. In India, from 1970-75 to 1981-85, the rural IMR fell by 19.5% (to 113) and the urban IMR by 28.1% (to 64), but by 1990 the rates were 86 and 51 respectively, so that in the 1980s rural IMR decline accelerated. In China, 'official' urban and rural IMRs in 1957-88 fell, respectively, from 50.8 to 13.9 and from 89.1 to 23.6, that is, at similar rates.[100]

As for the nutritional rich-poor gap, a 10% rise in income is associated with a 1-4% rise in dietary energy intake in household surveys; the rise is higher among the poor,[101] indicating that they, despite having the highest work-energy needs, are the most malnourished.

Rural-urban nutrition gaps are substantial and not narrowing. Though calorie intake per consumer unit does not differ much between rural and urban areas, rural people need more energy for work, travel, disease resistance and pregnancy, and have higher micronutrient deficiencies, impeding efficient energy utilization.

These different kinds of human capital deprivation reinforce each other's impact on the rural and the poor. Among children of illiterate mothers, mean weight-for-age in Bangladesh rises from 67% of the United States minimum acceptable National Centre for Health Statistics (NCHS) standard in the poorest quintile to 69% in the richest,

whereas with literate mothers the improvement is much more, from 65% to 75%. The interlocking disadvantages are passed on to the children of the rural, the poor, the unhealthy, the uneducated. The poor, and the rural among the poor, have higher child mortality, replacement fertility and thus child-to-worker and consumption-to-savings ratios. Uneducated women marry sooner, and have higher marital fertility. Their households are worse nourished, even at similar incomes, due to less knowledge of food and farming, higher worker/dependant ratios and more sibling competition. Where education is especially unequal (by region, gender or income group), malnutrition is higher than elsewhere, especially among small children (the most vulnerable), due to high fertility in uneducated households.[102]

More severe inequality in educational attainment in countries of Latin America and Africa than those of Asia explains about half their higher overall inequality.[103] So higher rural-urban inequality of human assets in Africa, and intra-rural inequality in Latin America, account for much of the high poverty there.

Productivity and poverty impact of rural human capital for the rural poor

Public or NGO outlay to steer human capital assets to the rural and the poor is unjustified if the same outlay cuts poverty more when directed to other capital for the rural poor, or to human capital for the urban poor. Does schooling, sanitation or better nutrition, though bringing double the benefit when directed to the rural poor as to the urban non-poor, cost three times as much? Does it convey sufficient welfare, capabilities or productivity gains to the rural poor to justify the cost of steering it to them?

Education

Education is good at reducing poverty for rural people who can use it to get better work or income from physical or natural capital, whether within farming or by leaving it; but it is much less so if they must stay where farm technology is sluggish. Where new technologies are rewarding, education speeds their adoption, often bringing large productivity and income gains for small farmers and farm workers. In Thailand four years' education triples the chance that a farmer will use new chemical fertilizers; educated farmers in India are more likely to use credit, irrigation and improved seeds. However, in Africa education appears to have a mixed and, where favourable, small impact on agricultural productivity. Education speeds adoption of new agricultural technologies and of cash crops, for example, in IFAD's efforts to help smallholders in Malawi to grow tobacco. Education can impart good farming practices in school; ease access to new information; facilitate access to others with information, like health professionals and extension agents; improve ability to make sense of new information; and so speed up innovation. This matters most during rapid change, as with the early Green Revolution in the Indian Punjab; then ability to master correctly new combinations of inputs and technologies can have high payoffs.[104] But if there are few new opportunities, or if their benefits are confined to those with substantial fixed assets, education alone may do little to help the poor. Education raises the rural poor's income only to the extent that they also have, or get, natural or physical assets or work yielding more if one is educated – and prices, policies, technologies or events raise demand for the products of the more educated poor, or make it more price-elastic.

This need not mean that the rural poor in agriculturally sluggish or dryland areas gain little from education. First, some such areas may be coming to show the best prospects for agricultural expansion given appropriate research. Second, adult education, which for demographic reasons must receive increasing emphasis in anti-poverty policy,

can help the poor to organize and lobby to improve infrastructure, health care, production, or access to information and power; NGOs such as Bangladesh Rural Advancement Committee (BRAC) in Bangladesh, interacting with microcredit and adult literacy training, have played a major role (Box 3.11).[105] Third, while the poor, to gain income from education, need to combine their new capabilities with other assets, work or technologies, these need not be rural or agricultural. Historically, education has reduced rural poverty mainly by helping people with few prospects in farming to leave it, and to seize non-rural or non-farm opportunities.

Nutrition and health, children and the rural poor: a virtuous circle

Human health assets comprise bodily and mental characteristics promoting longevity with full functioning, and resistance to (or rapid recovery from) illness and injury. The rural poor are especially handicapped by acute illness and injury (often untreated) in earning, learning and quitting poverty; and by chronic illness and injury due to unfavourable health-work-home and especially water-sanitation environments; and by low nutritional assets, such as height and lean body mass.

Inadequate food substantially reduced productivity of rural workers in India and cane-cutters in Guatemala, where calorie (rather than protein) shortage was the cause. For rural labourers in Sri Lanka, wages rose by 0.21% for each 1% rise in calorie intake. Anaemia has been found to reduce productivity and iron supplementation to raise it.[106]

Rural workers' incomes depend on the capacity to fight off illness, and on lifetime physical, learning and mental capacity and hence productivity when well. Both are much affected by child nutrition, including exposure to infections, mainly waterborne, that impede nutrient absorption. Caloric undernutrition and micronutrient shortage in childhood bring low height in adults. This reduces market wages for adult cane-cutters in the Philippines. For men of the same height and caloric intake, greater body mass brings higher wages, though height has more effect.[107] The nutrition-strength-productivity effects are much clearer, indeed there are thresholds,[108] for the smallest (and poorest) adults than for others, and for those likely to do heavy physical work: the rural ultra-poor. Undernutrition also harms learning, schooling, and hence later productivity,[109] again harming the rural poor most.[110] Child ill-health and undernutrition are thus causes, not just effects, of rural income poverty. A virtuous circle emerges from targeting on the rural poorest outlays for better child nutrition: it brings better adult health, education and productivity, which further improve child nutrition.

Yet even among the poor, calorie intake seldom rises by more than 4% when income rises by 10%. Direct approaches may be needed, notably interventions that help the poor cope with fluctuations in food supply. The IFAD/UNICEF-backed Andhra Pradesh Tribal Development Project in India (1991-99), established 230 grain banks and community nutrition workshops; and IFAD's inputs to the Special Programme for Africa include improved village cereal storage in Chad, and education on nutrient-rich foods and improved preparation techniques in the Kwale and Kilfi District Development Project, Kenya. Targeted nutrition interventions[111] can also be highly productive for the rural poor; increasing emphasis is now placed on micronutrients.[112]

Health and the rural poor

In Côte d'Ivoire and Ghana, an additional day per month of disabling illness brings a decline of 10% in male wages and of 3% in labour supply.[113] Nutrition-linked diseases (especially dysentery) remain the main affliction of the rural poor, but they are also exposed to other physical risks to their human assets. Agricultural workers' injuries from sickles, snakes and scorpions, and ill-health due to pesticides, are common and often untreated. So are burns from open fires and pollution from indoor cow-dung stoves. Investments in new types of fuel or stoves can help solve this problem, as with kerosene stoves in rural Nicaragua.

As for chronic illness, in parts of Africa and (though less recognized) Asia, HIV/AIDS not only kills many – life expectancy in several Southern African countries has regressed to levels not seen since the 1960s – but also condemns others to leave work in order to care for the sick and the orphaned. HIV/AIDS is a disease of poverty in that poverty pushes men into single-sex migration, women into prostitution, and children into undernutrition and hence impaired immune response. HIV/AIDS, though thought of as mainly urban, is spreading faster in some rural areas of India; in much of Africa urban and rural prevalence rates are similar. Rural areas along truck routes, or sources of migrant labour to towns, are especially vulnerable, as are nomadic pastoralists and farm women with seasonally migrant husbands. Yet in rural areas the infrastructure for prevention programmes (information; AIDS tests; counselling; condom availability) is less developed. So too are treatment facilities. Yet rural families bear the main burden of care and costs.[114] The burden of chronic rural sickness is also swollen by the spread of drug-irresponsive malaria and tuberculosis. Urban populations, tending to return to the village when sick or old, intensify the problem.

Any strategy for rural poverty reduction must include shifting asset formation towards building the health, education and nutrition of the rural poor, and away from concentration on tertiary urban health and education. But given resource scarcities, it is also essential to improve the efficiency and equity with which scarce resources for building rural human capital are used and maintained. Central issues include: reducing gender inequity in access to human capital assets; increasing user control over, and contribution to, providing such assets; and dealing with seasonality.

Human assets and the rural poor: addressing gender inequity and the new demographics

There are huge gaps between male and female educational access and literacy levels. These gaps are greater in rural areas, and greatest for the rural poor. Inequity helps cause inefficiency: female schooling does much more at the margin for income, poverty reduction, and child health and nutrition than extra male education. Women's lower adoption of agricultural innovations is due entirely to lower levels of education; at the same level, women farmers are as quick to adopt as men. Extra education raises household income more if it goes to females. Across Indian States in 1957-91, the responsiveness of poverty to initial female literacy was higher than to any other initial condition. Mothers' education is also associated with better child health in many studies, often holding income constant. Extra human capital for poor rural women and girls could well create a virtuous circle of better income, less poverty and better health and education, transmitted intergenerationally.[115]

This is underlined by the better impact of female income upon subsequent child nutrition and education and the rising proportion of rural people, and household heads, who are women. The growing age of the workforce means that a large, growing majority of the 2020 workforce is already well past its childhood. Human capital formation, for cost-effective impact on instrumental benefits (especially employment and labour productivity), must concentrate much more upon adults. IFAD experience of rural female literacy programmes[116] shows what can be done.

User fees and empowering the poor in health and education: helpful or perverse?

Decentralized user involvement in control over many public and NGO activities, despite the difficulty of ensuring that the poor have their say, improves participation, power, and often managerial efficiency. How does this apply to getting better human assets to the rural poor? It is not just poverty that makes so many of them work rather than attend a school or clinic, but, given the value of their working time, low school and clinic quality and their incapacity to improve it. Witness the contrast between rural school efficiency in South India and in Uttar Pradesh; in the latter case only, parents have little influence on teachers' performance or even attendance, with appalling results.[117]

In the 1980s user fees were widely thought to give consumers decentralized market power over health and education services, and to keep them going despite fiscal stringency. The effects of user fees on basic services for the rural poor have been, on balance, damaging. Without adequate exemption (targeting), user fees harm the poor; yet exemptions have proved very hard to manage cleanly and efficiently. Exemptions are absent in about one quarter of developing countries with user fees, and elsewhere seriously flawed by including the non-poor (such as health workers and the military) and excluding the rural poorest, or not reaching them in practice, as in Ghana and Zimbabwe.[118] The poor are more likely to give up such a service when a fee is imposed or raised. Even if they do not, since they typically devote 70-80% of the value of consumption to food, they almost certainly cut their own, or their children's, already inadequate nutrition to pay school or clinic fees.

Often user fees mean that treatment is delayed. In Zimbabwe, after the 1991 introduction of fees, the number of babies born premature increased by 10%. In four rural districts in Viet Nam, where fee exemption for the poor was ineffective, people delayed treatment and made less use of government health facilities (and the rich spent 3.9% of household income on health, compared with 19.3% for the very poor). In rural Kenya in 1989-90, curative out-patient attendance fell by over 30% after fees were introduced, and in-patient days by 20%. The poor reduced their use of health services most, as in rural Swaziland.[119]

Similar findings apply to primary education:[120] higher response by the rural than the urban, and by the poor than by the non-poor, to user fees. This led to declining school attendance in Zimbabwe, Malawi and Kenya, where nearly half the households in seven poor districts had at least one child who had dropped out due to inability to pay fees. In Ghana, Zimbabwe and Kenya, girls were more likely to be pulled out of school than boys, which is especially worrying given the higher private and social returns to their education.[121]

Efficiency and equity effects apart, the revenue-generating potential of fees is small, and exemption of the poor is difficult.[122] Credit is seldom feasible, let alone affordable, for school or health fees for the rural poor. As for insurance, middle-income countries with fairly dense and accountable public-service networks can operate with entitlement or exemption cards such as Chile's '*ficha CAS*',[123] but elsewhere insurance cards such as Burundi's *Carte d'assurance maladie* (CAM) have had serious problems; in the mainly rural Mayinga province they recruited only 23% of households, largely self-selected and higher-risk, making self-financing infeasible and risk-sharing difficult.[124]

The free provision, from China through Sri Lanka to Costa Rica, of much basic health and education; the sharp improvements in life expectancy and quality, and in poverty reduction, so generated; the disappointing revenues from user fees; the difficulties of exemption and insurance; above all the impact on the poor, the rural, and women, all suggest that fees should not be applied to basic services in low-income countries.[125] However, it makes sense to self-target or indicator-target some services on those at risk, such as nutrition supplements for children with faltering growth.[126] And the slack-season or spare-time work of rural communities, even the poorest, can be used to maintain, improve, or even construct, rural clinics or schools.[127]

CONCLUSIONS AND POLICY IMPLICATIONS

What makes an asset pro-poor? Typically, labour-intensity; capacity to build marketable skills; equal access for women and minorities; low seasonal and annual variation and risk; and focus on producing items that loom large in poor people's budgets, such as staple foods. Small and divisible assets are easier for the poor to acquire and manage. Fortunately, for important forms of rural asset, above all farmland, small scale brings advantages, such as low labour supervision cost and hands-on family-level overview. The persistently large share of farmland in smallholdings, and its labour-intensity combined with low unit costs in most branches of farming, provide strong arguments for (a) stimulating smaller and more equal landholdings, (b) steering more assets, especially education and water-yielding equipment, to rural areas, and (c) tackling the high risk and inadequate female access that limit the poor's gains from many rural assets.

Within rural areas, some countries such as China suffer from asset poverty mainly due to regional inequality; some, such as South Africa and Brazil, mainly due to land inequality within regions; and others, such as Ethiopia and Bangladesh, mainly due to low average per-person assets and GDP. But for many assets, notably human capital, rural-urban maldistribution is in many countries a main cause of asset poverty,

largely because governments and donors overlook rural and agricultural issues. In changing that, three main sorts of asset are most relevant to rural poverty reduction: farmland, water-yielding assets, and human capital.

Farmland

Over two thirds of the income of the rural poor is from farming. Most of the rest depends for growth on linkages to farming. Most of the rural poor still control some farmland; although the proportion mainly dependent on hired labour is rising, they too gain if land control is more equal and thus more labour-intensive. Land deprivation is strongly linked to poverty and vulnerability, and brings powerlessness, especially for ethnic minorities long compressed into remote and marginal lands.

Land redistribution to more equal family holdings has been massive, and has massively cut poverty. In much of Latin America and Eastern and Southern Africa, great land inequality still turns middle-income rural averages into widespread rural poverty, while probably reducing efficiency and growth. In most transitional economies much land remains in big state and collective farms; this harms the poor by being inefficient as well as reducing employment.

Yet classical land redistribution has slowed since the mid-1980s, partly because it was often unduly statist, centralized, slow to distribute land to the poor, insufficiently concerned with competitive inputs and services for new smallholders, and liable to create uncertain property rights. There is now a shift towards decentralized, substantially compensatory and market-led reform. Policy can help by removing selective subsidies to large farmers and their inputs, raising their incentive to sell land to the poor, and by direct donor support to appropriate land redistribution. Former large farmers can often profitably provide financial, marketing or processing services competitively to post-reform smallholders.

Given the distribution of land, the poor usually lose from laws against voluntary tenancy or communal tenure systems. Modes of formal and informal titling, tenure and tenancy are usually efficient forms of avoiding highly local transaction costs, provided the poor are not exposed to the market power of a few large landlords.

Neither unreformed nor reformed systems usually give women equal access to land. This is unjust, inefficient and bad for the health and education of children. Priorities in land reform should be: land for women; regions where extreme land inequality is the main constraint on poverty reduction; support services for post-reform smallholders; and incentives to sustainable post-reform farming systems.

Water-yielding assets
Increasing water scarcity coincides with big farm water subsidies: hence the pressure to divert water from farming. Yet the poverty-reducing Green Revolution was largely confined to water-controlled lands. The poor share even less in farm water than in farmland, and suffer serious drinking-water shortages. While persistent subsidy is wrong (and anti-poor), and while rural water-yielding assets should be redistributed and the economic efficiency of rural water use improved, unselective water transfer to urban areas would worsen rural poverty and pressure on marginal drylands.

Small farmer-controlled water-yielding assets irrigate large areas and are often pro-poor, but are not the whole answer. With large water-yielding assets, the non-poor often get special access, exacerbated for women by intra-household problems. Yet some projects have overcome such difficulties. Even if much asset management is centralized, water markets and full-cost pricing can assist access, instead, to the water itself.

Water-yielding assets can be redistributed to the poor by (a) restricting overpumping; (b) responding to poor user needs, for example, by supporting water harvesting; (c) credit, technical help or hydrological data to help the poor invest in wells; (d) facilitating private rent or sale of water-yielding assets to the poor; (e) substitution of employment for water in irrigation management and maintenance; (f) water user associations, representing the poor, to help control and manage systems; and (g) removing water subsidies, safeguarding the poor by allowing user groups to pay by maintenance work.

Drinking-water priorities reflect overwhelmingly urban interests, yet rural water deficiency is greater and harms health more. Cleaner water is more cost-effective in improving rural health and productivity if it complements other inputs; avoids technology dependent on unreliable external fuel, spares and maintenance; and trains and pays community maintainers. Finally, in some countries the rural poor's share of controlled water for production and clean drinking water is so tiny that substantial, open redistribution from urban and rich rural people is inescapable.

Human assets
Better health, education and nutrition help the escape from rural poverty by raising, first, innovativeness, income and food production of farmers and workers in low-income areas; and second, mobility to (and earning capacity from) cash-crops, rural non-farm production and urban work. In these roles human assets complement others: if the economy, physical capital, technology and employment stagnate, extra human assets for the poor may simply shift income among them. Moreover, while education, health and nutrition assets in developing countries have been improving unevenly and often slowly, the huge rich-poor and urban-rural disparities have mostly stagnated or widened. Shifts of human-asset-improving outlays to the rural poor, especially women, usually raise cost-effectiveness, partly because of mutual reinforcement among better

health, nutrition and learning, and smaller families, less poverty, and higher productivity.

Women's education disadvantage, greatest for the rural poor, explains low female innovation. If corrected, it cost-effectively improves child health, education and nutrition. The rising proportion of women farmers increases these prospects. Nutrition improvement raises subsequent learning, productivity and wage-rates, and cuts risk of income loss due to illness: it does most for the worst-off. The rural poor's gains from extra health can depend on complementary nutrition and schooling. The demographic transition, by sharply raising the proportion of workers 30 years hence who are aged over 15 now, implies productivity gains from shifting education and health assets towards poor adults.

Decentralized responsibility for asset formation in health, education and nutrition increases returns to the poor. But user fees for primary and preventive services in low-income countries have proved counter-productive. Exempting the poorest is seldom feasible; children suffer if they are denied basic human assets.

OTHER ASSETS

Other assets matter for rural poverty reduction: but they cannot replace policy to increase farmland, water and human assets of the rural poor, sometimes by redistribution.

Rural non-farm assets and work are large, growing parts of rural activity, but often mainly for the non-poor. Distress diversification from stagnant farming into languishing crafts seldom helps the poor. Growth linkages to dynamic sectors often do, but usually depend on prior, shared farm growth.

Livestock, especially small stock, can be crucial to the income, if seldom the diet, of many rural poor. The poor need institutions to acquire, manage and trade livestock and their products, and to help avoid crises in animal feed. Cattle ownership is often heavily skewed against the poor and women. Poverty reduction is advanced by refocusing livestock public-goods provision on small stock; by reducing artificial barriers to large stock ownership by the poor; and by furthering the practices by which the poor control and manage livestock they do not own.

Housing assets of the rural poor are often even worse than for the urban poor, yet almost all habitat policy is urban. The rural poor's houses need frequent repair. Traditional materials are getting scarcer, and need research on better durability and access. Public works can include off-season work in small local firms to test new house designs. Redistribution and service support for rural site-and-service and home gardens may also be feasible.

Transport and communications assets are often unsuitable for private or joint producer control by the poor. But the poor's weak access as consumers and producers carries huge handicaps and costs, both in market access and, especially for women, in domestic and inter-village farm, fuel and water transport. Non-motorized vehicles can greatly cut such costs, and are easily maintained.

The rural poor want assets to raise income and to provide buffers against shocks. The poor are more likely to control some sorts of assets than others; but farmland, water-yielding assets, and human assets are especially crucial. Pro-poor policy should be directed at improving access to and returns from assets. For land and water this may require redistribution; access to livestock, human capital and non-farm activities require mainly greater opportunity. Gender inequality in access to assets needs to be addressed in policy, and monitored. Rural people in most developing countries enjoy less, per head, of most sorts of assets allocable between city and countryside, especially human capital; these gaps, which in general are not falling, are inefficient as well as inequitable.

Annex 3.1

Non-distributive land options: collective, state and cooperative farms, titling communal land, tenancy restrictions

State, collective and cooperative farming

Attempts to compel cooperative asset use are self-defeating,[128] and cooperative use of farmland is seldom economic or preferred. However, there is scope for state or NGO help to rural people in cooperative management of assets (with scale economies) in use on farmland, especially where it is only managerial costs (including the costs of trust) that stop farmers from choosing cooperative institutions.[129] Such help for cooperative farm savings for joint irrigation in the Mexican *ejido* proved useful to the poor. Similarly some 60 000 of the 300 000-odd egalitarian family farmers, created out of the Armenian decollectivization in the early 1990s, chose to work through optional (but misnamed) 'collected farms', mainly for asset purchase, leasing arrangements, farm management advice and the consolidation and exchange of fragments. Though the poorest may be better reached if such cooperation is supported among landless suppliers of the input (for example, water from IFAD-supported Proshika groups in Bangladesh), state assistance to farmers can be helpful in bearing the managerial costs and externalities of otherwise desired joint activity. However, outside enforcement of joint (or state) farm activity not desired by the farmers is not land reform, but land 'deform'. It harms the rural poor.[130]

Communal tenure and titling

This is also true of enforcement of individual private property, if it runs against the grain of economics and of farmers' wishes. Where low-grade land is fairly plentiful and fencing expensive, common grazing rights have evolved, and cropland – while almost always farmed individually, with private usufruct rights – is owned communally. Rights to sell, rent or bequeath such land are highly variable and adapted to local situations, but often limited or absent.[131] Advocates of private titling argue that communal tenure impedes farmers' borrowing, because land is not acceptable as collateral; induces them to 'soil-mine'

and degrade land[132] (since in future years it may not be theirs to farm);[133] and diffuses and weakens demand for innovations.[134] However, in practice, communal tenure does not reduce production or efficiency, or even impede borrowing, as compared with freehold, in most conditions in Africa. Communal tenure is unlikely to reduce investment incentives, due to low risk of eviction.[135]

The balance between individual and communal tenure rights, unlike the distribution of power and control over scarce land, is mainly an effect, not a cause, of the prospects for profitable agricultural innovation, borrowing and conservation.[136] Private landholding normally develops in response to greater land scarcity,[137] new technical prospects, or different sorts of gain from conservation. But the adjustment involves conflicts of interest, transaction costs, and hence friction and delay,[138] which can justify public action to support land titling where most of the poor want it. But there is no case for enforced decommunalization or titling. This can disadvantage women, tribals with unwritten tenure records, and other vulnerable groups, without enhancing efficiency, as in Uganda.[139] In Rajasthan, India, Jodha[140] shows that privatization of common grazing lands was less favourable to the poor than use of the commons had been before titling, so that the process cost the poor substantial parts of income. Shanmugarathnam[141] shows that privatizing and titling reforms on grazing land disadvantaged pastoralists with small ruminants, mainly the poor.

There are exceptions. Titling can benefit the poor through improving the security of smaller, less well-documented holdings, since 'it is the holdings of [small farmers] that are especially likely to be untitled'. Where much land starts in the public domain, titling, as in Honduras, can help ensure that poor, not only rich, purchasers get security.[142] Where landlords are shifting tenants around, to stop them establishing the right to buy land under tenancy regulations, registration of title – as in West Bengal's 'Operation Barga'[143] – is a useful adjunct to land reform. But caution is needed. The above examples of titling that increases poor people's shares in land do not mainly come from areas of traditional communal tenure. There, the search for titling usually comes from better-off farmers and 'may offer more advantage to large ... farmers who have better access to markets'.[144] In communal areas, imposed removal of restraints on land sale can harm the poor, without efficiency gains. Unlike land-lease markets, land-sale markets, especially in progressive farm areas, tend on balance to transfer assets from poor to non-poor.[145] Higher farm efficiency does often require transfer of farming to better, nearer, or differently resourced farmers; but this can often be achieved by an emerging lease market, even without titling.

Control of land may best be redistributed not as ownership or title, but as common village or regional tenure – with secure individual usufruct rights. In China, this was linked to big increases in output and productivity. In Niger, land tenure insecurity is associated with reduced application of manure and hence lower output. In Ghana, density of tree planting is positively associated with tenure security, but not necessarily ownership.[146]

Tenancy and tenancy reform

The extent, type (sharecropping or fixed-rent) and terms of tenancy, such as collective, private and communal operation and tenure, are mainly consequences of agro-economic opportunity and incentives, and the initial distribution of control and power over land. If these causes do not change in the poor's favour, laws to restrict the type, extent or terms of tenancy seldom help the poor. Indeed, they are often counter-productive, inducing landlords to resume tenanted land for personal farming – usually larger-scale, more mechanized and less employment-intensive.[147]

Tenancy generally transfers farmland to smaller holdings.[148] In India, 'tenancy reallocates land from the large and middle farmers to the marginal farmers', leading 'to greater utilisation of land and labour';[149] in the mid-1980s some 19% of rural households leased in land, of which over 90% owned no land or below 1 ha – and more such households would lease land if legal restrictions were eased.[150] This flow of rented land to the poor is confirmed in a dis-

trict study.[151] Such flows allow poor households to sell and improve their managerial skills; to obtain income from land control; to save money to buy land later;[152] and to adjust their labour inputs, normally upwards, to suit their preferences. Also, rented holdings, being usually smaller, typically hire more labour per hectare than owned holdings. Efficiency losses due to type of tenure – for example, sharecropping – are usually prevented by explicit or implicit landlord-tenant deals. Usually, pro-poor agrarian policy should encourage tenancy (while creating an environment of greater equality in land access and political rights), not, as in the past, discourage it or restrict[153] its types or terms. The fact that barely 5% of farmland in Latin America is tenanted[154] indicates overemphasis on restricting or regulating tenancies, instead of on implementing or obtaining consensus for land redistribution.

Tenancy laws and restrictions, for example, to improve sharecroppers' terms, can help the poor, but only where power shifts sufficiently in favour of the poor to render credible the enforcement of ownership ceilings upon landlords who respond by eviction and resumption of large farms for personal cultivation. Land reform in Japan, the Republic of Korea, Taiwan and West Bengal consisted largely of tenancy restrictions, especially on sharecropping, yet greatly advanced equity and efficiency because it accompanied already widely dispersed land ownership and the reality or threat of effective implementation of ceilings legislation, so landlords could not resume large areas of land for personal cultivation. Further, the rural poor had already acquired considerable power. Operation Barga in West Bengal, India, after 1977 secured small tenancies and thus caused rapid growth in agricultural activity in the early 1980s.[155] Similarly, laws that set ceilings on rentals (especially for sharecropping) or on rented land, or entitle the tillers to buy it, usually cause evictions; but in Taiwan in 1949-53 such laws durably redistributed farmland to the poor, because evictions were prevented by credible ceilings for owned land.

Table 3.1: Gini Land Concentration Index

Country	1941-1950	1951-1960	1961-1970	1971-1980	1981-1990	1991-2000
Algeria				0.72s		
American Samoa	0.5716	0.7963	0.75		0.6705	
Antigua			0.7351			
Argentina		0.8625 0.836	0.873w		0.8598	
Australia	0.8391	0.8321		0.8206	0.9032	
Austria		0.7100	0.6953	0.6773	0.6581	
Bahamas				0.8956		0.8722
Bangladesh		0.47; 0.61	0.57	0.4187 0.54	0.549e	
Barbados			0.8996		0.9284	
Belgium	0.489	0.6137	0.5942	0.5668	0.5639	
Belize				0.7079		
Bolivia					0.7677	
Botswana						0.4369
Brazil	0.8329	0.8347	0.837	0.8521		
Brunei		0.5103				
Canada		0.534	0.5449	0.5119(71) 0.6016(80)		0.5531
Chile		0.933				
China				0.211	0.190	
Colombia		0.8598		0.8592	0.7742	
Cook Islands					0.4866	
Costa Rica	0.8072	0.782	0.7913	0.8133		
Cuba			0.35	0.21		
Cyprus				0.6061	0.6339	
Czechoslovakia	0.6772		0.9384		0.9195	
Denmark	0.4574	0.4513	0.4403	0.3961	0.4299	
Dominican Rep	0.7962	0.7999	0.79	0.8197		
Dominica			0.7957			
Ecuador		0.8642		0.8155		
Egypt	0.7144	0.6283		0.4587		
El Salvador	0.8309		0.8386	0.8075 0.61s(71)		
Ethiopia				0.4379	0.4701	
Fiji			0.5875	0.8508		0.7336
Finland	0.5984	0.5007		0.4388		
France			0.5165	0.5772(79) 0.5256(80)	0.5821	
Germany	0.6748	0.5391		0.5136	0.5142(87) 0.6674(90)	
Greece	0.4741			0.4835(71) 0.3974(80)	0.4621	
Grenada			0.7808		0.7356	
Guadeloupe					0.6009	
Guatemala	0.8588	0.828		0.8484		
Guinea					0.5099	
Guyana					0.6783	
Honduras		0.7512		0.7788		
Hungary	0.5636			0.9797		

(cont'd)

Gini Land Concentration Index (cont'd)

Country	1941-1950	1951-1960	1961-1970	1971-1980	1981-1990	1991-2000
India		0.6781(54) 0.5829(60) 0.607w(60)	0.59 0.64e(70)	0.6144	0.5924	
Indonesia			0.5535 0.62?(63)	0.5559 0.53s(73)		
Iran		0.623				
Iraq		0.7934(52) 0.8829(58) 0.902(58)		0.614		
Ireland	0.5702	0.5943			0.394	0.4659
Israel	0.8461			0.7549		
Italy			0.7452	0.7622	0.7386	
Ivory Coast				0.4229		
Jamaica			0.7909	0.8059		
Japan	0.3904	0.4114	0.4238	0.5212	0.3821	
Jordan			0.6671	0.6858	0.690	
Kenya		0.8184 0.822		0.6841(74) 0.7459(80) 0.81(77)	0.770e	
Korea			0.3535(61) 0.3108(70)	0.3512		
Kuwait			0.7635			
Lebanon		0.6862				
Lesotho		0.3738	0.362			
Liberia				0.7381		
Luxemburg	0.481		0.2905	0.4706		0.5013
Libya		0.6861				
Madagascar				0.804	0.800	
Malaysia		0.7507		0.5826		
Mali		0.4776				
Malta	0.352	0.4093	0.493	0.4863		
Martinique					0.7844	
Mauritania					0.5858	
Mexico	0.5915	0.6216	0.747			
Morocco		0.640	0.642			
Myanmar						0.4403
New Zealand	0.786	0.7159		0.7484(72) 0.7930(80)		
Nepal			0.57		0.6456	0.5181
Netherlands	0.546	0.5496	0.4787	0.699e	0.5024	
Nicaragua		0.8009		0.3177		
North Borneo		0.6442				
Northern Mariana					0.8235	
Norway	0.4131	0.3833	0.2959	0.4801		
Pakistan		0.5956 0.631 0.687w 0.61s(60)	0.63e	0.5363(80) 0.5081(72)	0.5835	
Panama	0.7129	0.7326		0.7778(71) 0.8441(80)	0.8712 0.840(81)	

(cont'd)

Gini Land Concentration Index (cont'd)

Country	1941-1950	1951-1960	1961-1970	1971-1980	1981-1990	1991-2000
Paraguay		0.8583 0.938		0.9281	0.939	0.7843
Peru		0.935	0.9355	0.9105 0.766(72)		
Philippines	0.5063	0.5076 0.580w		0.5093(71) 0.61s(80)		
Poland		0.5301	0.4638			
Port. Guinea		0.3971				
Portugal	0.7133			0.716	0.7249	
Puerto Rico	0.7253	0.7603	0.7749	0.7762	0.7569	
Reunion					0.6628	
Saudi Arabia				0.79	0.8262	
Senegal		0.4927				
Seychelles		0.9246		0.8206		
Sierra Leone			0.4432		0.4774	
South Africa		0.701				
South Korea	0.729	0.195 0.30s	0.384	0.301		
Spain		0.8368		0.8459	0.8583	
Sri Lanka		0.665		0.6670(73) 0.6398(80) 0.51e(73)	0.619e	
Sudan			0.5765			
Suriname		0.7289	0.6935			
Swaziland						0.3032
Sweden		0.7568	0.5082	0.2275(71) 0.5092(80)		
Switzerland				0.5159	0.4843	
Taiwan		0.4500	0.4678			
Tanzania				0.7899		
Thailand		0.455	0.4585	0.452	0.366	
Togo			0.4792(61) 0.5244(70) 0.41(70)	0.4673		
Trinidad			0.6838			
Tunisia		0.6456				
Turkey		0.6027	0.611w	0.5779		0.5984
U.K.	0.7206	0.7166	0.6939	0.6754	0.6214	
U.S.A.	0.7035	0.7132	0.7165	0.7455	0.7536	
Uganda		0.5079 0.485			0.5896	
Uruguay		0.82	0.8147	0.8034	0.84	
Venezuela		0.927	0.9244	0.9096		
Vietnam		0.5823				
Virgin Islands		0.8515	0.5863		0.8786	
Yemen					0.6648	
Yugoslavia		0.6203(51) 0.5181(60)	0.5641			
Zaire			0.5915			

Sources: el-Ghonemy (1990) unless otherwise stated. Where any confusion is possible data from el-Ghonemy (1990) are suffixed e. Data in the 1960 column are from Berry and Cline (1979; p38-9) unless otherwise stated. Data suffixed w are from Berry and Cline (1979; p41-2). Data suffixed s are from Arulpragasam (1990; p13)

Endnotes

1 This chapter excludes financial institutions – a source of borrowing for asset acquisition and a major focus of IFAD's work – because the poor do not borrow mainly to acquire assets. Likewise, it excludes 'social capital', i.e. institutions to increase and safeguard trust in social and economic transactions, since, however crucial to development, it differs radically from other assets. Both are dealt with in Chapter 6.

2 This is related to selection bias. Suppose some poor people, who obtain animals under a loan/subsidy scheme, escape poverty faster than others who do not participate. Such loans can be said to reduce poverty only if we allow for the initial endowments (skills, water access, etc.) of participants in the scheme, as compared with non-participants. Households selected to own livestock, or self-selecting to acquire it, tend to have initial endowments that render them relatively 'good at' managing it. If we do not allow for such selection bias, we overstate the poverty-reducing impact of assets and misjudge the balance of advantage among asset types (Morduch 1999; Haddad *et al.* 2000a; see also World Bank 2000a).

3 Pathak *et al.* 1977.

4 Allowing for rich households' smaller size (Sarvekshana 1979). Distribution in India has hardly changed since (Jha 1999), and is less unequal than in most developing countries (Deininger and Squire 1996).

5 World Bank: database on Demographic and Health Surveys.

6 Eastwood and Lipton 2000.

7 Kanbur and Lustig 1999; Birdsall *et al.* 1995; Deininger and Squire 1996; Tyler *et al.* 1993.

8 Demand for farm labour grows fastest when agricultural land, and growth, are based on fairly equal small farms. Large farms have much lower labour/land ratios, and are more likely to grow capital-intensively (Binswanger *et al.* 1995; Lipton 1983b). Demand for rural non-farm products and labour grows fastest when local agriculture – above all, small-scale farming – grows rapidly, raising local demand for farm tools, farm processing, and especially consumer services like construction, trade and transport (Bell *et al.* 1982; Mellor 1976; Hazell and Roell 1983; Hazell and Ramasamy 1991; Fisher *et al.* 1997; Mecharla 2000).

9 The developing world's share of total population mainly dependent on agriculture was 58% in 1990 and is projected to fall to 47% in 2010. By regions, respective data are: South Asia 60 (50); sub-Saharan Africa 69 (58); East and South-East Asia (including China) 51 (40); and Latin America and the Caribbean 26 (17) (FAOSTAT 1998).

10 Reardon *et al.* 2000.

11 Singh 1985.

12 Binswanger *et al.* 1995.

13 Hazell and Ramasamy 1991.

14 Singh 1990.

15 Psacharopoulos and Patrinos 1993.

16 Haddad *et al.* 2000, and World Bank 1998a, b; Dercon and Krishnan, 1999; Scott 1999; Jalan and Ravallion 1999; Knight and Song 2000; Grootaert *et al* 1997; Bevan *et al.*1989; Gaiha and Deolalikar 1993; Lanjouw and Stern 1991; Bouis and Haddad 1990; Gunning *et al.*, 1999.

17 Carter 2000.

18 Kanbur and Lustig 1999.

19 Mitra 1978.

20 Sen 1981.

21 Taiwan: Mao and Schive 1995; India: Besley and Burgess 1998; Zimbabwe: Gunning *et al.* 1999; Kerala: Herring 1983.

22 For references to these four points see, respectively, (1) Julka and Sharma 1989; (2) Bhalla and Roy 1988, Oberai 1988, and Lipton 1985; (3) Lipton, 1985: 9 and references, Christiansen 1999, Lipton and Ravallion 1995, and Ellis 1998; and (4) Agarwal 1994.

23 Bell 1990; Thiesenhuesen 1989; Lipton 1983b.

24 India: Saxena 1990: 116-7, 124-6; Pakistan: Singh 1990. On *Sim Terra*, the recent Brazilian civil-society analogue to India's *Bhoodan* reform movement: Liamzon 2000.

25 Vyas 1976; Yugandhar and Iyer 1993; Manor 1989: 7.18.

26 Sources for paragraph: Ray 1996; Mearns 1999; Singh 1990: 66; Sanyal 1976; Haddad *et al.* 2000. Measured increases in land equality omit the landless; in India the proportions of rural people who own no land, who neither own nor operate land, and even – in some agriculturally stagnant states – who operate no land, fell between 1960-1 and 1970-1 (Singh 1990: 72-3).

27 Malawi: Sahn and Alderman 1988; Kenya: Hunt 1984.

28 Lieten 1996.

29 Besley and Burgess 1998.

30 Tyler *et al.* 1993.

31 FAO 1991; Deininger 1999.

32 Carter and Mesbah 1993: 1.

33 Deininger and Binswanger 1999; Guinnane and Miller 1997; Brooks and Lerman 1994; Nicaragua: Jonakin 1996; IFAD projects: IFAD 1992a, 1999f, and 1999h.

34 Deininger 1999; cf. IFAD 1999g; Haddad *et al.* 2000.

35 Tendler 1991.

36 Tendler 1991; Liamzon 2000: 14.

37 Agarwal 1994. As the proportion of old persons grows (even in poor populations with weak social safety-nets), this becomes more important for poverty reduction,

because of women's greater survival prospects into old age. On the parlous state of widow-headed households in India, see Drèze and Srinivasan 1995.

38 For evidence on these three points, see respectively Alderman *et al.* 1995; Haddad *et al.* 1997; and Kennedy and Peters 1992.

39 Latin American title: Deere 1987; empowerment (and Bihar): Agarwal 1994; exit and marriage: Sen 1990; Mwea: Hanger and Moris 1973.

40 Agarwal 1998a.

41 For evidence see, respectively, Ncube *et al.* 1997; Rose 1998; Deere 1987, on Latin America; Gupta 1993; Agarwal 1994.

42 Agarwal 1994.

43 IFAD 1999c.

44 World Water Council 2000.

45 World Bank 1992: 47-9, 100; Rosegrant 1995; IFPRI 1997; Gleick 1999; IFAD, Communal Irrigation Development Project, Philippines 1982.

46 Kurnia *et al.* 1999.

47 Niger basin irrigation: Pearson *et al.* 1981; swamp development in Sierra Leone: Richards 1985.

48 For evidence on this paragraph see Bhalla and Roy 1988; Narain and Roy 1980; Mollinga 1998; Wade 1975.

49 Kenya: Adams *et al.* 1997; Burkina and Ecuador: Zwarteveen 1997; The Gambia: von Braun *et al.* 1989b.

50 Wood and Palmer-Jones 1991.

51 India: Narain and Roy 1980; Latin America: www.cgiar.org/irri/riceweb/g_overlatin.htm (CIAT 2000); the Philippines, and support for projects to improve farmers' water management: IFAD 1994a.

52 For successes, see Ostrom 1990.

53 Low maintenance is due partly to lack of incentives. Where many farmers share the same system, each has less incentive to maintain it than if one farmer is the sole owner/user. Water markets can give farmers an incentive to maintain the system. Alternatively, development of an institution responsible for water distribution and management can ensure maintenance.

54 North India: Mellor and Moorti 1971, Pant 1984, Shankar 1981. Mexico: Levine *et al.* 1998; Bangladesh: Aeron-Thomas 1992.

55 Howes 1980; Aeron-Thomas 1992; IFAD 1994b; Jaim and Sarker 1994.

56 IFAD 1999b: 43.

57 Such as a given share per unit of irrigable land, or depending upon crop grown where farmers negotiate timing.

58 Martorell 1995.

59 Esrey *et al.* 1990.

60 Nigeria: Huttly *et al.*, 1987, 1990; Blum *et al.* 1990; Imo State Evaluation Team 1989; Narangwal: Taylor *et al.* 1978.

61 Increased quantity of water means that food may be prepared more often and that hygiene standards in the household may be improved through bathing, washing clothes, washing dishes and cleaning the house.

62 Gleick 1999.

63 IFAD 1999c.

64 Churchill *et al.* 1987.

65 VLOM: Reynolds, 1992; Morgan, 1993; IFAD, 1994c.

66 UNICEF 1995.

67 Sara and Katz 1997.

68 Swajal: P. Iyer, pers. comm.; Tanzania: Cleaver and Kaare 1998, World Water Council 2000.

69 IFAD experience suggests that most of Eastern and Southern Africa is an exception, though transhumant herders still loom large among the poor in Kenya and Botswana.

70 Pingali *et al.* 1987.

71 IFAD 1994a.

72 In The Gambia, small stock are a store of wealth, used to buy grain or to 'save' and later exchange for cattle (Itty *et al.* 1997). For a Tanzanian case of cattle as a hedge against inflation and devaluation, see Gijsman and Rusamsi 1991.

73 Simmons 1981.

74 Gittinger *et al.* 1990.

75 Dercon 1998: 2, on Ethiopia.

76 Average number of livestock: landless (2), marginal (<1ha = 4), small (1-2ha = 5), medium (2-4ha = 6), large (4+ha = 7).

77 Botswana: Republic of Botswana 1975; Mongolia: Cooper 1995; India: Siroki and Siroki 1993, Farooqee and Nautiyal 1996, Sharma and Poleman 1994, Mellor pers. comm.; Pakistan: Kurosaki 1995.

78 Delgado 1999.

79 Poverty-focus of small stock: for Sukumaland, Tanzania, see Gijsman and Rusamsi 1991; Dercon 1998; for Mongolian villages, Cooper 1995; for Madhya Pradesh, India, Siroki and Siroki 1993. Senegal: Itty *et al.*1997; on costs of animal types, Seyoum 1992; on goats, Rao 1995.

80 It was motivated partly by a misperception (Sidahmed 2000): that most common lands were overgrazed. Even if they were, ranching would not help; private ranchers, subsidized to improve their herds' condition and hence increase offspring, avoid overgrazing *their* ranches by shifting offspring back to the commons.

81 Thomas-Slayter and Bhatt 1994.

82 On India's RNFS, FAO 1998a, and Fisher *et al.* 1997;

in Latin America, FAO 1998a; in Africa and overall, Reardon 1997.

83 China: Lin 1992; diversification versus linkages: Mellor 1976, Hazell and Ramasamy 1991; poverty-reducing prospects of modern vs traditional non-farm growth: Mecharla 2000 (on Andhra), Fisher *et al.* 1997, Bhalla 1994.

84 Binswanger *et al.* 1993.

85 Kingsbury pers. comm.

86 Hazell and Ramasamy 1991, Binswanger *et al.* 1993.

87 Hazell and Ramsamy 1991.

88 Lipton 1984.

89 Though some 2.5 million such homes are damaged annually by natural disaster, mud has benefits compared with modern materials, being cheap, nearby, ventilated, durable where there are few heavy rainstorms, and manageable with family (or local construction) skills (Mathur 1989; Satya Sundaram 1989).

90 Murthy 1989; Mathur 1989.

91 Herring 1983.

92 Dawson and Barwell 1993; Barwell 1996; Heidemann and Kaira 1984.

93 Barwell *et al.* 1985; Riverson and Carapetis 1991.

94 Microsoft's Bill Gates's massive support for research into malaria, Tuberculosis and AIDS was initiated by his realization, when visiting Soweto, South Africa, that these diseases and similar material constraints needed to be tackled locally, and that until this was done the 'communications revolution' was of limited relevance.

95 Alderman *et al.* 1996.

96 IFAD 1999a: 80.

97 The median 15-19 year old in the poorest quintile also had no schooling in Mali and Chad (top quintile, Grade 4), Benin (top quintile, Grade 5), Senegal, Niger, Côte d'Ivoire and Burkina Faso (6); Morocco and Bangladesh (8); and Pakistan (9); and grade 1 or 2 only in Mozambique and Central African Republic (5), Malawi, Haiti, Comoros and NE Brazil (6), Madagascar (7) and Guatemala (9) (World Bank 1999a: 43).

98 On educational gaps: Asia, Osmani and Lipton 1997; rich-poor: Haddad *et al.* 2000, Fig. 5, Jalan and Ravallion 1999 (China), Haddad and Ahmed 1999 (Egypt), McCulloch and Baulch 1999 (Pakistan) and Maluccio *et al.* 1999b (South Africa). On rural-urban gaps: Lipton 1977; Drèze and Gazdar 1997: 81 (on India); Eastwood and Lipton 2000.

99 World Bank, 2000b.

100 On rural and urban health: Sastry 1997; on IMR: Rajan 1993: 112, Goyal 1994: 104. Outside estimates for China are higher, but not split into urban and rural (Bhalla 1995: 237). Africa shows a large, persisting anti-rural health bias. In Malawi rural child mortality declined from 360 to 261 in 1972-84; the urban rate, from 239 to 121 (Palamuleni 1994: 72). In Cameroon in 1962-76 the remote rural areas and the capital city

showed the slowest IMR falls (Defo 1996: 411). In The Congo in 1985-92, a main predictor of child mortality risk – low birthweight – increased from 12% to 29% in rural areas, but from 12% to 16% in urban areas (World Bank 1997).

101 Alderman and Garcia 1993; Thomas 1986.

102 Haddad *et al.* 2000; Livi-Bacci and de Santis 1999.

103 Checchi 2000.

104 Lockheed *et al.* 1980; Chaudri 1973; Jamison and Lau 1982; Feder *et al.* 1985; Foster and Rosenzweig 1995; von Braun and Kennedy 1994; Thomas *et al.* 1991; Rosenzweig 1995; Huffman 1977; Schultz 1975, 1988. Peru: Cotlear 1990; India: Deolikar 1988, Raza and Ramachandran 1990, Chaudri 1973; Thailand: World Bank 1991; Africa: Appleton and Balihuta 1996, Haddad *et al.* 2000; Malawi: Carletto 1999.

105 Liamzon 2000.

106 Basta *et al.* 1979; Sudhardjo 1986. India: Deolalikar 1988; Guatemala: Immink and Viteri, 1981; Sri Lanka: Sahn and Alderman 1988.

107 Haddad and Bouis 1991.

108 Payne and Lipton 1994.

109 Combining such costs of chronic deprivation due to child undernutrition with those of current undernutrition, Horton (1999) estimates forgone annual GDP from iron deficiency in childhood and from iodine and protein energy malnutrition in adults to be over 5% in Pakistan. For Bangladesh, the cost of iron deficiency in children alone is nearly 2% of GDP.

110 Neonatal undernutrition damages later cognitive function (Lucas *et al.* 1998); hence nutritional supplementation and stimulation of stunted children aged 9-24 months have independent and additive impacts on the development of the children aged 7-8 years (McGregor *et al.* 1997). At the mean of a nationally representative sample from Ghana, a 10% increase in stunting causes a 3.5% increase in age of first enrolment at school (Glewwe and Jacoby 1995).

111 Berg 1987.

112 Deficient Vitamin A, iron and iodine seriously damage the poor's human capital. Vitamin A deficiency is normally responsive to dietary diversification and hence to major poverty reduction, but iodine deficiency is mainly localized in leached upland soils (and has been highly responsive to salt fortification). Anaemia – which cuts physical productivity and raises maternal mortality among over 2 billion people – has, alone of the deficiency conditions, shown no decline during recent decades. See FAO 2000.

113 Schultz and Tansel 1997.

114 FAO/UNAIDS 2000.

115 Lipton and Osmani 1997; Quisumbing 1996; Estudillo and Otsuka 1999; Datt and Ravallion 1997; Behrman and Deolalikar 1988; Strauss and Thomas 1995; Schultz 1999.

116 Kingsbury, pers. comm.

117 Drèze and Gazdar 1997: 62-81.

118 Russell and Gilson 1997; Hecht *et al.* 1992; Nyonator and Kutzin 1999.

119 Zimbabwe: Hongoro 1993; Vietnam: Ensor and San 1996; Kenya: Mbugua *et al.* 1995; cf. Gilson 1997; Swaziland: Yoder 1989.

120 Where health and school fees are introduced together, these effects are sharpened; in a rural district in Uganda, over a quarter of cash expenditure was on school or medical fees, and long-term illnesses were making the poor poorer (Lucas and Nuwagaba 1999).

121 Reddy and Vandemortele 1996; Colclough 1993; Zimbabwe: Chisvo and Munro 1994; Malawi: Bray and Lillis 1988; Kenya: World Bank, 1995j.

122 Appleton 1997.

123 Raczynski 1991.

124 Arhin 1994.

125 Payment does improve consumer involvement and control. There is a strong case for full-cost pricing of state services that enhance earning power mainly for the already well-off, e.g. university degrees, or residence costs in teaching hospitals; it is common, but unreasonable, for the state to give away or subsidize such largely urban elite services while charging user fees for basic health and education, especially in rural areas where both such services and their users are relatively poor.

126 Huffman and Steel 1995.

127 Hill 1991; Tamang and Dharam 1995.

128 Compulsion of collective, state or commune farms was motivated mainly by the search for economies of scale and by a wish to concentrate farming into points where food or timber could be cheaply extracted for urban use. These motives suggest that such modes of farm tenure are unlikely to help the poor, and also explain their near-universal failure. Forced collective or state farming helped cause millions of famine deaths in the Ukraine in 1931-35 and China in 1960-63, and tens of thousands in Ethiopia, Mozambique and elsewhere in Africa in the 1970s and 1980s. The objection is not to cooperation but to its top-down enforcement, inappropriate application to farmland, and use for extraction. If farmers and workers are permitted to reorder collective or cooperative assets, as in much of Latin America, they often prefer smallish cooperatives for assets with scale economies (milk-sheds, tractors); but for farmland they 'vote with their feet' for private, usually small-scale and equal, management (Thiesenhusen 1989: 497; Dorner 1992: 37, 41; Forster 1992: 575; Howard 1988: 5-14, on China; FAO 1991: 20, on Nicaragua; and Zevallos 1989: 50, on Ecuador).

129 Each farmer may refuse to contribute to management costs of (say) a marketing or irrigation cooperative, for fear that others will free-ride, raising his own cost.

Cooperative outcomes may also be frustrated in prisoner's dilemma situations – e.g. each farmer may overgraze the commons – if that game/situation is unlikely to be repeated in similar form, so that a tit-for-tat cooperative equilibrium (Axelrod 1984) does not emerge. In such cases, cooperative enforcement benefits all, but can be imposed only externally. That is the case for subsidies to some sorts of cooperative.

130 Mexico: Burke 1979; Armenia: Csaki *et al.* 1995; Bangladesh: Wood and Palmer-Jones 1991.

131 On institutional aspects of rural 'common property' and their role in poverty reduction, see Ostrom 1990.

132 Individual titling of common lands can affect incentives to sustainable land use. In semi-arid areas, titling may stimulate long-run investment in conservation, e.g. terracing; the title means that the traditional land authority cannot prevent inheritance, so the gains from terracing are assured for the investing family (on Mbere, Kenya, see Hunt 1996). But environmental effects of titling can be negative if traditional modes of land management are superseded without group incentives or institutions to replace them. This was IFAD's experience with an otherwise successful and poverty-reducing project for consensual titling in Orissa, India.

133 However, common graziers seldom, with self-destructive selfishness, overgraze and destroy the pasture; it normally pays them to accept controls on cattle numbers and/or land quality, and indeed to pay authorities, including chiefs, to exercise such control in acceptable ways (Drinkwater 1991; Tapson 1990).

134 In pre-independence Zimbabwe, Ranger and Werbner (1990) show that farming in so-called 'communal' areas remained individualistic; lower productivity was due to soil, climate, and colonial denial of markets, research and infrastructure. When that denial ended after Independence, smallholder maize output surged in communal areas. Communal tenure had not been a binding constraint (Roth and Bruce 1994: 34-6; Barrows and Roth 1989: 15-18).

135 See Noronha (1985) on communal tenure rights; on their consistency with efficiency also Blarel *et al.* 1991; Platteau 1993; Migot-Adholla *et al.* 1991; Place and Hazell 1993; and on investment incentives Sjaastad and Bromley 1997, and for Ghana, Besley 1995.

136 Lack of clear title did appear to constrain borrowing by small farmers in parts of Guatemala (Shearer *et al.* 1991: iv, 19) and Thailand (Feder *et al.* 1988), but individual, titled tenure has spread of its own accord.

137 Ault and Rutman 1979: 81.

138 Platteau 1992, 1993.

139 Nsabagasani 1997.

140 Jodha 1986.

141 Shanmugaratham 1996.

142 Shearer *et al.* 1991: iv, 9-10, 13.

143 Bandyopadhyay 1995.

144 Shearer *et al.* 1991: viii.

145 e.g. Mani and Gandhi 1994.

146 China: Lin 1992, McMillan *et al.* 1989; Niger: Gavain and Fafchamps 1996; Ghana: Besley 1995, Migot-Adholla *et al.* 1991.

147 In much of Latin America 'large landowners responded to the threat of tenancy reform by evicting all hired workers or tenants who could have claimed ownership under a reform program. The landlords either switched to livestock production and ranching or – aided by significant credit subsidies – shifted to highly mechanized cultivation' (Haddad *et al.* 2000; see also Deininger and Binswanger 1999; Binswanger *et al.* 1995; de Janvry and Sadoulet 1989). In India (Mearns 1999) tenancy reforms led to evictions, rotation among landlords' plots to prevent acquisition of occupancy rights, and worse tenure security (Appu 1997); and attempts to ban tenancy outright (e.g. in Uttar Pradesh, Orissa and Madhya Pradesh) led to concealed tenancy arrangements which were less secure, leading to loss, or at least 'informalization', of access to the poor of about 30% of their operated area (Ray 1996). In Nepal, tenancy regulations proved 'unenforceable [yet] harmful to the status of tenants [with] evictions, . . . shifting of tenants to informal settlements, and rent increases' (Riedinger 1993: 26).

148 It has other advantages (frustrated by removing the options of sharecropping contracts, which deters many leases). (1) Tenancy reduces transaction costs associated with labour: the large landowner must supervise employees if he farms commercially, but need not supervise the work of tenants so intensively (Agarwal 1993) since if they work harder they produce and earn more. The poor villager must incur search costs to find farmwork, but if he/she rents a farm it can be worked when he/she chooses. (2) Much tenancy, perceived as absentee landlordism (Thorner 1980: 159), in intensive small-scale surveys proves to be land exchange in time and space (Ghose 1983: 124-5): temporary emigrants rent out land; locals rent out remote plots, rent in nearby ones, and cut journeys among fragments. (3) Tenancy lets landowners, without draught oxen, rent out to those with oxen but not land. (4) Tenancy lets villagers farm even if poor, uncreditworthy, and unable to borrow to buy land. Note the re-emergence of tenancy following egalitarian individual land reforms in China (Bruce and Harrell 1989: 18) and Albania (Stanfield *et al.* 1992: 2).

149 Swamy 1988: 555, 562; Singh 1990.

150 Parthasarathy 1991.

151 Mani and Gandhi 1994.

152 In poor areas of Ecuador in the 1970s and 1980s, cash saved by sharecroppers, out of farm income, allowed them to climb the ladder by buying farmland later (Forster 1989: 7). Without land reform, tenancy restriction can cut the rungs of this 'agricultural ladder' (Spillman 1919) and prevent escape from poverty.

153 In particular, sharecropping is often restricted because, without landlord-tenant deals, the sharecropper would produce less output than under fixed-rent or owner-occupancy (having to surrender part of his output to the landlord). But such deals are almost always found; theory and evidence reveal no efficiency losses due to sharecropping (Otsuka and Hayami 1988; Otsuka and Chuma 1992). Moreover, sharecropping can induce better management and supervision than alternatives; fixed-rent lease and wage employment raise the cost of management and supervision would be low. Because share-rent (unlike fixed-rent) is less when crops are poor, sharecropping reduces transient poverty – and increases incentive to grow profitable but risky crops (Faruqee and Carey 1997).

154 de Janvry, pers. comm.

155 Lieten 1996.

CHAPTER 4

TECHNOLOGY, NATURAL RESOURCES AND RURAL POVERTY REDUCTION

Unless the poor have the power to participate in deciding which technology to use, they are unlikely to benefit from it. Better farm technology will most benefit farmers who are active partners in setting priorities for both research and extension.

TECHNOLOGICAL CHOICES AND OPTIONS

Over 70% of the world's extreme poor live in rural areas. They use over half their income to obtain staple food; receive over two thirds of their calories from this low-cost source; and, usually, produce it themselves. Yet often they cannot afford enough food to provide safe amounts of energy or micronutrients.

Improved bio-agricultural technology and water control took hundreds of millions of people out of poverty in 1965-90, mainly by raising food-staples production, employment and affordability. Yet large regions and large numbers of the rural poor gained little from this achievement; and progress has slowed down across the world. In many areas technological changes did not take place. In other areas the potential of existing technology seems to be nearly exhausted. New challenges arise, from land lost to erosion, salinity and urban expansion, and from water depletion and diversion to towns. Important, too, is the need to provide adequate, attractive rural employment incomes, as the numbers of working-age people in most poor regions double in the next 35-45 years. New science can meet the challenges if the poor are allowed to par-

ticipate in the process. Radical changes in research incentives, organization and management, above all in the relationship between private and public, are needed. This report on rural poverty gives a special emphasis to technology.

New agricultural technology has its opponents; many people prefer to explore other ways to cut rural poverty. However, these alternatives are generally complementary to technical progress and are unlikely, without it, to generate an adequate rate of poverty reduction.

- The empowerment of the rural poor – 'the soul of IFAD' – must include better technology in support of their labour, land and other assets. If technology is weak or unsustainable, the power to control it is worth little. Unless the poor have the power to participate in decisions which determine their use of technology, they will be unlikely to benefit from its implementation. Better farm technology will do more for farmers who are active partners in setting priorities for research, as well as extension.

- Improved land and water management is not an alternative form of technical change to rapid bio-agricultural progress. Without bio-agricultural progress, better land and water management will neither attract many farmers nor reduce poverty much.

• More available food, through technical development, is not an alternative to more food entitlements for the poor; it is often the most affordable way to provide entitlements, through extra income from small farms and hired work.

• Reducing urban poverty, and rural production of cash-crops, livestock or non-farm products, are not alternatives to the increased growth of staples through technology, but are helped by it.

• Better access to assets, institutions and markets for the poor are not alternatives to improved technology for production by the poor. Without such access, the returns to the poor from technical progress will be disappointing, as will their adoption of low-technology assets.

Why does this report emphasize the importance of staples in farm technology? The rural poor neither live by, nor produce, staples alone. Nonetheless, in South and East Asia, sub-Saharan Africa, marginal uplands and semi-arid lands, most of the poor still live mainly from farm or employment income from growing staples. Technical progress to raise income usually requires increases in the productivity of food staples, achieved by labour-intensive methods. In effect, most of the working poor continue to grow some food staples, and the poorest, having little land, usually buy more food than they sell. They gain in two ways if technical progress increases staples productivity – from cheaper consumption and higher income through more productive work. By reducing the risk of hunger, greater quantities, and reliability of food crops reduce the vulnerability of the poor.

Poverty is often concentrated in areas where the technology to improve the production of staples has not yet been introduced. The rapid reduction in poverty in 2000-20 requires technical progress that is substantial at smallholder level; that is quickly adopted by farmers across a wide range of

hitherto neglected areas; that creates productive employment; and that improves the growth of food crops, mainly staples.

To reach their targets, techniques to help the poor must be:

• capable of benefiting the mass of rural poor, whatever their status; and

• adapted to tightening constraints of water and land depletion and loss of biodiversity.

Agrotechnical progress has in the past usually occurred in small increments. It has spread slowly; in some cases, as with mechanization of draught, it has reduced employment without raising yields or making them more sustainable. The prospects of the rural poor have fortunately been transformed by the sharp acceleration since the 1950s of two very old forms of technical change that tend to raise staples yields and employment incomes: water control (greatly extended in South and South-East Asia and China in 1950-85), and plant and animal selection and breeding (culminating in the 1965-85 Green Revolution). Poverty incidence in affected rural areas fell, typically from 30-50% to 5-15%.

In spite of these advances, relevant outlays have plummeted since the early 1980s; and in some countries agricultural research, investment and extension are increasingly being privatized. Public and NGO outlays have not only been reduced but have also been diverted from water control and biological improvement. This has deflected effort from improving the production of poor people's food staples. Imaginative steps to reverse these trends are necessary for reviving the rapid reduction in rural poverty.

One plausible alternative – the substantial expansion of arable land – is not feasible for most rural populations in Asia, and increasingly in much of Africa and Latin America. In areas where it is feasible, it usually results in rising costs and falling returns. The expansion of staples into marginal areas has often exposed the crops to severe environmental stress (for example, maize in

Table 4.1: Rate of yield growth (percentage): cereals, roots and tubers, 1961-98

Cereals	Africa	Developing	E SE Asia	L. America & Caribbean	South Asia	Sub-Sahara
1961-71	1.03	2.76	1.96	1.43	1.88	(0.29)
1971-81	1.98	2.76	2.03	2.38	2.33	2.04
1981-91	(0.75)	1.86	1.67	0.74	3.09	(-0.07)
1991-98	(1.13)	1.55	0.86	2.72	1.7	(0.97)
1966-82	1.94	2.7	2.36	2.23	2.3	1.76
1982-98	0.75	1.67	1.35	2.05	2.69	(0.06)

Roots and tubers	Africa	Developing	E SE Asia	L. America & Caribbean	South Asia	Sub-Sahara
1961-71	0.65	2.95	(0.4)	1.57	4.13	0.65
1971-81	1.52	1.19	2.92	-0.77	1.73	1.44
1981-91	1.95	0.73	1.06	1.07	1.62	1.91
1991-98	(0.34)	0.99	(0.09)	1.02	1.09	(0.25)
1966-82	0.61	1.12	2.38	-0.56	2.04	0.52
1982-98	1.42	0.7	(0.21)	0.87	1.5	1.42

Entries are exponential growth-trend fit betas. Numbers in brackets not significant at 10%.

* significant at 10%. All other entries significant at 5%.

Source: FAOSTAT data tape 1999.

Southern Africa and rice in East Bangladesh). In most cases increasing farm income and employment requires a raising of yields. Yet growth in the yield of staples has declined sharply (Table 4.1).

Staples yield growth in developing countries fell from 3% annually in the 1970s to barely 1% in the 1990s, and staples employment growth from about 2% to below 0.5%, far below the projected growth in the rural workforce through 2015. In the leading-edge areas, farm progress has faltered. Many of the remaining rural poor live in areas largely untouched by modern farm technology. In leading and lagging areas alike, further irrigation and agrochemical use are limited by degradation in natural resources. Appropriate, sustainable land and water management is essential, and advances in livestock and cash-crop technology are desirable.

Meeting the UN target to halve dollar poverty in 1995-2015 demands a revival in technical progress to improve sustainable production of staple foods, with the potential to enhance further employ-

ment. Yields can be raised through extension, but it seldom pays farmers to incur the costs and risks of achieving yields beyond, say, 30-50% of research-station yield potential. If the varieties of seed available are not improved, the farmers' yields will not improve either.

Institutions, markets and governments, in their efforts to convert the rural poor to the use of new techniques and technology, should stimulate suppliers and advisers to encourage and support farmers in their adoption of new methods and products.

What techniques are most likely to help the poor? Pro-poor techniques are likely to concentrate on food staples; on better use of water; and on methods of production that raise demand for labour; they are especially well suited for smaller and more deprived farms, particularly those with fewer assets.

New techniques should be:
• more productive of output per unit of input, that is, should cut unit cost;

- more labour-intensive (uses more labour per unit of land or fixed capital); but
- adapted to seasonal labour demand and food needs;
- more robust against climatic, pest and labour-supply risks;
- more stable in labour use and product-flow across seasons and years;
- selecting products mainly made and/or used by the poor;
- cutting or stabilizing the price of staples; and
- more sustainable in terms of land, water and biodiversity.

There is often a trade-off between these features which wise policy can reduce. For example, land sustainability may be enhanced with higher labour/capital ratios by incentives for measures to improve land, by installing vegetative barriers rather than contour bunds. All the above features (except biodiversity) were advanced by the spread of high-yielding cereals in 1965-85, leading to unprecedented poverty reduction.[1]

TECHNICAL CHANGE TO BENEFIT THE POOR: LESSONS FROM HISTORY

In a time of popular politics and developed markets, it is now more likely than before that the poor will derive major gains from technology dedicated to improving farming output and employment. Agricultural progress has been driven by research on the farm for millennia; by formal public-sector research since the tenth century in China; and by the Darwin-Mendel scientific revolution which increased the power and pace of such research. Box 4.1 illustrates the process – and shows that some types of technical change have proved likely to spread fast and far and to the poor.

Information in Box 4.1 and recent experience confirm that technical progress in land and water management is usually slow to spread and to bring gains. First, innovations are slow to begin with, and resulting increases in national farm incomes or sustainability are gradual and small. Second, for hundreds of years the range of available techniques has not been enlarged by researched inventions (in land and water management) that substantially raise farm incomes and/or sustainability over a large area. Third, recent decades have seen little acceleration in research outputs. All this is not to deny major local advances.

Much faster gains are normal with technical progress in land cover (animals, crops, varieties), water availability and plant nutrient enhancement. Farmers' choice among available techniques – including shifts among crops, animals, or varieties, together with appropriate nutrient enhancement, and especially with irrigation – often double farm output and income over wide areas in 20 years. Each phase of biochemical advance (Box 4.1) has produced faster farm growth than the previous one; but there is a striking contrast between fast, widespread farm transformation by variety-irrigation-nutrient technology and slow, localized progress from land/water-management technology. Making farmers rely on this, rather than better germplasm or water control, sentences them to a slow reduction in poverty. Most farmers must choose from a slowly changing set of land-water and agronomic methods. Moreover, it pays the farmer to upgrade these only when better germplasm or water control makes it reliable and profitable.

The advances in irrigation over the last two millennia have made much new land usable and boosted crop production on existing land. However, these changes have often produced perverse incentives, with free or subsidized water. This is becoming increasingly hard to maintain as water becomes dearer and scarcer. Water on high-grade land, irrigable for much of the year, will be shifted away from cereals, especially rice, to higher-value crops, such as vegetables. Pressure will be applied to find sustainable methods for growing food staples with high yields, on less productive lands. The

Box 4.1: The global sequence of agrotechnical progress

Each of these advances reduced the amount of work needed to buy food, yet raised demand for – and hence the food-affording capacity of – labour, except 4b, which normally arrives when non-farm labour demand is predominant and expanding.

Time/place	Agrotechnical progress	Information source
1. China c. 5000-2000BC, West Asia 3500-900BC, Europe 2500-700BC-200AD.	Neolithic settlement: from hunter-gathering to crop/animal farming, using sparse labour on underused land. Early crop selection and transformation (maize in Central America).	Bray 1986: 9, 86; Piggott 1981: 30; Ammerman and Cavalli-Sforza 1971
2. Asia 200-800AD, Europe's 'mediaeval revolution' of 600-1200AD. Somewhat later in Africa	First agricultural transformation responding to very slowly rising person/land ratios: from shifting cultivation to stable groups of fields; land levelling, terracing; initial rotation – often cattle as well as crops, interdependent via manuring, draught, and feed.	White 1962; Boserup 1965; Ishikawa 1968
2a. China, much of East/South-East Asia, Near East and North Africa, South India and Sri Lanka; 200BC-1400AD.	Where indicated by water situations, land settlement was followed by the first irrigation revolution: big, centrally managed tanks, but also many small wells and some artesian systems.	
3. China c. 900-1000AD. Europe 1650-1850, 'European colonies' after 1800	Biochemical revolution 1: intense rotation, organic manuring, crop-animal integration, systematic plant breeding	Bray 1986; Mingay 1968: 11; Jones 1974: 78-9
4. Asia, Europe, America 1880-1940	Biochemical revolution 2: applied plant nutrient science (Liebig), formal plant selection; guano, inorganic fertilizers.	
4a. North India, Pakistan, Bangladesh, river valley schemes in China, some of North and East Africa. 1850-90 and 1950-80	Where indicated by scarcities, 'second irrigation revolution' (dams, tubewells).	Pingali et al. 1987
4b. After 1920	As farm density rose (Asia) or rural labour scarcity bit (North America, later Europe), draught revolution hoe-animal-tractor	
5. North America from 1930, c. 1955-88 South and East Asia and Europe, parts of Latin America, bits of Africa.	Green Revolution: huge acceleration of staples plant-breeding progress.	

issue of how to make this more sustainable and reliable will become more important.

The biochemical Green Revolution and major irrigation expansion have stalled, after early success. Yet there are three grounds for hoping that poverty will be substantially reduced through further transformation of farming technology.

First, less responsive lands might increase yield, employment and income through sustainable, low-input techniques. But these, however successful, cannot contribute enough to reduce global poverty. There are difficulties:

- If low-input techniques are also low-output, they do not generate much food or income.
- Low-input, high-output techniques that do not increase plant or livestock conversion efficiency of water and nutrients into economic farm output must use up soil nutrients or water and are therefore likely to be unsustainable.
- If such techniques safely and substantially raised conversion efficiency, they would have been adopted by farmers long ago. IFAD's support for extension to accelerate adoption is justified. Areas that received more extension in the past are far quicker to adopt research findings later on,[2] but repeated efforts to introduce rejected innovations seldom achieve much.

The second ground for hope for agrotechnical transformation lies with areas (and perhaps crops) that seem less responsive but in reality are not so, at least not in 2000. In India and China since the early 1990s some agriculturally backward regions show higher marginal returns to irrigation, roads and/or research than the forward irrigated areas.[3] In Southern and Eastern Africa, however, agricultural support outlays appear to have been skewed unduly towards slow-growing farming areas.[4] Also, plants and animals in many such areas are selected for hardiness, despite scarce or unreliable water or nutrients, not for high yield when such inputs are ample. Substantial yield improvements are therefore much less likely from crossing within species such as millets or goats, adapted to marginal semi-arid/arid environments, than within species such as rice or water buffalo, adapted to more resource-rich natural environments.

In these marginal environments, therefore, large rises in crop and livestock productivity may require introduced genes from other species. For many areas and crops, the best hopes lie in a revived Green Revolution, now being made more environmentally sensitive through biotechnology.[5] The scientific prospects are excellent,[6] but at present limited by the focus of research and development on a form of agriculture that caters mainly to rich people in rich countries, not to the food needs of the world's poor.[7] In spite of promising signs of change, substantial gains for the rural poor will require reorganization and revival of public research, and new incentives to private research, both in developing countries and globally.

However, while research is critical, even within the sphere of technology, it is not enough on its own. The rural poor need more information about technological options. Given that sources of "advice" are proliferating (increasingly including private-sector interests and NGOs), it is imperative that the capacity of the poor to evaluate advice is enhanced. This is the necessary social revolution in technology: elevating the poor from technology objects (or recipients) to technology subjects, involved in specification of need, evaluation of responses and choice of productive strategies.

BIO-AGRICULTURAL RESEARCH

Farmers and breeders raise yields by genetic selection for plant shape or chemistry that improves response to the normal environment, and to unusually good or bad seasons for, say, rainfall or insect populations. The selection and manipulation of crops and animals into high-yielding varieties (HYVs) is as old as farming. Breeders speed up the process by scientific selection, controlled

Box 4.2: Crop and animal improvement versus biodiversity

There is a conflict in biotechnical progress between biological improvement and biodiversity.

Improvement favours predominance of plant and animal species and varieties that better meet local human needs to raise and stabilize economic returns, cut costs and displace unwanted life-forms (such as weeds). Crop and animal improvement, plus farmers' responses to incentives, mean that plants and animals currently perceived as economically 'good' drive out 'bad'.

Yet this reduces biodiversity. Biodiversity permits complementarities (for example, among nutrient demands and supplies of different plants and animals). It prevents species attrition and losses that often prove disastrous later. Increasing reliance on a few carefully bred crop varieties contributes to a loss of spatial diversity in genetic resources, and to a common vulnerability to the same pest and weather-related risks. For example, IR-36 rice was planted on more than 10 million hectares in Asia. Such varietal specialization has occasionally led to widespread crop losses due to outbreaks of diseases and pests (tungro and brown planthopper in rice) and has necessarily diverted agricultural research expenditures from yield enhancement towards defensive research: maintenance research and germplasm conservation programmes (Anderson et al. 1987).

Farmers resolve the conflict by, for example, rotation and mixing of crops and herds; formal researchers, by such means as seed banks. The pressures towards fast improvement are strongest for the poorest, but so is the damage if lost biodiversity induces sudden heavy losses due to pest attack.

crossing, and access to an increasingly wide range of crossing materials and methods. This greatly accelerates farm improvement and rural poverty reduction but also sharpens an age-old conflict between two needs of the rural poor: biological improvement and biodiversity (Box 4.2).

Soil enhancement by manuring, to increase yield, is as old as varietal selection by farmers. But modern agrochemicals (fertilizer, herbicides, pesticides) are barely older than modern plant breeding, which began about 150 years ago. They often complement the yield-enhancing properties of HYVs and make them pay better, but biological HYVs can also substitute for agrochemical paths to higher, more robust yields. Farmers gain if they can keep seeds that incorporate pest resistance or high response to plant nutrients, so avoiding loans at interest to buy pesticide or extra fertilizer. Poor farmers gain most, because it is harder for them to borrow or repay loans. Also, wrapping up fertility and pest resistance in the seed rather than in agrochemicals, if feasible, helps sustainable management of natural resources.

But reducing inorganic fertilizer use is harder than reducing pesticide use. Even the Chinese, with their long experience of organic farming, have increasingly used inorganics as new varieties demanded more from the soil. If such varieties are more pest-resistant, the farmer uses fewer chemicals; but if they are more responsive to nutrients, it may pay him/her to use more chemicals. Use of chemical fertilizers, with careful planning and control, will probably continue to increase in most places as plant varieties improve. Current low fertilizer levels in most of Africa make good agricultural yields or incomes very hard to attain. With careful management, especially the prevention of nitrate and nitrite pollution of drinking water, health gains will far exceed ill-effects, as the poor acquire more income and food.

Agrochemicals and HYVs, when wisely used, have proved their great potential for reducing rural poverty. However, the transition since 1850 from farmer-dominated to scientist-dominated bio-agricultural research, and since 1980 its increasing privatization, threaten to deny, to poor farmers and consumers, both gains from and control over technology. If technical progress excludes the poor, poverty will be little reduced even by improvements in assets, institutions and markets. IFAD has supported participatory research methods that have potential to remedy this problem (Box 4.3).

The pace of varietal improvement in main food staples has been dramatic. Yields were expanded by maize hybrids, and even more by semi-dwarf rice and wheat varieties that turned nutrients into grain rather than straw and which could be heavily fertilized without lodging. These varieties were enhanced to deal with an increasing range of agro-ecologies, water conditions and pests (and pest biotypes). The Green Revolution was the main source of a more-than-doubled aggregate food supply in Asia in 25 years, with only a 4% increase in the net cropped area.[8] Tripled wheat and rice yields in that period were common over large areas of reliably watered cropland, in the Indian and Pakistan Punjab, Central Luzon, and the Muda scheme in Malaysia. By the late 1980s well over 80% of rice and wheat was planted to these high-yielding varieties, though yield gains in unirrigated areas were generally much smaller.

The Green Revolution kept food prices down and employment up. If an area doubled grain yields in the 1970s, as many did, employment per hectare normally rose by 40%, plus a further 30% due to extra farm demand for rural non-farm products.[9] Higher employment-based incomes meant extra food entitlements and cheaper food staples. Further, agriculture in the 1970s comprised 25-40% of GDP in the countries with a Green Revolution, which contributed substantially to their GDP and consumption growth. This typically accounts for 30-50% of international differences in speed of poverty reduction.[10] Without the Green Revolution, the continuation of the near-stagnant yield trends of 1955-65 would have induced massive intensification of production and expansion into previously forested areas and other environmentally fragile lands,[11] encroaching upon their use by marginalized rural people who were often ethnic minorities.

Nevertheless, in the early days of the Green Revolution, some argued that, although large farmers gained, poor farmers lost. Some of the new varieties of grains prospered only with high levels of input and involved high risks that poor farmers could not easily afford or manage. But poor farmers learned to manage the new varieties;

Box 4.3: IFAD-supported work in the CGIAR: focusing on poorer areas can succeed

Since 1979 IFAD has committed USD 99 million to research programmes at CGIAR-centres, focusing on input-output relations in marginal rainfed environments; institutions and incentives to maximize returns and conservation for smallholder assets; and building local capacity for participatory research:

- In 1979-89 IFAD invested USD 8.32 million in a pioneering partnership of the International Centre for Agricultural Research in the Dry Areas (ICARDA) with a NARS (Egypt) that achieved big yield rises, and nutritional improvements, for faba beans.

- Research through ICARDA on wheat and barley for farming systems in the Near East and North Africa produced high-yielding varieties, tolerant to moisture stress, adopted by drought-prone farmers in t12 IFAD investment projects in the region in 1981-85.

- In 1980-86, IFAD financed USD 5.3 million of ICRISAT and International Centre for Tropical Agriculture research on maize-sorghum-legume mixed cropping, leading to sorghum varieties for highlands, including rotation with field beans, initially benefiting some 600 000 rainfed farmers.

- IFAD-supported research at ICRISAT led to ICPH-8, the first pigeon-pea hybrid specific to resource-poor conditions; improved lines led to 10-30% yield rises in eleven Asian countries.

- IFAD's USD 3.1 million leveraged USD 35 million donor support for International Institute of Tropical Agriculture work that developed successful biological control for the cassava mealy bug in sub-Saharan Africa. Millions of poor or near-poor African cassava growers benefited. Estimated benefit/cost ratio: over 200:1.

rural institutions learned to widen access to relevant inputs; and crop scientists developed new varieties such as IR-20 rice emphasizing robustness against main pests and yield enhancement even at low input levels.[12] The landless rural poor gained from HYV spread. First, nearby employment rose and stabilized across seasons and years, because HYV seeds tended to be planted in less risky irrigated lands and in the formerly slacker dry season, and from the early 1980s to be more robust than traditional varieties. Second, HYV production increased the availability and reduced the price of local staples, and reduced fluctuations. The poorest, who are usually net food buyers even in rural areas and the most likely to depend on hired work, gained much from such changes.[13]

Rural poverty in HYV areas fell owing to the use of HYVs. Yet even there, partly due to rising land values and returns, inequality seldom declined. Even in non-HYV areas of countries with substantial HYV spread, the landless poor sometimes gained more from cheaper food than they lost from reduced employment opportunities; and some non-HYV areas shared in the gains through labour migration for work in HYV areas.

The anti-poverty record of the Green Revolution was excellent. Nearby rural areas and cities in affected countries enjoyed the gains from the reduction of poverty.[14] However, yields have risen much more slowly in the 1990s than in the 1970s, though the timing of the downturn varied among regions and staples (Table 4.1). The anti-poverty gains from the Green Revolution in well-watered wheat and rice areas were restricted in their spread by five factors.

1. Public agricultural research expenditure has fallen sharply in Latin America and Africa, and international outlays have been static in real terms since 1982; and from the mid-1980s outlays have been heavily diverted from biological crop improvement to other goals.

2. Yield growth has been slower for maize millets, sorghum, cassava, yams and sweet potatoes – staples eaten and/or grown by most of Africa's rural poor, and by many of the poorest elsewhere – than for wheat and rice.

3. Yield has grown more slowly even for the same crop in sparsely watered areas and in Africa.

4. Even in lead areas, yield growth has been slower since the 1980s. It has become harder to achieve gains in biochemically-based yields. Conventional research in breeding remains essential, but is used increasingly for defensive purposes: to select varieties less for higher yield *per se*, than for resistance against new pest biotypes, avoidance of micronutrient depletion, and adaptation to drought and more saline water.

5. The response of employment to a given yield enhancement in Asia is now about one third of 1970s levels owing to the increasing use of tractors and herbicides. This reflects, in part, rising real wage-rates and the retreat of poverty – but also the remaining subsidies on tractors, agrochemicals, fuel, or credit to obtain them.

Some of these trends are responses to the steady fall in global staples prices relative to fertilizer costs. Some reflect normal diminishing returns, as irrigation, improved varieties, fertilizers and research go first to the most promising areas and crops. These tendencies always slow down technical change, and are offset by extra demand for staples due to population and income growth and the livestock revolution.[15]

This does not explain why biological advance slowed down in the 1990s in the developing world more than elsewhere; or why it is less employment-intensive now than in the 1970s and 1980s. Two major factors are less emphasis on public research and its increasing need to be defensive. The success of the Green Revolution relied on the combination of international research developing improved varieties suitable for many conditions, and national agricultural research systems (NARS) screening and crossing such varieties to suit local conditions. This partnership breaks down if NARS are denied funds, especially as the need for local adaptation of improved varieties for more diverse areas increases.

What are the priorities in bio-agricultural research to help the poor? Since the mid-1980s, CGIAR[16] has sharply reduced the proportion of its expenditure committed to breeding for yield and yield potential. This would seem to correspond to: many poor farmers' preferences; the need to concentrate effort in regions of high poverty, where crop yield is harder to increase; and the new development agenda, which stresses priorities other than yield or income, such as risk reduction, gender equity and concern for the environment. Yet staples yield and yield potential need increased emphasis, to attack rural poverty by expanding income based on employment, while the growth of the workforce continues.

The CGIAR and IFAD observe increasing concentration of low yields and poverty on ill-watered areas, usually under environmental stress, with increasingly hazardous life chances for some poor groups. Diverting research towards these areas requires participation with local farmers and research institutions, not uniform varieties of single crops to suit all circumstances. Where farmers are consulted about their priorities, they often select priorities other than yield.[17] From 1980 the CGIAR moved away from breeding for yield, especially yield potential, towards such issues as environment, gender and distribution, and towards less promising crops and areas.

Yet this has probably helped to reduce the growth in the yield of staples even for lead areas of the Green Revolution, and has been ineffective in delivering growth to some of the areas where the poor are increasingly concentrated. Farm and food yields and output-per-person have fallen since the late 1960s in much of Africa. Research must now be refocused on yield.

The funding of the ICRISAT indicated a shift towards poor people's regions and crops (millet, sorghum, chickpeas and pigeon peas). Returns on some of this investment have been substantial. In India and China some of the initially neglected rainfed areas now show better returns to research – and more poverty reduction per extra research dollar – than do irrigated lead areas. There are cases of successful outreach to smallholders through bio-agricultural research in non-lead areas, usually in conjunction with improved water management and, more rarely, in drought-prone areas with higher-yielding coarse staples.[18]

The case for expansion of research for poorer areas faces several problems.

• Crops such as sorghum are selected to thrive with low, fluctuating moisture and nutrient inputs; but harsh environments punish plants with high input requirements. It is unsure, slow and costly to seek high-yielding yet safe varieties by breeding within the genetic range of these crops.

• Using marginal, low-humus lands to grow high-yield, continuous crops may be unsustainable, for example if adequate nutrient replacement is uneconomic.

• While well-watered deltaic or irrigated areas have many common features, rainfed – and especially rain-underfed – areas are diverse. A particular HYV or hybrid is therefore likely to have a limited range of usefulness.

• Although conventional breeding in HYV lead areas brings dwindling yield gains, it remains vital to defend yields against new pests, water scarcity and micronutrient shortage. Yet given the high proportion of staples output and employment in lead areas, the sharp slowdown of yield growth – probably due in part to a shift of research priorities elsewhere – harms the poor.

• Finally, growth in yield everywhere depends ultimately on increasing yield potential.

How can one reconcile the needs of the poor in three areas of bio-agricultural research: helping neglected groups in diverse drylands; revive yield growth in the breadbasket areas; and developing new technology to raise yields and yield potentials?

Bio-agricultural innovation can aim to increase conversion efficiency; partition efficiency (the proportion of the plant or animal comprising food or other economically valuable materials); or extraction efficiency (the capacity of plant or animal to find and use up nutrients or water). Extraction efficiency for a nutrient is exhaustive and not sustainable in soils that release little to the plant. Partition efficiency has been pushed near the limit with wheat and rice, but can still be improved by breeding in some crops, and perhaps animals, for less favoured areas. But the main emphasis for bio-agricultural research in less-favoured areas has to be on improving plants' or animals' conversion efficiency – especially if they are to be sustainably manageable by the poor.

Improving conversion efficiency has proved difficult within the range of genetic material of some species concentrated in less favoured areas: species can be adapted to robustness but at the cost of high yields. The possibilities made available by the ability to insert genetic material into crop and livestock species are vital. Wide crosses can achieve this within conventional plant breeding. For example, West African red rice (*O. glaberrima*), adapted to upland and swamp farming in parts of West Africa, is robust, of short-duration and weed-competitive, but gives very low yields. It has successfully been crossed by the West Africa Rice Development Association (WARDA) with Asian paddy (*O. Sativa*). Another example is triticale, which Borlaug produced by crossing high-yielding wheat with cold-resistant rye, producing a new crop that has substantially raised food yields on millions of hectares in cold climates.

Successes such as these are rare, because these approaches are technically difficult, inaccurate as regards gene transfer, and slow. Most developing countries can apply and develop usable varieties from genetic modification (GM), but not all have the resources on their own to do so. Increasingly the findings of research into GM are locked into patents held by a small number of powerful research institutions. Some companies may occasionally provide free information to low-income regions. More often, GM research is steered towards fields where those companies can gather most profit.

Moreover, although food safety and biodiversity issues raised by GM are in principle the same as those raised by other biological or chemical routes to farm product improvement,[19] GM has been a catalyst in public concern about these issues. Genetically modified crops have the potential to reduce the poverty of the poor by increasing their supply of food from difficult land, but it is only with the full participation of civil society and institutions that the technology can be shared and applied. The effects of ignoring new approaches to poverty, nutrition, hunger and survival could be very damaging.

Micronutrient enrichment of food staples illustrates how GM is a powerful weapon in the armoury of breeding. The extent of the poor's micronutrient deficiencies and the resulting deaths are well documented: cures need not wait until much higher incomes permit all to escape the problem through diverse diets. Medium-term progress is possible through food fortification (especially with iodine). But iron anaemia has not retreated globally; anaemia and Vitamin A deficiency remains widespread. Conventional non-GM plant breeding can address some of these issues; for example, an experimental rice variety rich in iron and zinc, IR-68144, has induced a leap in serum ferritin in an anaemic population in the Philippines. However, only by GM, Vitamin A could have been introduced into the rice endosperm. Both breakthroughs have been made available free to developing-country research institutions. If successful varieties can be developed for relevant agro-ecologies, they will contribute towards saving millions from blindness, mostly among Asia's rural poor. Only bio-agricultural research currently promises micronutrient benefits of comparable speed, spread and cheapness. Nevertheless, as is the case for any new variety, there are risks. These should be identified and judged against the expected benefit.[20]

Bio-agricultural research for crop-water response is crucial to the rural poor, both because the poor are most harmed by tightening water scarcity, and because they are most exposed to risks of drought and least able to bear them. Already in 1972, the International Rice Research Institute (IRRI) identified moisture stress resistance as the main rice breeding priority. For the poor in many arid/semi-arid borderline areas, there is a critical research choice between two goals, neither so far successfully pursued[21] but both more credible with GM: breeding much better yields into robust but low-yielding millets, or better moisture stress resistance (especially capacity to delay anther formation if rain is late) into fragile but higher-yielding hybrid maize.

Increasing water scarcities require breeding (and managing) plants and animals for water economy – that is, high yield per litre, including capacity to return reusable water to ground or surface sources. As responses to water involve many genes, knowledge of specific gene functions in each host plant or animal type (functional genomics) is needed for major progress with transgenics. Timed response to local water conditions and needs is essential. These are issues for joint land-water and bio-agricultural design, management and research, not for isolated and unconnecting studies. Few crop research agencies outside CGIAR employ economists or hydrologists; if they do, specialists are seldom involved in decisions on research priorities.[22]

Bio-agricultural research and its extension are crucial to pest management. Pesticides can stimu-

late new, resistant pest biotypes, requiring ever more expenditure on ever less effective chemicals. This pesticide treadmill harms poor farmers most: from pesticide-polluted drinking water which poisons many farmers,[23] to endangering of economically important non-targeted species, including pest parasites. Bio-agricultural research can reduce pesticide contamination by plant selection and breeding, and can control pests by introduced parasites (Box 4.4).

Overwhelmingly the main source of biological pest control, even within integrated pest management (IPM), will continue to be selection and breeding of host crops and animals. This can become defensive, to limit harm from new pest biotypes. The rural poor, being most risk-averse and least able to buy the right pesticides on time, gain most from this. Rice bioscience had to shift from TN1, IR8 and others – winners of yield competitions that proved to be museums of insect [and other] pests – to today's rice varieties, which are better than traditional varieties at coping with the six major rice pests. A series of IRRI varieties were crucial in providing more stable resistance to emerging biotypes of brown planthopper. Uganda's success in breeding cassava resistant to the new (Ugv) strain of cassava mosaic virus combined frontier plant genetics, important national research, donor support and skilful local extension in reversing huge economic and nutritional losses from this strain.[24] In 1997-99 GM research proved necessary to provide resistance to devastating rice yellow mottle virus in West Africa.

While safer than pesticides, some aspects of pest-resistant plant breeding could be safer still. First, most new varieties unduly stimulate emergence of new, virulent pest biotypes. These can be reduced by seeking: moderate resistance that allows the pest to damage, say, 5-10% of plants; tolerance, aiming not to destroy or avoid pathogens but to permit affected plants to survive damage; or horizontal control, using several plant

---

Box 4.4: Integrated pest management in Indonesia

In the early 1980s, Indonesian lowland rice was infested with the brown planthopper *Nilaparvata lugens*. Farmers applied pesticides intensively and IRRI conducted trials to breed plant resistance, but the scale of the problem prevented small farmers from controlling it economically. In 1986, the government (supported by FAO) announced its IPM policy, prompted by evidence that pesticide use was no longer increasing rice yields, and, by destroying natural-enemy populations, was destabilizing production systems. The main components of IPM were: banning many insecticides; reducing or removing pesticide subsidies; and strengthening crop protection and related research and extension institutions. By 1992, over 150 000 farmers had been trained to observe and understand the local ecology of the planthopper and its natural enemies and to follow simple threshold rules.

During 1987-90 the quantity of pesticides used on rice was halved. Yields increased by 15%. Extra net profits were USD 218 per IPM-trained farmer per season. The government saved USD 120 million a year (85%) of subsidies, which was partly used for the IPM initiative. Several lessons can be extrapolated to other high-potential rice-producing areas:

- Successful IPM requires access to education.
- Understanding the ecology of the rice field is a critical issue for IPM training.
- IPM training instructors must be aware of the local farming experience in the region.
- IPM should be part of extension worker training; farmers are the best candidates to be IPM trainers.

In high-potential areas, management-intensive IPM techniques offer low external input (and consequently low material cost) options for poor farmers. Through training in IPM and involvement in local initiatives to eradicate pests, farmers learn that they can jointly manage and improve their environments. Reduced health risks improves the livelihoods of rural farmers and farmworkers.

Whatever the IPM methods, natural selection implies that pests hit back with new biotypes. Hence an essential long-run component of IPM is a steady succession of improved pest-resistant varieties, such as IR-26, IR-36, IR-64 and IR-76, against evolving biotypes of the brown planthopper. This requires NARS in the field, working with farmers, to test, adapt and sometimes cross these emerging varieties.

Sources: Kenmore 1991; van Veen 1997; USDA/ARS 1993; van de Fliert *et al.* 1995; Hazell *et al.* 2000.

---

genes against the pest instead of a high barrier from just one. Second, in some crops and areas, breeders' very success has seriously lowered the biodiversity of farm populations: good, pest-resistant, profitable species and varieties drive out others. Although individual modern varieties tend to be more resistant to main pest species than traditional varieties, a population dominated by one such variety can be very vulnerable to virulent new pathogens, as with the resurgence in 1972 of southern corn blight (*H. Maydis*) in the United States and tungro rice virus in the Philippines. In each case researchers developed new resistant varieties in only two seasons.

Delays in research on plant breeding can harm the poor. How long can the poor wait without severe harm? And will research respond to new biotypes of pest, when they attack the new maize hybrids spread in Ethiopia, or adapted HYV rice in West Africa?

Lessons for pest management are:
- to improve biodiversity of modern plant and animal populations;
- to improve and duplicate both *ex situ* collections and *in situ* 'gene parks', so that a wide range of varieties remains available as a source of genetic material;
- to shift bio-agricultural research and extension towards horizontal, tolerant and/or moderate-resistant varieties;
- to assist in this, to stimulate genomics research to find pest-related roles of host and non-host

genes, and to improve pest management via inter-species gene transfer;[25]

- to see host pest resistance and tolerance in the context of IPM, including biological controls and appropriate pesticides; and
- to improve farmer participation (in pest research as well as reporting new pest problems: see the IFAD-supported example in Box 4.5).

Agricultural research and extension should focus on varieties that both suit the conditions of small and labour-intensive farmers, and that demand and reward workers rather than tractor-owners or herbicide manufacturers. Raising demand for labour, especially in slack seasons, is most needed where the rural poor rely mainly on employment for income. The researchers' main task is to enhance and stabilize yield; but their varietal choice affects the demand for employment and whether farmers demand more labour or more machines or chemicals. Publicly subsidized

research should not develop or improve tools or varieties that, without raising yields, cut employment for poor hired workers. Research policy should normally shift farmers' inputs towards labour and away from other inputs.

Allocating funds within research or extension requires economic analysis, both of benefit-cost ratios and of the distribution of benefits. This is still rare in NARS. The persistent absence of congruence between allocation of research among products and their importance for employing and feeding the poor means that poor people's products, such as sorghum and goats, are still under-researched, especially in traditionally neglected regions. Such species as sorghum and goats are under-researched at national level because they are written off as low-potential, yet are often low-yielding partly because under-researched, despite high returns to research. Seeking congruence makes no sense if the under-researched crops or animals

---

Box 4.5: Collaboration between farmers and researchers

- **Better varieties can stimulate revival and adaptation of traditional pest management methods.** Worldwide, over USD 300 million of pigeon pea, mostly grown by poor farmers, are lost yearly to pod-borer. In India by 1993, costly chemical controls predominated. At a farmers' meeting organized by an NGO (Research in Environment, Education and Development Society), an elder showed the defunct method of shaking larvae gently on to a plastic sheet and feeding them to chickens. In 1997 IFAD supported evaluation in a 15 ha watershed by ICRISAT. By 1999 the method had spread to thousands of farmers. It is a key component of the IPM strategy for pigeon pea.

- **Farmers creolise research-station releases;** ICRISAT millets and International Centre for Maize and Wheat Improvement maizes are crossed with landraces to suit local conditions and preferences, even at the cost of losing hybrid vigour in maize, as in the late 1990s by smallholders in Chiapas, Mexico.

- **Farmers experiment with new plant types,** as with the spread of cocoa in Ghana, or new combinations of plant type and land management, as in the indigenous agricultural revolution of mangrove rice in Sierra Leone.

- In many countries, a small subset of farmers, often on frontiers among agroecologies – e.g. for rice in Bumpeh village, Sierra Leone – specialize in **selecting new varieties,** planting out in various conditions, and selling – with advice – to others, often from hundreds of miles away.

- With appropriate amendments (testing larger populations of fewer alternative varieties), introducing collaborative even more than consultative **farmer participation** into **breeding staples** improves returns, biodiversity, speed and local relevance, especially in drier areas, as with rice in India and beans for women farmers in Rwanda.

- Where there is something worth extending, formal extension has substantial, documented returns. But farmers often get **bio-agricultural advice** from other farmers and/or migrants.

Sources: ICRISAT 2000: 5-6; Bellon and Risopoulos 1999; Hill 1957; Richards 1985; Witcombe 2000; Witcombe *et al.* 2000a, 2000b; Virk *et al.* 2000; Sperling and Berkowitz 1994; Evenson 1999; 2000: 264.

are unpromising for research; but new research methods offer new hopes. Even now, in Pakistan, if research outlays were in proportion to outputs, poor farmers' benefits would rise significantly.[26]

What about regional congruence? Current under-emphasis on some rainfed or less-developed regions harms output and efficiency, as well as the poor. In China, returns to extra agricultural research and development in the poorest (Western) region are 15% above the (already high) country average, and 140 people are brought out of poverty per 100 000 yuan of extra research investment, as against 34 nationally. In India in 1994, the impact of extra research on agricultural production in the sixth most fertile of 12 rainfed regions is double the impact in irrigated areas, and each million rupees of extra research investment takes 13 people out of poverty annually, as against one.[27]

The IRRI-supported Eastern India Rainfed Rice Project involved 'local scientists who had never conducted on-farm research' in learning as well as teaching improved management practices and farming systems in areas previously 'all but overlooked by advances in rice science'. Since 1996 these six States have produced all India's extra rice production, by shifting resources to the neglected area with future potential; better rice varieties, robust in rainfed conditions; and participatory research.[28] Box 4.5 provides evidence of the gains from linking formal research to farmers' own methods and experiments.

Farmer-researcher collaboration is needed to remedy another serious lack of congruence. Of formal non-commercial pest-control research, well below 10% goes to countering weeds, birds and rats. Yet these probably cause over half the poor's crop losses. A side-effect is that controls are over-dependent on agrochemicals. Only a large new research thrust, by farmers and formal systems together, can remedy this.

Participation is the ally, not the enemy, of formal research in benefiting farmers. But farmers are not the same as the rural poor in needs, tastes or preferences. Both participatory and conventional research give little say – less than most market research and much less than market demand or political action – to non-farmer food consumers or workers, or even tiny farmers who buy most of their food. Where such people comprise most of the poor, neither participatory nor top-down research, in current form, sufficiently involves the poor as agents.

Nevertheless, farmer participation in agricultural research usually raises poor people's welfare, for example, by stimulating choices that deal effectively with local problems, spread labour peaks, cut risks and improve or cheapen food. That impact will improve if indigenous research and extension are better integrated with the formal system. Issues relating to local farmers' priorities are still seldom considered in experimental design, especially in NARS; yet they are crucial, especially for the poor on marginal lands, in risk diffusion and labour and food planning.

IMPROVED LAND MANAGEMENT TECHNOLOGY (ILMT): LAND AS A NATURAL RESOURCE

ILMT is sorely needed to raise or maintain the quality of natural resources. Examples include range management to reduce overgrazing; the restoration of soil humus through the application of composts, rotational grazing, crop rotation, agroforestry[29] and fallow systems; land reclamation; and earth or vegetative barriers against erosion. ILMT can cut serious losses of farmland, which in developing countries around 1970 amounted to 200-300 000 ha a year from salinity and waterlogging alone, plus large areas to urban expansion. As for the loss of land quality, by 1990 about one fifth of land in developing countries (excluding wastelands) was affected by soil erosion or nutrient loss, two thirds of it badly enough to destroy or greatly reduce land usefulness for agricultural production. Every year the average cropped hectare in Africa loses over 30 kg of nitrogen, phosphorus and potassium. Land degradation in the late 1980s cost 3% of GDP each year in Java, 4-16% of agricultural GDP in Mali, and 10% of annual agricultural production in Costa Rica. Such estimates are controversial and may be somewhat too high, but the poor lose proportionately more, having fewer options or defences and being concentrated on poorest quality land. Land degradation is worst in hotspots, such as the foothills of the Himalayas, sloping areas in Southern China, South-East Asia, and the Andes, forest margins of East Asia and the Amazon, rangelands in Africa and West and Central Asia, and the Sahel.[30]

Bio-agricultural research seldom provides much of a remedy for this on its own. That makes a powerful case for ILMT. But unlike the adoption of fertilizer, new varieties, or many crops, ILMT innovation normally requires extra fixed capital and a time lag before benefits gradually accrue, which is not an attractive option for poor farmers. The rural poor may thus be slow to embrace ILMT. They need their scanty income for consumables now; they cannot afford sacrifices to invest in long-term land stability, and have more difficulty in borrowing money, especially for ILMT with perhaps small and distant returns. Moreover, poor rural people often interact with land in ways that give few incentives for long-sighted management: as labourers or short-term tenants, often with little security, supervision or extension.

ILMT is essential to prevent land degradation from threatening the poor's chances to improve employment incomes and food entitlements from the dwindling land remaining. However, the cause of ILMT is ill served by claims of large or fast gains in yields, employment, or the income of the poor, especially through low-external-input farming; because there is a weak empirical base for such claims.

Farmers know the problems of land degradation, but are reluctant to allocate resources with high opportunity costs for remote, uncertain or insecure benefits.[31] In India ILMT investments decrease where time spent in other activities has higher returns, or benefits are vulnerable to water use or drainage upstream – or insecure land tenure, as in Morocco, Mali, Tanzania, Ethiopia and Ecuador. There is much evidence that farmers take sensible conservation measures if they pay, limiting overgrazing[32] and maintaining forest islands and galleries.[33] The task is to ensure that incentives and institutions stimulate conservationist ILMTs.

To attract poor farmers, ILMT should not conserve at the expense of production, and preferably should itself be productive (for example, construction of vegetative bunds which provide fodder).[34] Pure conservation, even by simple methods, is seldom attractive to farmers.[35,36] Further, adoption of new techniques must suit the timed labour availability of the household (Box 4.6), and take

---

Box 4.6: Labour availability and new technology in land management/conservation

Timing construction to coincide with the slack season is desirable where feasible (when the soil is not too wet, hard or compacted) and if local labour remains available. However, vegetative barriers must usually be planted at the start of the rains. In the slack season many men in Africa migrate for funerals or weddings, or to seek work in the mines.

Male migration, which is often a consequence of past land degradation, means that many smallholder households become female-headed (30% in Malawi). Women have difficulty in finding replacement heavy labour, for example, to make stone bunds. In the Calicanto watershed, Bolivia, widespread migration to non-farm work, while desirable to raise and stabilize labour incomes, impeded labour availability for ILMT works. Research and extension should examine timing and needs, and match labour to techniques.

Sources: IFAD 1992b; Mangisoni and Phiri 1996; Zimmerer 1993; Reij *et al.* 1996; Chaker *et al.* 1996; Shaka *et al.* 1996.

account of other needs. Indian small farmers favoured boundary bunds over contour bunds as they could be used to demarcate property.[37]

Many disincentives to conservation by ILMT arise from public policy. Deforestation and use of lands for possibly unsustainable cropping in north-west Brazil have been stimulated by tax incentives and publicly subsidized roads.[38] Conservation activities are impeded if a farmer must share benefits with others, and institutions to ensure shared effort are weak, inequitable or costly to engage with; projects concentrating on individual users are more successful than wider efforts.[39]

ILMT and conservation seek to use labour to save land, but indigenous ILMT typically uses little labour. Farmers are not interested in a more labour-intensive approach proposed from outside. They see more rewarding uses for their time and need the income from labour quickly. But where a proposed new ILMT is moderately rewarding, safe and swift, farmers, including poor ones, use it – as in Ethiopia, but only where it does not reduce current yield, unless they have low discount rates or special incentives.[40] Most successfully extended ILMTs for conservation involve biological intervention enabling some swift, direct gain to be achieved as well, such as vetiver hedge barriers to erosion, and eucalyptus.

Conversely, inducing conservation ILMT by subsidy has sometimes diverted farmers' and public resources from better uses, whether because the works would have been done anyway or because they are not worth doing.[41] It makes sense to subsidize people to carry out ILMT conservation only if social benefits are sufficiently high relative to cost, while benefits to private conservation investors are not, except with the subsidy. This in turn requires at least one of three things. Net benefits, accruing to and not recoverable from other people, may be sufficiently large. Future losses, risks or thresholds, in the absence of conservation,

may be insufficiently discounted, because poverty requires high preference for quick income, or because of high credit costs. Or there may be distributional gains for the poor from the conservation ILMT not readily achieved otherwise.

Conservation tillage (CT)

This involves reducing or eliminating ploughing, resulting in a protective mulch on the soil surface (the residues from previous crops). This protects soil from wind and rain erosion, encourages water percolation, and improves the physical and chemical characteristics of the soil by retaining more soil organic matter, moisture and nitrogen. Yields may be increased slightly, but the main benefit is reduced land preparation costs.[42] However, CT applies only to soils that do not become too hard to be sown without first ploughing or hoeing. CT illustrates the complementary relationship between so-called low-external-input farming and external inputs. For many lighter textured soils, conventional tillage is mainly a means of weed control. Replacing it with CT may require the application of herbicides, especially in the first year or two without ploughing. For CT to be really attractive to farmers, yields should also increase. This can be achieved by introducing leguminous cover crops into the rotation, extra mulch or extra inorganic fertilizer.

In Latin America, the Latin American Conservation Agriculture Network (RELACO), a network promoting CT, was established in 1992. By 1998 more than 14 million hectares were under CT, with seed planted by a specially designed chisel plough which cut the costs of land preparation (Box 4.7, Table 1). Production costs per hectare of soybeans could be cut by USD 12 million in Argentina and USD 5 million in Brazil.[43] But, since distribution of cropland there is very unequal, most cost-cutting would benefit large, non-poor farmers. Much, too, would correspond to reduced demand for employment of very poor tillage workers: note the

Box 4.7: Conservation tillage in Chiapas, Mexico and Ghana

On the steep hillsides of Chiapas, Mexico, soil degradation is exacerbated by intensive maize and bean cropping to meet most local demand for food (though perennials such as coffee can improve matters). Conservation tillage offers promise. It requires farmers to use the residues of previous crops as protective mulch for soil; to minimize tillage, to avoid destroying the mulch; and to replace manual weed control with herbicides. CT also conserves water (reducing risk from drought) and reduces burning of crop residues and thus risk of forest fires. Net returns are higher when both the low tillage and mulch components of CT are practised, as are labour productivity and returns per day (Table 1). CT seems efficient while promoting sustainability and food security.

Table 1: Budgets for maize-bean intercropping, 1993 summer cycle, Motozintla, Chiapas

	Non-adopters	Mulch only	No-tillage only	Mulch and no-tillage
Gross benefit mxUSD/ha	1953	1941	1971	2210
Total var. cost USD/ha, inputs + labour	1291	1304	1227	1242
Total inputs mxUSD/ha	358	370	450	446
Total labour mxUSD/ha	933	934	777	796
Total fixed costs	326	539	326	539
Net benefit mxUSD/ha	336	99	418	428
Labour productivity (kg maize/day)	28.0	28.5	32.8	36.1
Return/day (mxUSD)	13.6	11.1	15.4	15.4

Source: Erenstein and Iniguez 1997.

In much of Ghana, slash-and-burn methods with traditional tillage are practised. This loses mulch and requires long fallow periods to allow for full land regeneration. These become less affordable as person/land ratios rise and shortening fallows degrade the land. Strategy to deal with this may include shifting to CT, with higher initial costs (and, even with hand weeding, some extra chemical inputs), but higher profits. This almost certainly permits shorter sustainable fallows. Labour costs (and incomes) are not recorded separately, but a fall might harm some of the poor.

Table 2: Costs and returns for three tillage systems in Ghana, 1997

Treatment	Variable costs (USD /ha)	Net profit	
		USD /ha	%
Slash and burn	56.25	360	100
Roundup + hand weeding	76.5	567	158
Roundup + Lasso + Atrazine	85.75	713	198

Source: Hazell et al., 2000, citing Ghana Crop Research Institute.

big fall in labour costs (employment income) from CT in, Ghana in Box 4.7. Unless land is fairly equally distributed and few labourers are landless, the poverty impact from CT in such conditions is at best dubious. It would be more appropriate in areas where land is more equally distributed and

where the proportion of cheap staples grown using CT would be higher, such as in parts of Africa.

Box 4.7, Table 2, shows the variable costs and profit of maize production under three tillage systems in 32 comparison plots. Farm income rises, and as less labour is used, returns per labour day rise too; but the poorest may lose hired work. However, heavy weed growth is usually transient and herbicide and spraying costs fall with time. CT offers the advantage of early planting: farmers do not have to wait for the rain to soften the soil prior to ploughing. Nevertheless, conservation tillage on African smallholdings remains constrained by lack of credit and the absence of commercial input suppliers of herbicides. Other constraints relate to difficulties in maintaining the surface mulch due to grazing; fast breakdown of organic matter; the use of crop residues for fuel; and consumption by termites.[44]

Land reclamation

Two main forms of land loss seriously harm the rural poor. In lowland irrigated regions, salinity has caused large losses of prime farmland. Each year, globally, land abandoned due to salinity is about equal to land developed for irrigation.[45] The other source of loss is erosion, especially on slopes in arid and semi-arid areas, and above all in Africa, where in 1992, 4% of the area under vegetation was seriously degraded and 18% lightly degraded – about half of this due to overgrazing.[46]

Degradation of such lands does not reflect ignorance or recklessness, but lack of incentives and the indifference of institutions serving the farmers. Some land reclamation might indeed boost farm incomes and productivity.

It is difficult, expensive and often slow to improve saline or waterlogged land. Labour-intensive reclamation is more pro-poor, but viable only on suitable terrain, and with high population densities. Techniques for reclaiming lands commonly include moving soil and installing drainage pipes. Mulching to modify the hydraulic properties at the soil surface can address secondary salinization. Ploughing, with tractors or livestock-pulling wooden ploughs that can cultivate to 30 cm, can rehabilitate abandoned soils.[47] More employment-generating reclamation practices include freshwater harvesting from ponds that form in gullies by constructing simple earth check dams, digging pits and refilling with the same soil, planting vegetative barriers with leguminous species, and afforestation with salt-tolerant species.

These practices are most relevant to the rural poor, who lack mechanized equipment, especially as establishing permanent vegetative cover with salt-tolerant trees and grasses provides income (firewood and fodder) as well as rehabilitating saline lands. The grasses provide some income for the poor while the trees grow (though the pool's access to the trees needs to be assured). In India, *prospis*, *acacia* and *casuarina* are useful trees and produce organic matter that enhances soil productivity. Soil pH fell (10.3 to 8.9 after six years) when salt-tolerant grasses were intercropped. *Prospis* and grass grown together, producing poles, woodfuel and fodder crops, provided a net income of Rs. 4866 per farmer.[48] However, income and employment levels for the poor after reclamation seldom approach those before the land became saline, except from Casuarina. Box 4.8 highlights IFAD's experience with reducing soil salinity in the North China Plain (Hebei Agricultural Development Project), combining mechanized and labour-intensive techniques.

Labour-intensive reclamation and subsequent maintenance techniques are usually more successful in reclaiming overgrazed or eroded than saline lands, but working populations tend to be sparser and more seasonal. Such techniques include earth or stone contour bunds; water harvesting; digging and refilling pits; and planting appropriate vegetative erosion barriers or species that can compete successfully with the thorn acacia which otherwise makes the areas ungrazable. Contour earth bunds were promoted by colonial extension officers in Western India for decades, but seldom worked well. Success depends on all, or almost all, farmers maintaining their part of the bund; that is, on high levels of collective action. How can benefits to secure

---

Box 4.8: Community-led land reclamation efforts in China

IFAD responded to a soil salinity problem in the North China Plain by supporting the *Hebei Agricultural Development Project* (1982-89). The soils of Quzhou and Nanpi, the counties where the project operated, are coarse, light silt loams, well suited to maize, wheat and cotton when adequately drained. However, years of irrigation and poor drainage made about half the farmland in the counties saline enough to inhibit agricultural productivity, particularly for the rural poor, who live on the most marginal lands.

Low-cost labour-intensive technologies were largely used to reclaim saline lands, though tractors were used at times. Drainage works to lower the water-table and reduce surface pooling of stagnant water involved excavating 17.6 million m^3 for drainage systems by manual labour, far surpassing targets. Land levelling of 11 000 ha allowed salt to be leached from soils, simplifying planting. Most tree-planting was less successful (propagation was inhibited by residual salt) but some community orchards were successfully established, providing nutritional and income gains.

Conditions improved greatly during the project. Landholdings increased, as did production of wheat, cotton and maize. Salinity greatly decreased and seemed likely to stay low, although continued monitoring and evaluation by the communities affected was a key requirement for long-term sustainability. Large labour requirements associated with the project worked against households with low adult/child ratios and unable to diversify. The communal philosophy of assisting neighbours and extended family alleviated some of the emerging disparity. The economic rate of return for the project was 19%; 23 000 ha of land were reclaimed through the project and 35 200 households lifted from poverty.

Source: IFAD data and project documents.

---

this be made faster, clearer, less unequal? Stone bunds require advance capital commitment and yield no obvious income. Vegetative barriers are more attractive to the poor, yielding quicker direct income (fodder) and, if not in competition with main crops, net benefits from nutrient cycling, and sometimes nitrogen fixation. Hedgerows, as in IFAD's East Java Rainfed Agriculture Project, have been called 'the most promising technique for soil and water conservation'. Vetiver, widely used traditionally, has advantages that assist extension: breaches are less erosive than in earth or stone bund, maintenance is light and the crop is drought-resistant and provides thatching, mulch or fodder. In Katsina State, Nigeria, vetiver reduced erosion both in boundary hedgerows and as grass contour strips. Where erosion has gone too far, humus and water management, building on traditional techniques, can reclaim some land (Box 4.9).[49]

Several points about these small-scale, locally based ILMT techniques should be noted.

- They tend to succeed with low-input techniques in part of the approach only because of high-input techniques elsewhere (manure and/or mulch with fertilizers, labour-intensive reclamation with initial bulldozing).

- They often achieve good results for the intended conservation aims, but, in contrast to many improved plant or animal varieties, yield or output growth is localized, small or doubtful (Box 4.8 may illustrate an exception).

- Some current income gain, for example from vetiver as fodder, is required to provide an incentive to expand the scope of what are, after all, usually familiar methods.

- Pro-poor distribution of benefit is not automatic; conservation should not be about rich farmers securing cheap gains by mobilizing poor clients who gain nothing.

- IFAD experience suggests that ILMT gains are often sustainable only if followed up with means, such as herd taxes, to discourage overgrazing of commons or situations where 'the better-off herders... graze their cattle on the common lands [and later move them to] well-fenced individual plots'.[50]

- Without good crop and animal varieties, poor farmers seldom find it pays to divert resources to

---

Box 4.9: Land reclamation through soil and water conservation, Burkina Faso and Niger

Where large-scale erosion control had failed, the IFAD-funded Special Programme for Soil and Water Conservation provided current income, while improving or reclaiming about 5 800 ha of abandoned and degraded lands on the farms of some 6 000 households in 77 villages, through *tassas* (called *zaï* in Burkina Faso). The soils had been sealed by a thin crust, hardened by wind and water, preventing infiltration by water. Such areas are usually abandoned, without vegetation, scattered with outcroppings of iron crust. They are prime sites for surface erosion. *Tassas* are 20-30 cm dug holes, filled with manure since the soils normally lack organic matter. This also promotes termites in the dry season, further enhancing infiltration. When it rains, the holes fill with water and farmers then plant millet or sorghum. *Tassas* are normally used with bunds from stones that farmers remove from fields for planting. These methods were learned by farmers of Illéla on a visit to Yatenga in Burkina Faso where, on the central plateau alone, some 100 000 ha have been restored – each now producing some 700-1 000 kg of cereal per year. Yields of millet without *tassas*, demi-lunes and bunds are 150-300 kg/ha. They rise to 400 kg with manure in a poor rainfall year, and 700-1 000 kg/ha in a good year. Fertilizer raises yields to 650 kg/ha in poor years and 1 400-1 500 kg/ha in good ones.

Tassas have allowed the region to attain average millet yields of 480 kg/ha, reaching 700 kg/ha with fertilizer (still uncommon). Fields of similar quality without *tassas* produced only 130 kg/ha. Food availability in participating households rose by 20-40%, depending on local rainfall. The average family in Burkina Faso and Niger using these technologies shifted from an annual cereal deficit of 644 kg (six and a half months of food shortage) to a surplus of 153 kg.

Tassas are best suited to landholdings with family labour, or where workers can be hired. The technique has spawned a network of young day-labourers who have mastered it. Rather than migrating, they move among villages to satisfy farmers' growing demands. Some farmers, recognizing potential profits from *tassas* early, bought back land. Three factors were key to developing and disseminating the technology:

(1) an action-research approach that is flexible, open to farmer initiatives, and conducive to negotiation;

(2) a technology that is quick, simple, compatible with existing cropping systems, and replicable; and

(3) a technological package that can adjust to the changing local context.

Source: Pretty 2000, citing Mascaretti, pers. comm.; Reij 1996; Hassan 1996; IFAD project documents.

---

wide-scale, long-term conservation and reclamation. Yet without these, the land to support better varieties may continue to degrade.

• There must be progress on research on ILMT and bio-agricultural research together for either to succeed.

WATER TECHNOLOGY AND THE POOR

The World Bank[51] has identified the main single environmental problem for the poor, alongside water quality, as water depletion, particularly in the context of scientific consensus on global warming, with less reliable rainfall and higher evapotranspiration. Technical progress in farming since the mid-1960s dramatically cut rural poverty where there had usually been earlier improved water control. For two millennia, the rural poor have reached sustainable prosperity, if at all, mainly by applying known innovations that enhance water reliability and control, or through biological inventions which allow swift yield-enhancement in already well-watered areas. Rapid poverty reduction has long eluded people in large semi-arid tracts, especially in Africa. Even if transgenics bring gains in drought tolerance, without more water for crops and animals, rapid reduction in poverty will be difficult to achieve.

Technology can promote better plant types that raise each litre's output or poverty impact; ILMT is often inseparable from water conservation and development (Box 4.10). Raising water-use efficiency (WUE) is possible: a good benchmark is 50%, but typically only 40% is achieved (60% of field water fails to reach the crop root zone), mainly due

---

Box 4.10: Water efficiency: conveyance, field, use; economic and social

Water engineers concentrate on **water-use efficiency** (WUE), i.e. the proportion of irrigation system water that reaches the crop root zone. **Conveyance efficiency** (CE) is the proportion of irrigation system water that reaches cropped fields and **field efficiency** (FE) is the proportion of water applied to the field that reaches the cropped zone: so WUE = CE x FE. Even technically, these are not the only determinants of **economic efficiency of water** (EEW). The worth of a given FE depends on whether the water reaches, and is drained from, the root zone at the right times; and on how much of the water that does is absorbed by the crop, transpired to manage moisture stress, or diverted to weeds. The worth of a given CE depends on the quality (non-pollution) of the water before and after conveyance.

EEW is the value added to output by the water, as a proportion of the extra cost incurred to obtain it. WUE can come at too high a cost, actually cutting EEW; for example, sprinklers usually show higher WUE than gravity systems, but are more maintenance-intensive. Excessive emphasis on WUE in Zimbabwe has led to costly, possibly unsustainable, schemes (Heinemann pers. comm.).

Private and social EEW can differ greatly if some costs or benefits of water accrue not to the user but to the taxpayer, or to downstream free-riders – or victims, if water becomes polluted on its travels, or causes salinity or flooding due to poor drainage. Private and social EEW are enhanced by growing crops with higher returns to water. Finally, even if WUE, private and social EEW all improve, some poor water users might lose. Some means to improvement, such as centre-pivot systems, save water by using much capital not accessible to poorer farmers – who thereby become less able to compete – and displace poor workers.

So in **principle** more FE or CE need not raise WUE; more WUE need not raise private EEW; more private EEW need not imply more social EEW; and more social EEW might not help the poor. All these need checking. Yet **in practice** the big technical inefficiencies suggested by disparities in WUE – together with the known under-performance, mismanagement and sometimes corruption of some big irrigation systems – suggest scope for increasing WUE compatibly with gains in EEW and equity alike. This suggests focusing on irrigation techniques and technologies to increase WUE. Changed irrigation frequency and volume, rotational irrigation, cross-bunding, new drainage systems, canal lining, and other methods need evaluation. These complement bioagronomic ways to improve WUE, e.g. changing crops, varieties, or timings of operations, or improving weed control (Joshi and Singh 1994), or to improve CE, e.g. by control of water hyacinth in canals.

---

to spillage, leakage, infiltration and evaporation.[52] In sub-Saharan Africa WUEs are normally around 20-30%.[53] Conveyance efficiency (CE) can also be raised by reducing seepage (for example, through unlined or badly maintained canals), percolation and evaporation (Box 4.10).

If prices, institutions or environment[54] are not too hostile, water management techniques can improve WUE, raise economic efficiency of water and help the poor. Canal lining reduces seepage and leakage, raising WUE and CE respectively by 5-10%.[55] But lining field canals may not reward farmers; or appropriate materials, hired skills, or extension may not be available. However, seepage, evaporation and percolation are also due to excess water storage in the field. Poor farmers can

address this problem by irrigating less frequently and making the best use of rains. Intermittent flooding in Asian paddies can reduce water requirements by about 40% with no significant decline in yields. However, while a farmer who cuts seepage and percolation enjoys more water, farmers downstream may then get less. In Northern Pakistan, overall WUE is only 30% due to mountains and coarse soil, but CE is 90% since downstream users benefit. In this case, greater upstream WUE – through technical progress or by water pricing – could cut CE, and thus water downstream.[56]

High evapotranspiration inevitably opens a gap between WUE and the benefit to the farmer in hot climates, but can sometimes be cut by cost-effective techniques that create employment. Covering reservoir surfaces is expensive, but there are alternatives. The irrigated area of Ethiopia might rise 20-40% if irrigation sources are used fully at night and weekends.[57] Any measure which reduces exposure time to atmosphere, or mean exposure temperature of irrigation water, reduces evaporation: for example, pipes to convey water, or tubewell irrigation. In the North China Plain piping irrigation water results in 90% CE, compared with 50-60% for earth canals.[58]

However, it is costly capital, rather than (poor people's) employment, that is saving the water. How accessible are such techniques for the rural poor? Sprinkler irrigation allows water to be applied gradually to large areas of crop. This commonly leads to 70-80% WUE,[59] but usually at high capital cost for installation and spares. Though still expensive, lower-cost, easy-maintenance gravity-fed sprinkler systems proved attractive to some poor farmers in Lesotho. Drip irrigation often involves underground pipes, applying water direct to the root zone. This can give the same potato yield as furrow irrigation with half the water, and in Israel cut water use per hectare by one third. Nutrients can be applied to the crop with the water. Since drip irrigation wets the soil only in the root zones, access to the field is easier. Again, this is capital-intensive and costly per unit of water saved. IFAD has encouraged its use in Egypt, where conventional ways to raise WUE are unattractive to farmers due to lack of direct irrigation charges. In Israel and Jordan, up to 60% of irrigated area has been converted to drip systems. Tubewell irrigation, though sometimes more expensive than canal irrigation, can work more in favour of the poor due to its modularity which enables water to be more easily controlled. Poor farmers can access tubewells via markets; this gives tubewell owners direct incentives to raise CE, provided there is little distance between tubewell and field compared with previous water sources.[60]

While such techniques suit middle-income or labour-scarce environments, more labour-intensive methods would be more cost-effective to reduce poverty in the poorest regions, which often have labour surpluses, at least in slack seasons. But invention and innovation in irrigation techniques and water management that replace water use with employment are scarce and slow owing to lack of water use and management research resources, their weak integration with crop research and with farmers, and their relative neglect of simple gravity-flow methods. Cross-bunding is an obvious simple option. Less well-known is porous pot irrigation – an affordable, efficient method which has spread from North Africa to other countries. It involves a series of interconnected unglazed pots buried in the soil with openings exposed. Seeds are planted round the pots, which are then filled with water. As with drip irrigation, water is applied to the plants very slowly. The technique is best suited to those with low opportunity-cost of labour, such as the rural poor: small farmers and family artisans who make the pots.[61]

New techniques are also relevant to improving WUE where alternatives are sought to desubsidizing irrigation and drinking water, which, while desirable, is sometimes not politically, or occasionally even technically, feasible.[62] Relevant techniques include computer-aided scheduling of water allocation, based on forecast needs allowing for weather, crop-water requirements and area cultivated, as in the Mae Klong scheme in Thailand. Such techniques will improve and spread as information technology gets cheaper. Yet small farmers may be disadvantaged unless they can reap economies of scale, access equipment and software, obtain information and hire expertise through an appropriate water users' group. The Bali Irrigation Project illustrates the need to involve such groups in innovation and technical choice. External agents tried to replace traditional weirs with structures that could vary distribution according to crop-water requirements. However, the technology was inappropriate to local needs and institutions, and drew management responsibility away from the water users' groups.[63]

Recycling can substantially improve conveyance efficiency. The Fayoum system in Egypt has WUE of over 60% because water unused by the crops, which seeps into the groundwater, is pumped up, increasing water availability on-site. Also downstream cultivators can collect run-off or pump groundwater which has resulted from low WUE up-stream. Conjunctive use of ground and surface water aims to optimize their joint use over time; one approach is to pump groundwater only in dry periods, and surface irrigation otherwise. In India, in theory, groundwater should normally be used for crops only from January to May, and rains plus surface irrigation should suffice at other times, especially for paddy.[64] But such rules of thumb are hard to enforce given power-structures, externalities,[65] downstream effects and sometimes corruption. They also allow too little for large local and short-term temporal variation in crop and other water uses and availabilities, in evapotranspiration rates, in preferences and costs, and in the needs of poor water users, who are less able to adapt to water failure or the resulting shortage of food or of employment income.[66]

There are many ways to improve the efficiency of both irrigation and drinking water delivery and use. The best way forward is often to work in partnership by combining rural people's own systems with technical expertise. This is shown by uses of water harvesting, sandrivers, valley-bottom systems such as *fadama* in Nigeria, and stream diversion methods such as *molapo* in Botswana. These systems were discovered by local farmers themselves, and are easily maintained by them. But without formal research and innovation, such systems spread and improve too slowly to reduce poverty enough. Most traditional methods have little application (without external scientific inputs) to rural management of drinking water, but bring dirty and dangerous water, stress and frequent water shortages.

What can water technology do to help eliminate rural poverty and address the problem of declining natural resources? There is much to be done to improve adequate rural drinking water for domestic and farm use. Old irrigation systems decline, and in large areas the lack of water precludes much benefit from improved seeds. Better plant and animal varieties have raised water demand by increasing the returns to extra water in well-watered areas, while doing little for parched areas. Rural water demand has also risen along with income, the livestock revolution with its higher grain requirements, and population. These pressures will continue, probably exacerbated by global warming. In spite of pressure to reduce agriculture's share in water use, water technology can be applied to offset these effects and reduce rural poverty.

More research is needed in developing countries on sustainable water use and supplementary systems, and for better integration of both with farmers' own techniques and preferences, and with bio-agricultural research. Discovery in water technology has been slow, despite huge growth in irrigated area in 1950-90. It is unlikely that the problems of water can be resolved without faster technical progress in farm water location, extraction, recycling and drainage.

The World Water Council[67] sets out the urgent case and priorities for expanded water research funding for the CGIAR and nationally. The special water needs of the rural poor must be integrated into such research. Infant mortality for the rural poor is much higher than for the urban poor. Such deaths are swollen by disease due to dirty water. The poor's productive progress is frustrated by lack of water control. Their main resource, labour, can earn incomes by constructing better water systems, but only if appropriate research choices are made early.

More controversial is the need for much more irrigation, including major schemes, in sub-Saharan Africa. Yields, income and employment from most unirrigated areas, especially for main staples, have stagnated or fallen for three decades, and, without dramatic breakthroughs in suitable plant varieties, are unlikely to increase fast enough to make an impression on extensive rural poverty. Yet only 1-5% of African cropland is irrigated (depending on how we classify traditional water management) as against 30-35% in Asia. Typically yields and farm incomes per hectare are between two and four times higher on irrigated land, and their growth has been far faster.

Africa's low irrigation levels are in part due to donors' change in support to farmer-managed schemes, which, although beneficial, have lower outreach and may divert from large schemes. Some of these have been partly successful: Mwea in Kenya, Gezira and Managil in The Sudan. However, from the costly failures of the 1970s, especially in West Africa, the World Bank, IFAD and others concluded that 'large-scale projects have not yielded the expected results and did not principally benefit [the poor;] small-scale farmer-managed irrigation [is] more suited to their needs'. The 14 IFAD-supported projects in Eastern and Southern Africa with 'important water management components aim to support irrigated production on about 40 000 ha, about evenly divided between rehabilitation and improvement of existing farmer-managed schemes and construction of new ones'. Capital costs were USD 3 000 per hectare[68] – far below the USD 8 300 per hectare cost of major schemes (Box 3.10). However, even a large and determined donor such as IFAD over several years could support irrigation for only 30 000-60 000 smallholders, in this region with tens of millions, overwhelmingly unirrigated. 'Small on-farm irrigation only' will not greatly dent African rural poverty.

Large-scale irrigation techniques in Africa have faced many problems:
- high construction costs due to monopolistic and sometimes corrupt foreign contractors;
- settlement, not of smallholders, but of capital-intensive, inexperienced government clients;
- top-down imposition of cropping patterns;
- uncompetitive farming systems, with water and (inappropriate) crops heavily subsidized at the expense of other areas (for example, irrigated rice vs. rainfed beverage crops in West Africa);
- weak and badly maintained distribution systems, linked to spreading water-borne diseases; and
- weak marketing and extension arrangements.

Though returns to irrigation in Africa have been improving (Box 3.10), partly because market distortions are much less, not all these issues have been fully addressed. Large-scale irrigation will fail if public managers abuse it, whether to reward clients with subsidies rather than to enable farmers to work more profitably, or to centralize farm decisions upon water controllers, turning irrigated farmers into pieceworkers. Yet such lessons have been learned in many countries. In Eastern and Southern Africa, the Food and Agriculture Organization of the United Nations (FAO) estimates that, of 38 million hectares suitable for cultivation, some 17 million have good irrigation potential, but only 3 million (mostly in Mozambique or on large farms in South Africa) are water-controlled.[69] While medium-to-large irrigation will be economical only for a minority of these lands, it should not be assumed to be economically or environmentally unacceptable. National water stress is increased by denying smallholder irrigation to areas, like parts of the Eastern Cape of South Africa or many riverine and lakeside areas throughout the continent, with underused water not suitable for use outside farming. It is time both to accelerate the spread of small-scale water management in Africa and to reassess the conventional wisdom about large-scale irrigation.

Excuses are offered for the delay in addressing the problem of irrigation in Africa. 'African irrigation is made less attractive by general inferiority, water-unresponsiveness, variation, or fragility in soils, climates or terrains': this makes little sense, given the huge and localized variation within both Africa and Asia. 'Costs of construction in Africa are much higher than in Asia': the gap has narrowed, and is partly due to excessive reliance in Africa on ex-colonial contractors with market or political power. 'Traditional irrigation systems occur where appropriate; these alone should be spread': they do show good sustainability, but spread slowly, perhaps because on their own they seldom improve income, output or employment fast. 'Crop, animal, and land-management research must concentrate on rainfed areas': this is reasonable while they occupy 95-99% of arable land, but this is only a consequence of past neglect and lack of alternatives in both irrigation and appropriate research. This neglect of irrigation has done vast harm by denying the African poor a Green Revolution.

It is vital to place more emphasis on researching and spreading pro-poor water control techniques, instead of assuming that they already exist but that farmers refuse to adopt them, or that traditional methods already serve the rural poor well. Crop and animal farming can and should increase value-added per unit of water; and in some areas (near many African lakes and rivers) irrigate with farmer-managed systems or medium or even large-sized schemes.

In many cases, especially in semi-arid lands and where there is little water control, external support for its improvement and expansion with farmer and client participation is pro-poor, and a precondition of rapid growth. This has to accompany desubsidization of water for productive use, and recognition that, with urbanization and development, agriculture's share of commercially extracted water should and will fall.

PRO-POOR TECHNIQUES IN OTHER RURAL ACTIVITIES

Although much could be said about the application of technology to many natural resources, we focus on technology where its prospects are most important for where the poorest live, what they work in, and what they eat. For most of the world's poor, economic advancement will continue to depend on crops, especially staple foods. Yet livestock are the main income and employment source for many poor rural people, especially in arid areas of Asia and the Horn of Africa. Elsewhere cattle are integrated into the farming systems as sources of draught and manure, and as users of crop residues. Indeed, their competing uses, for meat, milk, manure, draught, transport, store-of-value and so forth, render technology improvement harder, and policy generalizations less useful, than for crops. In spite of valuable work, research and innovation globally have been much slower, and more concentrated on the needs of wealthy farmers and consumers, for livestock than for crops. Chapter 3 examines ways to improve the benefits to the rural poor from livestock assets. The implications for research and technology are: a shift from cattle to animals more likely to be owned and managed by the poor (sheep, goats, pigs, poultry, donkeys); and, within cattle technology, a shift (in research on both productivity and disease control) towards small herds and their uses and feed.

A special issue relates to draught power. The shift from hoes via draught animals to machines is often desirable, as in parts of South-East Asia today, because wage-rates and employment are rising and labour is getting scarce. Too often, however, the causality is reversed: mechanization, especially the use of tractors, has received open or hidden subsidy, has displaced labour, and caused employment incomes to fall, causing harm to the poor with negligible production benefits. Aid-backed research into mechanization of ploughing, rice transplanting, reaping, weeding and so on for South Asia or sub-Saharan Africa reduces the incomes of the poorest, and is hardly ever justifiable. Despite such hidden subsidy to labour displacement, technology generation for animal draught (for example, better yokes and harnesses for animal traction in Africa), let alone hoe methods, is on a very small scale.

What of technologies for the rural non-farm sector? This sector is increasingly important, but the parts of it that can most effectively help the rural poor depend mainly on growing demand from nearby agriculture, and will prosper if farm technology drives ahead. As such, public rural non-farm sector research seems unlikely to succeed. In most developing countries, the rural non-farm sector, being much less homogeneous even than farming, lacks the professional organization, public-sector technical expertise, or common features that bring economies of scale and external benefits from publicly-supported research. In general, no overall technology policy for such a diverse sector makes sense (much less so than is the case for agriculture). State attempts to provide it often misperceive problems, build in inflexibility, and rest upon little public-sector expertise. It is more constructive to facilitate flexible sector growth, especially in trade, transport and construction, by providing training and stimulating the economic spread of relevant rural services while regulating monopolies.

TECHNOLOGY, THE SECOND INDUSTRIAL REVOLUTION AND THE RURAL POOR: CONCLUSIONS AND IMPLICATIONS FOR RESEARCH ORGANIZATION

Technical progress increased farm productivity and released labour, capital, food and timber to fuel the first industrial revolution in northern Europe and the United States. Many decades later, the new technologies revolutionized agricultural growth. In the North this was mainly through labour-saving innovations, from tractors to herbicides, suited to the demands of developed economies. But these innovations spread labour-displacing methods even to poor economies with fast-growing workforces. More appropriate land-saving techniques emerged only in the Green Revolution around 1965-85, largely where they were supported by water control and fertilizers. As discussed above, this reduced poverty in many countries, but that progress has slowed, leaving large parts of the developing world little affected. Renewed progress is essential for adequate advance in food staples yields, employment and hence rural poverty reduction. Land and water management techniques, meanwhile, have improved and spread very slowly; despite limited effect on yields, their acceleration is essential to contain soil and water degradation in the face of population growth, agrochemicals, growing effective demand for water diversion from agriculture, and probable climate change. In view of the reduced support for *pro bono* agricultural research, and increasing privatization and patenting of much agrotechnical progress, this raises serious difficulties for new pro-poor techniques in developing agricultures.

The 1990s saw great advances in biotechnology and the delivery of information. So far, these advances raised farm productivity mainly through labour displacement, favoured larger farms, and in spite of growing more food were not necessarily pro-poor in agriculture. Yet biotechnology and informatics in principle raise productivity through skills and communications; are neutral in scale; and may help small farmers to move from traditional to new methods with less reliance on innovations from the intervening stage of capital- and chemical-intensive farming.

For this to happen, and for farm income growth to revive and spread to the neglected areas where the poor now concentrate, changes are needed in agricultural research organization and funding.

Partnerships need strengthening between:
- farmers' own research and formal research systems;
- private and public or *pro bono* research;
- bio-agricultural and land-water research;
- low-external-input and high-external-input farm techniques; and
- work for leading regions and for backward regions.

Historically, poverty reduction has rested on pro-poor technical progress that raised entitlements to food staples. Since 1950 rising numbers of workers seeking employment income and, recently, the threat of land and water degradation made technical progress more urgent. Progress took two forms: the innovation of irrigation and water control especially in 1950-80; and the invention of new plant and animal types especially in 1960-85. Both irrigation expansion and biological yield-enhancement, especially for drylands, have slowed down. Environmental challenges, especially water depletion, require new ways to save and manage land and water, yet land-water management technologies have been historically slow to change, spread, or raise output or employment, though they are often successful at conserving resources.

There appear to be three ways forward. Low external-input agriculture faces a stark choice. With low outputs, employment and food entitlements will be inadequate. If high output is obtained by extracting water and nutrients, these are mined unsustainably; if by converting them more efficiently, farmers have generally discovered the methods already, yet remain poor. Accelerating conventional agricultural research and extension for previously backward areas is starting to show high returns in some cases, but is limited by the need to revive growth of employment and food output in the breadbaskets, and by the fact that farm crops and animals in resource-poor areas have been selected – by farmers and by nature – for robustness, not for high yields, restricting the scope for improving such species by conventional breeding. Thus genetic improvement of the species themselves, for which transgenics is the most promising method (as long as potential damage to human health and the environment are avoided), seems needed to revive growth in tropical yield potential. Output from economic best practice for farmers will always lag behind yield potential, but as best practice from existing crop and animal varieties spreads among farmers, new varieties with higher yield potential are needed to keep farm output, employment and food entitlements moving forwards. Genetic improvement of species also seems the only way to achieve some goals (such as rapidly reducing death and blindness from Vitamin A deficiency in very poor rice-eaters).

Whether by conventional or by transgenic techniques, bio-agricultural research can help the poor by wrapping the benefits in the seed rather than requiring costly purchases of inputs. Carefully planned seed research has raised farm output even at low levels of agrochemical inputs. The Green Revolution has induced a massive reduction in poverty for labourers and small farmers by increasing employment and restraining food prices, and has reduced the pressure to grow food crops on fragile land-water systems; yet its slow-down, and crop and geographic limits, have become evident. Though not the only causes, internal research and technology issues are strongly implicated: cuts in funding for public research; its diversion from germplasm improvement; and, within germplasm research, increasing concentration on defence against crop pests at the cost of yield expansion. There is a hard choice facing bio-agricultural research: concentrating on the diverse, recalcitrant farm circumstances of growing proportions of the rural poor, developing many fine-tuned varieties; or re-addressing the potential growth in yield by developing a few varieties to fit a wide range of conditions.

Improving the nutrition, income and employment of the poor requires advances on both fronts.

An important bio-agricultural contribution can be made to improved environmental sustainability, through both biodiversity and varieties of crops and animals able to produce high returns with less polluting and depleting methods of land-soil-water management. Yet progress on both fronts will require not just major new funding, but also the addressing of an overriding issue of research organization: the drain of leading-edge work from the public sector into a few large firms. Their concentration of research on assisting large farmers and processors, and their development of techniques (e.g. the 'terminator') to impede farm-to-farm spread of new varieties, deflect interest from the needs of the poor. The increasing drive for profits from research, and the increasing use of patents, should not preclude attention to reducing poverty.

Integration of bio-agricultural research with other activities to improve the robustness, sustainability and yields of poor people's farming is a priority. Stable pest management requires breeding for horizontal, less-than-total resistance and/or tolerance, with awareness of farmers' own pest management procedures and experiments, while reducing the risks that reduced biodiversity will stimulate unmanageable new pest biotypes.

Institutions such as IFAD can help the CGIAR and NARS to recognize how pro-poor research can involve not just smallholders but landless workers. Workers with no land need time-specific employment income; that is not simply a farm cost for researchers to minimize like other costs.

Water technology problems and options carry similar lessons and implications for research organization. Water supply to agriculture is under increasing pressure from falling groundwater tables, deteriorating surface irrigation systems, and diversion to domestic and industrial needs (although often justified), accompanied in many areas by increased evaporation, and probably less reliable (and reduced) mean rainfall due to climatic change. Yet the main contributors to the reduction of rural poverty since 1950 have been the spread of new staples varieties, and the extra irrigation that assisted their success. With the spread of irrigation reduced by decreasing returns and increasing price disincentives, ways to alleviate the water squeeze become vital for renewed growth in the yield of staples, rural employment, and hence poverty reduction. Prices and markets, institutions and water-yielding asset distribution can all help. But better methods of water delivery, economy and control are vital.

There has been less research in the field of water delivery; what there was, was less successful than bio-agricultural research, and these two areas were not integrated. Technical improvements in water-use efficiency are attainable, but if this is to increase the economic efficiency of water, let alone the share of benefit flowing to the poor, plant scientists and economists must work together with irrigation researchers and, above all, farm users themselves. As with other technical choices, so for water: farmers' traditional micro-methods and, building on these, collaborative, participatory methods in extension, trials and formal research itself, are not a populist alternative to research-station work: each needs to support the other.

Incentives and institutions should ensure that timely and available labour, rather than capital, is used and rewarded to save and control farm water. But some changes seem inescapable as current subsidies to over-use of farm water are phased out. Expensive and complex irrigation systems will increasingly be used to grow high-value crops, increasing the pressure on both biological and water research for technical paths to increased staples output, per litre and per hectare, from cheaper irrigation systems and sustainable rainfed production. Despite the growing water deficit in many countries, most of sub-Saharan Africa seems unlikely to achieve sharp improvements in the growth in staples yield and in the employment of the farmers growing staples without raising the proportions of cropland irrigated from the current 1-5% towards typical Asian ratios of 30-40%. Some progress is possible through small farmer-managed schemes, building on traditional methods, but improvement requires more expansion of implementation capacity in publicly supported domestic extension and maintenance, and in funds. For a large reduction in rural poverty, large formal schemes, as well as development of small farmer-managed water control, will be needed.

Technology and institutions ultimately determine not only the poor's access to assets and to local and global markets, but also to growth, distribution, and, in the end, poverty. This report on rural poverty places more than the usual emphasis on technical change. Many people see technical change as determined: by economic advantage as shown by crop and factor prices; by changing population or environment; or by institutions that set agendas for science and technology. But new science and technology affect economic, political, demographic and environmental outcomes, as well as being affected by them. New scientific breakthroughs, and new access to information, constantly change the boundaries of feasible technical progress in farming, and the cost and likelihood of different sorts of advances.

The CGIAR is the international agricultural research system with most effect on developing countries. Its funding has not improved since the early 1980s, while the number of member institutions reliant on its support has risen. Large and fast-growing proportions of CGIAR resources have been diverted from producing higher-yielding, less extractive and more robust germplasm towards new environmental and social goals;[70] yet the donors have failed to provide resources commensurate with such goals. (For example, the long-term experiments, needed to test environmental impact and sustainability of alternative varieties, farm systems, or watershed management, require longer-term and more resources than standard varietal trials). Research managers' ability to plan, or to move money where scientific success is most likely, has been further reduced by the growing propensity of donors to tie funds to particular goals. Despite continuing good performance and high rates of return, the CGIAR institutions have, under these conditions, been less and less able to compete with expanding private-sector research (especially biotechnology), and thus to keep sufficient leading scientists in institutions directed mainly to poverty reduction.

The CGIAR in the 1970s and early 1980s effectively advanced the concerns of the rural poor despite the tendency of much science and technology to serve the interests of the rich. The power of the CGIAR to do that is under threat. Renewed funding growth to meet new tasks is essential – as is a clearer focus on those tasks, a reversal of the tendency to tie them into special projects, and integration between bio-agricultural and land-water research and innovation. The most important issue is how donors, foundations, the CGIAR and developing-country NARS can work with private-sector researchers. If poor people's needs are to be met, biotechnology has to be redirected from its focus on the needs of the rich, and integrated into the environmental and food-safety concerns of developing countries. This can be done only with the cooperation of, and incentives to, the private companies involved, some of which realize the dangers, even to themselves, of their present isolation from the needs of the poor. Some are willing to contribute to remedies (in 2000 developing-country researchers obtained free seeds of provitamin-A-enhanced rice for crossing and trials; and Monsanto gave its working draft of the rice genome to the international public-sector group involved in this research). However, a wholly new public-private partnership is required. Such a partnership should: be led by the CGIAR (connected via its secretariat with both FAO and the World Bank); involve agricultural donors such as IFAD, using its experience of participation to discover and respond to the requirements of poor farmers, workers and nutrient consumers; and be mediated principally by developing-country scientists and economists.

We make no apology for discussing these institutions of international agricultural technology beside the local, immediate needs of the rural poor. Not only are many of these issues inherently international, so the welfare of the poor depends on their effective voice in agricultural technology institutions; but also, if the institutions continue to lose funds and freedom of action, and (to the private sector) both key staff and access to information, basic inputs to NARS will be missing. NARS will not recover, or in many areas even acquire, capacity to stimulate growth in yields or rural employment. If biological and land-water technologies fail to improve, rural poverty reduction will be slow at best.

Such improvement depends at least as much on NARS as on international research institutions. NARS in Latin America, sub-Saharan Africa and some of Asia have shown funding declines in real terms since the 1990s. Yet India, China, Brazil, Mexico and South Africa – with substantial world-class (bio)technology capacity that is responsive to the requirements of the rural poor – contain, between them, most of the world's rural poor. Many others inhabit agroscientific middle powers such as Indonesia, Kenya and Sri Lanka; the falling cost of transgenics, once a gene is identified, allows such countries to test and monitor

these options themselves, provided they are not patented. But many rural poor inhabit countries with severely underfinanced research systems; some have proud research traditions and achievements, but through lack of resources cannot follow their research through;[71] and in others there is effectively no research capacity at all.

Last but by no means least, we have said little about extension, the importance of which we fully recognize. The potential returns to investment in agricultural extension are high, but unfortunately the responsible organizations are frequently weak or politicized with poorly motivated staff and serious gender and other biases. Similarly, complementarities with research[72] are frequently inadequate. It should be recognized that extension is a pipeline. If congested, it slows down the transmission of research, harming the poorest most, but is unlikely to prevent farmers from eventually selecting the technology that suits them best. In other words, the issue is, first, refilling the pipeline with innovations that suit farmers' needs and are useful for the poor; and second, ensuring their access to relevant inputs. IFAD has been instrumental in supporting moves towards more participatory extension methods; it initiated Lesotho's Client Demand System (replicated in Cameroon and Haiti), by meeting client preferences for technique and location. But for any extension strategy – and indeed for empowerment as a whole – to achieve the desired results, it will have to be matched by renewed progress in the techniques that really matter to the poor: techniques that turn their power over land and water sustainably into output, employment and income.

Endnotes

1 Their sustainability benefit derives mainly from reducing the further spread of farming into marginal land, which in their absence would have been essential to feed growing populations. To do this at constant levels 'if world crop yields had not been tripled [in 1950-92], we would have ploughed 10-12 million square miles of additional uncultivated land' (Avery 1997).

2 Evenson and Kislev 1976.

3 Fan *et al.* 2000a, b.

4 Lele 1992.

5 We use this term interchangeably with 'transgenics' (insertion of a gene obtained from one species into another) and 'genetic modification'.

6 Conway 1997.

7 Nuffield Foundation 1999; Brazilian Academy *et al.* 2000.

8 Rosegrant and Hazell 1999.

9 Hazell and Haggblade 1993.

10 Lipton 1998.

11 Avery 1997.

12 See Lipton and Longhurst 1989; Kerr and Kohlavalli 1999; Hazell *et al.* 2000. Typically of perhaps 80% of the hundreds of high-quality studies cited in these sources, Hossain (1988) reports from a sample of 639 farms in Bangladesh that those operating below 1 ha allocated 52% of land to modern varieties, as against 45% on 1-2 ha and 42% on larger farms. Farmers owning below 1 ha devoted 42.3% of cropped area and 51.7% of rice area to rice HYVs, as against respectively 32.5% and 42.4% for owned farms above 2 ha. Fertilizer use per hectare of cropland on below-1 ha operated farms was 33% higher than on farms above 2 ha; yield was also more, despite less access to irrigation.

13 Singh and Byerlee 1990; Lipton and Longhurst 1989; Hazell and Ramasamy 1991.

14 By the early 1990s, an extra million rupees spent on agricultural research (overwhelmingly biological) for irrigated areas in India produced an expected reduction in the numbers in poverty of only 0.76 persons per year – despite a rise in gross farm output of 4.4 million rupees, of course far less net of extra inputs of fertilizer, etc. Outcomes were much more favourable in some, but not most, rainfed areas (Hazell *et al.* 2000: Tables 6-7).

15 The shift of land to grain for feed. To provide a given calorie intake per person requires some 3-7 times as much cereals land if the cereals are filtered through cattle, rather than eaten by humans direct (Delgado 1999).

16 The CGIAR, founded in 1972, comprises leading international institutes for research on tropical and sub-tropical food crops (e.g. IRRI and CIMMYT) and livestock, plus some 'topic' institutes (e.g. food policy, irrigation management) and some regional institutes.

The Secretariat is shared between the World Bank and the Technical Assistance Committee at FAO, with main financial and technical responsibility respectively.

17 IITA in Nigeria shifted from developing cowpea varieties for maximum monocrop yield because African farmers prioritized mixed cropping and fodder (Kingsbury pers. comm.).

18 Hazell *et al.* 2000; Fan *et al.* 2000a, b; Boyce 1987; Lipton and Longhurst 1989.

19 GM crops have spread from 1 million hectares in 1995 to 40 million hectares globally in 1999; some 60% of foods in US supermarkets contain them, with no known or recorded case of health damage. As with health, environmental risks are the same in principle as with other new plants (e.g. insect-resistant varieties can harm non-target insects), but GM crops are more carefully tested and screened. GM can be steered to increase biodiversity (e.g. the genetic similarity of many IRRI-based rice varieties has impaired field diversity, which should be increased following the insertion in 1999 of a dwarfing gene from wheat into rice). Environmental and health impacts of all introduced plants and foods should be screened, but potential benefits should be measured against risk (Nuffield Foundation 1999; Brazilian Academy *et al.* 2000; Lipton 1999).

20 On micronutrient deficiencies: FAO 2000; SCN Special Commission 2000. On iron-zinc-enriched non-GM rice: IRRI Press Release, Dr. R. Cantrill, 22/5/2000. On Vitamin A GM rice: Ye *et al.* 2000.

21 Hence 'do both' is unlikely to be a feasible way forward, even if funding constraints are somewhat relieved. Worryingly, the structure of international agricultural research (e.g. maize and millet are 'mandate crops' for independent institutions, respectively CIMMYT and ICRISAT) renders such choices hard to strategize or implement.

22 In crop/agronomic research to save water, an outstanding exception is IRRI's work in India, China and the Philippines on management to maintain rice yields under greatly reduced water use (IRRI 2000: 30-1).

23 Jeyaratnam *et al.* 1987.

24 Cockcroft 1997.

25 The main contribution of GM to pest management so far – inserting a gene expressing *Bacillus thuringensis* toxin into maize, soy and cotton – is single-gene, vertical resistance, intended to destroy as close to 100% of target pests as possible, and presumably as stimulative of virulent new biotypes as conventional breeding.

26 Byerlee 2000; cf. Mosley 2000, Lipton 1988.

27 Fan *et al.* 2000a: Table 6; 2000b.

28 IRRI 2000: 6.

29 These examples often involve mutual support between

bio-agricultural research and ILMT. More fodder-yielding cover crop varieties encourage the farmer to stabilize hilly land because they improve browse for cattle.

30 Lipton and Longhurst 1989.

31 Edwards 1995: 17 on Jamaica; IFAD/FAO 1999.

32 Drinkwater 1991; Tapson 1990.

33 Fairhead and Leach 1996.

34 Young 1998.

35 IFAD 1993.

36 Kerr and Sanghi 1992; Hudson 1992.

37 Kerr and Sanghi 1992.

38 Binswanger 1991.

39 IFAD 1992b.

40 Shiferaw and Holden 1997.

41 Lutz et al. 1998.

42 Erenstein 1999.

43 FAO 1998a.

44 Findlay and Hutchinson 1999.

45 Prathapar and Qureshi 1999.

46 World Resources Institute 1992; Yudelman 1993.

47 Prathapar and Qureshi 1999.

48 Singh, G. 1995.

49 On vegetative vs stone bunds: Kiepe 1995, Young 1998. On vetiver fodder: Grimshaw and Helfer 1995, Osunade and Reij 1996. Katsina: IFAD 1992b: 41.

50 Sidahmed 2000.

51 World Bank 1992.

52 FAO 1996.

53 Xie et al. 1993.

54 Seepage and percolation depend on soil permeability. WUE is around 70% in the Gezira Irrigation Scheme, Sudan, with impermeable soil. In Eastern India, rice irrigation reaches 85% WUE due to rock beneath shallow soils (Xie et al 1993).

55 Frederiksen 1992.

56 Paddy water: Tabbal et al. 1992, IRRI 1990, Hazell et al. 2000, IRRI 2000: 30-1. Pakistan: Wolters 1992.

57 Abate 1991.

58 Xie et al. 1993.

59 Wolff and Stein 1998.

60 On sprinklers: Wolff and Stein 1998; IFAD 1993. On drip: Stockle and Vilar 1993; Postel 1992;

IFAD 1999h; Abu Taleb et al. 1991.

61 Xie et al. 1993. See Chapter 2 on ultra-low-lift and treadle pumps in Bangladesh – like bamboo tubewells in Bihar, India, also irrigation assets especially well suited for ownership, use and manufacture by the poor, whose main asset is labour.

62 For example, farmer-specific metering or other irrigation charging is often infeasible (e.g. if water covers, and flows between, tiny paddies). Similarly, standpipes for several households are often far more cost-effective and affordable than individually metered drinking water. User consensus on sharing a group fee is then needed for efficient desubsidization, but usually obtainable only if the group has 'voice' in securing reliable water delivery.

63 Thailand: van Vilsteren and Srkirin 1987. Bali: Horst 1996.

64 Chitale 1991.

65 A striking example is 'water mining' – the effect of deep tubewell pumping in lowering the water-table, rendering shallower tube-wells (usually used by poorer farmers) useless. If a deep tubewell is privately owned (which usually pays only on a single large holding – absent public ownership, or collective action by many nearby small farmers), it is very hard to prevent water mining by legally enforceable pricing. Equity and equality effects apart, water mining steadily raises costs of pumping and of new tubewells, and may exceed recharge and exhaust the groundwater. Yet publicly owned or cooperative tubewells have familiar and serious problems too.

66 On Fayoum: Wolters 1992; conjunctive use: van Tuijl 1993; India: Chitale 1991; corruption: Wade 1982.

67 World Water Council 2000: 64-6.

68 IFAD 2000b.

69 IFAD 2000b.

70 Lipton 1999.

71 For example, Ethiopia in 1996-98 widely introduced two successful maize hybrids under the GLO-2000 programme of the Sassakawa Foundation. Maize research, split among federal and provincial bodies, will surely be called on to deal with new pest biotypes that 'like' a new hybrid. Resources and leadership will be needed to respond swiftly – and such responses elsewhere have too often been slow or missing. The poor and remote then suffer most.

72 Evenson 1999, 2000.

CHAPTER 5

MARKETS FOR THE RURAL POOR

Distance to markets, and the lack of roads, is a central concern for rural communities throughout the developing world. The rural poor need access to competitive markets not just for their produce but also for inputs, assets and technology, consumer goods, credit and labour.

MARKET ACCESS: CONSTRAINTS AND OPPORTUNITIES

The economic environment of the rural poor comprises several interlocking markets: for agricultural produce and for agri-inputs; for production support (agricultural extension) or financial services; for information; for assets, including land and water; for labour; and for food and other consumer goods. The terms upon which the rural poor enter and participate in such markets are sometimes inequitable. Many of the poor are currently passive participants, often obliged to sell low (immediately after harvest) and buy high, with little choice of where they conduct transactions, with whom, and at what price. With the liberalization of domestic markets and the globalization of international markets, these markets have become more open, with more choices, but also complex and uncertain. Today more than ever before, enhancing the ability of the rural poor to reach these markets, and actively engage in them, is one of the most pressing development challenges.

Rural people, especially the poor, often say that one reason they cannot improve their living standards is that they face difficulties of market access.

Low population densities in rural areas, remoteness from centres and high transport costs present real physical barriers in accessing markets. The rural poor are constrained by lack of information about markets, lack of business and negotiating experience, and lack of a collective organization which can give them the power they require to interact on equal terms with other, generally larger and stronger, market intermediaries. Cultural and social distance, and discrimination, may also be factors that at least partly exclude the poor from markets.

Farmers' inability to market produce means lack of income for production inputs, consumer goods and immediate cash requirements, and prevents asset accumulation. Market access thus influences farmers' production systems: those who live close to better roads and have more frequent and direct contact with the market are willing to produce more systematically for the market, while those with poor market access are forced to produce for domestic consumption. In such a situation food consumption is limited to what can be produced on-farm or within the community, in some cases resulting in poorly balanced diets.

How can the market access problem be solved, given the high cost of removing some constraints and the conflicts of interest, between rich and poor, rural and urban, involved in removing others? That is the challenge for NGOs, governments, donors and, above all, the rural poor, whose participation in finding and implementing solutions is needed for success.

The problem of market access may usefully be considered in three dimensions: the physical (the distance of the poor from markets); the political (their inability to influence the terms upon which they participate in the market); and the structural (the lack of market intermediaries). All of these must be tackled if the measures are to have the desired effect on productivity, output or incomes.

Until about 1980, the context for this challenge in most developing countries was state-led industrialization, regulation and protection. Increasingly, liberalization and globalization have changed the nature of the challenge. Liberalization of domestic and international markets gives the poor new opportunities for specializing in, and exchanging, their labour-intensive products. But these trends also increase exposure to world price fluctuations and thus increase the uncertainty of the economic environment within which the rural poor operate, and offer special competitive advantages to those in rural areas endowed with better market access and contacts. While trade liberalization and increased financial flows towards labour-intensive sectors offer big prospects for poverty reduction, they also bring big risks if initial market access is very unequal. Liberalization works best for the rural poor where the distribution of access, skills and probably land assets is not very unequal. Liberalization and globalization with initial gross inequality can allow the powerful to abuse their special access and so result in the poor becoming poorer. But huge poverty reduction in many cases shows that liberalization and globaliza-tion with fairly low initial inequality can bring widespread benefits to the rural poor.

Globalization of capital flows, access to technology and trade are leading to important changes in economic and social relations across the world, in developing and developed countries, promising new opportunities for growth and income-generating activities for households and firms. Within the rural sector, liberalization has reduced the price bias against farming, price distortions among farm products, and other government intervention. Trade and exchange-rate reform has been central to structural adjustment pro-grammes in developing countries since the 1980s. Most developing countries have liberalized their agriculture to some extent, changing its institu-tions and structure. This major change implies new conditions for the rural sector, and especially for the rural poor. It is true that, even without the intervention of governments and donors, private sector-led market development will almost cer-tainly take place over time. However, in the absence of intervention, it is quite possible that such development would be highly unbalanced in geographical terms, inequitable in socio-economic terms, and could even further exacerbate poverty for some rural people.

There is thus a role for intervention, with three objectives.

- To speed up the development of market access, choice and information.
- To remove or reduce barriers to market access, both by special support in places where markets are slow to develop spontaneously and by easing market participation of the poor.
- To establish a more equitable set of market rela-tions. This it would do by empowering small-holder farmers and agricultural workers, provid-ing them with the knowledge and skills that they require both to enter the market and to improve the terms upon which they participate in it.

PROBLEMS OF MARKET ACCESS

'A community without roads does not have a way out.'
Farmer in Juncal, Ecuador[1]

Market access problems can affect areas (due to remoteness or lack of infrastructure) and groups, such as the illiterate or poorly educated, minority ethnic groups or those not speaking the official national language, and women. The common problem of disadvantaged areas and disadvantaged groups is personal immobility, which frequently impairs responses to changing incentives. People from disadvantaged areas find access to markets restricted by high physical costs and by their lack of knowledge of market mechanisms, a consequence of lack of information and organization. This is compounded by the structure of the markets themselves, the limited market intermediaries and asymmetrical market power. (Box 5.1).

Remoteness and poverty both tend to reduce access to markets, increasing both the physical costs in reaching them and the costs of overcoming imperfect and often discriminatory institutional mechanisms that have sometimes evolved to handle those risks arising from remoteness and poverty themselves. Some of these physical costs and mechanisms work strongly against women and other disadvantaged groups. Indigenous and poorly educated people are over-represented in rural and remote regions: in large parts of Latin America, indigenous people are concentrated in rural areas, and have higher incidences of poverty, lower levels of literacy and generally less access to land and credit.[2] In other regions, remoteness combines with ethnic and language barriers to restrict market access, especially to labour markets.

The high physical cost of accessing markets

Five main aspects of remoteness, rurality and poverty create large physical problems, and often combined constraints, on market access by poor, remote or rural communities:

1. Lack of roads, or presence of seasonally impassable or poorly maintained roads.
2. High transport costs, arising from the lack of well-maintained roads, long distances and lack of affordable, appropriate transport.
3. Poor or non-existent communications infrastructure for disseminating information on markets, products and prices.

Box 5.1: Market access constraints: physical, structural, information and organization

Constraint	Disadvantaged areas	Disadvantaged groups
Physical	Poor roads, high transport costs, perishable goods, low value/weight produce.	Those located far from markets; women with heavy time burdens; those with poor access to transport and/or limited access to facilities.
Structural	Asymmetry of market relations: reliance on monopsonistic traders, agro-processors or marketing boards whose market power allows excess profit shares.	Those with poor access to land and credit to allow diversification, commercialization and/or marketing of goods in wider markets; those constrained by traditional or cultural norms.
Skills, information and organization	Lack of understanding of how markets operate, lack of information, lack of relevant skills.	Most of rural poor; those who lack education and collective organization.

4. Low value/weight ratios of much of what poor people make and sell, which make transporting it to market difficult and costly.

5. The perishable nature of much agricultural produce from the rural poor, especially women, combined with a lack of storage facilities and long distances to markets.

Distance to markets, and the lack of roads, is a central concern for rural communities throughout the developing world. In Ecuador, one farmer claimed simply: 'There are no good roads. To get the products out of the farm you have to use horses, but those who don't have a horse cannot do it.'[3] In Malawi, participants in research identified poor roads as a major problem in all but one of the ten communities visited. In Twabidi, Ghana, farmers complained of the high transport fees charged by truck drivers because of poor roads. As a result, a large share of food crops was locked up on farms, leading to post-harvest losses.

In Asia, high concentrations of rural poverty are found in remote hill and mountain regions. Chinese farmers living in rural areas close to cities with dense transport networks had higher incomes than those in remote locations, and much of their income came from non-farm industrial enterprises. In the Philippines, the incidence of poverty in upland areas is 61% compared with 50% in lowland areas.[4]

Remoteness and poverty go together especially in Africa. In areas such as Northern Angola, Northern Zambia, Southern Tanzania and Northern Mozambique, all isolated areas with weak market integration, up to 90% of the population are estimated to be chronically poor. Similarly, in the highland maize belts of Kenya and Tanzania, chronic poverty is not strongly linked to farm size but is concentrated among food crop producers in remote areas with poor road access. One study in Tanzania has estimated that households within 100 metres of a gravel road, passable 12 months a year with a bus service, earn about one third more per capita than the average.[5]

In Africa in particular, road quality is also a problem. Rural Africa has much lower population densities than rural Asia and lower road densities (population per road length and road length per area). But even where roads do exist they are often in a poor state: in Tanzania in 1990 only 24% of roads were in good condition; in Kenya 32%. Many roads are impassable during rainy seasons, which is often the peak season for raw material availability, affecting for example Tanzania's cashew nut industry and Kenya's dairy industry.[6]

High transport costs from the combination of scarce and poor roads in rural Africa make parts of the rural economy only semi-open and are the largest source of marketing margins, accounting for most of the 40% difference between marketing margins for food grains in Kenya and Malawi and those in Bangladesh and Indonesia.[7] The increases in commodity prices between farmgate and border, and in imported input prices between ports and rural areas, reduce incentives. Problems are particularly acute for areas specializing in roots and tubers (which are important in the forest and humid Savanna zones of coastal and Central African countries), as these have higher weight/value ratios and are more perishable than grains. Remote cassava-growing areas, while protected from cheap imports in local markets, find it difficult to compete in cassava chip exporting unless 'remoteness' can be reduced. Transport costs and storage constraints are particularly important for women, who tend to trade locally in vegetables and other perishables. Women in the Sahel who are involved in marketing vegetables are faced with massive oversupply in the local markets in the dry season, due to a lack of transport to urban markets and an inability to conserve produce for later sale.[8]

In Central and Eastern Europe and the newly independent states, poor farmers are also by and large those who live in mountainous and other remote areas, mostly at altitudes above 600 metres, notably in Romania, Albania, Armenia, Azerbaijan, Bosnia and Herzegovina, Georgia and Macedonia. Often entire communities live in extreme poverty: in the upland Bagramanian District of Armenia, 92% of farmers could not afford minimum requirements for food, heating and cooking fuel.[9]

In Latin America, too, remote areas face physical market access problems. In Peru, high transportation and storage costs attenuated price changes of potatoes following liberalization.[10] In Chile, consumer prices vary enormously throughout the country. In the extreme north and south, consumer prices are on average 20-25% higher than in the central zone and metropolitan area.[11]

Difficult market access restricts opportunities for income generation. Remoteness increases uncertainty and reduces choice: it results in more limited marketing opportunities, reduced farm-gate prices and returns to labour and capital, and increased input costs. This weakens incentives to participate in the monetized economy, and results in subsistence rather than market-oriented production systems. By contrast, improved infrastructure affects fertilizer and other input use, raising the responsiveness of producers to changes in prices and increasing market integration. In Africa villages with better physical infrastructure have fertilizer costs 14% lower, wages 12% higher and crop production 32% higher than villages with poor infrastructure.[12]

The physical costs of market access can be reduced by road construction, road maintenance, and improved transport, storage and information. Governments and donors have traditionally favoured building new roads which allow easier transportation of all produce, not just that of the rural, remote poor, to ports and markets within and beyond country frontiers. In 1995, Uganda successfully negotiated for a World Bank loan to build new roads rather than new primary schools, arguing that new roads would immediately raise national income and alleviate poverty, while the effect of primary education would not be felt until the medium or long term.[13] Certainly the poor in Africa regard new and/or improved roads as among the most successful initiatives to improve market access. In the Central and Nyanza provinces of Kenya, roads were most often cited as the most useful of government services. In Ghana and Côte d'Ivoire, rural roads ranked higher than educational needs, health and water supplies. The construction in Nigeria of a road from a village to the market centre provided the impetus to increase production.[14]

New roads do bring large benefits to poor, remote communities, in several ways (see Box 5.2 on estimating rates of return to roads). Rural roads improve market access not only for the rural poor but also for the less rural poor and urban population, opening up markets for both urban and rural producers and consumers. They encourage diversification in village economies by opening up the market for labour, artisanal products and agricultural produce. Road provision in Nepal and Bangladesh led to an influx of education services and provided access to health care in a wider area. In Egypt, villages enjoyed an increase in non-farm employment and in post-primary schooling availability when connected to a road network. In Sargodha district, Pakistan, unemployment decreased when a new road created opportunities for drivers, conductors, mechanics, filling stations, shops, tea-stalls near bus stops and other services for travellers.[15]

In India, Kenya and The Sudan, production improved through both intensification and specialization, though the extent of these varies across countries.[16] The use of commercial inputs like fertilizer and pesticides generally decreases with distance from the market, but differences are most

---

Box 5.2: Rates of return to road building

In India rates of return to road building have been estimated to be around 25%. But, just as for other types of investments, there are difficulties in estimating the rates of return to road building.

One of these arises from **mutual causation**: villages may be poor because they lack a road linking them to other villages or towns, or because they are in so-called 'unfavoured areas', with poor soil quality, low rainfall or lack of irrigation. Their poverty may prevent or deter a road from being built: villages may not be able to afford to build a road, if funded solely through local taxation; or the expected benefits of building the road, in terms of increased output, may be less than the costs. Adjusting for this mutual causation problem lowers rates of return to around 15-17% in India (Binswanger et al.1993).

A second difficulty arises from **trade diversion**. Some of the gains that accrue to a village through building a road connecting it to another village or a town may come at the expense of other remote villages which do not get a road and lose some of their already small market share. So far this difficulty has not been addressed, but it surely reduces rates of return further, bringing them closer into line with other investments.

---

notable for poorer rural people, especially in India. In The Sudan, the share of high-value perishable goods (fresh fruit and vegetables) increased, while the share devoted to dry, low-value crops fell, among all farm sizes.

In Malaysia, new roads greatly affected prices of food and inputs: trader vans started servicing roadside communities, and roadside shops had to reduce their prices. Food-crop production was also affected. In roadside villages, employment opportunities increased, offering an alternative source of cash income; paddy production fell, while off-road villages stepped up their hill paddy production to meet rising demand from the roadside villages.[17] In Sri Lanka, feeder roads in Kegalle had a positive impact on rural development: land value increased by over 700% along the Hingala/ Gogagama road within two years. The distance for a large village of 9 000 people to the main Colombo/Kandy road was reduced from 20 km to 1.8 km when a more direct road was constructed; cart tracks were made accessible to motors, resulting in improved marketing and reduced vehicle hire rates; 97% of respondents claimed that the roads had improved their marketing prospects, resulting in higher prices for their agricultural products and lower prices for their consumer goods. In addition there was a quickening of eco-nomic activity along the roads in the form of building construction, stalls, tea-kiosks and other services within two years.[18]

In Bhutan, feeder-road construction also had positive impacts on rural development. Extension workers on the IFAD-supported Tashigang and Mongar Area Development Project said that farmers were stimulated to take up extension opportunities and increase their use of inputs, credit and improved agricultural practices now that new roads gave them access to markets to sell their crops. In addition, the roads provided the only means by which farm families could reach health and education services, improved community life (through facilitating visits to friends and relatives) and better access to consumer goods.[19] Jacoby[20] argues that in Nepal the provision of extensive road access to markets would confer substantial benefits on average. Blaikie et al.[21] show that east-west roads were good for rural poverty reduction, through improved local market integration, but north-south road building was not, as it had the effect of subsidizing marginal-cost sales from India and China. However, recent moves to export horticulture to India will benefit from the north-south road.

The Nepal case suggests that the benefits of new roads would accrue mainly to landowners, not the very poor. However, the poor will also gain even if roads are not a targetable commodity and income inequality rises. Of course, the public nature of roads helps – roads benefit all members of the community, including women and the poorest, even if they do not gain as much as the rich – although the type of transport, timing and pricing may determine whether roads are *de facto* accessible to the poor.

One of the choices in improving physical access to markets is between building new roads and maintaining existing ones. Poorly maintained roads, however extensive or uncrowded they may be, will not meet the needs of rural populations. The World Bank estimates that returns on primary highway maintenance projects are almost twice as high as those on projects involving new construction.[22] In Tanzania, which has many miles of 'roads' per 1000 people, only 10% of rural roads are deemed to be in good condition.[23] In Zambia, the negative effects of removal of maize subsidies for remote rural producers have been exacerbated by poorly maintained roads, which prevent people in remote, rural areas from being able to access markets for inputs, outputs and consumer goods.

Maintenance of rural roads can have important effects on incomes and livelihoods of the rural poor.[24] The Rural Maintenance Programme in rural Bangladesh in 1984 aimed at maintaining earthen market roads using rural female labour. Market expansion associated with road maintenance resulted in an increase in food services, bicycle repair services and rickshaws on roadsides.[25] In Chile, during the 1980s, public employment schemes in poor rural areas, including maintaining roads, provided significant contributions to household income, reducing poverty and inequality.[26]

Market structure

Many rural markets are characterized by extreme asymmetry of relations between, on the one hand, large numbers of small producers/consumers and, on the other, a few buyers/sellers. Such market relations are inequitable, frequently uncompetitive, and rarely to the advantage of the small producer. Such market relations result from a number of factors. First is the physical aspect discussed above: either a complete lack of roads or roads that are impassable at crucial times of the year, which result in high transport and transaction costs, both to buyers and sellers. Second is the issue of market scale. Many rural communities, particularly those in more remote areas where population densities are low, have such limited demand for production inputs, or have so little to sell or barter, that traders do not find it worth their while to visit them.

Third, it should be recalled that farmers in many parts of the world, certainly prior to liberalization, were dependent on the government or on parastatal organizations to purchase their produce at a preset price. These marketing boards aimed to repress farm prices so as to keep consumer prices down. While keeping consumer prices for food staples low is one way of helping the poor, including many of the rural poor who are net food purchasers, it is far from the most efficient. Pan-territorial pricing (fixed, uniform prices, irrespective of distance to markets), where non-remote producers effectively subsidize remote producers, penalizes both rich and poor non-remote farmers with surpluses to sell. Relative prices, incentives and the farm-product mix, are all distorted by instruments of farm price repression.

Liberalization aimed to achieve efficiency gains through market determination of prices. It was predicated at least in part upon the assumptions that the withdrawal of the state from those activities in which it formerly engaged (input supplies, production support and financial services, produce marketing) would create the space for the private sector to enter, and that the private sector would operate more efficiently than the state. Progress in achieving market liberalization is now substantial, especially for food crops. With rare exceptions, domestic food markets for staple food crops have been almost completely liberalized, with impacts on producers and consumers generally viewed as favourable.

But the experience is mixed. In much of Southern Africa private-sector development has been slow and faltering, and the withdrawal of the state has resulted in a vacuum, which has not yet been adequately filled by the private sector. In other areas, the private sector has readily stepped into the gap temporarily created by state withdrawal from food crop marketing and processing. In West and Central Africa, the World Bank[27] judged that of 19 countries where agricultural policy reforms had been initiated during the 1980s, government intervention could be classified as either strong or moderate in 13 of these prior to reform for selected food crops. After reform in late 1992, only one country maintained a moderate level of intervention; the rest were characterized by zero public intervention, with the possible exception of maintenance of food security stocks. The exercise is considered to have been largely successful, particularly in the Sahelian countries, where the private sector has moved in fast to fill the gap created. The impact of liberalization of input markets has, by contrast, been far less successful, and has been associated with a decline in input use, with negative implications for sustained increases in agricultural productivity.

While reforms in many cases have no doubt been beneficial to non-remote farmers, large and small, and to farm labourers through increased employment and/or wages, farmers in remote areas have in the short term been left worse-off (Box 5.9). The contraction of the former market chain has left many farmers further from markets than they were previously: in northern Mozambique for example, the median distance to a market is today 20 km.[28] Removing the state buyer pushes the onus of marketing on to the farmer: under-investment in rural infrastructure, as in Zambia, means that often there is no buyer at all for their produce, or if there is a buyer, prices are extremely low because of the high physical transactions costs.[29]

Rural producers and consumers who face high physical costs in reaching markets often become dependent on traders coming to the village. Traders are essential lifelines for remote rural people, providing opportunities to sell agricultural produce and to purchase inputs and consumer goods. Small private traders also face high transaction costs arising from physical remoteness, which affect demand for small farmers' produce and the prices they receive (see Box 5.3).

In remote or flood-affected areas a trader may not arrive reliably or at all, and may well have monopoly and monopsony power when he/she does: farmers are then faced with little choice but to accept the first offer of the first trader who shows up, however unfavourable it might be. Also, rural people can become dependent on rural traders for information about agricultural products, supply of inputs and consumer goods, and price. Traders, especially if irregular or facing little competition, may be little concerned about reputation, and in such cases asymmetric information often forces the poor to accept low prices for products and to pay high prices for consumer goods. It is often hard for the poor to distinguish this effect from the already damaging effects on prices of remoteness and bad roads. Poor and remote people are more likely to be disadvantaged by non-contestable markets in this way: large farmers, or those closer to markets, can gather information more readily on prices and supply and demand conditions, and transport their produce to market themselves. In Zambia and Zimbabwe traders are often willing to engage only in barter rather than paying cash.[30]

In countries such as Zimbabwe, Zambia and Mozambique, with the privatization of the paras-

Box 5.3: Private traders in Zambia

Most trade in Zambia's Northern Province is through small independent traders who take cash or goods to barter, such as used clothing, soap, salt and blankets. Private traders in remote areas of Zambia face high transactions costs, including time and energy spent buying goods from farmers and hiring labour and transport to carry produce. Traders will travel to an area by public transport and often spend between two and three weeks in the area, camping overnight and travelling on foot between isolated villages buying small quantities of produce from farmers, until they have enough produce (beans, groundnuts or maize) for trade. The trader has to pay local labour to carry agricultural produce to the roadside, and the cost of hiring a truck to move purchases from the roadside into town is a substantial component of his costs.

Transaction costs of trade with remote villages are so great that it is often cheaper for large purchasers (such as maize mills) to buy from distant commercial growers than from small farmers located in the region.

Source: Winters 2000.

tatal commodity marketing agencies, there has been rapid expansion in export crop complex, with smallholders producing crops, particularly cotton, for sale to large agro-business concerns. However, monopolization of processing, credit, marketing and technical capabilities by the large companies makes the smallholders' re-entry to the market fundamentally inequitable. Although experiences have varied, and there are clear examples of companies acting with enlightened self-interest, smallholder farmers have in some cases found themselves unable to negotiate or withdraw their business, effectively operating as employees rather than as partners. They have ultimately derived very low net returns as the large-scale private buyers exercise economic power to take the lion's share of value added. This offers a scenario of growth of smallholder production without smallholder development.

In the case of production inputs, the problem is particularly complicated: the commercial firms that have replaced the parastatal input distribution companies have a very limited retail network in the interior and are only starting to develop their networks of agents. To the extent that the inputs get to the rural communities, the range is in many areas still limited (although perhaps increasingly based on demand), and the costs are high, both relative to what farmers have been used to paying – reflecting the removal of subsidy, and in absolute

terms – as the result of high transport costs, lack of competition amongst distributors, and farmers' lack of ability to negotiate favourable terms. In Mozambique the situation is particularly limiting: inputs are frequently in short supply, as traders prefer to deal in goods that are easier to transport and more profitable than most farm items; and, partly owing to the lack of available farm purchases, only 7% of farmers use fertilizer and, even less, improved seeds.[31]

One of the ways in which market structure can be influenced to promote greater competition, transparency and improved access of the rural poor to markets, and the terms and conditions upon which they interact with it, is to support the market intermediaries themselves. Over the past few years, a number of important and innovative programmes have been developed to do just this. For example, the Co-operative for Assistance and Relief Everywhere (CARE) in Zimbabwe has since 1995 been implementing a programme which seeks to facilitate the access of the rural poor to agricultural inputs, output marketing opportunities and improved agricultural know-how, through the establishment of a network of community-based, independent agri-input dealers. The programme, initially supported with seed funding from IFAD, has over the five-year period successfully established over 300 dealers: these have established commercial relations with the urban agri-input suppliers, and are each supplying farm inputs and other household provisions to between 100-200 smallholder farm families. The farmers are the most important beneficiaries of the programme: they are able to purchase inputs where they want, when they want and in the quantities they require. The effective prices they pay for the inputs are lower than formerly and, through their relations with the agents, many are able to purchase the inputs on credit.

In many countries, commercial banks provide little credit to rural traders. While some NGOs and non-bank financing agencies provide credit, the need far outstrips the supply. On account of its itinerant nature and the large size of established trade networks, rural trade is a marginal concern of the microfinance plans in many countries. Supplier credit offers an attractive alternative source of finance for cash-strapped rural retailers who do not easily qualify for a bank loan. The strategy of training rural traders in business management and helping them develop a commercial relationship with input supply or wholesaling companies can overcome this constraint.

Lack of skills, information and organization
Liberalization has substantially changed the environment in which smallholder producers operate, from one in which the production options were limited and the prices of inputs and produce were known, usually before the start of the growing season, to one which is open-ended and in which all prices can vary from day to day. In their dealings with this market, smallholder farmers find themselves at a major disadvantage.

Poor farmers in many areas do not understand how the market works or why prices fluctuate; they have little or no information on market conditions, prices and quality of goods; they are not organized collectively; and they have no experience of market negotiation and little appreciation of their capacity to influence the terms and conditions upon which they enter the market.[32] To the

extent that they have had contact with government agricultural extension services, they have received little guidance on these issues, as the services have tended to pass technologies with little reference to markets and prices. With no information, no experience and no organization, they have no basis upon which either to plan a market-oriented production system or to negotiate market prices and conditions, and are obliged to take the first offer made to them. Ultimately, their lack of knowledge means that they are passive, rather than active, players in the market; that they can be exploited by those with whom they have market relations; and that they fail to realize the full value of their production.

Since the early part of the twentieth century, marketing cooperatives (MC) have been considered an important vehicle to enable farmers to take advantage of economies of scale in transportation and storage so as to reduce the cost of marketing produce. Politically, MCs can give farmers greater control over trading activities than reliance on private traders alone, particularly in remote areas where traders may have considerable market power and greater bargaining power *vis-à-vis* traders. MCs enable farmers to raise their profit margins through reduced costs of marketing their produce and increased selling prices.

The experience of MCs in developing countries has been mixed. Many farmers have increased their profits by joining an MC, and MCs have provided employment in rural areas. In Nigeria, this has stopped the migration of young people to cities.[33] The building of cooperatives among women who weave screwpine mats in Kerala has helped them by stabilizing prices, organizing marketing and obtaining bank loans.[34] However, in numerous countries, during the 1960s and 1970s governments sought to influence, co-opt or directly control cooperative movements, generally with disastrous consequences. Problems would then arise from mismanagement through lack of business skills and training, lack of finances, corruption and state interference. For instance, the Cooperative Movement in the 1970s in Tanzania experienced misappropriation of funds, nepotism and corruption by the elite, and was disbanded in 1976.[35] In Cameroon some MCs had monopoly positions, leading to similar treatment of coffee and cocoa farmers to that by private traders.[36]

By the 1980s, the term 'cooperative' had come to be held in contempt by many farmers, particularly in Africa, who often saw them as nothing more than a particularly coercive and intrusive arm of government. However, with the liberalization of markets, there is renewed recognition of the importance of farmer organization and, in a number of countries such as Mozambique (Box 5.4), Uganda and Zambia, major efforts are being made to strengthen smallholder groups and associations.[37] Smallholders acting alone typically lack

the bargaining power to command on-time delivery of agricultural inputs at reasonable prices. By combining their needs for agricultural inputs, the group creates a larger and more important target market for vendors of seeds, agro-chemical inputs, market planning information, farming tools, land-preparation and harvesting services, post-harvest handling technology, credit and storage opportunities. For produce marketing, too, association provides enormous advantages: farmers who join a group can exercise more power when bargaining for sales terms and so enter into forward contracts for production, thereby offering improved access to future markets. Officially registered associations can enter into formal sales contracts: even those groups or associations still pursuing the process of formal registration enjoy better access to markets.

The key to success of group action (cotton primary marketing organizations in southern Mali,

---

Box 5.4: Rural group enterprise development in Mozambique

The Rural Enterprise Development Programme is a pilot initiative, designed and since 1995 implemented by the NGO CLUSA (Cooperative League of the United State of America), which is aimed at assisting Mozambican smallholders to develop a network of rural group enterprises (RGE) in order to increase agricultural productions and rural incomes. The programme is designed to provide services to RGEs and farmer associations in the areas of institution building, business management training and advice, functional literacy and numeracy training, auditing, market information and agricultural commodity broking, savings and credit training and information. To date, some 370 RGEs have been established, with a membership of around 13000 members.

Numerous interviews with group representatives and input supply companies revealed that organized groups of farmers are more likely to receive more timely supply of their seed requirements at the beginning of the planting season. CLUSA notes that 'One of the most important initial impacts of the RGE development process has been increased access to markets and improved transportation by rural producers for their produce. For the first time in 1996 and every subsequent year, producers were able to negotiate the prices of and market their own produce'. It also found that RGEs were able to obtain premiums on the prices at which they sell agricultural produce: cotton-buying companies are known to pay premiums of between 4% and 12% to groups and associations, in return for the group or association handling some of the company tasks such as gathering the cotton into warehouses, weighing, performing quality control and loading company trucks. An added benefit for the group in such an arrangement is better control through participation in the grading and weighing process, thereby lessening instances where farmers feel they have been unfairly treated. Even absorbing some of the premium to support the group infrastructure of personnel and facilities, the farmer members realized premiums over non-group prices. Cotton is not the only product for which organized farmer groups can obtain premiums for smallholders. CLUSA found that during the 1996 marketing season prices received by associations were 22% higher for maize and 93% higher for groundnut than the prices paid to individuals.

Source: CLUSA Rural Group Enterprise Development Programme, quarterly reports (various)

farmer groups at village level in Ségou, Mali, producer organizations at village level in the Centre Province of Cameroon) is the establishment of small-scale groupings in homogenous structures, with a particular purpose and where a sure market outlet is available.

Market information

The lack of market power that farmers experience (and complain about) when dealing with rural traders can be due to lack of market information, both in terms of price and price trends. This disadvantage is amplified when farmers are faced with a single buyer for their product. Farmer groups or associations can overcome this problem, in part at least, by canvassing a number of buyers with the promise of delivering a large quantity of uniform quality. Thus, delivery of more information on markets and prices has been shown to assist farmers with farmgate marketing decisions, particularly when faced with a single buyer.

Provision of market information, linked to training to help farmers to interpret and act upon that information, can also help them to understand better marketing processes and to develop strategies to achieve better and more stable prices for their agricultural produce. However, such information must be location-specific; it must be timely and accurate; it must be dynamic (track trends as well as absolute levels); and it must be locally available and in a language that is understood by all of the rural population. While government-run market information systems operate in many countries, few have adequately met the challenge of all the requirements associated with the information delivered.

Market information systems

Improved communications can also play a part in reducing informational asymmetries. The village pay-phones used by the Grameen Bank in Bangladesh were found to lower transaction costs

---

Box 5.5: Grameen Bank village pay phones

The Grameen Bank in Bangladesh started the Village Pay Phone (VPP) initiative in the mid-1990s: cellular phones were leased to poor rural female Grameen Bank members in order to provide a communication service to poor and non-poor rural dwellers alike. The cost of phones are paid for in weekly instalments over a three-year period.

A study of villages with VPPs within 50 km of Dhaka found the initiative to be pro-poor on a number of counts. While 50% of non-poor VPP users had used a phone within the last five years (before VPPs were introduced), only 40% of the non-poor had used one. Furthermore, absence of a VPP was found to result in greater transactions costs for the poor than the non-poor, through the need for the poor to be physically mobile and less likely to take up other sources of telephone service than the non-poor. Although 85% of the VPP users were non-poor, profits for (poor) owners amounted to between one fifth and one quarter of household income. This increase in household income meant improved food security, a greater ability to invest in health, education and clothes for children, and an increased propensity to save.

The phones have an impact on economic and socio-cultural spheres of users and owners. The presence of a phone in a village makes information about input and output prices readily accessible. As a result, prices of agricultural commodities such as paddy, eggs and vegetables are higher in VPP villages. Owners of livestock can quickly receive warning of outbreaks of disease. During the floods of 1998, VPPs helped in the relief effort. Law and order has improved since it is now easier to inform the police when crime takes place. One tenth of calls are health-related, enabling villagers to call a doctor or ambulance quickly. Kinship networks have been strengthened, particularly in villages with many overseas migrant workers. Empowerment of women is also evident. In addition to increased mobility around the village on receiving incoming calls, owning a phone increases prestige and respect within the village. Moreover, through receiving and overhearing calls, phone owners are able to expand their own knowledge about economic and social issues.

Source: von Braun et al. 1999.

Box 5.6: Commercialization and the rural poor

The move to commercial crops can bring about changes in a community that are not always to the benefit of the poorest. There are a number of scenarios where the poor might lose from commercialization.

Scenario	Consequences
(1) Inelastic demand	Declining prices: good for net food buyers, bad for net food sellers.
(2) Food production decline	Net food exports fall, or net food imports rise: bad for net food purchasers.
(3) Risk aversion/information	Delayed use of new technology among small farmers can lead to exclusion in markets.
(4) Weak tenancy contracts	Landowners evict tenants when new profitable cash crops are planted, leading to increased landlessness, malnutrition.
(5) Market distortions by state	Farmers plant inappropriate crops or are excluded from key crops in favour of large farmers.
(6) Gender roles	Traditional 'female' activities may not be compatible with market activities required by commercialization; increased employment by women may lead to increased use of child labour and poorer school attendance.

Source: Binswanger and von Braun (1991)

and to enhance the empowerment and status of women and households that leased phones as well as improving law-enforcement and communication during disasters (Box 5.5).[38]

MARKET ACCESS AND COMMERCIALIZATION

It is increasingly apparent that continuing exclusive emphasis on food crop production will not allow the agricultural sector to achieve the growth levels necessary for a significant impact on rural poverty, or generate the cash needed to sustain the development of economic and social services. Once food surplus is achieved, further increase of rural incomes and broad-based economic growth all hang squarely upon the ability of smallholder producers to diversify their production systems, base their production decisions on changing market opportunities, and so participate in the rapidly expanding cash crop complex. Such recognition is increasingly reflected in the agricultural sector policies of developing countries, many of which today give explicit attention to the commercialization of production systems.

There is also evidence that regions that produce commercial crops are generally better-off than regions under subsistence production, and that the poor in these regions are also better-off and have more secure jobs.[39] However, commercialization also poses challenges to producers beyond those of reaching the local market place or obtaining a fair deal from traders (see Box 5.6), and in the absence of an appropriate policy environment, it may even have a negative impact upon the poorest rural households. Reardon[40] establishes three groups of smallholders 'going commercial' in terms of welfare change. Commercialization most helps the group characterized by easy access to urban and export markets, infrastructure, human capital, technology and risk assistance. An intermediate group has moderate access to urban and export markets, close to the minimum requirements imposed by agro-industry companies, and lack of adequate capital, credit, technology and risk arrangements. An unfavoured group is in the hinterland, with very poor agroclimate, low access to technology, and almost no access to modern education, risk management or credit.

Traditional food crops produced for own consumption and local markets are still largely the domain of women in many developing countries. However, the growth of cash-cropping has in some cases increased the burden of women who work on their male relatives' cash-crop farms for no or little pay. Landless women in a coffee-producing area of Kenya set up collectives to produce bananas and vegetables to sell independently in local markets in order to control their own labour and benefits of production, as coffee prices were dwindling during the 1980s and women received less payment for their work on coffee farms.[41] Changes in crop-mix and/or changes in production can also influence who controls production: when rice in The Gambia became a crop with irrigation – also requiring market inputs such as fertilizer – and yielded significant marketed surplus, rice fields moved from women's to men's control.[42] However, as commercialization and agro-processing expands, women tend to be linked to the market through employment in such industries rather than being involved in trading themselves. This brings with it new obstacles and issues of working conditions, education, health and increased time burden.

Diversification is often prescribed as a way of reducing the vulnerability of farmers (particularly poor ones) to fluctuations in prices and production. However, poor farmers face difficulties in diversifying into or out of certain cash crops: for example, tree crops, including beverages, require long periods of gestation before providing a harvest; and rehabilitation of land, once the crop is discontinued, can take a long time. Delays in adopting new technology can mean foregoing opportunities when market channels have bottlenecks: for instance, the capacity of an established sugar mill may be filled up by the early users. The export vegetable cooperative in Guatemala has effectively stopped admitting new members because of concerns about bottlenecks in handling and capacity for cold storage.[43] In some cases smaller farmers may be excluded from new technology altogether. Poor farmers appear to have been excluded from the Central American flower boom of the late 1980s owing to lack of access to credit and information, even though many of the crops were suitable for cultivation on small plots of land.[44]

While many small farmers see commercialization as the way out of poverty, few sacrifice food security. The importance of growing cash crops and food crops simultaneously is illustrated in a number of studies (including India, the Philippines, Guatemala and seven from Africa).[45] Households that engaged in cash-cropping generally saw increases in net household income, attributable to higher returns to land and labour. Few households boosted cash crop income at the expense of own-food production. If land was spare, they increased the total land area cultivated where possible and hired additional labour; if, as in most cases, no spare land was available but technology was, they either invested some of the income from their own cash cropping in intensified food production or used income from employment in cash cropping to intensify food production. So, in order to maintain food security, access was required to one or more key inputs: land, labour and technology. With land becoming more scarce, the strategy of using income from cash cropping (as farmers or employees on commercial farms) to intensify food production will become more important, emphasizing the need for access to technology, labour and other agricultural inputs.

Access to markets in assets (including land and water), technology and credit is vital for consolidating and expanding production. Labour markets are also important for the landless and those with insecure property rights and for those seeking to hire labour to increase production, including the very poor during periods of peak activity.

Access to water and water markets

Access to water is crucial to agricultural development and poverty reduction, but markets for water for small farmers and the poor are often undeveloped or biased against the poor, who are often at the tail-end of irrigation systems.

In dry areas, water markets may provide access to water. Non-market allocation of water, often preferred by the state, has often been used to maintain control by 'despots' over a water-dependent populace or to appease the rich and powerful; further, prices have often not reflected the full opportunity cost of water, removing incentives to use irrigation only when it yields good returns, and resulting in gross waste.[46] There is a growing consensus, spurred by worsening water scarcities, that water markets, with full market pricing powers, are needed to tackle this, and to shift water to users and uses with the highest returns.[47] Water markets can encourage farmers to raise efficiency, to shift to high-value crops,[48] and to raise yields – rightly subject to their net value at the margin exceeding the marginal cost of water. The cost of available water induces farmers to adjust the amount and timing of supply to crops, and water providers to allocate water where it produces most returns and hence most farmer custom. Normally water trade gives economic gains to both seller and buyer: the seller can increase profits, while the buyer can access water relatively cheaply and easily, as competition encourages availability and low prices. But removing subsidies would have strong detrimental effects on users, especially the poor, which will require careful transition arrangements until returns are realized and safety nets established.

Water markets, both informal and formal, can be especially helpful to the poor by enabling them to acquire water without taking risks, or borrowing, to invest in water-yielding assets or to commit to specific technologies.[49] In the Pakistan Punjab and North West Frontier Province, only 15% of farmers own tubewells, but one third of these sell some of their water, securing access for those who would otherwise lack water for irrigation.[50] However, unregulated markets can help the poor less than the rich if the poor are less mobile or informed and thus less able to overcome barriers to access, information, or competitive suppliers. Further, market sales of water tend to settle down at prices that neglect the impact of the water use on third parties – for example, through increased scarcity,[51] salinity, waterlogging or pollution – especially if such third parties are many miles downstream, or too poor to transact. There are also practical problems. Some legal systems (like Roman-Dutch law as applied in Sri Lanka and until recently South Africa) give water rights 'from Heaven to the centre of Earth' to landowners, conflicting with efforts by downstream users' groups or the state, to account properly for water use as third parties. Elsewhere, custom rejects water pricing or even ownership – which sometimes safeguards sharing norms that protect the poorest in droughts, especially in remote communities. And there are technical difficulties in measuring water use (area, volume, or crop-specific), especially of flows across paddy land, and the opportunity-cost of water at different times.

In much of South Asia, informal water markets are well developed. In Northern India they usually involve trade between farmers on a watercourse, enabling them to balance supply and demand needs among themselves in each growing season at a time. Informal groundwater markets have helped the small-farming poor in Pakistan, buying from larger farmers, and the near-landless poor in Bangladesh, managing well-water and selling to poor farmers (Box 5.7). This can contribute to equity within the community.[52] Chile and Mexico have pioneered the development of formal water markets by introducing tradable property rights.

However, market access is not a perfect substitute for claims on assets. Farmers who actually own a tubewell benefit more than a water buyer, since they have earlier and stronger claims on water use. But it does not follow that providing poor farmers with credit to sink their own wells benefits them more than developing or formalizing water markets, since if water is unpriced and hard to buy or sell, the value of a well is reduced. In such conditions, owning a tubewell can reduce efficiency. Farmers overuse water because recurrent costs are low, especially where fuel is subsidized. They, or other poor farmers, with dug or shallow wells lose out if over-pumping causes the water-table to drop below the depth that they can reach, especially if they lack funds or credit to deepen the well, as in Tamil Nadu, India, early in the Green Revolution.[53]

So the water-yielding assets of the rural poor work best with water markets; and the poorest need water markets. Poor farmers are willing to pay large amounts for a reliable water supply for irrigation and, in the absence of a water market, these amounts find their way to allocators as bribes, with resulting corruption, centralization of funds and uncertainty. Many farmers pay in kind, often with water sharecropping. In India, in North Arcot district, farmers pay for their water with one third of their crop;[54] in Andhra Pradesh, water sellers provide the water and half the cost of fertilizer while the landowners provide land, labour and the other half of the fertilizer, sharing the produce equally.[55] Such flexible share arrangements adjust to local risks and supervision costs in formal water markets, just as they do in informal markets for rented land,[56] so helping the poor, who are the most risk-averse, and who have least labour supervision costs.

Often, informal water markets involve a simple one-off exchange: a fixed water volume, time, or area irrigated, against fixed cash or crop, or crop-share. Yet such informal markets are not always equitable. The location-specific nature of water, flows, and user farms and houses can create local monopolies. High prices often reflect monopoly access by water-asset-owners, including rich farmers, and can impede access for the very poor. In addition, third-party effects and externalities cannot be controlled as such markets are not regulated. Establishing formal markets through tradable water rights could reduce these negative

Box 5.7: Water sellers in Bangladesh

In rural Bangladesh, the NGO Proshika set up a project for groups of landless people to sink wells using local credit suppliers. The incomes of these water sellers have increased; some are now providing credit to small farmers; and their position in society has improved as their control over water resources gives them leverage over farmers when dealing with other issues. Farmers who buy water in this market are happier as this direct, one-to-one contact eliminates conflict (over distribution, labour inputs, operation and maintenance costs) with other farmers with whom water resources had previously been shared. Poor farmers are no longer tail-enders in irrigation schemes, but have equal access to water, provided they are able to pay.

Furthermore, they can interact with the landless water sellers on more equal terms, whereas before they may have always been the losers against other, richer farmers participating in their irrigation scheme. Increased control over irrigation water enables poor farmers to make a higher number of applications to their crops, which should produce higher yields. This has also created employment, especially in the winter rice season.

However, problems do exist, which can negatively affect equity. As the water sellers are largely paid for water in the form of crops per hectare, there is a bias towards providing water to farmers who produce higher yields per hectare, and these tend to be less poor. Also, when landowners have taken note of the higher yields secured by access to water markets, they tend to push poor tenants off the land in order to farm it themselves, or let it to richer farmers, as the presence of reliable water provision increases the value of the land.

Source: Wood and Palmer-Jones 1991.

aspects of informal markets, while promoting the advantages.[57] For example, enforcing laws and introducing regulations could help prevent monopoly power. Implementing reforms could stabilize informal water markets and work in favour of the poor.

Water pricing is inevitable where water markets exist (though the price may be 'wrong', reflecting monopoly or other price distortions,[58] or neglecting externalities), and normally desirable even where water is allocated otherwise. Water should be treated as an economic good and its price should reflect its true value. Price setting by the state or regulated private utilities should ideally reflect long-run marginal water supply costs, including transaction costs and third-party effects which can adversely affect the poor in particular. Otherwise, poorer farmers can lose out to better-off farmers both relatively (richer farmers can afford to buy more water than poorer farmers) and absolutely (lowering the water table through overpumping of the aquifer by owners of tube-wells, who tend to be better-off, means that the poor with shallow wells may no longer be able to access water). Volumetric pricing, used in some areas of India and Jordan, is normally efficient, and stimulates farmers towards efficient water-economizing choice of crop cultivated. However, due to the high cost of setting it up, volumetric pricing may be limited to public irrigation systems. Area pricing, or paying for water per hectare irrigated, may therefore continue to be popular for small-scale systems. The pricing of water using this method needs to be reviewed in order to achieve more efficient use. Normally the poor will gain from it; if they lose, they should be compensated by means that do not further stimulate water overuse.

Subsidies to the poor to protect them from higher farm water prices are difficult to target well, given that the rich farm more land, tend to use more purchased water per hectare and are politically well placed to divert subsidy. Also, subsidizing scarce resources encourages their overuse and ultimately rations them against the poor. Inequity is exacerbated where, as often, water subsidies are financed from regressive taxes. In Nigeria, 50% of subsidies were given for inputs and services for wheat cultivation, but dependent on a certain area of land being available for cultivation. This excluded poor farmers with small farms and deterred the expansion of irrigation.[59] In India only around 10% of irrigation subsidies in the mid-1980s ended up in the hands of the poor.[60] Subsidy on water-yielding assets is less likely to stimulate wasteful water use than is subsidy on purchased water itself, and can be confined to small and labour-intensive assets used mainly by the poor.

Labour markets

Access to labour markets is particularly important for many of the poor, who are highly dependent on their labour power. In many countries income from hired labour has become an important source of income (Box 5.8). Demand and supply factors account for this. For example, land subdivision may result in unused family labour and at the same time reduce the household's ability to subsist, while monetization of the local economy may induce an inflow of non-food goods and enhance a household's desire for cash. Commercialization, agro-industrialization and agri-exports have increased demand for labour in rural areas in some countries, particularly for women, although much of it is seasonal. Furthermore, the poor are particularly vulnerable to market conditions; for them, a decline in real wages or an increase in unemployment can be disastrous.

The ability of the poor to participate in the labour market is subject to a number of constraints arising from remoteness; lack of access to other assets, such as education; lack of participation in institutions such as credit groups; household characteristics such as family size and com-

---

Box 5.8: Wage labour and the rural poor

Often the rural poor are employed in farming, especially where there is skewed land distribution. Participation in the labour market is greater for those with few household assets, including land. Agricultural workers are vulnerable to seasonal change which influences agricultural labour demand throughout the year. Casual workers tend to be employed during peak labour demand, for example for weeding, ploughing and harvesting. Their wage may be higher than that of permanent workers due to the convenience of hiring labour only when needed and at a time of high demand. Opportunities are increasing for wage labour in non-farm work, particularly as rural financial markets become more established, allowing expansion of non-farm activities. Migrant labour is common in rural areas, with many households receiving remittances from members working in other rural areas, in towns and cities or in other countries. Cotton production in Peruvian coastal areas provides seasonal labour opportunities for those living in the rural Andes. The mines of Southern Africa are a good example of migrant labour both within countries and across international borders; remittances from mine-workers form an important part of household income and can be instrumental in maintaining the local economy.

Sources: Ryan and Ghodake 1980; Mukherjee 1994; Carter and May 1999.

---

position; cultural norms; and discrimination against women or ethnic minorities.

Remoteness

The provision of rural roads and transport can improve access to labour markets. In Colombia, rural road construction reduced out-migration as it improved access to urban amenities. In the Ecuadorian Andes, rural-urban migration was reduced by improved roads that facilitated the formation of small enterprises and increased access to urban amenities. The new road in Sargodha, Pakistan, while also providing new opportunities for the local population, facilitated migration, with around a quarter of those unemployed moving to urban areas.[61]

Lack of assets

Low access to land obliges many rural poor to work as hired labour. Levels of human and physical assets are important factors in determining earnings in labour markets. The rural poor are usually less educated and less healthy than the non-poor. Returns to education tend to be lower in rural areas than in urban areas, although the differences narrow once methods take account of migration,[62] as employment opportunities are typically in low-wage activities in agriculture. Low

coverage of social security systems, unaffordable private health insurance and lack of access to credit for smoothing consumption, oblige the poor to work even when ill. Low levels of productivity stemming from poor health attract low wages. This lack of access to assets forces labourers to rely on their employers for many services. In West Bengal, people are unwilling to work outside their own village, despite higher wages elsewhere, due to the trust and reciprocal information between workers and their employers from the same village, particularly when workers can call on their employer for credit provision and help in emergencies, and when employers can get extra work at times of crisis.[63]

Discrimination

Involving the poor in well-functioning labour markets not only leads to economic growth, but also helps them to a fair share of the benefits. However, labour markets do not always operate fairly, leading to disadvantage and exclusion of vulnerable groups. Gender wage differentials persist, even in urban labour markets in middle-income developing countries. Task-specific, productivity-adjusted gender wage differentials seldom exceed 10%,[64] but much more of the gender wage gap is due to female exclusion from rewarding tasks by educational or customary discrimination. Where men and women participate in similar jobs, women often receive lower wages. In Mexican agro-industries women make up the bulk of the labour force in packing plants, but men receive higher wages for carrying out similar tasks.[65]

Ethnic minorities also face discrimination in labour markets. They can be doubly disadvantaged: discrimination early on in life can leave them in a lower bargaining position in terms of education and experience when applying for jobs and receiving wages. In Bolivia and Guatemala, indigenous groups have lower levels of schooling, lower earnings and lower rates of return to schooling.[66] In Peru, Spanish-speaking workers have higher returns to schooling than indigenous people, and non-indigenous workers earn more than twice as much as indigenous workers. Human capital investment is the key to improving the position of these indigenous people within the labour market.[67] In parts of Asia, too, human capital endowments reduce wage rates among ethnic minorities, whose rural remoteness distances them from schools, clinics and other services.[68]

Household constraints

Often female participation in the wage labour force is conditioned by domestic needs, such as child-care. Decisions about which family member to send out to work vary with the demographic cycle of the household and its physical and human resource base. Opportunity costs are important in decision-making. These are dependent on wages that can be earned, and the experience, efficiency and abilities of various household members. In rural India, the opportunity cost of one person's time affects that person's time allocation, and that of other household members, and thus uptake of labour market opportunities. Domestic labour is frequently viewed as women's primary role, and only when this has been taken into account will their participation in the external labour market

be considered. In Andean Peru, highest female participation in the wage labour force is among young single adult women who have low demands on their labour within the household.[69]

Cultural norms

Men and women often undertake distinct types of work, reflecting their culturally determined roles within the home, or access to education. In the Peruvian Andes, young girls are mostly recruited into domestic service. In Masvingo Province, Zimbabwe, women are involved in domestic work, while men are solely responsible for looking after cattle. In semi-arid tracts of India where households diversify risk in the absence of insurance and capital markets by sending family members to work, female labour is often not used for social reasons, even though it may make economic sense. In Pakistan, women's low participation in the labour force (less than 10% of the labour force in rural areas in the early 1990s) is as much due to social norms as to economic constraints such as poor education, few opportunities and low wages. In rural Kenya, while men take on paid work, women must stay within the household, producing for subsistence purposes only.[70]

Improving access to labour markets

As with other types of markets, resolving problems of labour market access will need a pluralistic approach. Certainly improving rural schools would improve employment prospects for the rural poor, although they may have to migrate to seek work unless sufficient local employment opportunities can be created. The changing nature of export agriculture, with an increasing emphasis on grades and standards, has led, in some parts of Latin America, to rising demand for better educated workers.[71] Labour mobility can be increased through improved road, transport and information infrastructure, reducing the transaction costs of seeking employment, allowing rural labourers to migrate more easily to urban areas during slack seasons, so making their annual incomes and consumption more even.

Reducing remoteness allows the poor to respond to changes in labour demand wherever that may be: after farm price liberalization in parts of Africa (which allowed farm prices to rise), workers who had earlier migrated to urban areas returned to rural areas.[72] Some of the strategies aimed at reducing physical market access problems, such as building and maintaining roads, can significantly affect local employment opportunities through increased economic activity along roadsides and in transportation. Labour-intensive public works may help in some areas. In Africa, where liberalization has resulted in labour displacement due to inability to compete in the world market, rural remoteness from well-functioning labour markets can be overcome. Although in the past rural public works have been associated with short-term relief, these can be a long-term solution to rural problems: not only is surplus labour absorbed, but assets (such as roads) are produced for use in rural areas, which can promote rural growth.[73] But however successful employment generation schemes are in creating sustainable jobs, some groups, women and ethnic minorities will remain excluded because of discrimination and persistent social and cultural norms, although removing biases against educating girls and improving access to education by ethnic minorities may help.

LIBERALIZATION, MARKET ACCESS AND RURAL POVERTY

Advocates of trade liberalization argue that open economies fare better overall in the long run than do closed economies, and furthermore that open trade can play a positive role in poverty alleviation.[74] Faster growth accounts for about half of the international differences in rates of poverty reduction and is not systematically linked to worse income distribution. Freer trade, by accelerating

growth, should help the poor. If poor countries, being mostly well-endowed with labour relative to capital and other factors of production, increase their exports of labour-intensive goods, trade and growth will benefit poor people more.

Agricultural liberalization removes distortions that create biases both between the agricultural and industrial sectors and within agriculture (and industry). In general, liberalization has removed or reduced biases against farm prices, which had often been kept down in the past in order to keep consumer prices low; it has also helped the net food sellers among the rural poor, but harmed net food buyers.[75] If further liberalization of trade allows cheaper food imports from other countries, sometimes also poor, then the gains will be distributed in different ways: consumers will benefit while producers lose, at least until – if not constrained by lack of credit for example – they shift production to other food and/or non-food products where they do have a cost advantage.

Trade liberalization can affect the poor through their access to market distribution channels. In many developing countries, monopsonistic marketing boards are used to distribute products from farmers to local, national and international markets. Even when exchange-rate or tariff liberalization raises export-crop prices in the domestic currency, these boards, because they extract farm income as tax or because of corruption, inefficiency or market-related power, often fail to pass on increases in world prices for export goods further back in the supply chain. However, removal of these distribution channels often leaves farmers either dependent on a private monopsony buyer, who may be just as extractive, or isolated from markets, and, in some cases, from markets for sale of farm products as well as purchased inputs, and credit, since many of these boards had a multiple role.

In the short term, until competitive private sector markets develop, the rural agricultural population, and especially the poor given the difficulties they face in non-contestable markets, may suffer smaller income gains or even losses from this type of trade liberalization, and the shocks may be transmitted to a number of markets (see Box 5.9). Trade liberalization has helped the rural poor when linked to measures to improve market performance and access; missing markets can mean that liberalization worsens poverty.[76] 'Getting prices right' by removing market distortions that affect incentives between agriculture and industry, and within agriculture, brings important efficiency gains. Attention must also be paid to ensuring that the constraints to the development of competitive and transparent markets are overcome.

Liberalization is predicted to reduce the bias against agricultural growth, productivity and prices. Table 5.1 shows farm efficiency effects of liberalization for five countries. In Chile, agricultural prices rose dramatically, with a large increase in output and productivity. Most other countries in this study felt smaller but positive impacts. However, the impact on poverty will depend on whether small farmers and farm-workers participate in the gains, to what extent the poor are net food buyers or sellers, and how they respond to

these changes. In Madagascar, small rice farmers comprise most of the country's poor, and most of them are net rice buyers: the rise in the price of rice meant these farmers faced higher consumer prices for rice, but they responded by increasing effort, leading to increased productivity and output, and so a reduction in how much rice needed to be purchased.

Trade liberalization eliminates policies that hold down low domestic food prices. It has led to an increase in both the mean and variance of all major food crop prices, particularly rice. While rising prices are likely to have a negative impact on the urban poor, who are on the whole net food purchasers, the effect on the rural poor will depend on the composition of their production and consumption and on whether higher consumer prices are passed on to producers. Rising food prices after liberalization had a negative impact on the rural poor in India, the Philippines and China.[77] If rising consumer prices are passed on to the producers and the country has a relatively egalitarian agrarian structure, as is the case in China, then liberalizing border trade as well as internal trade markets probably cuts rural poverty. However, if the economy is characterized by an

---

Box 5.9: Changing market access after trade liberalization

Better market access: cotton in Zimbabwe.

Prior to liberalization, the monopsony buyer (Cotton Marketing Board) held producer prices low to subsidize inputs into the textile industry. While large producers were able to diversify out of cotton into other, unregulated products, such as tobacco, small farmers could not do so and suffered from the low prices. After deregulation and privatization, three buyers have emerged, producing price competition and better prices for producers, and competing to offer extension and input services.

Worse market access: maize in Zambia.

In contrast to the Zimbabwean cotton success story, some rural poor in Zambia have had a bad experience in liberalizing maize markets. Prior to liberalization, pan-territorial and pan-seasonal pricing meant that remote farmers were subsidized by those living close to rail lines, small farmers were subsidized by those with storage facilities, and the whole sector was subsidized by mining. Non-remote maize sellers and consumers, who include deficit maize producers, have benefited from the reforms, but remote producers have lost: very high physical transaction costs arising from remoteness, compounded by a severe deterioration of transport infrastructure, make it difficult for traders to reach producers far from main roads.

Sources: Winters 2000; Oxfam/IDS 1999.

Table 5.1: The impact of reforms on agricultural prices, output and productivity
(percentage changes during post-reform five-year period compared with pre-reform five-year period)

	Real agricultural prices	Real exchange rate[a]	Real GDP growth[b]	Agricultural output	Multi-factor agricultural productivity growth
Chile	+120	+105	+28	+40	+8.2
Mexico	-24	+22	-3.7	+14	+1.3[c]
Ghana	+5	+230	+3.9	+50	+12.2
Madagascar	+11	+94	+2.0	+15	+2.9
Indonesia	+20	+75	-0.6	+42	+2.3

a/ + Signifies that the currency depreciated in real terms relative to the dollar.

b/ The change in the annual growth rate of real GDP is measured in percentage points: for example an increase from 2.0 to 3.0% receives an entry of +1.0 not +50.

c/ Productivity growth was negative in the five years after reform but was even more negative in the five years before reform.

Source: Gardner 1995.

unequal agrarian structure (as in India and, much more, the Philippines) allowing consumer and producer food prices to rise to international levels is likely to benefit the non-poor.

Price fluctuations or price risk are bad for the poor, whether they arise internationally or domestically. Reducing a small or poor family farm's food or staple deficit reduces exposure to price fluctuations of purchased market staples, since less has to be purchased. On the other hand, increasing food surpluses increases exposure to market staples price fluctuations, since more has to be sold.[78]

Where rural infrastructure is good, the poor have been better able to respond to new incentives and opportunities. For instance, competitive markets developed rapidly in China after commerce was freed, thanks to good infrastructure in roads and irrigation and adequate production of fertilizer and other inputs. In contrast, in large parts of Africa, supply response to price and institutional liberalization has been slow, due to poor infrastructure and the slow development of commerce.[79]

However, within Africa distinctions must be made. Supply response to devaluation has been significant in Côte d'Ivoire, where road and communications networks are better developed. Cocoa harvests reached record levels in 1996 (at least 20% higher than the previous record), and non-

traditional exports also increased substantially. In contrast, in The Congo devaluation produced an extremely modest supply response, largely because of years of total neglect of the road network and other key rural investments. Distances are similar, but whereas in 1995 it cost 10-15 Central African francs (CFAF) per kilo to transport coffee from Ivorian production zones to the coast, in The Congo it cost CFAF 60 per kilo. These extra costs are passed on to the farmer in the form of lower purchase prices for their produce, and such costs also rise with devaluation, attenuating the farmer's gain from higher output prices.[80]

Trade liberalization has had a mixed impact on women. In sub-Saharan Africa women have often been unable to participate in the export crop market, lacking land rights, access to inputs and marketing channels. However, in Uganda, women own-account farmers are finding it easier to start growing non-traditional agricultural export crops than traditional export crops such as coffee. Women have gained through employment creation associated with trade liberalization in industry, services and agribusiness and food processing, although these are often seasonal and dependent on good yields. In southern Mexico trade openness improved the quality of life and earnings of women. Whereas two decades ago women were heavily over-represented among poor farmers, they are now frequently working, often full-time, in urban businesses and factories or their own rural businesses.[81]

MARKET ACCESS AND GLOBALIZATION

Under globalization, market access becomes increasingly important as only those who have it can exploit the new opportunities. Without market access, the potential benefits of higher product prices and lower input prices are not transmitted to poor households. With closed markets, such households can be protected against lower product prices, higher input or consumption prices, and price fluctuations, though usually at high economic cost. Remoteness also restricts access to information about new technologies and changing prices, leaving the poor unable to respond to changes in incentives. Of course, supply response will also be affected by many other factors, such as access to assets, skills and credit.

The evidence suggests that there are benefits associated with globalization that can be realized by the rural poor, in a variety of different ways: as independent producers, as contracted producers or outgrowers, or as employees working in association with large commercial agricultural or agribusiness enterprises. In Guatemala, new export marketing channels for vegetables boosted the production of high-value labour-intensive crops. Small farmers (average 0.7 ha) realized large income gains from specialization, while employment in agriculture increased by 45%. In Central America, the value of fruit, vegetables and flower exports increased by 17.2% a year in 1985-92. Though they still represent a small fraction of total exports, expanding production has generated hundreds of thousands of jobs, especially for women drawn from poor rural households.

In Colombia flower exports employ about 80 000 people, 80% of them women. The trade boom has spurred growth in transport, packaging and marketing. Similarly, global demand for year-long fresh fruit has brought new opportunities for women in Chile. They comprise over half the labour force in the Chilean fruit industry, primarily in packing, concentrated in peak season months between December and March. Women are popular for their dexterity and their willingness to accept unstable employment and rates of pay. The jobs open to them are very insecure, with long hours of work without a break during the season, and no source of income during the winter months. Conditions are also poor, with no proper health insurance, social insurance or pension rights. Yet at the peak of the season rural women can earn some of the highest incomes in the sector, and be the main wage earners for a period each year. Their integration into formal paid work has given them greater independence, social recognition and enhanced status within the household.[82]

In the 1990s national and overseas supermarkets have become increasingly important (Box 5.10). There are potential rewards: vegetables for supermarkets are increasingly not only picked and shipped, but locally washed, chopped, wrapped, combined into multi-product packs, labelled and barcoded, creating off-farm employment opportunities. But the process also contains dangers. The power of large buyers means that even the larger producers and exporters are left vulnerable: in the words of one large Zimbabwean exporter, removed from Sainsbury's (United Kingdom supermarket food chain) list, 'You can be replaced at the drop of a hat ... you are only as secure as your last day's delivery'.

As independent producers, smallholders find it particularly hard to meet supermarket requirements for quality (and consistency of quality), reliability of supply, and health, safety and ethical assurances.[83] However, they are occasionally contracted to service the export food market. In Zimbabwe, they are becoming increasingly involved in horticulture, producing for larger commercial farms engaged in packing. Around 3 000 smallholders are growing for export on a contract basis, but face high quality requirements: much of their (sub-standard) produce is sold in the local fruit market.[84]

Smallholder farming offers important advantages. Indeed, researchers generally agree that smallholder farms use resources, labour, land and inputs more efficiently in land- or capital-scarce, labour-surplus economies than large-scale farms.[85] Nor is scale always the issue. In the Chilean fruit sector, while there are economies of scale in post-harvest activities that the small-scale producers cannot capture, the problem appears to be more one of the asymmetric distribution of power and the over-dependence of smallholders on export

companies. The large-scale export firms have established a contract system tailored to their needs; small growers have little choice but to accept the conditions. Elsewhere, marketing cooperatives have been able to provide small farmers with alternatives (like vegetable export cooperatives in Guatemala) but no such associations have yet developed in Chile.[86]

Including the smallholder is possible – many agricultural products, like bananas, rubber, cotton and sugar, have been produced and marketed through contracting many small-producers – but there are issues of quality and standards particularly important for horticulture. An increasing number of foods for both export and urban markets are now subject to grades and standards.[87]

Box 5.10: International supermarkets and local growers

The rise of large supermarket chains in the United Kingdom is an important example of global retail concentration. The top four supermarkets there account for almost 75% of food sales. Consumers have become accustomed to buying a wide range of affordable fresh fruit and vegetables all year round, sourced directly from southern-hemisphere growers, offering developing-country suppliers access to this lucrative market. However, although this trade can offer positive benefits, it remains buyer-driven, liable to change according to the supermarkets' customer needs.

Supermarkets now deal with a small number of larger producers, favouring longer-term relationships with suppliers. This helps suppliers improve standards and quality, but in return they are obliged to make greater investment and face greater risks. Kenya and Zimbabwe supply off-season speciality vegetables; South Africa is a major exporter of off-season fruit; Chile is now a world leader in supplying fruit to European Christmas markets.

Developing country producers and exporters can reap rewards, but are precariously placed in buyer-driven commodity chains. Supermarkets' demands have favoured the concentration of a few large firms in the export trade, sourcing mainly from large commercial farms, marginalizing small farmers to the diminishing wholesale market. But consumers benefit from increased product variety.

Two of Africa's largest exporters, Kenya and Zimbabwe, have shown that smallholder sourcing can meet the quality requirements of supermarkets. The exporter takes responsibility for organizing growers, arranging finance, providing technical support and ensuring traceability. In Latin America there is some evidence that smallholders can benefit if they organize into cooperatives, where they can gain better access to information and technical services and spread potential risks.

Employment in export agriculture can be an important source of income for poor rural households. Export crops generate more demand for labour per hectare than traditional agriculture, especially at key seasonal peaks and in post-harvest activities such as packing. Flexible labour requirements have favoured the employment of women in seasonal work in export agriculture, providing a pool of temporary skilled labour that can be mobilized each season. But working conditions are often poor and unregulated, with punishing production schedules and exposure to pesticides and chemicals putting women's health and safety at risk. The health and education of the family can also be adversely affected by women working long hours.

Source: Vogel 2000.

Farmers who do manage to meet quality and safety standards stand to gain from increased national and global trade. In Chile, small lettuce growers with access to clean irrigation water marketed their products as superior and earned significant premiums. However, meeting agri-food standards often requires substantial investments, in technology and monitoring, often out of reach of small farmers and processors. The costs to producers when they fail to meet grades and standards is high: between 1984 and 1994, the United States Food and Drug Administration detained more than 14 000 shipments from ten Latin American and Caribbean countries because the produce failed to meet United States pesticide standards.[88]

One of Africa's largest horticultural exporters found that while smaller producers can get involved with larger exporters so that transaction costs seem to be overcome, problems in ensuring quality were unresolvable (see Box 5.11). Persuading the supermarkets that smallholders can cope, and that smallholder sourcing will not endanger quality or safety, is possible, though rare. Supermarkets remain wary, appearing to feel that there is less risk in sourcing from a small number of large producers. Ironically, ethical trading standards increase this tendency: supermarkets do not want to be caught out, on child labour for example, and other labour standard issues, and so need to know who their producers are.

Smallholders have been more successful in integrating into global markets through niche markets, such as fair-trade products, environmentally friendly products and, to a limited extent, organic products (Box 5.12). Niche markets such as organics may represent a way to tap into premium markets and reduce reliance on agrochemicals. This 'agro-ecological approach' relies mainly on labour and organic material, as well as on being sustainable. However, significant improvements in information, knowledge and farm management would be needed. In addition the relatively low yields of such farming, and the land used up by some techniques (such as production of green manure), make this approach inappropriate in most land-scarce areas.[89]

Conclusions

Contrary to the stereotyped image of their isolation from trade and markets, the rural poor are already closely involved in local, national and, to some extent, global markets. Rural households earn much of their income from non-farm activities and are active in non-farm labour markets and food markets. This view of the small farmer as a 'multi-sectoral firm'[90] contrasts with the predominant image of small farmers in low-income countries. Many farming households appear willing to accept the new opportunities of commercializa-

---

Box 5.11: Two African exporters

Homegrown, Kenya's largest horticultural exporter, grows over 90% of its crops on its own farms using sophisticated irrigation systems and greenhouses, and has a fleet of refrigerated vehicles to transport produce from field to packing stations and on to the airport, where it has an ongoing agreement with MK Airlines to transport on every evening freight flight. It has also recently built a factory for preparing salads, guaranteeing that salads are picked, prepared, labelled and on supermarket shelves within 48 hours.

Pumpkin exports beans, snowpeas, papaya and mango from Kenya to a United Kingdom importer. Pumpkin initially sourced from smallholders, but realized it could not control product quality. The cost was calculated as 50% higher than the cost of produce grown on large farms because of the waste of produce that failed to meet European Union quality standards. It decided the market for second-grade produce was not large enough and in 1997 leased two farms in order to control its own production.

Source: Dolan et al. 1999.

Box 5.12: Fair trade

To address small producer poverty issues and in response to rising consumer demand for 'ethical' products, both alternative trade organizations (ATOs) and some mainstream firms engage in so-called 'fair trade'. Over 60% of the 2500 products bearing the fair trade mark are primary commodities such as coffee, tea, honey, cocoa, sugar, and bananas, and minimally processed foodstuffs. (The fair trade range does not include industrial and manufacturing goods but does include crafts – an important source of income for both rural and urban producers.) Producer stakeholders are therefore overwhelmingly rural. Global estimates of producers range from 1 to 5 million. Seven food product groups registered with the Fair Trade Labelling Organization (FLO) account for 235 cooperatives and 39 plantations in over 45 countries. One such cooperative alone, in Costa Rica, has distributed USD 1260000 to some 4000 affiliated small coffee producers.

In the United Kingdom, 70 fair trade products are sourced from over 100000 producers, not including family members and community externalities. Although much emphasis has been placed on the higher farm-gate prices producers earn as a result of fair trade pricing policies, producer groups tend to identify capacity-building in trade relations as a key fair trade benefit. The absence of adequate risk-sharing mechanisms and full information tends to marginalize many small-scale producers. Fair trade, with its long-term contractual commitments and technical/quality control services mitigates some of these marginalizing failures in international commodity trade as well as increasing the returns accruing to producers.

The fair trade retail market in the United States and Europe amounts to some USD 400 million each year. Although this accounts for only 0.1% of world trade, it represents explosive growth from the time of the first OXFAM shop in 1964. Improvements in product quality, combined with increasing consumer awareness and recognition of the fair trade mark and wider mainstream retail distribution, have facilitated some startling market penetrations. The introduction of a fair trade banana in Switzerland resulted in an immediate market share of 10% in 1997, growing to 20% of the Swiss banana market by the beginning of 2000. A more typical pattern of fair trade consumer market behaviour can be seen in the Netherlands, where the fair trade banana enjoyed an initial share of 10%, only to settle to a stable niche level of 5% of the market. The 2-5% market share range is characteristic also of the more popular fair trade products, including the market leader: coffee. With wide mainstream retail distribution in the United Kingdom, fair-traded coffee brands like Cafédirect and Ashby's Fairtrade have captured roughly 3% of both the ground and instant coffee markets. Similarly, fair trade ground coffee market shares in the rest of Europe average 2.6%. These somewhat low market shares coincide with high rates of growth for fair trade as a whole. In the United Kingdom, sales increased by 40% in 1998-99 alone and fair trade revenues to producers tripled from their 1996 level to £4.5 million in 1998. Finally, fair trade is reported to be growing at European rates of 10-25% per year.

These growth rates, however, are due mainly to the introduction of new goods in new markets since individual commodity patterns show an initial and rapid market penetration, typically followed by little expansion beyond the 1-5% market share level. The most recent fair trade product launches, namely bananas, as well as commercial penetrations such as the signing of Starbucks coffee to fair trade blends in the United States, suggest that this pattern, though typical, is not inevitable. It is therefore difficult to ascertain whether fair trade will remain a niche or is at the beginning of an important growth path.

Source: Ronchi 2000.

tion, in the hope that they will be released from poverty, but are constrained from doing so fully. The rural poor see that commercialization and globalization can bring increased employment opportunities and income-generating activities.

Small farmers and the rural poor often cannot take advantage of these opportunities. The transactions costs arising from poor physical access, the asymmetric structure of many markets, and their lack of skills, information and organization can represent substantial barriers to accessing markets. Remoteness, scarce and poorly maintained roads, inadequate transport and storage facilities, and difficulties in accessing reliable information on products and prices prevent the rural poor from participating in competitive markets, often restricting them to non-contestable markets dominated by a few, powerful purchasers.

Reducing these transaction costs is a priority for improving access to markets. The difficulties lie in selecting policies that will have the greatest impact on reducing rural poverty while using scarce resources efficiently. Investing large sums in road-building schemes linking remote villages may be less appropriate than alternative infrastructure policies aimed at maintaining roads and improving transport and communications. A complementary approach would tackle not just the physical aspects of market access but the institutional transaction costs: encouraging competition by reducing information asymmetries, and removing farm price controls and other distortions that bias food and staples production.

If the rural poor are to escape poverty they need access to competitive markets not just for their produce but also for inputs, assets and technology, consumer goods, credit and labour. Many of the transaction costs that affect farm prices also affect availability and distort prices of other goods and services. Confronting the physical and institutional transaction costs through market reform and infrastructure development will raise productivity and incomes through greater farm output and more rural farm and non-farm employment. 'Getting prices right' needs to be tackled alongside infrastructure development.

However, the new opportunities presented by liberalization and globalization are accompanied by new risks, and the poor are often ill-equipped to take these unless they have safety-nets. This is one more reason why some degree of food security is a precondition for the poor's enthusiasm for, and safe involvement in, crop-export-based globalization. Most smallholders with cash-crops, exports and/or supermarket links nevertheless keep some land in food for subsistence, diversifying into cash crops while maintaining food crop production.

Poverty can be reduced as the poor acquire access to wider market exchanges, but there are a number of provisos. First, mass poverty is normally reduced by the acquisition and technical improvement of land assets to enhance local staples production. There are exceptions to this general rule, as in the case of smallholder beverage crops. Second, the poor's progress through market development is strongly complementary with asset redistribution. Control by the poor over some human capital and, if in farming, some land, enormously helps in the willingness to take those risks required for successful involvement in expanded markets. Third, just as the case for liberalization embodies the truism that people are seldom helped by hampering their trade and exchange, so the case for globalization risks importing a fallacy: that the further away one trades or invests the better, that local linkages are second-best, that it is fine to subsidize trade and exchange, from free road access to internet-access subsidies.

Endnotes

1   Narayan *et al.* 2000.

2   Wodon 1999.

3   Narayan *et al.* 2000.

4   IFAD 1999e: 20.

5   IFAD 1999a.

6   IFAD 1999a.

7   IFAD 1999a.

8   World Bank 1995a.

9   IFAD 1999d: 62.

10 Glewwe and de Tray 1989.

11 Ferreira and Litchfield 1999.

12 IFPRI 1990, cited in IFAD 1999b: 41.

13 Channel 4 Television, London 1997.

14 These reviews of poor people's preferences are drawn from Platteau 1996: 197.

15 Howe 1984; Nepal: Blaikie *et al.* 1977; Bangladesh: Howe 1984; Egypt: El Hawary and El Reedy 1984; Pakistan: Ali Shah and Azam 1991.

16 Von Oppen *et al.* 1997.

17 Windle and Cramb 1997.

18 IFAD 1994a.

19 IFAD 1994a.

20 Jacoby 1998.

21 Blaikie *et al.* 1977.

22 World Bank 1994a.

23 EIU 1999.

24 Winters 2000.

25 Moslehuddin *et al.* 1993.

26 Scott and Litchfield 1994;

27 World Bank 1994a.

28 ENXX. (IFAD [1999j]. Appraisal Report, PAMA Support Project. IFAD: Rome.)

29 Winters 1999.

30 Oxfam/IDS 1999.

31 IFAD 1999j.

32 IFAD 1999a: 74.

33 Abbott 1987.

34 Jaitly 1996.

35 Mrema 1994.

36 Oosterlee 1988.

37 IFAD 1999a: 87.

38 von Braun *et al.* 1999.

39 Binswanger and von Braun 1991.

40 Reardon 2000.

41 Turner *et al.* 1997.

42 von Braun *et al.* 1989b.

43 von Braun *et al* 1989a.

44 Thrupp *et al.* 1995.

45 Von Braun and Kennedy 1994, cited in Killick *et al.* 2000.

46 Use of water, since it is cheap or free, for purposes such as drowning weeds, where returns are low; and lack of incentive to devise or adopt techniques, product mixes, or asset types that save water.

47 World Water Council 2000.

48 However, this challenges the growth of staples and could result in reversal of self-sufficiency in staples (reached in some countries, like India, during the Green Revolution) and increased pressure on foreign exchange resources. Furthermore, large staple-producing countries such as the United States and Australia will not be able to grow enough to feed the entire world in the future.

49 Water markets are particularly common where groundwater is extracted since this provides a more dependable and easily controllable and measurable supply than canal irrigation. Such markets perform best where medium farmers own wells, as they are more likely than large farmers to use water efficiently and to want to gain income through selling surplus.

50 IFPRI 1997.

51 Often confined to earlier acquirers of water-yielding assets, or poorer users of water. Water markets encourage construction of tubewells to produce water for sale. The extra extraction lowers the water-table and renders useless the cheaper dug wells, or shallow tubewells, owned or acquired previously by the poor.

52 Fujita and Hossain 1995.

53 Chambers and Farmer 1977.

54 Chambers *et al.* 1989.

55 Shah and Raju 1988.

56 Otsuka and Chuma 1992.

57 Thobani 1997.

58 For example, if governments artificially depress farm prices, for example by trade and exchange-rate policies favouring industrial products, the market price of water usable only for farm products is artificially forced down, leading to wasteful water use.

59 Kimmage 1991.

60 Adiseshiah 1994.

61 Colombia: Udall 1981; Equador: Rudel and Richards 1990; Pakistan: Ali Shah and Azam 1991.

62 Schultz 1988.

63 Bardhan and Rudra 1986.

64 Lipton 1983a.

65 Appendini 1995.

66 Patrinos and Psacharopoulos 1993.

67 MacIsaac and Patrinos 1995.

68 World Bank 2000a.

69 India: Skoufias 1993; Peru: Radcliffe 1990.

70 Peru: Radcliffe 1990; Zimbabwe: Adams 1991;
    India: Kanwar 1995; Pakistan: Sultana *et al.* 1994;
    Kenya: Neitzert 1994.

71 Barrientos 1996.

72 Horton and Mazumdar 1999.

73 Bryceson and Howe 1997.

74 Winters 2000.

75 Krueger *et al.* 1991.

76 Winters 2000.

77 Tendulkar and Jain 1997; Balisacan 1997; Khan and
    Riskin 1998. Liberalization affects poverty through
    employment as well as prices. Rising staples and food
    prices, while potentially bad for the poor if they are net
    food purchasers, may increase employment in food
    production, as long as price distortions between capital

and labour are also removed which favour capital-
intensive agricultural production.

78 Fafchamps 1992.

79 World Bank 2000a.

80 IMF 1998, cited in IFAD 1999b: 41.

81 Uganda: Fontana *et al.* 1998; Mexico: Gladwin
    and Thompson 1995.

82 Guatemala: Binswanger and von Braun 1991;
    Colombia: Thrupp *et al.* 1995; Chile: Barrientos 1996.

83 Dolan *et al.* 1999.

84 Oxfam/IDS 1999.

85 Deininger and Binswanger 1999.

86 Murray 1997.

87 Reardon 2000.

88 Thrupp *et al.* 1995.

89 Pinstrup-Andersen *et al.* 1999.

90 Reardon 2000.

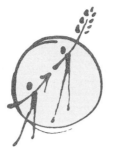

CHAPTER 6

INSTITUTIONS AND THE RURAL POOR: BUILDING COALITIONS
FOR RURAL POVERTY REDUCTION

What we need now is to move from a system in which the poor participate in officially-led develop-
ment programmes towards one in which governments and external donors support people-initiated
development. That must be the true objective of all of us: the empowerment of the poor, allowing them
to gain greater control over their lives and futures.

Fawzi H. Al-Sultan, President of IFAD
Conference on Hunger and Poverty, 1995

INSTITUTIONS AND EMPOWERMENT

The last decade has witnessed rapid change in policies to reduce rural poverty. Greater emphasis is now placed on devolution and local management of common property resources and the extension and strengthening of partnerships with civil societies to nurture and develop human assets. These new approaches emphasize local participation, supporting the construction of social capital and linking the poor to dynamic sectors of the economy.[1] Participation allows the poor a voice, and through a transfer of responsibility gives them the power to discover and determine ways to improve their lives. Empowering the poor is the foundation of rural poverty alleviation.

This policy shift thus involves a new emphasis on institutions: on the organizations (for example, families, banks and trade unions) that mediate the access of the poor to assets, technologies and markets, and on the rules (laws, customs and administrative practices) that determine whether the poor benefit from such access. The poor's chance

to influence rules, and to help control organizations, depends on their power and influence. These, in turn, depend on their knowledge, access and, perhaps above all, whether alternative courses of action are open to them.

This report recognizes the paradox that, while we want institutional change to help the poor, institutions, including the state and NGOs, tend to be controlled by the powerful non-poor. Often, those who control one institution also control others. For instance, even after land redistribution, the large farmer may continue to have better access than the ex-landless labourer to production, credit, information and marketing networks, and the capacity to diffuse and insure against risk.[2] How can the poor and weak use and benefit from those institutions, which were initially controlled by the rich and powerful and run mainly in their interest?

It may be necessary for the poor to seek empowerment at the centre to restrain both the non-poor from arranging things to their own advantage and the rural elite from wielding 'decentralized' power over rural financial institutions or over natural resources. In some cases, the poor may benefit by uniting with some of the rich in a coalition to raise their income shares at the expense of others. In most developing countries the poor can vote. Many non-poor, for whatever reason, often support forms of insurance or universal coverage amounting to pro-poor redistribution: for example, to provide basic health care or social safety nets. In all these cases, much depends on whether the poor use their resources and power jointly, or are fragmented by distance, caste, ethnic group or gender. It also matters whether the poor can afford the time and cost of political mobilization.

Institutions may often persist, but they are not immutable. Channeling appropriate resources such as land, education, and technology to raise the productivity of assets, and markets to improve sales and purchases for and from asset use, improve the poor's 'exit options' that over time may also help them alter institutions for their sustained benefit. For instance, by changing the political structure in the village, land redistribution gives more voice to the poor and induces them to get involved in local institutions and management of the local commons.[3]

This chapter examines three institutional approaches to empowering the rural poor in their quest for poverty reduction: (a) a blend of devolution and collective action for natural resources management; (b) delivery of financial services to the poor to enable them to access and secure financial assets; and (c) developing linkages with NGOs and the private sector as partners for service delivery. The issue of developing global partnership is dealt with in the concluding chapter.

DECENTRALIZATION

Decentralization is often recommended as a way of redefining the boundary between state and market. It is an umbrella term for a number of related policy reforms, in which central government agencies transfer rights and responsibilities to local institutions. Decentralization's merits include easier access to local information, greater sensitivity to local needs, and accountability to the local community. In theory, as the decentralized system becomes more attuned to local preferences it becomes more transparent and accountable. But in practice things may not always turn out that way. The result depends on the context of decentralization.

Recent Indian legislation granting rights of ownership and management over categories of natural resources to *gram sabhas* (village assemblies) of forest villages is a step that can be used by disadvantaged local minorities to assert rights to their share of resources. But whether at local, provincial or even national level (witness East Timor), such devolution of powers and revenues has inevitably been linked with struggles of the concerned minorities.

Devolution of powers to the village has also worked well in making possible high rates of accumulation and elimination of poverty in some Chinese villages where there has been a reasonable level of agreement between the leaders and the village as a whole on the development goal of raising incomes.[4] In the absence of mechanisms of public debate, the ability of these villages to meet crises could be limited.

When conscious and aroused, the rural poor are more likely to be able to influence decisions at the local level than in distant metropolitan centres. Supporters of decentralized targeting claim that information about who is poor is more readily available at the local level than at the centre, and that as local institutions tend to be more accountable to local people, they have an incentive to use information to improve programme performance.[5] That may be so in a few cases (Box 6.1), but, by and large, the claim that local institutions are accountable to the poor is controversial, as decentralized institutions may be controlled by powerful elites that reduce the efficacy of programmes. Viable alternatives are few, however, since non-local institutions have often proved to be even less accountable to the poor.

The case for decentralization depends partially on the extent to which the local programme has been free from capture by the non-poor.[6] This status is also likely to influence the actions the centre may need to take to set the 'rules of the game' for efficient and equitable local operation. This was successful for drought-relief operations in Brazil.[7] Again, the relative success of decentralized government in Karnataka, India, is attributed to the effective system of democratic accountability.[8]

Anecdotal evidence exists of local capture of decentralized anti-poverty programmes and development projects. Rich local farmers in Bangladesh captured a World Bank-funded local irrigation facility intended for poor farmers.[9] More recently, the World Bank's participatory poverty assessment in Bangladesh suggests that the rich in the community tend to dominate the local power structure; they tend to be the first, and possibly only,

people consulted when a development programme is undertaken in the community.[10]

Such observations warn against assuming that local communities are homogeneous, whether in terms of class, ethnicity, age, or gender, and point to serious accountability problems with anti-poverty programmes. Differences in the relative power of the poor, and marginal groups particularly, in local decision-making can make a big difference to the distributional outcomes of programmes within villages. Thus, while there are many benefits from decentralization, local institutions will not necessarily be more accountable to the poor than centralized ones. Analogous to the risks of centralized alternatives, the poor face a real threat of capture of decentralized social programmes by local elites unless some safeguarding measures are deliberately introduced (Box 6.2).

It is therefore necessary, in implementing institutional interventions to reduce poverty, to examine the interaction between central government, civil society, and NGOs and popular institutions, and the options for intervention. The issues are whether these institutional arrangements reach,

---

Box 6.1: Increased accountability and performance through decentralization: does nature of polity matter?

Even in otherwise centralized bureaucracies, the institutional design for the delegation of tasks to local-level agencies is not uniquely related to the nature of the political regime at the centre. The modes of operation of the irrigation bureaucracies in South Korea and in India make an interesting contrast. The Indian canal systems are large, centralized hierarchies in charge of all functions (organization and management as well as design and construction), insensitive to the need for developing and sustaining local social capital. In Korea there are functionally separate organizations in the canal system. The implementation and routine maintenance tasks are delegated to the Farmland Improvement Associations, one per catchment area, which are staffed by local part-time farmers, knowledgeable about changing local conditions, dependent for their salary and operational budget largely on the user fees paid by the farmers, and drawing upon local trust relationships.

In some otherwise democratic countries, if the institutions of local democracy and local accountability are weak (as in large parts of North India), absenteeism of salaried teachers in village public schools and of doctors in rural public health clinics is a serious problem. The villagers lack the institutional means of correcting the problem, as the state-funded teachers and doctors are not answerable to the villagers in the insufficiently decentralized system. On the other hand, in non-democratic China, there is much greater provision of primary education at the local level. There are similar accounts of more effective public pressure in rural basic education and health services in Cuba compared with some of the more democratic regimes in Latin America. There are, of course, many authoritarian countries where local accountability is completely absent; and the situation is much worse than in parts of North India.

Source: Bardhan 1996.

benefit and empower the poor to enhance their capacity to benefit from economic growth; and whether participation in these institutions enables the rural poor to increase their welfare and bargaining capabilities.

The devolution of natural resources management
The daily livelihood of many of the rural poor depends on the success with which common property resources (CPRs) are managed, and on the environmental consequences of their management. The poor depend more on CPRs for income than the rich, but rural income from CPRs is falling sharply as they are privatized or statized.

Recent years have witnessed an increasing trend towards devolution of control (Box 6.3) over natural resources from government agencies to local communities. These resources include farmland, water (especially irrigation), and other common pool resources such as rangelands, forests, fisheries and wildlife.

Experience has shown that centralized and technocratic 'top-down' conservation is effective only with large expenditures on enforcement or under undemocratic circumstances. Usually the rich evade top-down conservation laws, e.g. by poaching from national parks in Africa and exploiting reserved forest resources in Latin America, while the poor are effectively excluded from livelihoods without compensation. On the other hand, participation of different types of local stakeholders – an effectively enforced condition prior to IFAD funding of many projects – has proved essential for effective and sustainable management and conservation of natural-resource systems, and, in general, is fostered by a significant degree of decentralization to local communities.

Privatization of CPRs is, however, seldom a sensible alternative if poverty is to be reduced, since this may create problems of access for the poor, as documented in India.[11] Moreover, community programmes aimed at protecting forests against overexploitation by restricting access could be harmful to the rural poor.[12] Where the poor are heavily dependent on CPRs for survival, there is little hope for poverty reduction if access by the rural poor to these dwindling resources becomes less certain. Devolution of management of CPRs to local com-

---

Box 6.2: Decentralization with control: Bangladesh's Food-for-Education Programme

Food for Education (FFE) is implemented in two stages. First, the participating Union *Parishads* (UP) are chosen. It is a local government area and there are 4500 UPs in Bangladesh, each of which belongs to a *Thana*, of which there are 490. One thousand two hundred UPs were chosen to participate in the programme through a process that assured that all *Thanas* participated. Initially, one UP from each *Thana* was selected; 450 councils were added in 1994-95, and another 250 councils in 1995-96. The stated aim is to select UPs that are 'economically backward' and with a low literacy rate. The selection is done by the centre in consultation with the Thana Education Committee and the minister in charge of coordination of development activities in that area of the country. The centre clearly controls the UP selection process, though there is scope for local lobbying to attract the programme.

In the second stage, eligible households are identified within the selected UPs. Distressed widows, day-labourers, low-income professionals (defined as fishermen, weavers, cobblers, potters and blacksmiths, and so forth), landless or near-landless farmers, and households with school-aged children not covered by other similar targeted programmes are officially eligible to receive the programme benefits. The FFE relies heavily on community involvement in the selection of the households. The selection is typically done by the School Management Committee (SMC): this is composed of teachers, local representatives, parents, education specialists and donors to the school. The food is distributed by the SMC, or sometimes by the UP or a local NGO. Each participating household is entitled to receive 15 kg per month for each child enrolled in school, up to 20 kg for more than one child.

Source: Galasso and Ravillion 1999.

Box 6.3: Devolution: what's in a name?

Devolution programmes are given a number of names. When control over resources is transferred more or less completely to local user groups, it is often referred to as **community-based resource management**. In these cases, the government generally withdraws, and either cuts or redeploys agency staff. When the state retains a large role in resource management, in conjunction with an expanded role for users, it may be referred to as **joint management** or **co-management**. However, these are often not clear-cut, with most cases involving some form of interaction between the state and user groups. Specific terms may vary by sector and country. In irrigation, for instance, **irrigation management transfer** generally refers to programmes that go farther in divesting state agencies of their role, while **participatory irrigation management** programmes seek to increase user involvement, usually as a supplement to the state's role. **Joint forest management** and **fisheries co-management** are other examples of programmes that transfer some management responsibilities to user groups, in conjunction with state agencies.

Source: Meinzen-Dick and Knox 1999.

---

munities can, however, greatly reduce poverty, both directly through sustaining or enhancing food security, and through empowerment, and increased capacity for local management, which should occur as a result of the institution-building required to manage the resources.

Yet the rationale behind many efforts at devolution of CPR management to local communities continues to be sustainability of resources for use by all, including the non-poor, rather than poverty reduction through securing livelihoods for the poor *per se*. Poverty reduction is too often a secondary goal: the poor, who are the main users of CPRs, are in the most strategic position to conserve them[13] – yet, unless proper incentives are provided, also under most pressure to use them.

In short, it is essential to question two assumptions when decentralizing CPRs, or to take action (or persuade local communities to work out actions) to validate those assumptions. The first assumption is that community CPR management will automatically give the rural poor better control over, or access to, those resources and thus help them become less poor. The second assumption is that it will make sense for the decentralized CPR managers, especially poor ones, to give high priority to conservation, given that this depends largely on affordable techniques for making conservation methods quick income-yielders.

Benefits

Devolution of natural-resources management has two sets of advantages. For the users, devolution leads to increased accountability of those responsible for its management. Local users may have a comparative advantage over government agents in managing resources. Being nearer to the resource and having a greater understanding of its importance to users means that more efficient rules can be designed. In addition, the monitoring and enforcement of such rules are easier at the local level. Close scrutiny of resource use by the users themselves leads to greater accountability.

For the government, devolution helps to reduce the cost of delivering these interventions. The active involvement of beneficiaries may lower the informational costs associated with anti-poverty interventions.

Devolution also helps government to overcome lack of knowledge of local conditions. Local participants have the advantage of local knowledge necessary for the conservation of natural resources, and maintenance of resources requires considerable local knowledge and inputs. This is important where the cost of the acquisition of such knowledge by outsiders is high. Irrigation systems are a good example of this. Local factors such as soil conditions, water velocity and shifting watercourses are important considerations in their design; external planners and engineers often lack detailed information. Community involvement in water and sanitation projects is important in ensuring that these are sited where they are most likely to be used.[14] In public works projects in South Africa, communities had knowledge about local conditions such as safety hazards and vandalism, with relevance for road design.[15] Local decisions can take into account the locally valuable functions (like the role of forests in local soil formation, nutrient recycling, water control, and so on) that are usually neglected in decisions by external authorities.

Through devolution, government can get a sense of user preferences. Beneficiary participation offers the potential for the design and implementation of interventions that reflect the preferences of the population they are designed to assist. However, since communities are rarely homogeneous, it is important to examine whose preferences are being voiced.

As we noted above, devolution of natural resource management enables the local community to take account of local costs (external costs) that are ignored in higher-level decisions. These local costs can be balanced against the incomes and overall livelihood impacts to get more balanced natural resource management decisions.

Further, such local management can be designed to link investment with returns: for instance, fish-stocking and infrastructure maintenance with the returns from selling fish. Such a link between investment and returns, secured by assured user rights, is likely to result in higher levels of production, as observed in the Oxbow Lakes Small-Scale Fishermen Project in Bangladesh.[16] But although there is the potential to lower the costs of implementing interventions, it does not necessarily follow that beneficiaries will always be the lowest-cost providers.

Conditions for effective devolution: emergence of collective action

Because their benefits cannot be withheld from anyone, and also because of their size, most irrigation systems, forests, rangelands and fisheries cannot be managed individually or by the household, and require coordinated regulation. Programmes to devolve natural resources management are generally based on the assumption that users will take on the roles formerly assigned to the state. This requires some form of collective action to coordinate individuals' activities, to develop rules for resource use, to monitor compliance with the rules and sanctions against violators, and to mobilize the necessary cash, labour or material resources.

Moreover, natural resources have multiple uses and users. Many of these uses have high economic value or are essential to the livelihood of different households. Several IFAD-funded projects of the early 1980s have demonstrated that external approaches which focus on resource management to maximize a single use are not likely to be as appropriate in these situations as rules that are developed locally through negotiation between different users. Local collective action can be instrumental in finding rules and allocation of the resource between different users in a way that is seen as equitable by the users themselves. There are therefore equity as well as productivity arguments for collective action in natural resources management. But under what conditions will collective action emerge? Some key factors that may increase the likelihood of collective resources management are presented in Box 6.4 and are discussed subsequently.

Size

Small groups have lower negotiation costs, are better able to recognize illegal users of the CPR, and are less prone to free-riding by members.[17] On the other hand, because relationships within a small group are highly personalized, there is more potential for conflict, and as there are fewer people to monitor CPR use, poaching by non-members may go unnoticed. The latter difficulty was experienced in a community forestry programme in Almora District, India.[18] For these reasons, a precise specification of the appropriate group size is difficult. However, several IFAD-funded projects have been successful in reducing conflict between group members through a conscious choice of more marginalized people and areas and with a special focus on ethnic minorities and women. Such groups enjoy a considerable amount of homogeneous and shared sense of both deprivation and expectations.

Group homogeneity and homogeneity of interests
Must groups always be homogeneous or heterogeneous? This may be a more important aspect of community management of CPRs than size, since how a community group of any size actually interrelates through institutional arrangements is more crucial to successful CPR management.[19] In a study of people's management of upland forests in Orissa, homogeneity along caste lines was felt to be important in the development of successful institutions.[20]

In the Zanera Danum irrigation system in the Philippines, users were given fragmented parcels of land along the irrigation system so that there was homogeneity of interests in management, as all users benefited equally from the resource.[21] A similar experience is cited in South India, where corporate institutions are mainly a feature of downstream villages.[22] Given the scarcity of water in these villages, unrestrained access to canal water is likely to result in frequent conflicts and disruption of the crop production cycle. Corporate institutions with effective enforcement machinery have evolved to regulate access to water. Although there was considerable inequality in the villages, elite support for these institutions was guaranteed by the fact that plots of the large landowners were widely scattered. Since any individual arrangement would not have been workable, it was in everybody's interest to cooperate.

Conflict of interests can also be reduced, if compensation is provided to overcome differential gains from cooperating.[23]

Poor users may be reliant on a resource for their very survival, but non-poor villagers may make large financial contributions to institutional costs and take up leadership if gains from the CPR are large enough. This applies to irrigation schemes where non-poor farmers may require a larger share of available water to irrigate their larger landholdings.[24] However, even in such cases, the poor could benefit from the management of CPRs by collectives, provided their bargaining skills are enhanced and coalition is fostered among the poor.

Rangeland management is another CPR that induces the non-poor to play an important part in collective action, exemplified in Lesotho and Karnataka, India.[25] Since the non-poor often own more and larger animals, they are likely to take advantage of common land for grazing, while freeing up their own land for other productive uses.

Box 6.4: Key factors that facilitate collective action

- **Size** of the group: large enough to defy capture by a few powerful individuals, but not so large as to pose monitoring problems by the group.
- A **history of cooperation** and networks among group members (or 'social capital').
- Group **homogeneity** or homogeneity of interest.
- **Returns** from the resource and its importance for local people's livelihoods.
- Clearly demarcated **property rights**.

Here again, homogeneity of interest of the poor and non-poor could be promoted by building on the coalition of the poor.

Tradition of trust

In some situations, traditional patron-client relationships are sustained during the development of viable CPR management institutions. For example, in the High Atlas Mountains of Morocco, senior members of society have full rights to any part of the range for a greater length of time than other members who must negotiate with the local council for access.[26] Indeed, cooperation can develop under unequal conditions in some situations.[27] Confidence and trust among members of user groups are not ruled out even when there is inequality of endowments. In landlord-initiated and funded irrigation projects in Tokugawa, Japan, collective action was possible because of existing patron-client relations.

IFAD's experience in the Oxbow Lakes Small-Scale Fishermen Project in Bangladesh, however, shows that it is possible to create trust where strong traditions of collective economic action did not previously exist. The preconditions were the granting of secure, long-term user rights to the fishers and cooperation incentives in the form of substantially higher incomes. The fishermen set up systems of equity in income and cost sharing, democratic rotation of leadership, and monitoring by group members, which themselves depended crucially on the acquisition of relevant knowledge by members.[28]

The costs and tangible benefits of participation have long been at the heart of the collective-action debate. One aspect of participation that is often not recognized is that people often choose to participate in natural resources management because it offers them an opportunity to socialize and form stronger relationships. Such networks contribute to greater livelihood security, especially in situations of poverty and vulnerability,

where mutual support among family, neighbours and community becomes vital. In Haiti, even landless households would contribute labour to watershed management activities, in part to strengthen networks with landowners who might later offer employment or other help. Such social capital could be an important survival strategy of a poor household.[29]

An examination of the effectiveness of community-based water projects in Central Java found that 'in villages with high levels of social capital – in particular with active village groups and associations – household participation is likely to be high and monitoring mechanisms are more likely to be in place'. But, 'Village leaders and outsiders do not necessarily represent the preferences of households: household participation in service design and decision-making led to different – typically more expensive and convenient – water technology choices in Central Java'.[30]

Clearly demarcated property rights

For local users to be willing to take on responsibility for CPR management, the rights and responsibilities must be transferred from the state to users. Property rights play a central role in the management of natural resources, conveying authority and shaping incentives for management. They give necessary authorization and control over the resource; and can enforce collective action. However, privatization of these common resources often implies disenfranchisement of the poor.[31]

Table 6.1 outlines other important prerequisites for successful devolution of CPR management that have been identified in different contexts. There are no blueprints, only a few guiding principles.

Problems of equity

A community institution for natural resources management is not inevitably or necessarily pro-poor.

A study of four watershed development projects in India[32] that were designed primarily to promote eco-restoration and improve the natural-resource base, with poverty reduction as a secondary concern, found that their (direct) benefits to the poorest were relatively small. While significant improvements were achieved overall in crop yields, diversification, income from farming, and women's participation in meetings, the benefits to the poorest (through higher employment) were much lower.

There was also negligible participation by the poor in project design, and no distinction was made between poor and non-poor in the decision-making process. In such projects, designs generally made reference to small and marginal farmers and women, but less emphasis was placed on the landless and to scheduled castes and tribes. No specific indicators were used to monitor periodically how far the benefits of the project interventions were reaching the poor and marginalized groups: it was just assumed they were doing well.

Community management of resources can lead to improvements in productivity and sustainability of the resource. In Nepal, a study of 86 community-managed and 22 government-managed irrigation schemes found that community-managed schemes were more efficient in terms of crop yield, cropping intensity, and so forth.[33] Similarly, Oxbow Lakes in Bangladesh managed as CPRs of poor fishermen showed much higher rates of investment and yield per hectare than both privately leased and government-managed lakes.[34] A study of Ugandan forests found that state-owned forests were heavily exploited due to lack of incentives to staff to enforce the law. State and private forests which allow villagers to use their traditional rights to access forest resources in return for mon-

Table 6.1: Successful local CPR management

Management variable	Important factors
Attribute of the resource	Worth investing in, that is, a feasible improvement Predictable availability of resource Strong resource-base
Attribute of the user group	Small size: fewer than 40 members, but not too few Clearly defined boundaries Clearly defined rights to use Sanctions against rule-breaking designed and enforced Consensus about who the users are Strong leadership and prior organizational experience Localized system of justice Autonomy: access and use rules determined without interference by external authorities Fair distribution of decision-making rights Remoteness of user group reduces the chances of poaching and enhances mutual obligation All users similarly affected, that is, fairly homogeneous with similar time preferences
Relationship between user group and resources	Location overlap between resource and user Demand for resource Knowledge about level of yields that is sustainable Discount rate low in relation to future benefits Equity in sharing of costs, including labour, and benefits
Relationship between users	Recognition of the effect of one's actions on others' use of the resource Trust

Sources: Farrington and Boyd 1997; Hobley and Shah 1996; McKean 1995; Ostrom 1990, 1999; Wade 1988; Turner 1996; Saxena 1996; Appu et al. 1999.

itoring duties are much less over-exploited.[35] The condition of forests in Nepal varies with the presence of community institutions for monitoring use and restricting harvesting.[36]

In the Philippines, participation in irrigation schemes resulted in greater project sustainability: resources were mobilized, loan repayments were greater, and area under cultivation expanded.[37] Similarly, the Aga Khan Rural Support Programme's work with natural resources management institutions in Gujarat, India, found that where programmes were managed by local institutions, farmers were willing to make greater investments in resource conservation, and agricultural productivity increased by up to 100% within three years.[38]

All this makes a strong case for encouraging and strengthening local-level institutions for the management of local commons. But how equitable are these institutions? How well do they serve the interests of the poor? Three distinct but related issues need to be addressed in this context.[39]

1. Can cooperation emerge when vast inequalities and asymmetries of power exist among the potential appropriators of a resource?

2. If institutions do evolve, even under these circumstances, are the weakest members of society likely to be covered at all under the evolved framework?

3. Even when they are covered, are they likely to enjoy equitable access?

Extreme diversity and inequality among the potential appropriators of a resource may inhibit cooperation, whereas equality may promote it. Across a number of countries, greater equality of endowments among the irrigators was associated with a higher degree of rule compliance and good maintenance. The relatively egalitarian structure of the community was an important factor in the farmers' willingness and ability to organize irrigation projects in Gujarat.[40] Similarly in the Indian State of Meghalaya, villages with greater equality of ownership of land, including forests, showed a greater propensity to overcome collective problems in regulating both distribution of ownership and methods of harvesting of forests for timber. On the other hand, in villages with greater inequality of landholding, even investments in land improvement were not forthcoming because of problems in combining the interests of large landowners and those of numerous tenants. The absentee landowners suspected that land improvements by tenants would lead to claims over land and blocked such investments.[41]

For example, in South India, inequality of landholding among the irrigators generally reduces cooperation on water allocation and field channel maintenance; but at very low and high levels of inequality, conservation is possible, while for some, at middle range of inequality it is not.[42] An analysis of 54 farmer-managed surface irrigation systems in central Mexico yielded similar results.[43]

In general, however, the relationship between inequality and collective action is complex.[44] There are distinct but opposite effects of inequality. Those who benefit most from collective action are more willing to bear the costs involved and thus to make collective action possible. But those likely to benefit least have little incentive to participate in the collective effort: free riding then may be the more lucrative option for them. Besides, the transaction and enforcement costs for some cooperative arrangements may rise with inequality.

Inclusivity of local institutions

Are the institutions that do emerge under unequal conditions inclusive enough to cover the poorest and socially excluded segments of the society?

Although self-managed irrigation schemes may yield an equitable distribution of water among participating farmers, the criteria for membership in these irrigation groups tend to exclude women. Weaker categories of users are frequently excluded by dominant groups in order to achieve efficient use of resources.[45]

Although a number of forestry and drinking-water projects have been aimed at women as primary users of the resources provided, most CPR institutions exhibit a virtual absence of women. In several IFAD-funded projects it was commonly observed that women are invisible farmers. As a result, women's needs are less likely to be taken into account. The impact is two fold. In addition to the disadvantages faced by women themselves, the overall productivity of the CPR system is often impaired. For example, water users' associations have been particularly dismissive of women's needs due to the misconception that only men require water for irrigation.

Both Joint Forest Management (JFM) and Community Forest Management (CFM) in India have tended to ignore the demands of women and the poor in general. This is demonstrated in case studies of the UP hills (now Uttarakhand) and Orissa.[46] When communities closed their forests for regeneration they prevented poor women from collecting firewood, whether for consumption or for sale.

Cultural taboos such as fear of ritual pollution in Nepal stop women from contributing labour for irrigation system maintenance.[47] In Malolo, Tanzania, women are prohibited from maintaining canals, so that they feel they cannot complain if they do not get their fair share of water.[48] Government policy in the Philippines excludes women from construction work.[49] Not surprisingly, female participation in water user associations in Sri Lanka, Nepal, Pakistan and India is lower than that of men.[50] Women often refuse to provide labour to, or participate in, agricultural development projects because they believe that the benefits will accrue only to male household members.[51]

In India and Nepal, fewer than 10% of community forest group members are women,[52] perhaps because, in almost half of Indian States where the JFM Programme exists, only one member of the household may become a member, which tends to

be the man as head of the household. Women may be worse placed than men in their ability to attend meetings. A woman in the Parapegama irrigation system in Sri Lanka is quoted as saying,

I never participate in the FO meetings. If I go there I have to spend about two or three hours, but if I stay at home I can make 200-300 beedis [cigarettes].[53]

In the Ambewelar irrigation system in the hills of Sri Lanka meetings are held at night to accommodate men who work all day, but it is not thought to be suitable for women to go out at night.[54] In Nepal, women gave their illiteracy as a reason for not attending meetings. They thought they would not understand what was being said and would not be able to contribute.[55] Women seldom speak at forest management meetings and their opinions are rarely listened to.[56]

Given that so few women are members of natural resources maintenance groups or attend meetings, it is not surprising that more women are not present on executive decision-making committees. The few women who are involved in forestry committees often participate because it is mandatory for the committee to include one or two women. As a result, and as there are few female members to represent, women on such committees tend to have 'nominal rather than effective presence'.[57]

Despite these barriers to women's participation in CPR management, in India and Nepal women are active in protecting the forests as they feel that men's patrolling is not effective; but their inability to take part in decision-making has consequences for equity and efficiency. For example, several times more forest resources can be extracted sustainably than is actually permitted.[58] An important implication is that knowledge about resource levels is lacking, as the most regular and frequent users are excluded and gender differences in preferences for forest species are not taken into account.

To overcome this problem, the IFAD-funded Tamil Nadu Women's Development Project has been encouraging women to take a greater interest in watershed management projects. Participating NGOs such as MYRADA and OUTREACH have now adopted an approach of facilitating the emergence of women's self-help groups (SHGs). One of the typical discussions is about the management of the natural resources around them. The women group members then try to help men to organize activities for natural resources management. Once this is achieved, women SHGs leave it up to the men, but they do have a representative in the decision-making group.

Sometimes women are fully included in management of irrigation systems. In the Provincial Irrigation Unit, Nyanza Province, Kenya, women's contribution to rice farming is recognized and, accordingly, a minimum of 50% attendance by women is required at the preparatory meeting of new water users' associations, where women are organized in order to articulate their needs.[59]

Similarly, in Dodoma, Tanzania, the Water Supply and Health Project in Marginal Areas encouraged allocation of water rights in quantities sufficient for irrigating one acre to both men and women. As a result, men and women find it is worth hiring agricultural land from landowners. To overcome many of the issues mentioned above, many NGOs now encourage formation of women's CPR management groups. In Nepal, 3% of community-forest groups consist only of women.[60]

Women directly bear the cost of poor participation in community institutions designed for natural resources management. Village forest protection committees regulate forest access for its sustainable use. The cost of foregoing forest use is disproportionately borne by the women through a larger amount of time spent in fuelwood collection. Women's collection time increased from between one and two hours to between four and five hours for a headload of firewood, and journeys of half a kilometre lengthened to eight or nine kilometres soon after the start of protection in the Indian States of Gujarat and West Bengal.[61]

Wherever possible, women shift to alternative fuels such as twigs, dung cakes and agricultural wastes. While some of these hardships have been alleviated in some areas, they have not been eliminated entirely. 'The persistent shortages women face in these contexts thus appear to have more to do with their lack of voice and bargaining power in the [village protection committees], than from a lack of aggregate availability'.[62]

Yet the various JFM and CFM initiatives show that where women and the poor do organize they are able to make some impact on the agendas of the community institutions. In Meghalaya, for instance, the strongly male-dominated village assembly, after continuous pressure from the IFAD project, has begun to include women in its deliberations. Women's issues of access to fuelwood and fodder have also been included within the forest management programmes.

The inclusion of women and other poor does not come about as a matter of course. Changing age-old traditions is a matter of struggle to change gendered or caste-based norms of behaviour, a struggle involving mainly the local participants but also facilitated by external agencies, including project agencies, NGOs and government legislation and orders. The various laws and rules in different South Asian countries, including most recently Pakistan, mandating a certain proportion of women members in village committees create a strong climate in favour of women's public and community roles. While such representation of women often starts out as nominal, over time it also tends to become more real and effective; but, of course, not without struggle.

Lessons [63]

Participation is necessary but insufficient by itself. It needs to be built upon improving the livelihood security of the poor.

The poor who live at the edge of subsistence necessarily place a high value on their time: if conservation of natural resources comes into conflict with meeting the immediate need for survival, then they will disregard the concern for conservation. For instance, in northern and western Senegal, immediate safeguarding of the food supply has become the first priority of ordinary peasants because of the low fertility of land, insufficient rainfall and incidental swarms of locusts. Long-term investment in soil or trees is not undertaken because it would in fact endanger the food supply.[64]

For the poor to be interested in conservation, a mechanism has to be devised that incorporates it into the livelihood security of the poor. This is especially true in a differentiated society where the poor might be tempted to free ride in the hope that the wealthier section would make the necessary investments for conservation. Of course, the wealthier section may not oblige, especially if increasing links with the external economy allow them alternative opportunities for investing their surplus. In that case, depletion of resources would become inevitable. The solution is to take advantage of links with the external economy in a way that simultaneously promotes conservation and improves the livelihood security of the poor.

Such a solution has been successfully attempted by the Communal Areas Management Programme for Indigenous Resources (CAMPFIRE) Project of Zimbabwe. This project has devolved power over wildlife and other resources to local people and has enabled them actually to gain from conservation (Box 6.5).

Conservation has also been linked with security of livelihood with the JFM programme announced in 1988 in the Indian State of Madhya Pradesh. The policy accepts that the biotic pressure from villagers seeking fuelwood, fodder and timber, both for their household needs and for generating cash income, is the main cause of forest degradation. But, unlike previous policies, which tried to prevent degradation by depriving the villagers of their traditional right to forest produce, the new policy recognizes that the life of tribal people and other poor communities living within and near forests revolves around those forests, and that their domestic requirement of fuelwood, fodder, minor forest produce and construction timber should be the first charge on forest produce.

An integrated village resource development programme is now an important aspect of the JFM pro-

---

Box 6.5: CAMPFIRE, Zimbabwe

Mahenye is a collection of villages extending over about 600 sq. km on the border of the Gonarezhou National Park in the south-east of Zimbabwe. Most of the people were located there to make room for the national park. At independence in 1980, rural people were desperately poor, poached as often as they dared, and were extremely hostile to the wildlife, particularly elephants, which raided their fields.

To counter this situation, in 1984 the government permitted safari hunting, within Mahenye ward, of elephant and buffalo migrating out of the park. The dividends of this hunting were channelled into the local community, which was given security of tenure and the right to manage its wildlife resources in the long term. Today, the people have their own committees and other internal government structures, and make responsible decisions. Ten years after the scheme was initiated, there is a welcome resident population of over 300 elephants in Mahenye.

At a meeting of the Mahenye community in 1995, attention was drawn to the fact that a successful entrepreneur from the neighbouring community who owned 500 heads of cattle was in the habit of grazing them on Mahenye land that had not been used for anything else. What were they to do? They could charge him a nominal rent, or ask him to take his cattle elsewhere and put that land under wildlife. They decided unanimously to put it under wildlife.

Mahenye is an example of how decision-making by consensus can lead to the sustainable use of wildlife resources to alleviate rural poverty.

Source: Kikula et al. 1999.

gramme, which presumes that if forests support village development, then people will appreciate their forests and help protect them. In other words, if resources outside forest lands become more productive, people will give up gathering from forests. There are some success stories (Box 6.6), but these are still mostly in the nature of pilot experiments, and have yet to be tried on a large scale. A recent study of JFM in India and the Community-Based Natural Resource Management Programme in the Philippines, carried out by the Centre for International Forestry Research (CIFOR) under an IFAD-funded technical assistance grant project, revealed that decision-making in such programmes was still centralized and access by the poor to forest produce was restricted. There will be no improvement in this situation unless high priority is given to coalition-building of the poor.

Institution-building must be just, genuinely participatory and inclusive

If the poor are to benefit from cooperative arrangements for resource management, they must participate fully in setting them up. Such arrangements can be built on the basis of patron-client relationships, but these are unlikely to advance the living standards of the poor much beyond the level of survival. The alienation of the clients from the residual income accruing from their labour makes it difficult and costly, even impossible, to monitor their performance effectively. This alienation within patron-client relations would reduce productivity itself; while a more inclusive situation is likely to enhance productivity.

As traditional hierarchies are being eroded everywhere with the spread of education and democracy, a new basis of cooperation must be created so that the appropriators can themselves devise viable institutions by mutual consent. Even in this case, however, the poor might be excluded. It is essential that the poor are encouraged and welcomed to participate in the decision-making process. Today, this is a fundamental requirement of most IFAD-funded projects. Evidence from Mexico shows that successful management requires vigorous, regular and well-attended community

---

Box 6.6: Joint forest management in Madhya Pradesh: transformation of a village society

In recent years, under JFM the government has made considerable progress in involving communities in forest protection and management. Primarily, the benefits have been in building awareness, establishing linkages, and convergence between different government schemes. The example of Karidongri illustrates this.

Karidongri is a forest village in Bilaspur district. Out of 57 families of the village, 15 were landless, while the others had un-irrigated land. All families were traditionally dependent on forests for their livelihood. These families, together with officials, formed a village forest committee in 1995 to manage the development of the village and the forest resources. After agreement, they created a diversion channel, a new tar dam, bunding of 20 acres of agricultural land, wells with eight electric pumps, levelling of lands, and a general store with the help of funds from government and other sources. The villagers also started raising fish to generate income. Gradually, all the families came to earn their livelihood from sources other than forests. A SHG of women assisted by the Development of Women and Children in Rural Areas has started manufacturing bricks. A grain bank which provides social security to the village has also been established.

The committee members have protected the forests assigned to them from illicit felling, grazing, fire and encroachment. They have also helped in registering 51 forest offence cases. Besides protection, the village forest committee has taken an active interest in afforestation and has planted 54 780 plants on 60 acres of land. It has sown 192 kg of seed in 1996-97 in blank forest area out of which 13 300 seedlings have been established. The members have resolved to plant 1000 seedlings in non-forest area and name it 'Shakti Van'. The sole objective is to raise fuelwood plantation to supplement their fuelwood requirement.

Source: Government of Madhya Pradesh, India 1998.

assemblies, and the existence of accounting and reporting practices that provide community members with a healthy flow of accurate information.[65] Outside agencies interested in institution-building for the poor will need to adopt special measures to ensure that participation is genuinely all-encompassing.

The example of the En Nehud Cooperative Credit Project in The Sudan shows that this is possible.[66] In The Sudan, the state-run water supply services are in the process of being privatized. In many villages, water shortages are severe and prices high; families can spend up to half their income on water alone. The IFAD-funded project in the En Nehud district aims to restore the water-supply system and transfer ownership and management of water stations to community groups set up for this purpose. Communities themselves selected individuals for receiving training in system operation and maintenance, while legislation was passed providing for the transfer of ownership to the community groups. The communities now manage most of the water stations. Living conditions in the villages have improved greatly, reducing migration from them: a clear indication that the poor have benefited.

IFAD's Special Programme for Africa has revealed some difficulties. This programme was launched in 1986 to assist governments in sub-Saharan Africa in responding to the devastating droughts of the 1980s. A sub-programme on Small-Scale Irrigation and Water Control (SSI/WC) was a major component of this programme. Its objective was two fold: (1) to increase the productive capacity of smallholders and improve household food security, and (2) to build the capacity of the farmers to take over operation and maintenance responsibilities of the scheme by involving local communities or beneficiary organizations. A participatory demand-driven approach was considered a prerequisite for ensuring sustainability. Beneficiaries were expected to be key partners involved in selec-

tion, design and implementation. The strategy was to construct small-scale irrigation schemes which farmers would own and therefore take responsibility for their subsequent operation and maintenance.

The water users' associations did reasonably well in operating and maintaining the schemes, especially in view of the complexities involved.[67] But participation at the stage of project design was minimal. The primary reason for this failure was the absence of a recognized local community or beneficiaries' organization able to deal on equal terms with the government or project representatives. As a result, participation was limited to consultation with village chiefs, local farmers' leaders and individual farmers. This experience emphasizes the importance of devoting time and resources to building organizations of the poor if genuine participation is to become a reality.

But it also has to be recognized that in most rural societies it would be practically impossible to ignore or bypass the traditional power structure altogether. The power base of the traditional elite may be eroding, but it still exists, and no large-scale project of common property resource management can possibly be undertaken without their involvement, even if that implies agreeing to hand over portions of community assets to the poor. The difficulties well-off lessees face in instituting 'social fencing', whether of forests or water bodies, and thus in securing their investments can itself be an important factor in persuading them to agree to such redistribution.

Both the Oxbow Lakes Small-Scale Fishermen Project in Bangladesh and the Hills Leasehold Forestry and Forage Development Project in Nepal are examples of successful redistribution of community assets to coalitions of the poor. The latter project in Nepal selects the marginalized members of the community, families below the poverty line, women, small and marginal farmers, and landless and deprived ethnic or tribal people, and forms them into groups that are then given a 40-year lease of designated forest areas, which often amounts to a lease for life.

It was found that targeting marginal groups would not produce positive results unless the agreement of the whole community was obtained. These leases were given out on what had been *de facto* community land, used by the richer as well as poorer farmers. A long period of time was spent persuading first the officials and then the rest of the community – in particular the village leaders – that the project would benefit everyone and not just the leasers.[68] In the same way, in the Oxbow Lakes Small-Scale Fishermen Project in Bangladesh, the local elite could see that fish culture by the poor increased local availability of fish, both reducing price and improving freshness. But at the same time, the success in large-scale aquaculture has also made the lakes attractive targets for takeover by local vested interests.

In the present economic and political climate it may be necessary to present the case for equality in terms of its contribution, or likely contribution, to efficiency in use of resources. Egalitarianism needs to be cast in terms of asset transfer rather than outright income transfers. While income redistribution may have no effect on productive efficiency (though the experience of East and South-East Asia shows that income redistribution in terms of higher public spending on health and education can have positive effects on productive efficiency), asset redistribution would link labour and investment with returns and income. For instance, the granting of property rights in forests to local communities and families, as in China or in North-East India, could improve microman-agement of the forest and link investment with returns. Thus, a generalization of this equality-enhancing property reform is likely both to be more just and to increase productivity of forest for products, including ecological services such as flood control and carbon sequestration, for exter-

nal stakeholders. At the same time, we should also consider restrictions on property rights, in terms of excluding absentee claims or of excluding the right to sell or otherwise transfer forests.[69]

Asset redistribution can contribute to sustainable poverty reduction only if it increases the productive capacity of the poor and of the economy as a whole. The generally superior yields on small farms *vis-à-vis* large farms makes an important case for land redistribution to the landless. Similarly, even in the case of common pool assets, like forests or water-bodies, the success of the Nepal Hills Leasehold Forestry and Forage Development Project and the Bangladesh Oxbow Lakes Small-Scale Fishermen Project shows that coalitions of the poor can increase the productivity of community resources.

Inclusive local community institutions are inconsistent with the exclusion of women from effective community roles. The question of enhancing women's roles in public and community affairs is critical even in matrilineal and forest-based communities, let alone in patriarchal ones.[70] Women have gender-specific knowledge of local resources and processes, and have gender-specific economic and other household responsibilities. Men tend to dominate inclusive community organizations; encouragement of separate public and community organizations for women would promote their greater participation in the management of the community.

DELIVERY OF FINANCIAL SERVICES FOR RURAL POVERTY REDUCTION

Credit helps the poor to smooth consumption, and later to acquire assets greater than the value of the liability. Consumption smoothing is especially important for the rural poor; agricultural incomes and rural health fluctuate widely and will destabilize consumption if households cannot fall back on savings or access to credit. Once poor households feel that consumption is safe, they are more ready to risk borrowing for investment in physical, natural or human capital assets. But the poor can sustainably service credit only if the new asset yields more than enough to repay interest and, eventually, the capital element of the loan. Thus finance for investment can reduce poverty, but not while basic consumption remains at serious risk or if technology (or market access) does not enable the poor to earn a decent return on assets. Yet investment by the rural poor is often constrained because they cannot borrow. At the same time, if formal lenders are to reduce moral hazard and adverse selection to affordable levels, they must avoid high unit transaction costs on tiny loans; especially if they cannot effectively screen poor borrowers (who lack collateral). Informal (local) lenders are put off providing loans to the poor (again lacking collateral) by high co-variance (a bad harvest means loans fail together) – and often it does not pay to price-discriminate, charging more to poor/risky borrowers, because that stimulates even more risk-taking. The rural poor often lack reliable access to financial services as a whole – including not only competitive credit, but also savings and insurance services – whether from public, formal private, or informal sources.

From the early 1950s, developing-country governments and international donors provided massive doses of credit to the agricultural sector at concessional interest rates, often negative in real terms, through either cooperatives or state-run banks. This approach achieved little in reaching the poor, raising output, using credit efficiently, or developing sustainable rural financial institutions. Subsidized interest may even have destroyed competitive private lending and stimulated low-yield investment. There is now a widespread consensus that problems in state intervention in rural financial markets arose as much from interest-rate ceilings as from distorted incentives and weak governance structures of the public-sector financial

institutions (Table 6.2). Yet the international development community recognized that, if state monopoly was bad for growth and poverty, untrammeled markets alone were unlikely to do the job either. Could decentralized, participatory management be a better solution?

Increased access of the rural poor to financial services was achieved by rapid increase in microcredit provision during the last 20 years.[71] Targeted microcredit programmes seek a strong anti-poverty focus, and aim to increase incomes and smooth consumption. Enthusiastic and large-scale support for these innovations from multilateral and bilateral donors has ensured a rapid growth of microfinance institutions across the world.[72]

The predominant financial product offered by most microfinance institutions (MFIs)[73] is an advance of a lump sum of money, with capital and interest to be repaid in regular instalments. To ease collection and enforce repayment, individuals are often federated into groups that are collectively responsible for loans extended to its members ('peer monitoring'). Further incentive for regular repayment is provided in the form of quick, easy and increased access to repeat loans. The repayment-by-instalment arrangement provides an opportunity for clients to take the maximum advantage of fungibility of cash by managing regular instalments from existing income sources. The financial product is insensitive to seasonal demand and risk (which can be a disincentive for poorer clients using credit as quasi-insurance substitutes), and does not take into account the cash-flow cycle of client enterprises. Nevertheless, in sharp contrast to subsidized and loss-making state-backed rural credit, many (though not all) of the new microfinance agencies achieve sustainability by combining high repayment rates with interest at the market rate, thereby confirming that 'the poor need credit, not cheap credit'.[74]

But this is not costless. Though part of the package is that the state (and donors) phase out

Table 6.2: Recent developments and shortcomings hampering outreach and sustainability of MFIs

Topic	Recent developments in some countries	Continued shortcomings in the majority of countries
Policy environment	Macroeconomic stability; interest rate deregulation; ease of setting up banks or branches; low minimum capital requirements for MFIs	Inadequate policy and legal environment; slow implementation of deregulation; inadequate property rights and judicial procedures
Microfinance institutions	New legal forms for commercially operating MFIs; privately financed start-up; increasing numbers of self-sustaining MFIs.	Lack of appropriate legal forms; excessive capital requirements
Non-formal financial institutions	New legal framework provides opportunities for upgrading to formal levels and for financial market integration	The potential for upgrading millions of informal financial institutions remains largely untapped
NGOs	Innovative approaches to poverty-lending in repressive environments; some successful conversions to formal intermediaries	NGOs are slow in mobilizing domestic resources and in striving for self-reliance; donors support unviable NGOs
Agricultural development banks	Incipient reforms towards autonomy, viability and self-reliance, with or without privatization	Political interference; lack of viability; failure to meet demand for credit and deposit services
MFI regulation and supervision	Controversial discussion on the need for effective regulation and supervision of MFIs	Financial authorities unable to supervise MFIs; agricultural development banks escape supervision; lack of MFI self-regulation
Agricultural finance	Self-financing from profits and savings plus non-targeted commercial credit replaces preferential sources	Self-financing and commercial credit insufficient to meet the demand for short- and long-term finance; inadequate savings mobilization
Access of the poor to financial services	Outreach of viable MFIs (including rural and other banks) to the poor as users and owners drastically increased	Vast numbers of poor people, particularly in marginal areas, lack access to savings and credit services

subsidies of interest rates, initial administrative subsidies to create sound microfinance intermediaries for the rural poor have been huge. They are incurred, in part, because of the belief that poor populations can implement income-generating economic activities, and that the main limitation on their initiative is the lack of access to capital in contexts where: (1) financial markets are not well developed; (2) commercial banks are reluctant to commit themselves because of the extent of the risk, and also because of their lack of familiarity with the sector; (3) development projects and banks have most often failed; and (4) the informal sector is neither sufficiently large nor capable of responding to the challenges of development.

Initially, then, the challenge for microfinance was to demonstrate that, once financial tools specifically adapted to the needs and constraints of 'poor' populations were developed, then people would be able to use these tools for productive purposes and incorporate themselves into the financial milieu, repaying the loans and accumulating savings. Based on this assumption, many microfinance systems have been developed in South and Eastern Asia, with different institutional forms, and often giving preference to disadvantaged areas and to the most disadvantaged groups within these areas.

In the second phase of the development of the microfinance sector, the need to create sustainable financial markets became evident, and the legal and financial sustainability of microfinance systems became a priority. Microfinance systems were set the goal of breaking even, and thereby being able to liberate themselves from grant-funding within a reasonable period of time, and this very rapidly became the fundamental orientation of microfinance 'best practice'.

The emphasis was on providing small loans, often focused on women entrepreneurs, as a means of reducing poverty. These loans have three objectives: to generate productive income streams; to reduce poverty; and to support sustainable rural financial institutions. There is no reason to expect that these three objectives will point to the same set of loans or even of lending institutions, or that they will be consistent; and where there is no sufficiently productive/profitable safe opportunity that the poor can take up, the objectives will not be achievable. In short, production-oriented credit success needs assets and/or technology, usually with market access. While many agree that microfinance can make a difference to people's lives, the extent to which it contributes to poverty reduction remains uncertain. The relationship between microfinance and poverty reduction is fairly complex: just as poverty is multidimensional, so there are many pathways to its reduction. Welfare indicators relate not only to income, but also to human, physical and social capital.

The existing evidence of the impact of microcredit is not clear-cut. Some research suggests that access to credit has the potential to reduce poverty significantly,[75] but there is also research suggesting that microcredit has a minimal impact on poverty reduction.[76] It is now increasingly recognized that microfinance alone is not a magic bullet for poverty reduction, but only one of many factors that may contribute to it. In fact, in an effort to dispel the impression that microfinance is a cure for poverty, it is argued that 'the claims that microfinance assists "the poorest" and "the poorest of the poor" are

unfounded within national contexts. MFIs virtually never work with the poorest . . . and many MFIs have high proportions of clients who are non-poor [using the national poverty lines]'.[77] This may be because the poorest households tend to shy away from MFIs. Also, because of moral hazard, a poor person is rarely welcome in a group of five.

In many cases, the poor face significant structural challenges, which marginalize them not only in economic terms but also in social and political terms. This makes them 'invisible'. Many very poor people migrate seasonally for wage employment; some consciously avoid joining the mainstream, such as the *banjaras* in parts of India; some households, such as the 'Kamaiyas' in Nepal, are 'attached' to other households in semi-bonded relationships. Such 'invisibility' makes targeting difficult. It is hard to arrange loans or repayments from short-term migrants. Further, microfinance agencies (and members of peer groups) emphasize regularity in attending meetings and depositing savings – which penalizes employees in general and migrants in particular.

Poorer participants are less able to sustain benefits from these programmes and might drop out disproportionately, perhaps because the products offered are not appropriate to their needs. The rural poor need a range of financial services, including savings and insurance, not just credit. The poor operate in a micro-economy in which production, consumption, trade and exchange, saving, borrowing and income-earning occur in very small amounts, which increases the per unit transaction costs and makes it unattractive for them to borrow from the formal sector. They are also exposed to high levels of risk arising from violence, natural disasters, health, harvest failure, and price and labour market fluctuations; the different forms of these risks weaken the capacity of community-based social security networks to provide support.

These features mean that the poor must devise ways to spread risk, by economic diversification and the development of informal financial networks. Savings and credit mechanisms are used by the poor as substitutes for insurance, so savings, credit and insurance have to be treated in a unified way.

Under these circumstances, the provision of microcredit has been found to affect crisis-coping mechanisms positively by allowing the diversification of income-earning sources and building assets. For example, even where there may be no evidence that access to microcredit leads to increases in consumption, it does contribute to reducing household vulnerability. According to estimates, consumption variability is 54-47% lower for eligible microcredit borrowing households than for the control group. Such consumption smoothing is driven by income smoothing, which is shown by the significantly lower labour-supply variability experienced by households using microcredit than by the control group.[78]

This is important as poverty is so closely associated with risk and vulnerability. These results suggest that programme participation by the poor is driven largely by the benefits of risk reduction rather than the benefits of greater consumption levels. But this finding says more about the finan-

cial service preferences of the poor than the product itself, which, as argued, is rather insensitive to risk and vulnerability dimensions of poverty. In Sri Lanka, for example, SANASA's poorest clients use savings services more than credit services[79] and small, high-cost emergency loans more than large, low-cost investment loans.

Designing financial services for the poor must focus on risk and vulnerability if they are to extend their outreach and prove more useful. One obvious response is insurance. However, quasi-insurance can be built into existing products, such as more frequent, but also more flexible, repayment; giving the opportunity to use savings for loan repayment; more flexible repayment schedules suited to client preferences; and purpose-specific contractual savings products for events such as marriage, death and so forth. Some possibilities are catalogued in Table 6.3.

Building sustainable financial systems
Recently, the emphasis has shifted from the link between microcredit and poverty alleviation to the intrinsic importance of building sustainable financial systems offering wide-ranging services comprising microcredit, microsavings and insurance

Table 6.3: Financial products for the poor and possible innovations

Product	Elements not sensitive to risk and vulnerability	Possible changes
Microcredit	Fixed instalments	More frequent but flexible instalments
	Fixed maturity	Variable maturity
	Loan size treadmill	Savings-balance determined loan size
	Mandatory repayment	Client-determined option for the use of savings for repayment
	Complete collective responsibility (repeat loan access denied if group repayment imperfect)	Partial collective responsibility (repeat loan access sanctioned, not denied, if group repayment imperfect)
Microsavings	Fixed savings	More frequent but flexible savings
	Compulsory savings	Transparent compulsory and voluntary savings
	Limited savings products	Purpose-specific contractual savings
	Unclear rules about access to pooled savings	Clear rules about access to pooled savings

Source: Matin 1999.

facilities. This is because the poor need access to financial services, particularly:[80]

- deposit facilities for accumulating and safe-keeping their savings, consumption-smoothing and self-financing of economic operations;
- credit for consumption-smoothing and external financing of their operations; and
- insurance for social security and loan protection.

Provision of a wide range of financial services will not only serve clients' needs more effectively, but also improve outreach depth and improve access to external sources of funding.[81]

Improved access to financial services can enable the poor rural household either to augment income generated by the production process or to reduce the cost of smoothing consumption at sufficient levels. Smoothing disposable income generated by borrowing for consumption, or by saving in highly liquid but less remunerative assets, is expected to be relatively more important for households that face the risk of transitory or chronic food insecurity.

This perspective of financial service allows us to understand the difficulty that poorer households face in participating in and sustaining benefits from some of the current innovations. The importance of financial-service provision to the poor is of intrinsic value, irrespective of its promise as a poverty-alleviating tool. Viewed thus, the issue is the design of suitable financial-service products that the poor would find useful. This in turn warrants an understanding of the financial behaviour and preferences of the poor.

The importance of saving

Households all around the world have always saved: as insurance against emergencies, for religious and social obligations, investment and future consumption. The importance that poor people attach to saving is also demonstrated by the many ingenious, but often costly, ways they find to save in addition to keeping small amounts of cash secreted at home. These methods include investing in assets that can be sold in case of emergency (for example, corrugated-iron sheets, livestock or jewellery), participating in local initiatives such as Rotating Savings and Credit Associations or funeral funds, or lending between family and friends. But these mechanisms can often fail to meet the needs of poor people in a convenient, cost-effective and secure way. If a poor household is given a safe, accessible opportunity, its capacity to save and the amounts it manages to save are remarkable.

Savings were previously the forgotten half[82] at the MFIs and were typically extracted from clients through compulsory systems. There was a notion that 'the poor cannot save', and compulsory savings systems often required members to deposit small token amounts each week as well as levying more substantial amounts at source from loans. These compulsory savings were then often 'locked-in' until members left the organization, thus denying them access to their own money. Until recently, compulsory, locked-in savings systems, in one form or other, were a prevalent model for MFIs throughout the world.

However, compulsory savings systems have come under increasing pressure not only from the professionals involved with financing, managing and reviewing MFIs but also from clients themselves. The Consultative Group to Assist the Poorest has stressed that 'possibly the greatest challenge in microenterprise finance is to expand the provision of savings services to the poor'. This is driven by the fact that 'there is substantial evidence from many parts of the world that: (1) institutional savings services that provide the saver with security, convenience, liquidity and returns, represent a crucial financial service for lower-income clients; and (2) if priced correctly, savings instruments can contribute to institutional self-sufficiency and wide market coverage'.[83]

Nonetheless, for MFIs with a history of credit-driven services that have levied compulsory savings as part of a package, the shift to flexible financial services, including savings products, is often hard to effect. MFIs need to acquire more sophisticated management capabilities to manage liquidity, risks and cost, as well as develop a more complex organizational structure and information and reporting systems in order to act as financial intermediaries.

Furthermore, several other factors often provide significant impediments to promoting savings. These include macroeconomic problems such as high inflation rates as a result of political turmoil and/or economic imbalances, and financial repression through interest rate controls and subsidized credit schemes. In addition, in many countries there are no appropriate systems of regulation and supervision for MFIs leaving them either operating outside a legal framework or pinned down by traditional formal-sector banking laws. Thus, despite the huge demand for savings facilities for the poor, the supply of such services is inadequate, in terms of both quantity and quality.

The need for insurance

Insurance can complement the provision of credit services for institutions seeking to help their clients to smooth their consumption. Insurance is a powerful poverty-reducing tool, as well as a means for the institution to reduce risk. As institutions mature they are in a good position to provide insurance to smooth consumption of the poor and to enhance institutional profitability. Insurance goes even further than savings to minimize dips in basic needs consumption. It also gives the poor a sense of security that allows them to dare to pursue profit-maximizing income strategies, and hence to borrow, because they know that an income shock will be minimized when the claim is settled. With the repayment rate of a lending institution closely linked to clients' return on investment, insurance has considerable potential as a complement to an institution's credit programme.

Insurance provision in the semi-formal sector is still not viewed as a policy goal: hence the large surplus of premiums over claims that MFIs' insurance products typically generate. Resources attracted by MFIs through insurance provision are generally used to build up capital for smoother operations rather than to improve upon the insurance services provided to clients. While capital accumulation is certainly an important advantage of providing insurance, neglecting to improve insurance products is short-sighted and keeps the institution from developing a valued service.

Developing insurance products will help address an institution's long-term profitability and protect members against larger, more destabilizing economic shocks. Insurance instruments are a profitable complement to credit delivery for a mature MFI. As the average loan size of an MFI increases, it becomes increasingly risky to disburse credit, since if a family's return on investment from borrowed capital is less than anticipated, the larger repayments cannot be mustered from the family's normal income. The opportunity for profits through lower-risk insurance instruments could significantly help keep microfinance operations profitable, even as default pressures increase with larger loan sizes. With increased profits from insurance services, credit disbursement could be more selective with respect to screening and follow-up. The likely result would be more efficient and profitable credit delivery for income generation.

From a social welfare standpoint as well, a more fully developed insurance market is desirable. Absorbed savings in the form of insurance premiums are disbursed when beneficiaries are most likely to spend additional income on basic necessities. For the institution, therefore, insurance provision means more effective poverty alleviation, improved loan repayment rates and improved profitability. Consumption-smoothing strategy is strengthened with insurance provision. Demand for savings services could in part be accommodated by insurance services that would have a more direct and positive effect on poverty.

Microfinance institutions

The preceding discussion establishes that different types of financial institutions and strategies are required; there is no single best type (Box 6.7). Institutions must be tailored to the potential of the area, the cultural environment and the requirements of the clients.

• There are marginal areas with a predominance of subsistence agriculture and low-return activities. Here, user-owned SHGs or small cooperatives which are savings-oriented and operate at nominal costs may be most suitable.

• There are high-potential areas with high-return agriculture and profitable rural microenterprise activities. In these areas, credit-oriented rural banks with professional management, large financial cooperatives and commercial bank branches with individual or group technologies may be more appropriate.

The choice of institutions that are suitable in a given situation will depend on the situation and environment specifics. The degree to which financial disciplines and cost-recovery principles can be applied will depend on the extent to which the local production environment is developed, that is, the rate of return from activities taken up through MFIs. It will also depend on the effects of

---

Box 6.7: An approach to promoting MFIs for rural poverty reduction[85]

Depending on the situation, IFAD encourages variety and competition rather than the replication of single models. It engages dialogue with stakeholders and is prepared to support initiatives such as:

• promoting informal financial institutions at retail level, such as the SHGs in India, Benin, Indonesia and the Philippines, including financial grass-roots organizations of indigenous origin, as in Ghana;

• mainstreaming savings and credit cooperatives, as in the United Republic of Tanzania;

• supporting networking and apexing among MFIs, as in Cameroon;

• strengthening private and community-owned rural banks, their bank associations and apex organizations, as in Ghana, Indonesia, Nigeria and the Philippines;*

• transforming credit programmes into user-owned institutions, as in Nepal;

• reforming agricultural development banks as major microfinance providers, as in Indonesia and Thailand, or closing them if unreformable;

• linking banks and SHGs, as in Ghana, India, Indonesia and several other Asian and African countries;

• promoting commercially operated apex organizations for refinancing MFIs, such as the People's Credit and Finance Corporation in the Philippines and the Small Industries Development Bank in India, and apexes with additional functions like liquidity exchange, credit rating, credit guarantees and reinsurance;

• supporting trader, processor and supplier credit** and promoting their access to refinancing institutions, as in various East African countries;

• promoting institutional innovations, such as (micro-) leasing companies;

• strengthening microfinance units in central banks, as in Cameroon and Ghana; and

• providing non-credit enterprise development services to reduce the risk of clients, as in the case of the Maharashtra Rural Credit Project in India.

* The terms 'rural bank' and 'community bank' refer here to regulated institutions which fall under the banking law or a special law for rural or community banks, as in Ghana, Indonesia, Nigeria and the Philippines. IFAD does not use the term bank or village bank for unregulated institutions such as *caisses villageoises*, *sanadiq* (sg. *sanduq*) or other informal and semi-formal MFIs.

** Traders, processors and suppliers may act as important channels of credit, particularly in the absence of a functioning local financial system. These channels tend to be less sustainable than institutions and less efficient in terms of transaction costs, but may provide interim solutions in the process of building up smallholder assets and rural financial systems.

various man-made and natural disasters on the normal flow of economic events. Large gains can be wiped out overnight, making recovery of loans difficult, if not impossible. Such circumstances will need provision of additional resources for supporting the development of MFIs. If such costs are to be internalized, many of the microfinance initiatives may cease to be viable.

The viability of MFIs will also depend on how far these institutions can reduce transaction costs. This is a major challenge. Informal financial markets in many parts of Asia and Africa have been demonstrated to be efficient mobilizers of savings and providers of financial services.[84] They can often show the way for cutting down on costs and ensuring fuller recovery. Efforts need to be made to integrate the positive features of informal financial market behaviour into the formal MFIs.

PARTNERSHIPS FOR ENDING POVERTY

Poverty reduction is a complex task, requiring sustained commitment to consistent, yet flexible, joint action. There are no quick fixes and no easy solutions. No one institution, national or multilateral, public or private, and no unique strategy can hope to deal effectively with the different contexts and causes that underlie poverty. So coherent anti-poverty strategy requires stable partnerships, based on trust as well as self-interest.

The most fundamental partnership is with the poor. Poverty reduction is not something that governments, development institutions or NGOs can do for the poor. They can help create the conditions in which the poor can use their own skills and talents to work their way out of poverty. This requires putting the poor at the centre of the process, as full partners in determining the priorities and the directions of change, emancipating them from the constraints that trap them in poverty, empowering them. It is therefore misguided bureaucratic centralism to plan for the poor; partnerships for poverty reduction should,

wherever possible, start with the agency of the poor themselves, with their preferences and potentials. But it is naïve to suppose that the poor can make bricks without straw; technologies, information, schools and skills have to be built in conjunction with outsiders. The evidence of the success of partnerships with the poor even in such apparently unlikely areas as plant breeding – not passive farm trials but farmers' active varietal selection and development – is telling. Whatever kind of resource is involved – technologies for plants; animals; housing; asset choices among skills; types of rural road; forms of consensual land distribution – involving the poor through the institutions of partnership assists success. The problem is that doing this locally with decentralized systems means opening opportunities to the articulate, the strong, or the unscrupulous.

That said, outsiders can support partnerships with the poor at different levels (Table 6.4). Micro-level partnerships are institutional arrangements – formal or informal organizations and rules – among nearby people, e.g. to manage common property resources. Meso-level partnerships – of government with civil society, NGOs or the private sector – are increasingly used for service delivery, with the NGOs implementing government projects, often working jointly for lobbying and advocacy, or with donors. Micro- and meso-partnerships are necessary not only to deliver services, but also to identify and develop demand for them. Macro-partnership, the overarching global framework for anti-poverty strategies, is discussed in Chapter 7.

NGOs as Service Providers

National government institutions and external donors have long collaborated with NGOs and other civil-society institutions as service providers in the context of development projects and programmes. Currently, NGOs in developing countries reach directly an estimated 250 million people.[86] These organizations now supplement, and in some

Table 6.4: A typology of partnerships

Level	Type of partnership	Objective (s)	Example (s)	Threats
Macro	Donor-donor	Improved aid disbursement Cofinancing Knowledge sharing Devising common policy	DAC Guidelines	Lack of coordination among different donors
	Donor-govt.	Influence domestic policy Capacity building	UNDAF, CDF PRSPs, ADB's Poverty Partnerships, multi- and bilateral support	
	Govt.-govt.	Sharing of natural resources Management of global public goods	Regulation of ozone layer; Control of CFC emissions; Sharing of river waters	Narrow political considerations can derail agreements
	Donor-Govt.-NGO	Service delivery Encourage government ownership	Most World Bank's partnerships with NGOs	
Meso	Govt.-NGO	Service delivery Subsidize cost of O&M	Primary education, health	Pressure of scaling up the programme
	International-Local NGO	Relief and/or development work		Imposition of an international agenda
	Donor-NGO	Service delivery	Bilaterals	Funding constraints; Changing priorities
	NGO-NGO	Lobbying/advocacy	ADAB, NGO Forum in Cambodia	Inability to agree to a common strategy
Micro	Govt.-people	Local management of natural resources	Joint forest management; Water users' associations	Tussle over control of resource in an environment of mistrust
	NGO-people	Improve service delivery, local skills and capacity	Most NGO projects	
	People-people	Increase demand for provision of public goods Management of CPRs	Associations and networks; ROSCAs, user groups; micro-credit groups	Heterogeneity; lack of social capital

UNDAF: United Nations Development Assistance Framework; CDF: Comprehensive Development Framework; PRSPs: Poverty Reduction Strategy Papers; ROSCAs: Rotating Savings and Credit Associations; O&M: Operation and Management; CPRs: Common Property Resources; ADAB: Association of Development Agencies in Bangladesh. Membership NGOs, trade unions, peasant associations are not included.

cases have displaced, state agencies in the provision of relief and welfare, social services and development projects. The delivery of international development assistance has also been transformed with increased NGO involvement in various projects. Resources disbursed for development projects increased steadily from USD 0.9 billion in 1970 to USD 6.3 billion in 1993 (in constant 1970 dollars).

In an international finance institution like IFAD, for example, virtually every project in recent years involves civil-society institutions and NGOs.

In several Latin American countries, the responsibility of providing a number of social and development services has been delegated to NGOs. In some cases the state has withdrawn from financing as well as delivering services, such as rural credit and agricultural extension in Peru. In other cases the state has delegated delivery and management to NGOs while maintaining its financing responsibilities in activities such as running schools, national parks and agricultural extension in Bolivia, agricultural extension in Colombia and Chile, and primary health care in El Salvador. NGOs are playing a similar role in some Asian and African countries where they deliver a significant proportion of health services and are often the only service agencies operating in remote rural areas.

The involvement of NGOs has often been found to enhance the prospects for successful project implementation. Such organizations have a comparative advantage in reaching the poor. Often they have better information about the poor because of local contacts, and they reduce the leakage in delivering benefits that results from corruption in government bureaucracies.

NGOs typically work in communities or settings where the reach of the government is weak. In the West Bank and Gaza an estimated 1 200 NGOs provide 60% of primary health care, up to half of secondary and tertiary health care, most agricultural services, low-cost housing, and microcredit. The same is true of primary health care and education in many African countries in remote rural areas where NGOs run by Christian missionaries are often the only service agencies operating.

Decentralization initiatives have also enhanced NGO involvement, in part because of government budgetary limitations. A majority of public-private partnerships over the last 15 years in Latin America have involved local or municipal governments. NGO expertise in targeting, the ability to access the poorest groups, and experience and technical knowledge in the fields of education, health and the environment, have been the main factors driving such relationships.

In a pilot project in El Salvador the Ministry of Health delegated the management of health care to an NGO while retaining financial responsibility; the

NGO's dedicated and well-trained volunteers and doctors travelled to parts of the countryside that public health services could never reach. In Bolivia the government retains responsibility for research and development expenditures and an NGO has built an extension system to serve farmers. Careful planning of responsibilities is particularly important in fully collaborative efforts – such as joint farm trials – in which a successful outcome requires carefully scheduled inputs from both sides.[87] In this case, the NGO owns and operates the extension service, while the government has a comparative advantage in research and development.

In the city of Itagui in Colombia, the local government was responsible for the construction of school buildings, and an NGO with a distinguished track record in providing education was responsible for managing the curriculum and staff.

In India, recognizing the expertise of NGOs in the health sector and the shortcomings of the outreach of official agencies, the government has begun handing over its primary health centres for the NGOs to run, as opposed to its earlier policy of giving subsidies and tax advantages (Box 6.8). In an official document, the Ministry of Health and Family Welfare[88] stated: 'The government has envisaged a very prominent role for voluntary organizations/NGOs in the implementation of health and family planning programmes. India is second only to the United States in terms of the number of hospitals outside the public health sectors and run by NGOs and these organizations are doing a very creditable job in organizing and running hospitals and dispensaries.'

Partnerships may also arise where an NGO develops an appropriate technology or extension methodology (such as group-based training, farmer-to-farmer dissemination) and 'passes them up' to the government for replication elsewhere. As small organizations acting alone, NGOs have limited impact beyond the boundaries of a pilot project area. In contrast to governments, they do not have a broad (as opposed to deep) presence in many areas. Hence expanding an effective rural development programme beyond a small area has necessitated collaboration with the government.

The comparative advantage of NGOs in reaching beneficiaries at the grass-roots level has been one of the most important reasons for government-NGO partnerships. But being merely the government's delivery agency, or dependent on government funds, often obliges NGOs to tone down their social and ideological objectives, which in turn can undermine the spirit of voluntarism or credibility with the group of beneficiaries which lies at the heart of their comparative advantage.[89]

Partnership with the Private Sector

Partnerships between governments, development agencies and civil-society institutions are of long standing. More recently, it has been recognized that, in a world of liberalization and globalization, with development processes increasingly market-driven, partnerships need to be built with the private sector.

Governments and donors have always dealt with the private sector for the supply of goods and serv-

ices. Private sector entities are now showing an interest in private/public partnerships that seek to reduce rural poverty.

The United Nations Secretary-General has called for a global compact with business to work together to promote human rights and raise environmental and labour standards. This represents a new partnership and concern for objectives that are in the long-term interest of human society as a whole, even if they do not immediately add to profits. Of central importance is the need to mobilize the private sector within countries in support of poverty alleviation. The scope for this is illustrated by an IFAD project in Uganda. There, a private oil-processing firm has agreed to join a project to help smallholder cultivators of oil palm and vegetable-oil seeds to improve their productivity and output. The private firm, which is contributing more than half of the project's USD 60 million investment cost, will provide an assured market and fair prices as well as technical support to the farmers. In turn, it will benefit from a reliable raw material supply source, allowing it to increase production levels. Such partnerships to benefit poor farmers and other poor

---

Box 6.8: Community participation in health delivery for the poor

The IFAD-funded Andhra Pradesh Tribal Development Project in India provides an example of how the health delivery system can be made more responsive and effective in a poor tribal area through the active participation of the community. Major elements of this system include the placement of well trained community health workers, who are selected and paid by the community as front line agents of health delivery system; enhanced mobility for women health supervisors; operationalization of specific strategies for control of communicable diseases, malnutrition, infant and maternal morbidity and mortality though community-based interventions; establishment of mobile units for primary health care extension; strengthening of referral services; development of infrastructure for subsidiary health centres; capacity enhancement of staff, especially the medical officers; and health education. Strengthened outreach services have stimulated community demand for better health care delivery. Important benefits of this system include significant reduction in maternal and infant mortality due to improved surveillance and early treatment of communicable diseases; increased immunization of pregnant women and children; increased awareness about environmental hygiene; improved nutrition due to enhanced food production and increased family incomes from other interventions of the project; and enhanced confidence on the part of the community that it can maintain health standards through community management. The success of this scheme led the State government to accept it as a viable strategy for primary health care in remote rural areas. Consequently, the World Bank has adopted several elements of the strategy for its project covering a wider area of the State.

Source: IFAD's internal documents.

groups are one of the keys to promoting pro-poor economic growth and allowing the rural poor to participate in, and benefit from, market processes on a fair basis.

Public-private partnerships could also play a major role in developing agricultural and medical technologies supportive of the poor. At present large private agricultural and health firms do not see markets or profits in developing new technologies for the poor. A number of interesting ideas have been put forward in recent years to create incentives for private firms to undertake such research using a combination of public funds and tax benefits. These can be used to promote research into the crops and animals suitable for the dryland, rainfed conditions where most poor farmers live, and to address diseases such as malaria, tuberculosis and AIDS strains prevalent in Africa.

Most people now agree that governments, national institutions and external development agencies usually have to work in partnership with civil society and the private sector if development goals are to be attained. Many practical instances have been cited to illustrate the scope, and limits, of this approach. What is relatively new is the perception that rural development works best when poor rural people are agents, not recipients of charity. The poor can sometimes initiate successful development partnerships, can often share their aims, and should always be empowered by participation in them.

CAPTURE OR COALITIONS?

In many regions, development programmes have in effect been captured by vested interests, with either the active collusion or the passive acquiescence of state elites. Lack of people's organizations that actively promote the coalition of the poor is usually a major contributory factor in capture by powerful interests. Although there is a risk of being over-optimistic on the basis of limited evi-

dence, the temptation to rule out a strong coalition of the poor on the grounds of ethnic, religious and caste differences must also be resisted. A recent synthesis draws attention to key factors in promoting coalitions of rural poor.[90]

Cooperation depends on whether cooperative action was successful in the past. The latter may be associated with the shared norms of trust in a community. Whether such norms would be observed in vertical social networks (as opposed to horizontal ones, involving people of similar status and power) is debatable. There is some evidence that if the gains are large, these could overcome the disadvantages of a socially heterogeneous membership.[91] The problems of social heterogeneity are nevertheless compounded by those of economic inequalities. Capture of local organizations by the rural elite often remains unchallenged by the poor, who are trapped in a dependent role. An agricultural labourer, in debt to his regular employer, will be disinclined to cooperate with other labourers to demand an increase in the agricultural wage.

It is commonly believed that the only reliable way to achieve an increase in participation and the collective action potential of poorer groups is to increase the resources available to them through redistributive policies. For instance, access to land through a market-mediated land redistribution programme could weaken elite dominance and induce more effective participation by the poor in local bodies.[92] However, while earlier land reform helps facilitate later success, decentralized institutions have also worked well in areas where land reform has had little success, such as in Bangladesh or in the Indian State of Karnataka. Manor argues:

Poor as well as prosperous people participate more and increase their collective action potential as a result of decentralization even where it works mainly to the advantage of elites. Over time, the greater transparency offered by democratic systems at lower levels, the increased participation of poorer groups, and their developing skills at influencing those systems may well assist them in curbing the power of the rural elites to appropriate benefits.[93]

Participation by the poor in local self-governing institutions does help in evolving a sense of collective identity and building social capital, which over time can lead to empowerment. But this process of empowerment is often slow, incremental and uncertain. A more rapid process of empowerment usually follows through a coalition-building process (Box 6.9).

Case study 1: The mobilizing potential of the Employment Guarantee Scheme, Maharashtra

The Employment Guarantee Scheme (EGS) was formalized in the mid-1970s in the Indian State of Maharashtra. It is an innovative scheme that guarantees paid unskilled work for the rural poor for building public infrastructure. All rural adults are eligible for such work, which is paid on a piece-rate basis, employment being guaranteed within 15 days of demand and within 8 km of residence. Unemployment benefit is promised if the government is unable to provide work for job-seekers. At the onset, at least 60% of project expenditures were to be spent on wages. In general, the project has been hailed as a success for poverty alleviation due to its ability to target the poor through wages being just below the usual agricultural wage.[94]

Worker organization has been catalysed by the introduction of the EGS, which also increases the bargaining power of the poor.[95] The EGS is the cause rather than the effect of mobilization of the poor.[96] Furthermore, by making employment an entitlement under the EGS, workers have a right to work which stimulates collective action should the right not be met. Indeed, the Employment Assurance Scheme, introduced in all Indian States in 1994, did not guarantee work and, as a consequence, mobilization was not forthcoming.[97]

A number of organizations have arisen as a result of the EGS. Activism is of two types. Some organizations, such as Bhoomi Sena in Thane district, educate people about their rights to work.[98] Villagers are encouraged to fill out forms to petition for work and to pressure the government to start EGS works in the vicinity of their village. At State level, some organizations provide training camps for EGS workers to give them basic skills.[99] The second type of action confronts the state for initiation of projects or modification of working conditions (such as payment of minimum wages and unemployment allowance and provision of amenities on work sites). This is achieved through sit-ins and demonstrations, whether at the workplace or at government offices. In 1981, an apex organization established to coordinate demands by the late-1980s consisted of 19 organizations.

However, most of these demands were not met. For example, the Employment Guarantee Workers' Union made persistent efforts to demand projects in Pune district, through filling out work applications, making a list of possible projects and meeting with various EGS staff, but

---

Box 6.9: Women's empowerment through income gains

In India, promotion of women's producer groups by the Self-Employed Women's Association and of women's credit and thrift societies by the Cooperative Development Foundation – despite initial scepticism among the members – has led to more than moderate income gains among the members on a regular basis. Income gains coupled with experience of managing producer groups/cooperatives have imparted to them greater self-confidence, security and independence both within and outside the household. There is a sense of solidarity among them. Caste divisions have weakened. Women now advise their husbands on cropping decisions. Their advice is also sought on community matters, like sanitation. Greater political awareness has led to more active participation in local elections.

Source: Carr et al. 1996.

without success.[100] Even when activism instigated reforms, these have often been ineffective. Although demands for the distribution of food-grains for workers were met, few merchants would honour the food coupons. In addition, paid maternity leave was attained, but only two women benefited. The EGS did not lend itself to activism as workers did not tend to work on the same project for any length of time. EGS employment was viewed as only temporary, and the projects were managed by various government departments, which made agitation a challenge.[101]

The doubling of the minimum wage in 1988, in part due to EGS activism, was a milestone in the history of the EGS. Contrary to expectation, this resulted in a decrease in labour attendance.[102] Some argue that there was an unmet demand for work because it became too costly for the government to guarantee work. In this case, one would expect activism to increase as the guarantee of work was not being honoured. However, activism dwindled after 1988, which suggests that people were not as reliant on the EGS as once thought. Indeed, a run of good crop years and positive impact of EGS assets increased productivity and hence agricultural employment opportunities; so the supply of agricultural employment could also have been responsible for the drop in EGS attendance.[103]

In addition to the drop in the number of EGS participants, targeting of the poor was less successful during the 1980s. The proportion of poor workers in the scheme decreased from 48% in 1979 to 27% in 1989,[104] possibly as a result of reforms in 1986 which meant that work no longer had to be offered within 8 km of the home. The poorest therefore find that transport costs do not justify taking part in the scheme. The weakening of self-targeting was exacerbated when the Planning Department decided to finish incomplete works before taking up new ones. Furthermore, wages did not keep up with infla-

tion and were often late; thus the EGS became unattractive for many of the rural poor.

However, despite the lack of success of activism to address issues such as these, the poor have gained from the presence of the EGS and success of activism even if they have not participated. Adherence of the EGS to the minimum wage legislation, which was lobbied for by activists, led to a rise in agricultural wages. The EGS had an impact on agricultural wages of about 18% in the long term, reflecting a rise in agricultural productivity as a result of the increased reservation wage due to guaranteed employment in the EGS during slack periods.[105] In addition, the sense of collective identity created by the EGS improved the bargaining position of the rural poor *vis-à-vis* large landowners. Thus, even though the EGS became less well targeted to the rural poor and activism was largely unsuccessful in improving working conditions within the EGS, the rural poor did benefit from the EGS through indirect agricultural wage increases.

Activism has been revived somewhat since the mid-1990s, but its nature has a more general rural development flavour through national campaigns for legislative action to protect the rights of rural workers. Specific to EGS workers has been a writ petition against the State government in 1998 to fight for a minimum wage above the poverty line. However, limited public funds for EGS inevitably means that rising wages reduce both total EGS employment and the targeting of the programme on the neediest; activism can sometimes exclude as well as include.

Case study 2: Increasing accountability through local organization

Since the late 1980s, Mazdoor Kisan Shatki Sangathan (MKSS), or Workers and Farmers Power Organization, has been active in attempting to improve the accountability of local governments through undertaking right-to-information agitation in Rajasthan. MKSS demands, and is frequently successful in gaining, access to official government expenditure records which are then exposed for a people's audit. It is unique in that it is the only organization in India that both addresses theft of public resources and challenges bureaucratic culture. Although formal membership of the organization is small, it has a large informal following of local socially-excluded groups and committed activists from elsewhere, which has played an important part in MKSS's success.[106]

At the centre of MKSS's activities is the fight for the right to information. This has often been viewed in India as synonymous with freedom of expression associated primarily with the press. Action by the MKSS has transformed the notion by applying it to the concerns of the rural poor. Exercising the right to information through access to official documents is a vitally important element in ensuring accountability of local government authorities. Indeed, the 'public-hearing process has allowed the MKSS to develop a radical interpretation of the notion that ordinary citizens have a right both to know how they are governed and to participate actively in the process of auditing their representatives in minute detail'.[107] Corruption seems to be rife in local governments, for example, influencing estimates for projects, using poor quality materials in projects and billing central government for amounts above what workers are paid. In January 1998 a study of five village councils found that as much as Rs.100 000 (USD 2 500) of public funds were unaccounted for in each village.[108]

After acquiring balance sheets and supporting documentation, a 'social audit' can be used to expose wrongdoing. This involves reading aloud official documents to villagers in public hearings. Local people then testify to discrepancies. For example, a camel cart driver may report the number of bags of cement he has delivered to a work site and compare this with the figures given in official project documents. Some people have discovered that even though they had received no payment, they were listed as beneficiaries in means-tested anti-poverty schemes. Such social action has been largely successful. Local politicians and bureaucrats frequently attend these public hearings and are asked to account for any inconsistencies raised. Occasionally they own up to their corrupt behaviour and even return funds.

However, due to the difficulty MKSS faces in acquiring government accounts, social audits are rare. Instead, large-scale public protests are used to get reforms to enable local people to legally obtain official records. After four years of protest, in 1999 the new chief minister of Rajasthan established a committee to improve access to information. However, the results are disappointing. Only specifically indicated information in digested form can be made available to the public.

One measure of the impact of MKSS is resistance by government officials. For instance, there was a state-wide strike of village level development officers in 1996 because one district chief allowed a village to photocopy official documents before a hearing.[109] The MKSS has successfully promoted transparency of local governments, albeit on a small scale. It has demonstrated great skill in mobilizing the rural poor in seeking to fulfil their rights at local level. In addition, it has developed a network of support from the elite, intellectuals, activists and the media, which has spread MKSS's influence beyond village level and may have greater bearing on state legislature in the future.

As the review of evidence suggests, people's participation does not follow rules, even if these create incentives for the flow of benefits. This is so especially where we are attempting to involve in the participatory process people who have been deprived of their rights for generations. To prevent the capture of the institutions that have the potential to benefit the poor, it is important to mobilize the poor. But it is essential to provide them assets, technologies and markets, so they have a fall-back position, if 'punished' or excluded because they have sought or exposed inconvenient facts.

Case study 3: A peasant-led agrarian reform

The Movimento des Trabalhadores Rurais Sem Terra (MST, Landless Peasants' Movement) of Brazil rose out of the struggles of the peasants in the late 1970s, when Brazil was going through a phase of political openness following the end of the military regimes. Brazil has one of the highest concentrations of land ownership in the world, with 1% of the population owning some 46% of the landholdings, many of which are inefficiently utilized. Of the 400 million hectares under private ownership, scarcely 60 million hectares are cultivated, with the vast majority of the lands either lying idle or given to pasture or held simply for speculative purposes. Currently some 4.5 million families are landless.

The MST has three major objectives: attainment of land, agrarian reform, and a more just society. Specifically, these translate into: expropriation of the large land areas in the hands of multinational corporations; an ending of the unproductive *latifundio*; and the defining of a maximum allowable ceiling for number of hectares for ownership of rural properties. The agrarian reforms proposed by MST seek to:

- guarantee social welfare and improved living conditions for all Brazilians, with special concern for the poorest working people living in the country's interior;
- guarantee food in sufficient quantity and quality and at an affordable price for the entire population;
- ensure work for everyone, harmonizing job creation and income distribution;
- develop small- and medium-size agro-industries as a means to develop the country's interior; and

- secure a permanent striving for social justice, equality of rights in the economic, social, cultural and spiritual spheres.

The movement is operative in 22 States and, in its 12 years of existence, some 6 million hectares have been acquired with the settlement of over 140 000 landless families on these lands. Many of the settlers are organized into producer cooperatives, linked with the Confederation of Agrarian Reform Cooperatives of Brazil (CONCRAB), founded in 1992. The CONCRAB brings together 45 agricultural cooperatives, ten regional marketing cooperatives, dozens of associations and eight central Agrarian Reform Cooperatives. And in settlements where agro-industries, such as the coffee and tea-processing units, milk and cheese production, flour mills, and so forth, have been developed, average incomes have risen from between 3.7 and 5.6 times the minimum monthly family wage. MST's current slogan 'Agrarian Reform – Everybody's Struggle' reflects its main strategy to involve the whole Brazilian society in the campaign for land even as violence against agrarian reform continues unabated.

Case study 4: Leakage of poverty programmes as a form of coalition building

Research from lending programmes in Bangladesh reveals that there is leakage or mistargeting of programme benefits to the relatively better-off households who constitute the non-target group (NTG) of the Bangladesh Rural Action Committee (BRAC).[110] One possible explanation is that the pool of target households who wish to join becomes saturated and as a result non-target households are included. However, evidence of significant numbers of households who could have taken part but did not suggests that this cannot be the whole story. Programme administrators and field staff suggest that pressures exerted by target-group members themselves to include some influential NTG households may compel programme administrators to relax the official targeting criterion. These pressures could arise due to poor members wanting to get a wealthier household involved in the rural development programme (RDP) in order to tide over loan repayment difficulties within the group. As Mosley[111] points out when analysing Banco Sol in Bolivia, these transfers from better-off to poorer borrowers are not necessarily 'altruistic' as they are often in the form of loans. Moreover, there may be powerful factions within the village who could disrupt the daily operations of RDP if their representatives are not given access to BRAC's inputs.

While the general 'community approach' has been tried and discarded by BRAC due to the impression that the elite was benefiting most, the target-group approach may have to be flexible enough to incorporate a number of socially influential households to maintain a link with the other socio-economic classes in the village. This line of argument fits in with Besley's[112] model which shows that the limited inclusion of the non-poor may be necessary in order to induce them to limit their claims on benefits that are meant for the poor.

Another reason for the inclusion of non-target households may be the belief that they are better credit risks than poorer households. They are also likely to deposit more savings and demand larger loans, thereby improving a branch's self-financing ratio. However the 'loan absorptive' capacity of these NTG households is still a matter for investigation, as it will determine the full extent of the revenue-earning potential for an MFI.[113] The extent to which NTG members are above the eligibility threshold is crucial. If the NTG household is marginally above the cut-off point, then the inclusion may simply be merited on the grounds that BRAC's land and occupation-based eligibility criterion is not perfectly correlated with poverty and that the NTG household could be below the poverty line. There is a strong possibility that the typical 'non target' BRAC member is either poor or part of the 'vulnerable non-poor' group. If the policy-maker's objective is to reduce the proportion of people below the poverty line, then targeting the moderate poor and even the vulnerable non-poor may be justified.[114] If the aim is to reduce the severity of poverty then incentives need to be targeted to the poorest sections.

The central argument here is that the inclusion of non-target households in microcredit programmes may not be necessarily a sign of programme weakness. On the contrary, inclusion of a few NTG households may just help to increase sustainability of flow of benefits to the poor by preventing capture attempts by the richer households.

CONCLUSION

One of the most important conclusions of this report is that decentralized institutions are created and run in the interests of those with power. These may come under political, economic or ethical pressure to benefit the poor, from the poor themselves or otherwise. But on the whole the powerful will run – or allow the poor to help run – pro-poor institutions only if the powerful expect to gain (or to avoid loss) by so doing. This is a special problem for institutional reform seeking to help the rural poor: if centralized, because of the facts of urban government, concentration, power and bias; if decentralized to rural areas, because the determination of institutional outcomes is placed in the hands of rural 'big men' – and the rural gap between big and small (and men and women) is especially huge, not only in poverty, but also in literacy, information and other prerequisites of political success. That rural big men run local institutions in their interest is a fundamental difficulty for current modes of top-down institutional devolution, decentralization and participation. That the modes are usually initiated from the top is a defect, but inevitable. And participation, even if initiated from above, is often essential to efficiency.

Furthermore, we review in the four case studies above striking examples – but only in open societies – of learning-by-doing by the rural poor of how to enhance political power, influence and agility in the 'civic culture'. The case study from Bangladesh describes how the inclusion of non-poor in targeted programmes may be necessary to a limited degree in order to prevent them capturing more benefits that are meant for the poor.

Nevertheless decentralized institutions for natural resources management and financial services rarely help the rural poorest 'directly' (e.g. by steering credit or natural resources to them) but often reach the moderately poor, and help all through increased efficiency and sustainability, as the locally powerful are driven to recognize their shared interests with the poor in these. Two of the most important types of decentralized rural institutions thus share the experience of some success in improving sustainability and efficiency, but little redistributive effect or outreach to the poorest. To the extent that they participated, the poor did so by sharing general gains, not by insisting on a larger share: by coalition, not redistribution. This can achieve something, but seldom for the very poorest, and seldom very fast.

More generally, development programmes can be captured by elites or vested interests; or they can give rise to broad coalitions which share the gains. The rich may get the lion's share, or may find that it pays them to do with less, especially if the poor have political voice, or can organize themselves into counter-coalitions with other persons (including politicians) of power. Several examples of successful actions by women's and poor people's groups illustrate the point; but they need options and voice; hence the importance of a reserve of land (even if tiny) and of literacy and political openness.

Finally, the dilemma of 'willing participation into being from above' is increasingly softened, if not solved, by partnerships involving donors, governments and NGOs. But careful selection – of governments, NGOs and projects – is essential if this process is to lead cost-effectively to gains for the rural poor. Experience suggests some quite detailed rules for such selection.

While there are grounds for optimism, it would be naïve to presume that collective action among the rural poor to bring lasting benefits to their communities can be initiated and strengthened only through government support. As noted earlier, organizing the rural poor is not easy without profound research and reliable information on their local practices. The learning process for them may be slow and frustrating. Locally powerful groups may divide the poor, and the bureaucrats may resent local organizations designed for the benefit of the poor. Yet for poverty reduction, strengthening the coalitions of the rural poor is an important consideration.

The shift from simple delivery of goods and services to participatory programmes or projects draws attention to process, and the role of women and men in those programmes. As all resources have to be transformed into consumption units, the efficiency of the process will be affected by those who acquire access to the resources. This area has not been much researched in the analysis of organization and development. But there are more than a few pointers: in the case of micro-enterprises, for instance, the advantages are realized to lie in 'self-employment … [that] makes workers the residual claimants of the fruits of their ideas and efforts and … provides motivation for hard and imaginative work'.[115]

Resources are critical, and without access to adequate resources there can be no elimination or reduction of poverty. But they are not the entire story. The ability to transform resources into production involves the agency of the producers and the development of this capability is central to the process of poverty elimination. The transformation of social, including gender, relations is part of the process of poverty alleviation.

The scale of poverty and its multiple forms make ending poverty a complex task requiring commitment and the willingness to cooperate over a long period of time. No one institution, national or multilateral, public or private, and no unique strategy can hope to deal effectively with the different contexts and causes that underlie poverty.

As our understanding of the dynamics of poverty has increased in the last 30 years, it has been widely recognized that ending poverty is not a matter of simple-minded economic approaches whether based on central planning or on 'getting the prices right'. It is now widely recognized that there are many pathways for ending poverty. Building partnerships at various levels that enable the poor to build up their assets, develop labour-intensive management techniques and improve access to assets and techniques, largely by making markets work for the poor, provide the best prospects for poverty reduction.

Endnotes

1   This exposition is taken from the comments of Alain de Janvy on earlier draft of this chapter.

2   Binswanger *et al.* 1995.

3   Bardhan 1999.

4   Nathan and Kelkar, 1997.

5   Galasso and Ravallion 1999.

6   Bardhan and Mookherjee 1998.

7   Tendler 1997.

8   Crook and Manor 1994.

9   Hartmann and Boyce 1983.

10 World Bank 2000c.

11 Pasha 1992.

12 Carney and Farrington 1998.

13 Cornista 1993.

14 Manikutty 1998.

15 Adato *et al.* 1999.

16 Appu *et al.* 1999.

17 The incentive to free-ride increases with size because the share of a group's income from which a free-rider will benefit is smaller (Baland and Platteau 1996).

18 Agarwal 1998b.

19 Agrawal and Gibson 1999.

20 Saxena 1996.

21 Tang 1992.

22 Wade 1988.

23 Kanbur 1992.

24 Wade 1987.

25 Swallow and Bromley 1994; Pasha 1992.

26 Gilles *et al.* 1992.

27 Osmani 2000.

28 Osmani 2000.

29 White and Runge 1995.

30 Isham and Kahkonen 1999: 53, 52.

31 As emphasised by Bardhan (1996: 142-3), '…from the enclosure movement in English history to the current appropriations of forests and grazing lands in developing countries by timber merchants and cattle ranchers, it has been the same sad story'.

32 Ninan 1998. The four projects are DANIDA-aided Karnataka Watershed Development Project; EU-aided Doon Valley Integrated Watershed Management Project, Uttar Pradesh; KFW-aided Integrated Watershed Management Project, Karnataka; and an ODA project in Karnataka.

33 Ostrom 1994.

34 Nathan and Kumar 2001.

35 Banana and Gombya-Ssembajjwe 1998.

36 Varughese 1998.

37 de los Reyes and Jopillo 1988.

38 Pretty 1996.

39 Osmani 2000.

40 Jayaraman 1981.

41 Nathan 2000; Contreras *et al.* 2001.

42 Dayton-Johnson 1998.

43 Bardhan 1996.

44 Bardhan 1999.

45 Andre and Platteau 1997

46 Sarin and Singh 2001.

47 Meinzen-Dick *et al.* 1997.

48 Van der Grift 1991.

49 Van Koppen 1998.

50 Meinzen-Dick and Zwarteveen 1998.

51 Whitehead 1990.

52 Agarwal 2000.

53 Kome 1997.

54 Kome 1997.

55 Zwarteveen and Nepuane 1995.

56 Agarwal 2000.

57 Agarwal 2000: 286.

58 Shah 1997.

59 Hulsebosch and Van Koppen 1993.

60 Moffat 1998.

61 Agarwal 2000.

62 Agarwal 2000: 287

63 This section draws upon Osmani 2000.

64 van den Breemer *et al.* 1995.

65 Klooster 2000.

66 IFAD 1999e.

67 FAO 1998b.

68 IFAD 1999d.

69 Roemer, in Bowles and Gintis 1998.

70 Kelkar and Nathan 1991; Kelkar 2001.

71 Schneider and Sharma 1999. Sustantial increase in microfinance provisions took place in Bangladesh, India, Indonesia, among many. There are some 15 000 formal amd semi-formal MFIs in Indonesia alone. NABARD in India works through 160 000 primary lending institutions, including 92 000 cooperatives with 105 million members.

72 According to World Bank there are more than 900 active microfinance programmes in 101 countries. Based on a survey conducted in September 1995 which included 206 programmes from 900 institutions, total lending is nearly USD 7 billion with deposit mobilization of over USD 19 billion, Sinha 1998.

73 'Microfinance institution' is used as a collective term for formal banks such as Grameen Bank (now a full-fledged bank) and NGOs that provide financial services to their members. This term itself is new. The earlier term, 'microcredit', is still widely used (as the Microcredit Summit exemplified), underpinning the belief that credit is the vital element for poverty alleviation.

74 Morduch 1998.

75 Khandker 1998.

76 Morduch 1998.

77 Hulme 2000.

78 Morduch 1998.

79 Hulme and Mosley 1996.

80 IFAD 2000a.

81 von Pishcke and Adams 1992.

82 Adams and Vogel 1986.

83 Robinson 1996.

84 Rahman 1992, Ghate 1992.

85 Drawn from IFAD 2000a.

86 UNDP 1993.

87 Farrington and Bebbington 1993: 153.

88 Government of India 1985.

89 Clark 1995.

90 Gaiha and Kulkarni 1999.

91 Seabright 1997.

92 Gaiha 1993.

93 Manor 1997: 43.

94 Ravallion et al. 1991.

95 Drèze 1988: 75-6.

96 Dev 1996.

97 Joshi and Moore 2000.

98 Dev 1996.

99 Joshi 1998.

100 Echeverri-Gent 1993.

101 Joshi 1998.

102 In 1986-87 employment in the scheme was 196.7 million person days. By 1989-90 it was only 78 million person days. Gaiha 1997.

103 Gaiha 1997.

104 Gaiha 1997.

105 Gaiha 1993.

106 Jenkins and Goetz 1999b.

107 Jenkins 2000.

108 Jenkins and Goetz 1999a.

109 Jenkins and Goetz 1999a.

110 Zaman 1998.

111 Mosley 1996.

112 Besley 1997.

113 A further argument that can be made to include 'non-target' households is that they have the potential to create employment opportunities for the poorest by setting up small/medium-scale enterprises. BRAC has recently set up a new project lending to 'graduated' or NTG members with proven entrepreneurial ability in order to create such enterprises. The average loan size is around ten times more than the typical microcredit loan and the loan screening and monitoring process is a combination of microcredit and formal banking methods.

114 Ravallion 1991.

115 Fafchamps 1994.

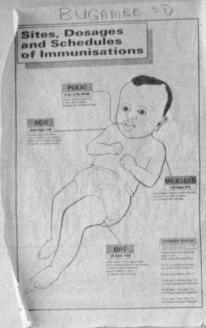

CHAPTER 7

ENDING RURAL POVERTY: CHALLENGES AND OPPORTUNITIES

Poverty reduction is not something that governments, development institutions or NGOs can do for the poor. The poor themselves have to seize responsibility, as agents of change, for their own development.

The 20 years between 1970 and 1990 saw the fastest and most widespread retreat of poverty, hunger, premature death and illiteracy in history. Most of those affected were the rural poor of the developing world. However, large rural areas, containing hundreds of millions of people, remain trapped in poverty; since 1990 its retreat has been much slower. This report has explored the nature of the rural poor; who they are; where they are; what accounts for the successes, gaps and failures of rural poverty reduction; and what can be done about rural poverty and by whom.

A global report on rural poverty is not the place for policy advice to any particular country. Each chapter has set out conclusions about needs for better policy, and about types of policy that work or fail in specified conditions. But some themes have emerged from the analysis, which underlie policy and have operational implications.

EMERGING THEMES AND CHALLENGES

The nature of rural poverty and the inadequate response

Most of the world's poor are rural, and will remain so until at least 2035. The urban-rural gaps in poverty, health and literacy are large and, on the whole, not narrowing. These gaps are not only unjust but also inefficient: shifting resources, assets and access from urban to rural, and from rich to rural poor, often advances economic growth. Now that most donors and developing countries are reorienting their policy towards poverty reduction, one would expect investment and aid to concentrate substantially on the poorest countries, and on support for agricultural and rural activity. Yet this is not the case; for example, in 1988-98, aid to agriculture fell by almost two thirds in real terms.

The poor themselves report distress that stems not only from low consumption but also from ill-health, lack of schooling, vulnerability, lack of assets and disrespect from officials. Those who suffer from one of these conditions tend to suffer from others as well. Disproportionately many are rural women, ethnic minorities in remote areas, landless, casual workers, or children: poverty and lack of education are inherited conditions. Breaking the 'interlocking log-jams of disadvantage' may require attacking several barriers. For example, we document shocking educational disadvantages among the rural poor. To address these, more nearby schools and teachers are needed, but so are better health and nutrition. Lack of these human assets stops children from learning, compels parents to send them to work, and perpetuates poverty.

Fertility decline and the dramatic rise in worker-dependant ratios in 1990-2030 can help the poor to escape poverty, if the extra workers can find decent work. This was achieved in East Asia through early gains in farm yields, smallholder incomes, and hence farm employment – soon followed by increases in employment and growth in the non-farm sector. South Asia and Africa can follow this path if their agricultural and rural policies can be set right, and if right policies can be translated into favourable outcomes in terms of the assets and opportunities of the rural poor at the local level and their livelihoods.

Women's disadvantage and exclusion in education, landholding and, in some countries, nutrition and health care reduce their security and esteem; in some countries they slow the fertility transition. These disadvantages are greater in rural areas: they can be reduced by redressing the under-allocation of rural resources.

Poverty and asset policy

The extreme poor spend almost three quarters of their income on food. They receive over two thirds of their calories from staples, and earn perhaps half their income from growing them. So the control of farmland by the poor tends to be a safeguard against extreme poverty. 'Classical' land reform has transferred more land, and with more success in reducing poverty, than is widely believed; but it has run into many problems. Consensual and decentralized land redistribution is a promising way forward, with the largest farmers attracted to sell land in small amounts to the poor; but it requires some land fund in support. This is in tune with the policy preferences of many donors, recipients and civil-society organizations, as well as those of many of the poor. However, especially with the new requirements of global markets, post-reform smallholders require access to competitively marketed inputs and services and to research, roads and other resources that normally only governments can supply.

Water-yielding assets are also increasingly important to the rural poor as more areas are affected by water scarcity and diversion. Removal of water subsidies is desirable, but caution has to be exercised against further transfers of water away from rural areas, which will endanger the already inadequate farm water control (and drinking water) of the rural poorest.

The heavy biases against rural people, the poor and women in acquiring 'human assets', especially health and education, are inefficient as well as unjust, and in most cases not shrinking. Reducing these biases, and providing the poor with access to land and improved farm technology, are complementary; each increases the economic gain and poverty reduction from the other.

Technology policy, poverty, and natural resource sustainability

The value of human, land, water-yielding and other assets depends on the technologies that turn those assets, together with labour, into adequate incomes. The poor's shortage of assets compels them to live mainly by selling their labour-power. So increasing the market value of that labour-power, through choices in asset-building and in technology that are employment-intensive, is vital for poverty reduction. But subsidies to farm equipment, such as combine-harvesters and weedicides, displace human labour and ultimately harm the poor. There are also positive requirements of pro-labour policy. If the poor have some farmland, their bargaining power in labour markets is increased. Agricultural researchers need to perceive that the use of labour itself, while a cost, has social advantages for poverty reduction.

Rural technologies face two tasks: to reduce poverty through more and better distributed output and welfare; and to improve resource sustainability. On the whole, the former has been best achieved by bio-agricultural research, and the latter by improved land and water management technology. The two are strongly complementary, though separated by fashion and by barriers between researchers and institutions. Poor farmers can seldom afford to buy into conservation technology unless there is a production gain. And all types of formal research are complementary with farmers' own research and succeed best with participatory methods. But the lack of progress in the spread of water control (especially in Africa) and the slowdown in historically fast rates of food-crop yield improvement are serious causes for concern. The stagnation or decline in many areas of public agricultural research must end. The increasing locking-in, or patenting, of agricultural research results by a few private companies, with few incentives to structure their work towards the needs of the rural poor, has to be replaced by appropriate public-private partnerships and by new incentives for scientific endeavour.

Just as rural poverty reduction, growth in staples yield and farm income expansion in developing countries have slowed down, before the gains have spread to many areas, exciting new scientific prospects have been opened by transgenics. These have produced intense debate and polarized arguments. Careful consideration of trade laws, environment and safety regulations sympathetic to developing countries are important to ensure that neither the poor, nor the world, are exposed to undue risks. However, from the perspective of ending poverty, a greater risk is that gains from transgenics will not reach the poor and the hungry. Decisions must not be confined to the world of business and politics, but should be open, drawing on the experience of professional research, the rural poor themselves (labourers and consumers as well as farmers) and organizations in direct contact with them.

Poverty, markets, liberalization and globalization

The poor need technologies to increase output from their assets, and they also need markets to exchange that output freely and to best advantage. Yet the poor are dogged by the market power of others, market failure, bad distributional outcomes from market 'success', and barriers to market access. Rural areas are dispersed: in remote areas, market access problems are most serious, and competition and information least adequate. Action by civil society, government, donors and often the poor themselves can greatly improve their relative access and strength in markets. Globalization can bring significant benefits to the rural poor. But it will bring most benefits if attention and support are directed towards helping small producers to make the best of their market-mediated relations with vastly more powerful and international private-sector operators.

Access to information is an overlooked area for the rural poor; more information would enable farmers to take better decisions on markets and services. Investment in rural roads brings striking returns in both GNP and poverty reduction. It is less affordable in remote or sparsely populated areas, but here, more imaginative solutions can improve physical market access or reduce the cost to the poor. 'Getting the prices wrong' is seldom sensible, but getting them right often does nothing to solve the market access problems of remote areas, and can even make them worse.

Liberalization and globalization are changing the landscape of many poor rural areas. Despite their economic advantages of labour intensity, poor farmers have difficulty meeting exacting supermarket or export standards. Donors can work with NGOs and cooperatives, as well as governments, to provide support and to increase the bargaining power of the poor through trade and marketing associations.

Policies for pro-poor rural institutions

The poor are largely excluded from the institutions and partnerships that can enable them to share and control the decisions that affect their lives. This is because institutions often tend to be controlled by the powerful non-poor. Channeling appropriate assets such as land and education, technology to raise the productivity of assets, and markets to improve sales and purchases, improve the poor's 'exit options' that over time may also help them alter institutions for their sustained benefit. Decentralized institutions for natural resources management and financial services have not always been successful in reaching the poor, although they have been important in helping the poor, through increased efficiency and sustainability, as the local elites are driven to recognize their shared interest with the poor.

Poverty reduction is a complex task, requiring sustained commitment to consistent, yet flexible, joint action. There are no quick fixes and no easy solutions. No single institution, national or multi-lateral, public or private, and no single strategy can hope to deal effectively with the different contexts and causes of poverty. Coherent anti-poverty strategy therefore requires stable partnerships, based on trust as well as self-interest.

It is important to recognize the need for sustaining the management of change towards pro-poor institutions and programmes through support from below. The coalition of the poor among themselves and with others provides the best hope for the poor to get integrated with a process of sharing wealth and development more equitably than before. The best guarantee of good policy is effective accountability.

RESUMING AND SPREADING THE RETREAT OF RURAL POVERTY: BUILDING A GLOBAL PARTNERSHIP AMONG THE STAKEHOLDERS

Micro- and meso-level partnerships were discussed earlier. Macro-partnerships provide the overarching global framework for anti-poverty strategies. An important purpose of the macro-level partnership is enhanced aid effectiveness through improved donor coordination.

Since the 1995 United Nations Social Summit, the international community has been reconstructing the global partnership with the poor. The most recent expression was at the Millennium Summit in September 2000, when Heads of Government and State confirmed the commitment to halve the incidence of extreme poverty by 2015. For some time, therefore, the United Nations system has regarded poverty alleviation as its overarching objective. Major donor countries under the auspices of the OECD have agreed to realign aid towards similar poverty targets at national level. The Poverty Reduction Strategy Papers (PRSPs) being prepared by each recipient of World Bank and IMF support underpin this process.[1]

Unfortunately, the material basis for achieving this global poverty target in terms of development assistance has not been strengthened, and indeed has eroded over recent years. As we have seen, the bulk of the poor are in rural areas, drawing their livelihood from agriculture and related activities; yet development assistance to agriculture fell by nearly two thirds between 1987 and 1998. Assistance has also tended to shift from supporting productive activities by poor farmers towards social sectors.

Thus, there is a paradox: an ambitious target for poverty alleviation with fewer resources to achieve it. If the target of reducing extreme poverty by half by 2015 is to be achieved, overall development assistance must be raised and the share going to agriculture should reflect its importance in generating livelihoods for the majority of the poor.

Once that condition is met, the challenge is to develop and foster genuine cooperation, good governance and a policy framework in which the rural poor in developing countries can participate.

Box 7.1: Development partnerships

The Comprehensive Development Framework (CDF) is a holistic approach to development. It seeks a better balance in policy-making by highlighting the interdependence of all elements of development – social, structural, human, governance, environmental, economic and financial. It is based on the following principles:

- ownership by the country. The country, not the assistance agencies, determines the goals and the phasing, timing and sequencing of its development programmes;
- partnership with government, civil society, assistance agencies and the private sector in defining development needs and implementing programmes;
- a long-term vision of needs and solutions, built on national consultations, which can engender sustained national support; and
- structural and social concerns treated equally and contemporaneously with macroeconomic and financial concerns.

CDF is still at the experimental stage but, once operational, will offer a global partnership framework for selective IFAD participation at the country-level within the ambit of its central mandate and strategic framework.

The United Nations Development Assistance Framework (UNDAF) is a strategic planning and collaborative framework that helps to identify priorities for UN action. It is a key component of the Secretary-General's reform proposal of July 1997, and is designed to bring greater coherence, collaboration and effectiveness to UN development efforts in the field. Participation by many UN agencies, including IFAD, in UNDAF provides the operational framework for donor coordination, and a pilot phase has been launched in 19 countries.

Developing country governments and donor agencies need partnerships to ensure a cost-effective attack on poverty; the rural poor need partnerships to support their own initiatives, but free of the intrusiveness for which donors are sometimes criticized.[2]

Hence donors are emphasizing partnership-building to improve the efficiency and effectiveness of poverty reduction efforts and to build a consensus on:

- setting development priorities;
- reforms necessary to pursue these priorities;
- the programmes and/or projects in support of the reforms; and
- the successful implementation of these programmes and projects with better definition of the responsibilities of the stakeholders in the process.

One response to the scarcity of development resources has been efforts to coordinate available aid funds around shared initiatives against poverty. Both the CDF proposed by the World Bank and the UNDAF provide frameworks for such mutuality (Box 7.1).

Effective coordination among donors is of increasing importance to reduce duplication and avoid placing too great a burden on the host country's administrative and management capacity. Multiple donors and programmes may also cause confusion within the government. Grateful as they may be for assistance, governments might come to see donor activities as more of a hindrance than a help, given the extra burden on government personnel in trying to manage different overlapping activities.

The global initiatives to forge coalitions and partnerships among and with developing countries donors are welcome. However, success requires the substance to be made 'bottom-up' in two ways.

First, each government has to be responsible for country policy. History shows that imposed conditionality in aid, and anti-poverty planning from Northern capitals for the Asian or African poor, seldom works. So each government in the PRSP process has agreed to 'chair' a national poverty partnership, constructing an anti-poverty strategy with civil-society agencies, to be embodied in the

PRSP. In Asia eight countries are working with the Asian Development Bank on strategies directly geared to the Social Summit's 2015 targets on poverty, health, education and gender equality.

Second, the poor themselves have to take responsibility, as agents, for their own development; the poor, not just an abstract 'civil society', which can be biased towards the rich and strong. Even where the poor can overcome that bias, civil-society institutions are underdeveloped in some countries and repressed in others. The key issue is whether the poor have room for manoeuvre by capturing particular local or central institutions, or by coalitions with some of the strong. If poverty reduction is to reach the poorest, often linguistic minorities in remote rural areas, the problem is more difficult.

FUTURES OF SUCCESS, FUTURES OF FAILURE

The future outcomes of rural poverty could be worsened by matters not reviewed in this report, such as increasing war or civil violence, or worse-than-expected effects of AIDS or global warming. Conversely, competent and stable public policy in large countries with substantial mineral resources, such as Nigeria or D. R. Congo, could bring much larger and swifter falls in poverty than are now expected. We close, therefore, by looking 20-25 years ahead, and asking: what policies might then be needed to cope with the consequences of success or failure at dealing with rural poverty? How might policies put in place now make the task easier?

Success in reducing mass poverty in low-income countries initially depends on progress in farm yields and employment, and later on a transition towards employment-intensive non-farm products, alongside a fall in the number of people engaged in agriculture, and increasing urbanization. Improved small-scale agriculture in developing countries is essential for meeting immediate poverty reduction targets, and can contribute decisively to the overall development process, including the emergence of quite new opportunities for income and employment in other sectors. It is a stepping stone to larger solutions, but it is not itself the whole solution.

Several East Asian countries, following breakthroughs in farming, have made the transition to broad-based non-farm growth. This tends to make urbanization faster, not slower, creating new problems, but problems that are more soluble because migration is spurred by rural success rather than by desperation.

However, widespread labour-intensive rural non-farm growth appears to have been central to East and South-East Asian success. We know that such growth is, in its early stages, fastest when there is demand, especially for consumer goods, from a not-too-unequal, fast-growing local farm sector. Such rural non-farm growth readily broadens to wider markets later. Hence, the strategies of labour-intensive technical progress, and wide distribution of land and human capital, not only reduce poverty in the short run, but also ease the transition from agriculture-based to more broad-based poverty reduction.[3]

What of the effect, 20-25 years hence, of failure to achieve rural economic growth or to translate it into widespread poverty reduction? Periods of faster growth, overall, are associated with faster poverty reduction, but there are big differences among countries in their success in turning growth into rural and urban poverty reduction. The failure of African rural poverty to fall is surely explained mainly by agricultural stagnation; recent exceptions to stagnation, such as Uganda, Ghana and parts of Ethiopia, appear to show some poverty decline too. On the other hand, India enjoyed faster growth in 1992-99 than in 1975-89, but much slower responsiveness of rural poverty to agricultural or overall growth, and hence slower rural poverty reduction. It is hard to believe, especially with the fertility transition so that poor rural people have fewer and better-educated children, that the slowdown in rural poverty decline in India will continue if agricultural growth is maintained. It is, unfortunately, plausible however that poverty will persist in much of rural Africa if agricultural growth does not speed up, especially where land distribution is also very unequal.

This report documents great progress in the reduction of rural poverty, but shows a worrying slowdown and a failure to reach large areas. The sources of progress lie in getting assets, appropriate technologies and market access to the poor, and in their obtaining more influence on decentralized and national-level institutions. The poor themselves, NGOs and organizations such as IFAD have been instrumental in securing participation by the poor in decisions on credit, farm technology, natural resources management and much else that affects their chance to escape poverty.

We are now at a turn in the road. Some of the old effective solutions, like classical land redistribution, the Green Revolution and irrigation expansion, have run into limitations. Yet the reasons these solutions were effective remain valid: the poor still need access to labour-intensive, security-enhancing assets and technologies. The institutions, the required local and global partnerships (linking the poor especially with scientists and with the private sector), and the market forms best suited to obtain such access for the poor, have changed. But the need for the poor to participate in their own emancipation remains the same.

Endnotes

1 Initially a country PRSP is a precondition for debt relief under the Highly-Indebted Poorest Countries Debt Initiative (HIPC DI), but will soon become a precondition also for loans from the Bank on aid terms (via the International Development Association, IDA), or medium-term support under the IMF's Poverty Reduction and Growth Facility, formerly the Enhanced Structural Adjustment Facility.

2 Sceptics argue that even 'partnership . . . is essentially a [way] for donors to become more intrusive . . . for a more effective, more collective enforcement of the liberalisation agenda' (Abugre 2000).

3 Perhaps that is why, even when agriculture has shrunk to 10-20% of GDP, differences among nations in farmland inequality continue to explain much of their variance in overall inequality (Carter 2000).

Bibliographical notes

Abate, Z. (1991). Planned national water policy: a proposed case for Ethiopia. Unpublished paper for the 1991 June International Workshop on Water Resources Management, Washington DC.

Abbott, J. C. (1987). *Agricultural marketing enterprises for the developing world.* Cambridge University Press.

Abu Taleb, M. F., Salameh, E. and Kefaye, B. (1991). Water resources planning and development in Jordan: problems, future scenarios, recommendations. Unpublished paper for the 1991 June International Workshop on Water Resources Management.

Abugre, C. (2000). *Partners, collaborators or patron-clients? Defining relationships in the aid industry: a survey of the issues.* mimeo, ISODEC, Ghana.

Adams, D. W. and Vogel, R. C. (1986). Rural financial markets in low-income countries: recent controversies and lessons. *World Development* 14(4): 477-87.

Adams, J. (1991). The rural labour market in Zimbabwe. *Development and Change* 22(2): 297-320.

Adams, R. and He, J. J. (1995). Sources of income inequality and poverty in rural Pakistan. International Food Policy Research Institute: Washington DC. Research Report 102.

Adams, W. M., Watson, E. E. and Mutiso, S. K. (1997). Water, rules and gender: water rights in an indigenous system, Marakwet, Kenya. *Development and Change* 28: 707-30.

Adato, M., Hoddinott, J., Besley, T. and Haddad, L. (1999). Participation and poverty reduction: issues, theory and new evidence from South Africa. Background paper for World Development Report 2000/1. World Bank: Washington DC.

Adiseshiah, M. S. (1994). No good for this big task. *Yojna* 20(20-1): 16.

Aeron-Thomas, M. (1992). *The equity impact of deep tube-wells: evidence from the IDA Deep Tubewell Project.* ODI Irrigation Management Network. Network Paper No. 12.

Agarwal, B. (1994). *A field of one's own: gender and land rights in South Asia.* Cambridge: Cambridge University Press.

— (1998a). Disinherited peasants, disadvantaged workers: a gender perspective on land and livelihood. *Economic and Political Weekly* March 28: A2-14.

— (1998b). Group size and successful collective action: a case study of forest management institutions in the Indian Himalayas. In Gibson, C., McKean, M.A. and Ostrom, E. (1998) (eds), *Forest resources and institutions.* Forestry, trees and people programme, FAO: Rome. Working Paper 3.

— (2000). Conceptualising environmental collective action: why gender matters. *Cambridge Journal of Economics* 24: 283-310.

Agrawal, A. and Gibson, C. C. (1999). Enchantment and disenchantment: the role of Community in Natural Resource Conservation. *World Development* 27(4): 629-49.

Ahuja, V., Bidani, B., Ferreiro, F. and Walton, M. (1997). *Directions in development: everyone's miracle?: revisiting poverty and inequality in East Asia.* World Bank: Washington DC.

Alderman, H. and Garcia, M. (1993). *Poverty, household food security, and nutrition in rural Pakistan.* International Food Policy Research Institute: Washington DC. Research Report No. 96.

Alderman, H., Chiappori, L., Haddad, L., Hoddinott, J. and Kanbur, R. (1995). Unitary versus collective models of the household: Is it time to shift the burden of proof? *World Bank Research Observer* 10: 1-19.

Alderman, H., Behrman, J. R., Ross, D. R., Sabot, R. (1996). The returns to endogenous human capital in Pakistan's rural wage labour market. *Oxford Bulletin of Economics and Statistics* 58(1): 29.

Alesina, A. and Dollar, D. (1998). *Who gives foreign aid to whom and why?* National Bureau of Economic Research. Working Paper No. W6612.

Ali Shah, Q. and Azam, M. (1991). Impact of rural roads on employment (a case of District Sargodha). *Journal of Rural Development and Administration* 23(4): 87-103.

Allison, C., Cheong, K., and L. Yap. (1989). *Rapid population growth in Pakistan.* World Bank: Washington DC. Report 7522-Pak.

Amid, M. J. (1990). *Agriculture, poverty and reform in Iran.* Routledge: London.

Ammerman, A. and Cavalli-Sforza, L. (1971). Measuring the rate of spread of early farming in Europe. *Man* 9: 6.

Anderson, J., Hazell, P. and Evans, L. (1987). Variability in cereal yields: sources of change and implications for agricultural research and policy. *Food Policy* 12(3): 199-212.

Andre, C. and Platteau, J. P. (1997). Land relations under unbeatable stress: Rwanda caught in a Malthusian trap. *Journal of Economic Behaviour and Organisation* 34(3): 1-47.

Appendini, K. (1995). *Revisiting women wage-workers in Mexico's agro-industry: changes in rural labour markets.* Center for Development Research: Denmark Working Paper 95.2.

Appleton, S. (1997). *User fees, expenditure restructuring and voucher systems in education.* World Institute for Development Economics: Helsinki. Research Working Paper No.134.

— and Balihuta, A. (1996). Education and agricultural activity: evidence from Uganda. *Journal of International Development* 8(3): 415-44.

Appu, P. S. (1997). Land reforms in India: a survey of policy, legislation and implementation. *Economic and Political Weekly* 32(38): 2394.

Archer, D. and Cottingham, S. (1996). *Action research report on REFLECT: the experiences of three REFLECT pilot projects in Uganda, Bangladesh, El Salvador.* Overseas Development Administration: London.

Arhin, D. C. (1994). The health card insurance scheme in Burundi: a social asset or a non-viable venture? *Social Science and Medicine* 39(6): 861-70.

Ault, D. and Rutman, G. (1979). The development of individual rights to property in tropical Africa. *Journal of Law and Economics* 22: 163-82.

Avery, D. (1997). *Saving the planet with pesticides, biotechnology and European farm reform.* Bawden Lecture, Brighton Conference, British Protection Council.

Axelrod, R. (1984). *The evolution of cooperation.* Basic Books: New York.

Ayako, A. B. and Katumanga, M. (1997). *Review of poverty in Kenya.* Institute of Policy Analysis and Research, Nairobi and Actionaid Kenya. The Institute: Nairobi.

Baland, J. M. and Platteau, J. P. (1996). *Halting degradation of natural resource: is there a role for rural communities?* FAO/Oxford University Press.

Balisacan, A. (1997). *Philippines: policy reforms and poverty alleviation.* International Labour Office: Geneva.

Banana, A. Y. and Gombya-Ssembajjwe, W. (1998). Successful forest management: the importance of security of tenure and rule enforcement in Ugandan forest. In Gibson, C., McKean, M. A. and Ostrom, E. (1998) (eds), *Forest resources and institutions.* Forestry, trees and people programme, FAO: Rome. Working Paper 3.

Bandyopadhyay, D. (1995). Reflections on land reform in India since independence. In Sathyamurthy, T. V. (ed.), *Industry and agriculture in India since independence.* Oxford University Press: Delhi.

Bardhan, P. (1996). Decentralised development. *Indian Economic Review* 31(2): 139-56.

— (1999). *Democracy and development: a complex relationship.* University of California: Berkeley.

Bardhan, P. and Mookherjee, D. (1998). Expenditure decentralisation and the delivery of public services in developing countries. Mimeo, University of California: Berkeley.

Bardhan, P. and Rudra, A. (1986). Labour mobility and the boundaries of the village moral economy. *Journal of Peasant Studies* 13(3): 90-115.

Barrett, C. (1994a). *On price risk and the inverse farm size-productivity relationship.* Department of Agricultural Economics, University of Wisconsin: Madison.

Barrientos, S. (1996). Flexible work and female labour: the global integration of Chilean fruit production. In Auty, R. M. and Toye, J. (eds). *Challenging the orthodoxies.* Macmillan: Basingstoke.

Barrows, R. and Roth, M. (1989). *Land tenure and investment in African agriculture: theory and evidence.* Land Tenure Center: Madison. Paper No. 136.

Barwell, I. (1996). *Transport and the village.* World Bank: Washington DC. Discussion Paper No. 344.

Barwell, I., Edmonds, G. A., Howe, J. and de Veen, J. (1985). *Rural transport in developing countries.* International Labour Organisation: Geneva.

Basta, S. S., Soekirman; K. D., and Scrimshaw, N. S. (1979). Iron deficiency anaemia and the productivity of adult males in Indonesia. *American Journal of Clinical Nutrition* 32: 916-25.

Basu, A. M. (1999). *Poverty and AIDS: the vicious circle*, in Livi-Bacci, M. and de Santis, G. (eds). *Population and poverty in developing countries.* Clarendon Press: Oxford.

Baulch, R. and Hoddinott, J. (1999). Economic mobility and poverty dynamics in developing countries. *Journal of Development Studies*, 36 (6).

Baulch, R. and McCulloch, N. (1998). *Being poor and becoming poor: poverty status and poverty transitions in rural Pakistan.* Institute of Development Studies: Brighton. Working Paper 79.

Behrman, J. R. and Deolalikar, A. (1988). Health and nutrition. In Chenery, H. B. and Srinivasan, T.N. (eds), *Handbook of development economics* 1. North Holland: Amsterdam.

Bell, C. (1990). Reforming property rights in land and tenancy. *World Bank Research Observer* 5: 2.

Bell, C, Hazell, P. R. B. and Slade, R. (1982). *Project evaluation in regional perspective.* John Hopkins University Press: Baltimore.

Bellon, M. and Risopoulos, J. (1999). *Expanding the benefits: farmers' transformation of a CIMMYT technology to suit the poor.* San Jose workshop on impact of agricultural research on poverty. CIAAT.

Berg, A. (1987). *Malnutrition: what can be done? Lessons from World Bank experience.* John Hopkins University Press: Baltimore.

Berry, A. R. (1984). Land reform and the adequacy of world food production. In Montgomery, J. D. (ed.), *International dimensions of land reform*. Westview: Boulder.

Berry, A. R. and Cline, W. S. (1979). *Agrarian structure and productivity in developing countries*. John Hopkins: Baltimore.

Besley, T. (1995). Property rights and investment incentives: theory and evidence from Ghana. *Journal of Political Economy* 103(5): 903-37.

— (1997). *Political economy of alleviating poverty: theory and institutions*. Annual Conference on Development Economics Proceedings. World Bank: Washington DC.

Besley, T. and Burgess, R. (1998). *Land reform, poverty reduction and growth: evidence from India*. London School of Economics, Suntory and Toyota Centres for Economics and Related Disciplines DP No.13. London School of Economics: London.

Bevan, D., Collier, P. and Gunning, J. (1989). *Peasants and governments: an economic analysis*. Clarendon Press: Oxford.

Beynon, J. (1999). *Assessing aid and the Collier-Dollar poverty efficient aid allocations: a critique*. Department for International Development: UK.

Bhalla, A. S. (1995). *Uneven distribution in the Third World: a study of China and India*. Macmillan: Basingstoke.

Bhalla, S. (1994). Poverty, workforce development and rural labour markets. *Indian Journal of Labour Economics* 37(4): 609-22.

Bhalla, S. and Roy, P. (1988). Mis-specification in farm productivity analysis: the role of land quality. *Oxford Economic Papers* 40(1): 55-73.

Bharadwaj, K. (1974). *Production conditions in Indian agriculture*. Cambridge University Press: Cambridge.

Bhargava A, and Osmani, S. R. (1998). Health and nutrition in emerging Asia. *Asian Development Review* 16(1): 31-71

Binswanger, H. P. (1991). Brazilian policies that encourage deforestation in the Amazon. *World Development* 19(7): 821-30.

Binswanger, H. P. and Khandker, S. R. (1995). The impact of formal finance on the rural economy of India. *Journal of Development Studies* 32(2): 234-62.

Binswanger, H. P. and von Braun, J. (1991). Technological change and commercialization in agriculture: the effect on the poor. *The World Bank Research Observer* 6(1): 57-80.

Binswanger, H. P., Deininger, K. and Feder, G. (1995). Power, distortions, revolt and reform in agricultural land relations. In Behrman, J. and Srinivasan, T. N. (eds), *Handbook of Development Economics* 3b. North Holland: Amsterdam.

Binswanger, H. P., Khandker, S. R. and Rosenzweig, M. R. (1993). How infrastructure and financial institutions affect agricultural output and investment in India. *Journal of Development Economics* 41(2): 337-66.

Birdsall, N., Ross, D. and Sabot, R. (1995). Inequality and growth reconsidered: lessons from East Asia. *World Bank Economic Review* 9(3): 477-508.

Blaikie, P., Cameron, J. and Seddon, D. (1977). *The effects of roads in West Central Nepal, Part I*. Overseas Development Group, University of East Anglia.

Blarel, B., Hazell, P., Place, F. and Quiggin, J. (1991). *The economics of farm fragmentation: evidence from Ghana and Rwanda*. World Bank: Washington DC.

Bloom, D. and Williamson, J. (1997). *Demographic transitions, human resource development, and economic miracles in emerging Asia*. Harvard Institute for International Development, Cambridge, Mass. Background paper for Asian Development Bank Emerging Asia Study. Forthcoming as HIID working paper.

Blum, D., Emeh, R. N., Huttly, S. R. A., Dosunmu-Oganbe, O., Okeke, N., Ajala, M., Okora, J. I., Akeijobi, C., Kirkwood, B. R. and Feachem, R. G. (1990). The Imo State (Nigeria) drinking water supply and sanitation project, 1. Description of the project, evaluation methods, and impact on intervening variables. *Transactions of the Royal Society of Tropical Medicine and Hygiene* 84: 309-15.

Boserup, E. (1965). *Conditions of agricultural progress*. Asia: Bombay.

Bouis, H. E. and Haddad, L. J. (1990). *Agricultural commercialization, nutrition, and the rural poor: a study of Philippine farm households*. Lynne Rienner: Boulder

Bouis, H. E., Palabrica-Costello, M., Solon, O., Westbrook, D. and Limbo, A. B. (1998). Gender equality and investments in adolescents in the rural Philippines. International Food Policy Research Institute: Washington DC. Research Report 108.

Bowles, S. and Gintis, H. (1990). *Recasting egalitarianism: new rules for markets, communities and states*. Verso: London.

Boyce, J. K. (1987). *Agrarian impasse in Bengal: institutional constraints to technological change*. Oxford University Press: Oxford.

Bray, F. (1986). *The rice economies: technology and development in Asian societies*. Blackwell: Oxford.

Bray, M. and Lillis, K. (1988) (eds). *Community financing of education: issues and policy implications in LDCs*. Pergamon Press: New York.

Brazilian, Chinese, Indian, Mexican, US and Third World Academies of Science and The Royal Society (2000). *Transgenic plants and world agriculture*. The Royal Society: London.

Brooks, K., Krylatykh, E., Lerman, Z., Petrikov, A. and Uzun, V. (1996). *Agricultural reform in Russia: a view from the farm level.* World Bank Discussion Paper No. 327.

Brooks, K. and Lerman, Z. (1994). *Land reform and restructuring in Russia.* World Bank: Washington DC. World Bank Discussion Paper 233.

Bruce and Harrell (1989). *Land reform in the Peoples' Republic of China,* 1978-1988. Land Tenure Center, University of Wisconsin: Madison. Research Paper No. 500.

Bryceson, D. F. and Howe, J. (1997). African rural labour and the World Bank: an alternative perspective. *Development in Practice* 7(1): 26-38.

Burke, R. V. (1979). Green Revolution technology and farm class in Mexico. *Economic Development and Cultural Change* 28(1): 135-54.

Burnside, C. and Dollar, D. (1998). *Aid, the incentive regime, and poverty reduction.* World Bank: Washington DC. World Bank Policy Research Working Paper No.1937.

Byerlee, D. (2000). Working Paper for CIAT Conference on the impact of agricultural research on poverty, San Jose.

Carletto, C. (1999). *Using market-orientated policies for poverty alleviation: empirical evidence from Southern Africa.* International Food Policy Research Institute: Washington DC.

Carney, D. and Farrington, J. (1998). *Natural resource management and institutional change.* Routledge: London

Carr, M., Chen, M. and Jhabvala, R (eds) (1996). *Speaking out: women's economic empowerment in South Asia.* Vistaar Publications: New Delhi.

Carter, M. R. (2000). Land ownership inequality and the income distribution consequences of economic growth. In Cornia, G. A. (ed.), *Inequality, growth and poverty under the Washington consensus.* World Institute for Development Economic Research: Helsinki.

Carter, M. and Alvarez, E. (1989). Changing paths: the decollectivization of agrarian reform agriculture in coastal Peru. In Thiesenhusen, W. (ed.), *Searching for agrarian reform in Latin America.* Unwin Hyman: Boston.

Carter, M. R. and May, J. (1999). Poverty, livelihood and class in rural South Africa. *World Development* 27(1): 1-20.

Carter, M. R. and Mesbah, D. (1993). State-mandated and market-mediated land reform in Latin America. In Lipton, M. and van der Gaag, J. (eds), *Including the poor.* World Bank: Washington DC. Proceedings of a symposium organized by the World Bank and the International Food Policy Research Institute.

Chaker, M., El Abassi, H. and Laouina, A. (1996). Mountains, foothills and plains: investing in SWC in Morocco. In Reij, C., Scoones, I. and Toulmin, C. (eds), *Sustaining the soil: indigenous soil and water conservation in Africa.* Earthscan Publications Ltd: London.

Chambers, R. and Farmer, B. H. (1977). Perceptions, technology and the future. In Farmer, B. H. (ed.), *Green Revolution? Technology change in rice-growing areas of Tamil Nadu and Sri Lanka.* Cambridge University Press: Cambridge.

Chambers, R., Saxena, N. C. and Shah, T. (1989). *To the hands of the poor: water and trees.* Oxford and IBH Publishing Company: New Delhi.

Channel 4 (1997). *The Bank, the President and the pearl of Africa.* Channel 4 documentary.

Chaudhri, D. P. (1973). *Effect of farmer's education on agricultural productivity and employment; a case study of Punjab and Haryana states of India* (1960-1972). Working Paper No. 11. World Employment Programme of the ILO

Chaudhuri, S. and Ravallion, M. (1994). How well do static indicators identify the chronically poor? *Journal of Public Economics* 53: 367-94.

Checchi, D. (2000). Does educational achievement help to explain income inequality? In Cornia, G. A. (ed.), *Inequality, growth and poverty under the Washington Consensus.* World Institute for Development Economics Research: Helsinki.

Chisvo, M. and Munro, L. (1994). *A review of social dimensions of adjustment in Zimbabwe, 1990-94.* UNICEF: Harare.

Chitale, M. A. (1991). Comprehensive management of water resources: India's achievements and perspectives. Unpublished paper for the 1991 June International Workshop on Water Resources Management: Washington DC.

Christiaensen, L. (1999). *Mali case study.* International Food Policy Research Institute: Washington DC.

Churchill, A. A., de Feranti, D., Roche, R., Tager, C., Walters, A. A. and Yazen, A. (1987). *Rural water supply and sanitation: time for a change.* World Bank: Washington DC. World Bank Discussion Paper No. 18.

CIAT (2000). www.cgiar.org/irri/riceweb/g-overlatin.html

Clark, J. (1995). State, popular participation and the voluntary sector. *World Development,* April.

Clarke, G. (1995). More evidence on income distribution and growth. *Journal of Development Economics* 47(2): 403-27.

Cleaver, F. and Kaare, B. (1998). *Social embeddedness and project practice: a gendered analysis of promotion and participation in the Hesawa Programme, Tanzania.* University of Bradford for SIDA.

Cleland, J., Onuoha, N. and Timaeus, I. (1994). Fertility change in SSA – a review of the evidence, in Locoh, T., and Hertich, V. *The onset of fertility transition in Sub-Saharan Africa*. Ordina editions: Liege.

Cockcroft, L. (1997). *'Mastering Mosaic': the fight for cassava production in Uganda*. Gatsby Foundation: London. Occasional Paper.

Cohen, B. (1998). The emerging fertility transition in Sub-Saharan Africa. *World Development*, 26(8): 1431-61.

Cohen, M. (2000). *Microfinance, risk management and poverty*. World Bank: Washington DC. Background paper for World Development Report 2000/1.

Colclough, C. (1993). *Education and the market: which parts of the neo-liberal solution are correct?* UNICEF International Child Development Centre: Florence. Innocenti Occasional Papers. Economic Policy Series No. 37. Special Subseries: Fiscal Policy and the Poor.

Collier, P. and Dollar, D. (1999). *Aid allocation and poverty reduction*. World Bank: Washington DC. Policy Research Working Paper No. 2041.

Connell. J., Dasgupta, B., Laishley, R. and Lipton, M. (1976). *Migration from rural areas: the evidence from village studies*. Oxford University Press: Delhi.

Contreras, A., Dachang, L., Edmonds, D., Kelkar, G., Nathan, D., Sarin, M., Singh, N. and Wollenberg, E. (2001). *Creating space for local forest management*, CIFOR: Bogor (forthcoming).

Conway, G. (1997). *The doubly Green Revolution*. Penguin: London.

Cooper, L. (1995). *Wealth and poverty in the Mongolian pastoral economy*. Policy Alternatives for Livestock Development in Mongolia Research Report No.11. Institute of Development Studies: Brighton.

Cornia, G. A. (1985). Farm size, land yields and the agricultural production function *World Development* 13: 4.

Cornista, L. B. (1993). Community-based management of natural resources: an answer to environmental stress? Paper presented at *Common property in ecosystems under stress*, the fourth annual conference of the International Association for the Study of Common Property, Manila, Philippines, June 16-19.

Cotlear, D. (1990). The effects of education on farm productivity. In Griffin, K. and Knight, J. (eds) *Human development and the international development strategy for the 1990s*. Macmillan in association with the United Nations: Basingstoke.

Crook, R. and Manor, J. (1994). *Democratic decentralisation in South Africa and West Africa*. Department for International Development/Overseas Development Administration: London. Final Report to ESCOR.

Csaki, C. and Lerman, Z. (1997). *Land reform in Ukraine: the first five years*. World Bank Discussion Paper No. 371.

Csaki, C., Brook, E., Lundell, H., Zuschlag, A., Arakelar, R. and Moury, S. (1995). *Armenia: the challenge of reform in the agricultural sector. Based on a mission in May-June 1993*. World Bank: Washington DC. World Bank Country Studies.

Cumpa, M. and Webb, R. (1999). Mobility and Poverty Dynamics in the 1990s. Paper presented at IDS/IFPRI Workshop on Poverty Dynamics, April 1999, Institute of Development Studies: Brighton.

Datt, G. and Ravallion, M. (1996). *Macroeconomic crises and poverty monitoring: a case study for India*. World Bank: Washington DC. Policy Research Working Paper 1685.

— (1997). *Why have some Indian states done better than others at reducing rural poverty?* World Bank: Washington DC. World Bank Policy Research Working Paper No.1594.

Dawson, J. and Barwell, I. (1993). *Roads are not enough: new perspectives on rural transport planning in developing countries*. IT Publications: London. Intermediate Technology Development Group.

Dayton-Johnson, J. (1998). *Rules, inequality and collective action in poor hydraulic countries: a model with evidence from Mexico*. University of California: Berkeley.

de Haan, A. and Lipton, M. (1999). Poverty in emerging Asia: progress, setbacks, and log-jams. *Asian Development Review* 16(2): 135-76.

de Janvry, A. (1981). *The agrarian question and reformism in Latin America*. John Hopkins University Press: Baltimore.

de Janvry, A. and Sadoulet, E. (1989). A study in resistance to institutional change: The lost game of Latin America land reform. *World Development* 17: 1397-407.

de los Reyes, R. and Jopillo, S. (1988). The impact of participation: an evaluation of the NIA's Communal Irrigation Programme. In Korten, F. F. and Siy Jr, R.Y. (eds), *Transforming a bureaucracy - the experience of the Philippine National Irrigation Administration*. Kumarian Press: Connecticut.

Deere, C. D. (1987). The Latin American agrarian reform experience. In Deere, C. D. and Leon, M. (eds), *Rural women and state policy: feminist perspectives on Latin American agricultural development*. Westview Press: Boulder.

Defo, B. K. (1996). Area and socioeconomic differentials in infant and child mortality in Cameroon. *Social Science and Medicine* 42(3): 399-420.

Deininger, K. (1999). Making negotiated land reform work: Initial experience from Colombia, Brazil and South Africa. *World Development* 27(4): 651-72.

Deininger, K. and Binswanger, H. (1999). The evolution of the World Bank's land policy. *World Bank Research Observer* 14(2): 247-76.

Deininger, K. and Squire, L. (1996). A new data set measuring income inequality. *World Bank Economic Review* 10(3): 565-91.

— (1998). New ways of looking at old issues: inequality and growth. *Journal of Development Economics* 57: 259-87.

Delgado, C. (1999). *Livestock to 2020: the next food revolution*. International Food Policy Research Institute: Washington DC. IFPRI 2020 Vision for Food, Agriculture and the Environment, Discussion Paper 28.

Demery, L. (1999). *Poverty dynamics in Africa: an update*. World Bank: Washington DC.

Deolalikar, A. B. (1988). Nutrition and labour productivity in agriculture: estimates for rural South India. *Review of Economies and Statistics* 70(3): 406-13.

Dercon, S. (1998). Wealth, risk and activity choice: cattle in Western Tanzania. *Journal of Development Economics* 55: 1-42.

Dercon, S. and Krishnan, P. (1999). Poverty, seasonality and intra-household allocation. Paper presented at IDS/IFPRI Workshop on Poverty Dynamics, April 1999, Institute of Development Studies, Brighton.

Dev, M. (1996). Experience of India's (Maharashtra) Employment Guarantee Scheme: lessons for development policy. *Development Policy Review* 14(3): 227-53.

Dev, S. M., Parikh, K. S. and Suryanarayana, M. H. (1991). *Rural poverty in India: incidence, issues and policies*. Indira Gandhi Institute of Development Research: Bombay. Discussion Paper No. 55.

Diskin, M. (1989). El Salvador: Reform prevents change. In Thiesenhusen, W. (ed.), *Searching for agrarian reform in Latin America*. Unwin Hyman: Boston.

Dolan, C., Humphrey, J. and Harris-Pascal, C. (1999). *Horticulture commodity chains: the impact of the UK market on the African fresh vegetable industry*. Institute of Development Studies: Brighton. IDS Working Paper No. 96.

Dollar, D. and Pritchett (1998). *Assessing aid: what works, what doesn't, and why*. World Bank: Washington DC.

Dorner, P. (1992). *Latin American land reforms in theory and practice: a retrospective analysis*. University of Wisconsin Press: Madison, Wisconsin.

Drèze, J. (1988). Social Security in India. Mimeo. STICERD London School of Economics.

Drèze, J. and Gazdar, H. (1997). Uttar Pradesh: the burden of inertia. In Dreze, J. and Sen, A. (eds), *Indian development: selected regional perspectives*. World Institute for Development Economics Research. Oxford University Press, Delhi.

Drèze, J. and Srinivasan, P. V. (1995). *Widowhood and poverty in rural India: some inferences from household survey data*. London School of Economics: London. Suntory and Toyota Centres for Economics and Related Disciplines DP No. 62.

Drèze, J., Lanjouw, P. and Stern, N. (1992). *Economic mobility and agricultural labour in rural India: a case study*. Development Economics Research Programme DEP 35, STICERD, London School of Economics.

Drinkwater, M. (1991). *The state and agrarian change in Zimbabwe's communal areas*. Macmillan: Basingstoke.

Eastwood, R. and Lipton, M. (2000). Impact of changes in human fertility on poverty. *Journal of Development Studies* 31(1): 1-30.

Echeverri-Gent, J. (1993). *The state and the poor*. University of California Press: Berkeley.

Edwards, D. T. (1995). *Small farmers protection of the watersheds: the experience of Jamaica since the 1950s*. University of Bradford Development and Project Planning Centre, New Series Discussion Papers 55.

EIU (1999). *Country profile: Tanzania*. Economist Intelligence Unit.

El-Ghonemy, M. R. (1990). The political economy of rural poverty: the case for land reform. Routledge: London.

El Hawary, M. A. and El Reedy, T. Y. (1984). Rural roads and poverty alleviation in Egypt in Howe, J. and Richards, P. (eds.) *Rural roads and poverty alleviation*, IT Publications.

Ellis, F. (1998). Household strategies and rural livelihood diversification. *Journal of Development Studies*. 35: 1-38.

Ensor, T. and San, P. B. (1996). Access and payment for health care: the poor of northern Vietnam. *International Journal of Health Planning and Management* 11(1): 69-83.

Epstein. S. (1973). *South India: yesterday, today, tomorrow*. Manchester University Press: Manchester.

Erenstein, O. (1999). The economics of soil conservation in developing countries: the case of crop residue mulching. PhD Thesis. Wageningen University, Netherlands.

Erenstein, O. and Cadena Iniguez, P. (1997). *The adoption of conservation tillage in a hillside maize production system in Motozintla, Chiapas*. Mexico, D.F.: CIMMYT. Natural Resources Group Paper 97-01.

Esrey, S. A., Potash, J. B., Roberts, L. and Shiff, C. (1990). *Health benefits from improvements in water supply and sanitation: survey and analysis of the literature of selected diseases*. USAID: Washington DC. Water and Sanitation for Health Technical Report No.66.

Estudillo, J. P. and Otsuka, K. (1999). Green Revolution, human capital and off-farm employment: changing sources of income among farm households in Central Luzon 1966-94. *Economic Development and Cultural Change* 47(3): 497-523.

European Union (2000). *Agriculture and rural development policy in developing countries.* EU, Brussels. Policy Orientation Paper.

Evenson, R. E. (1999). *Economic impact studies of agricultural rest extension.* Yale University: New Haven.

— (2000). Agricultural productivity and production in developing countries. *The State of Food and Agriculture.* FAO: Rome.

Evenson, R. E. and Kislev, Y. (1976). *Agricultural research and productivity.* Yale University: New Haven.

Fafchamps, M. (1992). Cash crop production, food price volatility and rural market integration in the Third World. *American Journal of Agricultural Economics* 74(1): 90-9.

— (1994), Industrial structure and microenterprises in Africa, *The Journal of Developing Areas*, 29, No. 1, 1-30.

Fairhead, J. and Leach, M. (1996). *Misreading the African landscape: society and ecology in a forest-savanna mosaic.* Cambridge University Press: Cambridge. Centre of African Studies, University of Cambridge.

Fan, S., Linxiu, Z. and Zhang, X. (2000a). *Growth and poverty in rural China: the role of public investments.* International Food Policy Research Institute: Washington DC.

Fan, S., Hazell, P. and Haque, T. (2000b). *Targeting public investments by agroecological zone to achieve growth and poverty alleviation goals in rural India.* International Food Policy Research Institute: Washington DC.

FAO Food Balance Sheets.

— (1991). *Third progress report on WCARRD* (Conference on Agrarian Reform and Rural Development 1979, Rome, Italy). Programme of Action. FAO 26th Conference 1991, Rome.

— (1996a). *World food security.* World Food Summit, Rome 13-17 November.

— (1998a). The state of food and agriculture. FAO: Rome.

— (1998b). Evaluation of the special programme for African countries affected by drought and desertification: thematic study on small-scale irrigation and water control activities, 1. Mimeo. FAO, Rome. Report No. 98/073 IFAD/SSA.

— (1998c). *Fish Farming in Vietnamese Rice Fields Fights Golden Apple Snail.* FAO: Rome. FAO News and Highlights, 10 April, 1998.

— (2000). The state of food and agriculture. FAO: Rome.

FAO/UNAIDS (2000). *Sustainable agriculture/rural development and vulnerability to the AIDS epidemic.* FAO/UNAIDS: Rome.

FAOSTAT (1998). FAO: Rome.

— (1999). FAO: Rome.

— (2000). Website of August 2000. FAO: Rome.

Farrington, J. and Bebbington, A. (1994). *Non governmental organisations and the state in Latin America.* Routledge: London.

Farrington, F. and Boyd, C. (1997). Scaling up the participatory management of common pool resources. *Development Policy Review* 15(4): 371-91.

Faruqee, R. and Carey, K. (1997). *Research on land markets in South Asia: What have we learned?* World Bank: Washington DC. Policy Research Working Paper No.1754.

Farooqee, N. A. and Nautiyal, A. (1996). Livestock ownership patterns among transhumants in high-altitude villages of the central Himalayas. Nomadic People 39: 87-96.

Feder, G., Just, R. E. and Zilberman, D. (1985). Adoption of agricultural innovations in developing countries: a survey. *Economic Development and Cultural Change* 33(2): 255-98.

Feder, G., Onchan, T., Chalamwong, Y. and Hongladarom, C. (1988). *Land policies and farm productivity in Thailand.* Published for the by Johns Hopkins University Press.

Ferreira, F. G. H. and Litchfield, J. A. (1999). Calm after the storms: income distribution in Chile, 1987-1994. *World Bank Economic Review* 13(3): 509-38.

Findlay, J. B. R. and Hutchinson, N. C. (1999). Development of conservation tillage in African countries: A partnership approach. In Breth, S. A. (ed.), *Partnership for rural development in sub-Saharan Africa.* Center for Applied Studies in International Negotiations: Geneva.

Finkelstein, I. and Chalfant, J. A. (1991). Marketed surplus under risk: do peasants agree with Sandmo? *American Journal of Agricultural Economics* 73(3): 557-67.

Firdausy, C. M. (1994). Urban poverty in Indonesia: trends, issues and policies. *Asian Development Review* 12(1): 68-89.

Fisher, T., Madajan, V. and Singha, A. (1997). *The forgotten sector: non-farm employment and enterprises in rural India.* Intermediate Technology Publications: London. Intermediate Technology Development Group.

Fontana, M., Joekes, S. and Masika, R. (1998). *Global trade expansion and liberalisation: gender issues and impacts.* BRIDGE Briefings on Development and Gender Report No. 42.

Forster, N. R. (1992). Protecting fragile lands: new reasons to tackle old problems. *World Development* 20: 4.

— (1989). *When the state sidesteps land reform: alternative peasant strategies in Tungurahua, Ecuador.* University of Wisconsin Land Tenure Paper 133.

Foster, A. and Rosenzweig, M. (1996). Technical change and human capital returns and investments: Evidence from the Green Revolution. *American Economic Review* 86: 931-53.

Frankenberg, E., Thomas, D. and Beegle, K. (1999). The real costs of Indonesia's economic crisis: preliminary findings from the Indonesian family life surveys. RAND Corporation: USA. Working Paper.

Frederiksen, H. D. (1992). *Drought planning and water efficiency implications in water resources management.* World Bank: Washington DC. World Bank Technical Paper No.185.

Fujita, K. and Hossain, F. (1995). Role of the ground water market in agricultural development and income distribution: a case study in a north west Bangladesh village. *Developing Economies* 33(4): 442-63.

Gaiha, R. (1988). Income mobility in rural India. *Economic Development and Cultural Change* 36(2): 279-302.

— (1989). Are the chronically poor also the poorest in rural India? *Development and Change* 20: 295-322.

— (1993). *Design of poverty alleviation strategy in rural areas.* FAO: Rome.

— (1997). Do rural public works influence agricultural wages? The case of the Employment Guarantee Scheme in India. *Oxford Development Studies* 25(3): 301-14.

Gaiha, R. and Deolalikar, A. B. (1993). Persistent, expected and innate poverty: estimates for semi-arid rural South India, 1975-1984. *Cambridge Journal of Economics* 17(4): 409-21.

Gaiha, R. and Kulkarni, V. (1999). Policy reforms, institutions and the poor in rural India. *Contemporary South Asia* 8(1): 7-28.

Galasi, P. (1998). *Income inequality and mobility in Hungary 1992-96.* UNICEF: Florence. Innocenti Occasional Paper 64.

Galasso and Ravallion, M. (1999). Distributional outcomes of a decentralised welfare programme. Mimeo. World Bank: Washington DC.

Gardner, L. B. (1995). *Policy reform in agriculture: an assessment of the result of eight countries.* University of Maryland: College Park.

Gavain, S. and Fafchamps, M. (1996). Land tenure and allocative efficiency in Niger. *American Journal of Agricultural Economics* 78: 460-71.

Ghate, P. (1992). Informal finance, some findings from Asia. Oxford University Press: Oxford.

Ghose (ed.) (1983). *Agrarian reform in contemporary developing countries.* Croom Helm: London. An ILO-WEP Study.

Gijsman, A. and Rusamsi, E. (1991). *Food security, livestock and sustainability of agriculture systems in Sukumaland, Tanzania.* International Course for Development Oriented Research in Agriculture: Wageningen. Farming Systems Analysis Paper 15(E).

Gilles, J. L., Hammoudi, A. and Mahdi, M. (1992). Oukaimedene, Morocco: a high mountain agdal. In Bromley, D. (ed.), *Making the commons work: theory, practice and policy.* Institute for Contemporary Studies, San Francisco.

Gilson, L. (1997). The lessons of user fee experience in Africa. *Health Policy and Planning* 12(4): 273-85.

Gittinger *et al.* (1990). *Household food security and the role of women.* World Bank: Washington DC. Report of the Symposium on Household Food Security and the Role of Women, held Jan. 21-24, 1990, in Kadoma, Zimbabwe, organized by the Women in Development Division of the World Bank.

Gladwin, C. H. and Thompson, C. M. (1995). Impacts of Mexico's trade openness on Mexican rural women. *American Journal of Agricultural Economics* 77: 712-8.

Gleick, P. H. (1999). *The world's water 1998-99: The biennial report of freshwater resources.* Island Press: Washington DC.

Glewwe, P and de Tray (1989). *The poor in Latin America during adjustment.* World Bank: Washington DC. LSMS Working Paper No. 56.

Glewwe, P. and Jacoby, H. G. (1995). An economic analysis of delayed primary school enrolment in a low-income country: the role of early childhood nutrition. *Review of Economics and Statistics* 77(1): 156-69.

Glewwe, P. and van der Gaag, J. (1990). Identifying the poor in developing countries: do different definitions matter? *World Development* 18(6): 803-14.

Government of Madhya Pradesh, India (1998). The Madhya Pradesh Human Development Report 1998, Government of Madhya Pradesh: Bhopal.

Government of India (1985). *Collaboration with NGOs in implementing the national strategy for health for all.* The Ministry of Health and Family Welfare: New Delhi.

Goyal, A. (1994). Mortality in India: trends and prospects. *Demography India* 23(1-2): 103-16.

Greeley, M. (1987). *Postharvest losses, technology, and employment: the case of rice in Bangladesh.* Boulder: London.

Gregson, S. (1994). Will HIV become a major determinant of fertility in Sub-Saharan Africa? *Journal of Development Studies* 30(3): 650-79.

Gregson, S., Garnett, G., and Anderson, R. (1994). Assessing the potential impact of the HIV-1 epidemic on orphanhood and the demographic structure of populations in Sub-Saharan Africa. *Population Studies* 40: 435-58.

Grimshaw, R. G. and Helfer, L. (1995) (eds), *Vetiver grass for soil and water conservation, land rehabilitation, and embankment stabilisation: a collection of papers and news letters compiled by the Vetiver Network.* World Bank: Washington DC. World Bank Technical Paper 273.

Grootaert, C. and Kanbur, R. (1995). The lucky few amidst economic decline: distributional change in Côte d'Ivoire as seen through panel datasets, 1986-88. *Journal of Development Studies* 31(4): 603-19.

Grootaert, C., Kanbur, R. and Oh, G. (1997). The dynamics of welfare gains and losses: an African case study. *Journal of Development Studies* 33(5): 635-57.

Guinnane, T. and Miller, R. (1997). The limits to land reform: the acts of Ireland, 1870-1909. *Economic Development and Cultural Change* 45: 591-612.

Gunning, J. W., Hoddinott, J., Kinsey, B. and Owens, T. (1999). Revisiting forever gained: income dynamics in the resettlement areas of Zimbabwe, 1983-97. Paper presented at IDS/IFPRI Workshop on Poverty Dynamics, April 1999, Institute of Development Studies: Brighton.

Gupta, J. (1993). Land, dowry, labour: women in the changing economy of Midnapur. *Social Scientist* 244-6, 74-90.

Haddad, L. and Ahmed, A. (1999). *Poverty dynamics in Egypt,* 1997-1999. International Food Policy Research Institute: Washington DC.

Haddad, L. J. and Bouis, H. E. (1991). The impact of nutritional status on agricultural productivity: wage evidence from the Philippines. *Oxford Bulletin of Economics and Statistics* 53(1): 45-68.

Haddad, L., Hoddinott, J. and Alderman, H. (eds) (1997). *Intrahousehold resource allocation in developing countries: models, methods and policy.* John Hopkins University Press: Baltimore.

Haddad, L., Hoddinott, J. and Mukherjee, S. (2000). *Assets and rural poverty.* Thematic paper for IFAD's Rural Poverty Report 2001: the challenge of ending rural poverty.

Hanger, J. and Moris, J. (1973). Women and household economy in Mwea: An irrigated rice settlement in Kenya. In Chambers, R. and Moris, J. (eds) *Africa Studien No. 83.* Weltforum Verlag: Munich.

Harris, B. (1986). *The intrafamily distribution of hunger in South Asia.* WIDER: Helsinki.

Harris, J. and Todaro, M. (1970). Migration, unemployment and development: A two sector analysis. *American Economic Review* 40: 126-42.

Hartmann, B. and Boyce, J. (1983). *A quiet violence: voices from a Bangladesh village.* Zed Press: London.

Hassan, A. (1996). Improved traditional planting jobs in Tahoua Dept., Niger. In Reij, C., Scoones, I. and Toulmin, C. (eds), *Sustaining the earth: indigenous soil and water conservation in Africa.* Earthscan Publications Ltd: London.

Hayami, Y., Quisumbing, A. R. and Adriano, L. S. (1990). *Toward an alternative land reform paradigm: a Philippine perspective.* Ateneo de Manila UP: Manila.

Hazell, P. and Haggblade, S. (1993). Rural-urban growth linkages in India. *Indian Journal of Agricultural Economics* 46(4): 515-29.

Hazell, P. B. R. and Ramasamy, C. (1991). *The Green Revolution reconsidered: The impact of high-yielding rice varieties in South India.* Johns Hopkins University Press: Baltimore.

Hazell, P. and Roell, A. (1983). Rural growth linkages: household expenditure patterns in Malaysia and Nigeria. International Food Policy Research Institute: Washington DC. Research Report No. 41.

Hazell, P., Jagger, P. and Knox, A. (2000). *Technology, natural resources, management and the poor.* Thematic paper for IFAD's Rural Poverty Report 2001: the challenge of ending rural poverty..

Hecht, R., Overholt, C. and Holmberg, H. (1992). *Improving the implementation of cost-recovery for health: lessons from Zimbabwe.* World Bank: Washington DC. World Bank Africa Technical Department Population. Health and Nutrition Division Technical Working Paper No. 2.

Heidemann, I. C. and Kaira, C. K. (1984). Transport planning in rural regions in developing countries. *Economics* 30: 142-57.

Herring, R. J. (1983). *Land to the tiller: the political economy of agrarian reform.* Yale: New Haven.

Hill, P. (1957), *Migrant cocoa farmers in southern Ghana: a study in rural capitalism.* Cambridge University Press: Cambridge

Hill, M. J. D. (1991). *The Harambee Movement in Kenya: self-help, development and education among the Kamba of Kitui District.* London School of Economics Monographs on Social Anthropology No. 64. Athlone Press Ltd.

Hobley, M. and Shah, K. (1996). *What makes local organisation robust? Evidence from India and Nepal.* Overseas Development Institute: London. Natural Resource Perspectives 11.

Hongoro, C. (1993). *The effect of user fees on health care delivery in Zimbabwe.* Report prepared for the Ministry of Health and Child Welfare by the Health Systems Research Unit and the Blair Institute, funded by UNICEF.

Horst, L. (1996). *Irrigation water division technology in Indonesia: a case of ambivalent development.* International Institute for Land Reclamation and Improvement; Department of Irrigation and Soil and Water Conservation, Wageningen University.

Horton, S. (1999). *Opportunities for investment in nutrition in low income Asia.* Asian Development Bank. Paper prepared for RETA 5671.

Horton, S. and Mazumdar, D. (1999). *Vulnerable groups and the labour market: the aftermath of the Asian financial crisis.* Paper prepared for the World Bank/ILO seminar on 'Economic crisis, employment and labour market in East and Southeast Asia', Tokyo, October 1999.

Hossain, M. (1988). *Nature and impact of the Green Revolution in Bangladesh.* International Food Policy Research Institute, Washington DC.

Howard, P. M. (1988). *Breaking the iron rice bowl: prospects for socialism in China's countryside.* Sharpe, M. E.: Armonk, New York, London.

Howe, J. (1984). The impact of rural roads on poverty alleviation: a review of the literature. In Howe, J. and Richards, P. (eds), *Rural roads and poverty alleviation.* Intermediate Technology Publications.

Howes, M. (1980). The creation and appropriation of value in irrigated agriculture: a comparison of the deep tubewell and the handpump in rural Bangladesh. In Greeley, M. and Howes, M. (eds), *Rural technology, rural institutions and the rural poorest.* Center on Integrated Rural Development for Asia: Comilla.

Hudson, N. (1992). *Land husbandry.* B. T. Batsford Ltd: London.

Huffman, W. (1977). Allocative efficiency: the role of human capital. *Quarterly Journal of Economics* 91: 59-77.

Huffman, S. L. and Steel, A. (1995). Do child survival interventions reduce malnutrition? The dark side of child survival. In Pinstrup Andersen, P., Pelletier, D. and Alderman, H. (eds), *Child growth and nutrition in developing countries: priorities for action.* Cornell University Press: New York.

Hulme, D. (2000). Is microdebt good for poor people? A note of the dark side of microfinance. *Small Enterprise Development* 11(1): 26-8.

Hulme, D. and Edwards, M. (eds) (1995). *Non-governmental organisations: performance and accountability: beyond the magic bullet.* Save the Children Fund. Earthscan Publications: London.

Hulme, D. and Mosley, P. (eds) (1996). *Finance against poverty.* Routledge: London.

Hulsebosch, J. and van Koppen, B. (1993). *Increasing women's benefits from irrigation development: smallholder irrigation in the Kano Plains, Kenya.* Irrigation Management Network. Network Paper 24.

Hunt, D. (1984). *The impending crisis in Kenya: the case for land reform.* Gower: Aldershot.

— (1996). *Rural livelihood systems and farm-nonfarm linkages in lower Embu, Eastern Kenya: 1972-4 to 1992-3.* End of project report to Overseas Development Administration.

Hussain, S. (1998). Micro-credit and income generation in rural Pakistan. *Asia-Pacific Journal of Rural Development* 8(1): 95-107.

Huttly, S., Blum, D., Kirkwood, B. R., Emeh, R. N. and Feachem, R. G. (1987). The epidemiology of acute diarrhoea in a rural community in Imo State, Nigeria. *Transactions of the Royal Society of Tropical Medicine and Hygiene* 81: 865-70.

Huttly, S., Blum, D., Kirkwood, B. R., Emeh, R. N., Okeke, N., Ajala, M., Smith, G. S., Carson, D. C., Dosunmu-Ogunbi, O. and Feachem, R. G. (1990). The Imo State (Nigeria) drinking water supply and sanitation project, 2. Impact on dracunculiasis, diarrhea and nutritional status. *Transactions of the Royal Society of Tropical Medicine and Hygiene* 84:316-321.

ICRISAT (2000). *Science with a human face.* Annual Report, ICRISAT: Patancheru.

IFAD (1982). Communal Irrigation development Project, Philippines.

— (1992a). *Egypt West Beihera Settlement Scheme interim evaluation report.* IFAD: Rome.

— (1992b). *Soil and water conservation in Sub-Saharan Africa: towards sustainable production by the rural poor.* IFAD: Rome.

— (1993). *Lesotho Local Initiatives Support Project mid-term Evaluation.* IFAD: Rome.

— (1994a). *Thematic study on lessons learned from evaluations in selected Asian countries.* IFAD: Rome.

— (1994b). *Bangladesh country portfolio evaluation.* IFAD: Rome.

— (1994c). *Sudan country portfolio evaluation.* IFAD: Rome.

— (1999a). *Regional assessment: supporting the livelihoods of the rural poor in East and Southern Africa.* Africa II Division. IFAD: Rome.

— (1999b). *Assessment of rural poverty in West and Central Africa.* Africa I Division Project Management Department. IFAD: Rome.

— (1999c). *Rural poverty assessment part I.* Near East and North Africa Division Project Management Department. IFAD: Rome.

— (1999d). *Regional assessment of poverty in Central and Eastern Europe and the Newly Independent States.* Near East and North Africa Project Management Department. IFAD: Rome.

— (1999e). *Rural poverty assessment: Asia and the Pacific region.* Asia and Pacific Division Project Management Department. IFAD: Rome.

— (1999f). *The North West Agricultural Services Project and Irrigation Rehabilitation Project, Armenia.* Report of Supervision Mission. IFAD: Rome.

— (1999g). *Zimbabwe: Community Based Resettlement Approaches and Technologies Project* (CREATE). financing proposal. IFAD: Rome.

— (1999h). *Arab Republic of Egypt: Newlands Agricultural Services Project mid-term evaluation.* IFAD: Rome.

— (1999i). *Rural poverty: a regional assessment.* Latin America and the Caribbean Division. IFAD, Rome.

— (1999j). *Appraisal Report, PAMA Support Project,* 1999. IFAD, Rome.

— (2000a). Rural Finance Policy Paper. IFAD: Rome.

— (2000b). Technical assistance grant to strengthen implementation of water management and irrigation components of IFAD projects in East and Southern Africa. Africa II Division. IFAD: Rome

— (2000c). Armenia: Country Strategic Opportunities Paper. Near East and North Africa Division, Programme Management Department. March 2000.

IFAD/FAO (1999). *The role of indirect incentives.* Environmental Report Series 2. FAO Investment Centre. FAO: Rome.

IFPRI (1985). *Annual Report.* International Food Policy Research Institute: Washington DC.

IFPRI (1997). Groundwater sales promote equity. International Food Policy Research Institute: Washington DC. *IFPRI Report* 19(1).

Immink, D. C. and Viteri, F. E. (1981). Energy intake and productivity of Guatemalan sugarcane cutters: an empirical test of the efficiency wage hypothesis, Parts I and II. *Journal of Development Economics* 9(2): 251-87.

Imo State Evaluation Team (1989). Evaluating water and sanitation projects: Lessons from Imo State, Nigeria. *Health Policy and Planning* 4 pp 40-49.

IRRI (1990). Irrigated rice program: 1991 budget presentation. International Rice Research Institute: Los Baños, Laguana, Philippines.

— (2000). *The rewards of rice research: Annual Report 1999-2000.* IRRI: Los Baños.

Isham, J. and Kahkonen, S. (1999). What determines the effectiveness of community-based water projects? Evidence from Central Java, Indonesia on demand responsiveness, service rules and social capital. Mimeo. World Bank: Washington DC.

Ishikawa, S. (1968). *Economic development an Asian perspective.* Hitotsubashi: Tokyo.

Itty, P., Ankers, P., Zinsstag, J., Trawally, S. and Pfister, K. (1997). Productivity and profitability of sheep production in The Gambia: Implications for Livestock Development in West Africa. *Quarterly Journal of International Agriculture* 36(2):153-72

Jacoby, H. G. (1998). *Access to markets and the benefits of rural roads.* World Bank: Washington DC. Policy Research Working Paper No. 2028.

Jaim, W. M. H. and Sarker, R. K. (1994). Irrigation through treadle pump: A technology for alleviating poverty in rural Bangladesh. *Journal of Rural Development* 24(1): 81-90.

Jaitly, J. (1996). The impact of trading policies on the screwpine mat weaving women of Kerala, India. *Global trading practices and poverty alleviation in South Asia.* UNIFEM: New Delhi.

Jalan, J. and Ravallion, M. (1998). Transient poverty in postreform rural China. *Journal of Comparative Economics* 26: 338-57.

— (1999). *Do Transient and chronic poverty in rural China share common causes?* Paper presented at IDS/IFPRI Workshop on Poverty Dynamics, April 1999. Institute of Development Studies: Brighton.

Jamison, D. T. and Lau, L. J. (1982). *Farmer education and farm efficiency.* John Hopkins University Press: Baltimore

Jarvis, L. S. (1989). The unravelling of Chile's agrarian reform. In Thiesenhusen, W. (ed.), *Searching for agrarian reform in Latin America.* Unwin Hyman: Boston.

Jayarajah, C., Branson, W. and Sen, B. (1996). *Social dimensions of adjustment: World Bank experience, 1980-93.* Operations Evaluation Department, World Bank. Washington DC.

Jayaraman, T. K. (1981). Farmers' organizations in surface irrigation projects: two empirical studies from Gujerat. *Economic and Political Weekly,* 26 September.

Jenkins, R. (2000). Reconceptualising transparency: movements for accountability to the poor in India. 3rd version of submission for: *The Global Report on Human Settlements. Centre for Human Settlements,* United Nations.

Jenkins, R. and Goetz, A. M. (1999a). Accounts and accountability: theoretical implications of the right-to-information movement in India. *Third World Quarterly* 20(3): 603-22.

— (1999b). Constraints on civil society's capacity to curb corruption: lessons from Indian experience. *IDS Bulletin* 30(4): 39-49.

Jeyaratnam, J., Lun, K. C. and Phoon, W. O. (1987). Survey of acute pesticide poisoning among agricultural workers in four Asian countries. Bulletin of the World Health Organization 65(4):521-27.

Jha, R. (1999). *Reducing poverty and inequality in India: has liberalisation helped?* Draft paper for World Institute for Development Economics Research project meeting. Rising income inequality and poverty reduction: are they compatible?

Jodha, N. S. (1986). Common property resources and rural poor in dry regions of India. *Economic and Political Weekly* 21(27).

— (1988). Poverty debate in India: a minority view. *Economic and Political Weekly Special* 23: 2421.

Jonakin, J. (1996). The impact of structural adjustment and property rights conflicts on Nicaraguan agrarian reform beneficiaries. *World Development* 24: 1179-91.

Jones, E. (1974). *Agriculture and the industrial revolution.* Blackwell: Oxford.

Jones, W. I. (1995). *The World Bank and irrigation.* World Bank: Washington DC.Operations Evaluation Department.

Joshi, A. (1998). Mobilising the poor? Activism and the Employment Guarantee Scheme, Maharashtra. Mimeo. Institute of Development Studies: Sussex.

Joshi, A. and Moore, M. (2000). *The mobilising potential of anti-poverty programmes.* Institute of Development Studies: Sussex. IDS Discussion Paper No. 374.

Joshi, N. L. and Singh, D. V. (1994). Water use efficiency in relation to crop production in arid and semi-arid regions. *Annals of Arid Zone* 33(3): 169-89.

Julka, A. C. and Sharma, P. K. (1989). Measurement of land inequality in India: A revision of the Lorenz Gini ratio. *Indian Journal of Agricultural Economics* 44(4): 423-9.

Kanbur, R. (1992). *Heterogeneity, distribution and cooperation in Common Property Resource Management.* World Bank: Washington DC. Policy Research Working Paper 844.

Kanbur, R. and Lustig, N. (1999). *Why is inequality back on the agenda?* Paper prepared for Annual World Bank Conference on Development Economics, April 1999. World Bank: Washington DC.

Kanwar, S. (1995). Do farm households use the labour market as a hedge against revenue risk? Evidence from female labour supply. *Indian Journal of Agricultural Economics* 50(4): 660-74.

Kelkar G. (2001). *Gender relations in forest-based societies.* Sage Publications: New Delhi (forthcoming).

Kelkar G. and Nathan D. (1991). *Gender and tribe: women, land and forests in Jharkhand,* New Delhi, Kali for Women.

Kenmore, P. E. (1991). Indonesia's integrated pest management: policy, production and environment. Paper presented at USAID-ARPE Environment and Agricultural Officers Conference, 11 September, Colombo, Sri Lanka.

Kennedy, E. and Peters, P. (1992). Household food security and child nutrition: the interaction of income and gender of household head. *World Development* 20(8): 1077-85.

Kerkvliet, B. and Selden, M. (1998). Agrarian transformations in China and Viet Nam. *The China Journal* 40: 37-58.

Kerr, J. and Kohlavalli, S. (1999). *Impact of agricultural research on poverty alleviation: conceptual framework with illustrations from the literature.* International Food Policy Research Institute: Washington DC. Environment and Production Technology Division Discussion Paper No. 56.

Kerr, J. and Sanghi, N. K. (1992). *Indigenous soil and water conservation in India's semi-arid tropics.* International Institute for Environment and Development: London. Sustainable Agriculture and Rural Livelihoods Gatekeeper Series 34.

Khan, A. R. (1998). *Poverty in China in the period of globalization: new evidence on trend and pattern.* Development and Technical Cooperation Department. International Labour Organisation: Geneva. Issues in Development Discussion Paper No. 22.

Khan, A. R. and Riskin, C. (1998). Income and inequality in China: composition, distribution and growth of household income, 1988 to 1995. *China Quarterly* June.

Khandker, S. R. (1998). Micro-credit programme evaluation: a critical review. In *IDS Bulletin* 29(4): 11-20.

Kiepe, P. (1995). *No run-off, no soil loss: soil and water conservation in hedgerow barrier systems.* Wageningen Agricultural University. Tropical Management Papers 10.

Kikula, I. S., Dalal-Clayton, B., Comoro, C. and Kiwasila, H. (1999). A framework for distinct participatory planning in Tanzania Vol. I. Institute of Resource Assessments of the University of Dar-es-Salaam and the International Institute for the Environment and Development.

Killick, A., Kydd, J. and Poulton, C. (2000). *The rural poor and the wider economy: the problem of market access.* Thematic paper for IFAD's Rural Poverty Report 2001: the challenge of ending rural poverty.

Kimmage, K. (1991). Small-scale irrigation initiatives in Nigeria: the problems of equity and sustainability. *Applied Geography* 11: 5-20.

King, R. (1977). *Land reform : a world survey.* Westview: Boulder

Kirk, D. and Pillett, B. (1998). Fertility in Sub-Saharan Africa in the 1980s and 1990s. *Studies in family planning* 29(1): 1-22.

Klooster, D. (2000). Institutional choice, community and struggle: a case study of forest co-management in Mexico. *World Development* 28(1): 1-20.

Kodderitzsch, S. (1999). *Reforms in Albanian agriculture: assessing a sector in transition.* World Bank Technical Paper No. 431. World Bank: Washington DC.

Knight, J. and Song, L. (2000). Economic Growth and Economic Reform and Rising Inequality in China. In Riskin *et al.* (eds.) *Equality in Retreat.* Routledge and Sharpe, M.E..

Kome, A. (1997). *Gender and irrigation management transfer in Sri Lanka: IRMU, ID and IIMI.* Wageningen Agricultural University, The Netherlands.

Krongkaew, M. *et al.* (1994). Thailand. In Quibria, M. G. (ed.), *Rural poverty in developing Asia 2.* Asian Development Bank: Manila, Philippines.

Krueger, A. O., Schiff, M. W. and Valdes, A. (eds) (1991). *The political economy of agricultural pricing policy.* John Hopkins University Press: Baltimore.

Kurnia, G., Avianto, T. and Bruns, B. (1999). Farmers, factories and the dynamics of water allocation in West Java. In Meinzen-Dick, R. and Bruns, B. (eds), *Negotiating water rights.* Sage Publishers: India.

Kurosaki, T. (1995). Risk and insurance in a household economy: role of livestock in mixed farming in Pakistan. *The Developing Economies* 33(4):464-85.

Kutcher, G. P. and Scandizzo, P. (1981). *The agricultural economy of Northeast Brazil.* John Hopkins University Press: Baltimore.

Laderchi, C. R. (1997). Poverty and its many dimensions: the role of income as an indicator. *Oxford Development Studies* 25(3): 345-60.

Lanjouw, P. and Stern, N. (1991). Poverty in Palanpur. *World Bank Economic Review,* 5(1): 23-55.

Lanjouw, P. and Stern, N. (1993). Agricultural changes and inequality in Palanpur, 1957-84. In Hoff, K., Braverman, A. and Stiglitz, J. E. (eds), *The economics of rural organisation: theory, practice, and policy.* Oxford University Press: Oxford.

Lastarria-Cornhiel, S. (1989). Agrarian reforms of the 1960s and 1970s in Peru. In Thiesenhusen, W. (ed.), *Searching for agrarian reform in Latin America.* Unwin Hyman: Boston.

Lele, U. (1992). *Aid to African agriculture: lessons from two decades of donors' experience.* John Hopkins University Press for the World Bank: Baltimore.

Levine, G., Cruz Galvan, A., Garcia, D., Garces-Restrepo, C. and Johnson III, S. (1998). *Performance of two transferred modules in the Lagunera Region.* International Water Management Institute: Colombo, Sri Lanka. Water Relations Research Report 23.

Liamzon, C. M. (2000). *Civil society organizations and their role in people's empowerment and rural poverty eradication.* Background Paper for IFAD's Rural Poverty Report 2001: the challenge of ending rural poverty.

Lieten, G. K. (1996). Land reforms at centre stage: the evidence on West Bengal. *Development and Change* 27(1): 111-30.

Lin, J. (1992). Rural reforms and agricultural growth in China. *American Economic Review* 82: 34-51.

Lipton, M. (1977). *Why poor people stay poor: a study of urban bias in world development.* Australian National University Press: Canberra.

— (1982). Rural development and the retention of rural population in the countryside of developing countries. *Canadian Journal of Development Studies* 3(1): 12-37.

— (1983a). *Demography and poverty.* World Bank: Washington DC. Working Paper No. 623.

— (1983b). *Poverty, undernutrition and hunger.* World Bank Staff Working Paper No. 597. World Bank: Washington DC.

— (1984). Family, fungibility and formality: rural advantages of informal non-farm enterprise versus the urban informal state. In Amin, S. (ed.), *Human Resources, Employment and Development, 5: Developing Countries.* Macmillan: London

— (1985). *Land assets and rural poverty.* World Bank: Washington DC. World Bank Staff Working Paper No. 744.

— (1988). The place of agricultural research in the development of sub-Saharan Africa. *World Development* 16: 1231-56.

— (1998) *Successes in antipoverty.* International Labour Office: Geneva.

— (1999). *Reviving global poverty reduction: what role for genetically modified plants?* Sir John Crawford Memorial Lecture. Consultative Group on International Agricultural Research: Washington DC.

Lipton, M. and Eastwood, R. (1999). *Changes in rural urban inequality and urban bias.* Prepared for WIDER conference 1999. University of Sussex: Brighton, UK.

Lipton, M. and Longhurst, R. (1989). *New seeds and poor people.* Unwin Hyman: London.

Lipton, M. and Osmani, S. (1997). *Quality of life in emerging Asia.* Asian Development Bank: Manila. Background paper for Emerging Asia: Change and Challenges.

Lipton, M. and Ravallion, M. (1995). Poverty and policy. In Behrman, J. and Srinivasan, T. N. (eds), *Handbook of development economics* 3b. North Holland: Amsterdam.

Livi-Bacci, M. and de Santis, G. (1999). *Population and poverty in developing countries.* Clarendon Press: Oxford.

Lockheed, M. E., Jamison, D. T. and Lau, L. J. (1980). Farmer education and farm efficiency: a survey. *Economic Development and Cultural Change* 29(1): 37-76.

Lucas, A., Morely, R. and Cole, T. J. (1998). Randomised trial of early diet in preterm babies and later intelligence quotient. *British Medical Journal* 317: 1481-7.

Lucas, H. and Nuwagaba, A. (1999). *Household coping strategies in response to the introduction of user charges for social services: a case study on health in Uganda.* IDS Working Paper No. 86. Institute of Development Studies: Brighton.

Lutz, E., Binswanger, H., Hazell, P. and McCalla, A. (1998) (eds), *Agriculture and the environment: perspectives on sustainable rural development.* World Bank: Washington DC.

MacIsaac, D. J. and Patrinos, H. A. (1995). Labour market discrimination against indigenous people in Peru. *Journal of Development Studies* 32(2): 218-33.

Mahmood, M. (1993). A macro analysis of time change in the distribution of land. *Pakistan Development Review* 32(4) Part 2:771-87.

Maluccio, J., Haddad, L. and May, J. (1999a). Social capital and income generation in South Africa, 1993-98. Paper presented at IDS/IFPRI Workshop on Poverty Dynamics, April 1999, Brighton.

— (1999b). *Income and social capital in South Africa, 1993-89.* FCND Discussion Paper No. 71. International Food Policy Research Institute: Washington DC.

Mangisoni, J. H. and Phiri, G. S. (1996). New perspectives on local conservation techniques: a case study from Malawi. In Reij C., Scoones, I. and Toulmin, C. (eds), *Sustaining the soil: indigenous soil and water conservation in Africa.* Earthscan: London.

Mani, G. and Gandhi, V. (1994). Are land markets worsening the land distribution in progressive areas? A study of Meerat District in western Uttar Pradesh. *Indian Journal of Agricultural Economics* 49(3): 330-8.

Manikutty, S. (1998). Community participation: lessons from experiences in five water and sanitation projects in India. *Development Policy Review* 16(3): 373-404.

Manor, J. (1989). Karnataka: caste, class, dominance and politics in a cohesive society. In Frankel, F. R. and Rao, M. S. A. (eds), *Dominance and state power in India. Vol 1.* Oxford University Press: Dehli.

— (1997). The political economy of decentralisation. Mimeo. World Bank: Washington DC.

Mao, Y. K. and Schive, C. (1995). Agriculture and industrial development in Taiwan. In Mellor, J. (ed.), *Agriculture on the road to industrialisation.* John Hopkins University Press: Baltimore.

Martorell, R. (1995). Promoting healthy growth: rationale and benefits. In Pinstrup Andersen, P., Pelletier, D. and Alderman, H. (eds), *Child growth and nutrition in developing countries: priorities for action.* Cornell University Press: New York.

Mathur, G. C. (1989). Rural housing technology and poverty eradication. *Kurukshetra* 37(12).

Matin, I. (1998). Mis-targeting of Grameen Bank: a possible explanation? *IDS Bulletin* 29(4).

— (1999). Risk and vulnerability: the role of microfinance. Sprigfield Centre for Business and Development. Mimeo.

Mbugua, J. K., Bloom, G. H., and Segall, M. M. (1995). Impact of user charges on vulnerable groups: the case of Kibwezi in rural Kenya. *Social Science and Medicine* 41(6): 829-35.

McCulloch, N. and Baulch, B. (1999). *Distinguishing the chronically from the transitorily poor: evidence from rural Pakistan.* Institute of Development Studies: Brighton. IDS Working Paper No. 97.

McGregor, S. M., Walker, S. P., Chang, S. M. and Powell, C. A. (1997). Effects of early childhood supplementation with and without stimulation on later development in stunted Jamaican children. *American Journal of Clinical Nutrition* 66(2): 247-53.

McKean, M. (1995). Common property: what is it, what is it good for and what makes it work? Paper presented at the International Conference on Chinese Rural Collectives and Voluntary Organisations: Between state organisation and private interest, Sinological Institute, University of Leiden, 9-13 June.

McMillan, J., Whalley, J. and Zhu, L. (1989). The impact of China's economic reforms on agricultural productivity growth. *Journal of Political Economy* 97: 781-807.

Mearns, R. (1999). *Access to land in rural India.* Policy Research Working Paper 2123. World Bank: Washington DC.

Mecharla, P. R. (2000). Distress diversification or growth linkage? Explaining rural non-farm employment variations in Andhra Pradesh, India. PhD Thesis submitted to University of Sussex, May.

Meinzen-Dick, R. and Knox, A. (1999). Collective action, property rights and devolution of natural resource management: a conceptual framework. Workshop draft, Mimeo. International Food Policy Research Institute: Washington DC.

Meinzen-Dick, R., and Makombe, G. (1999). Dambo Irrigation Systems: Indigenous Water Management for Food Security in Zimbabwe. In Knox McCulloch, A., Babu, S. and Hazell, P. (eds). *Strategies for poverty alleviation and sustainable resource management in the fragile lands of Sub-Saharan Africa*, Proceedings of the International Conference held from 25-29 May, 1998 in Entebbe, Uganda. Food and Agriculture Development Centre, DSE, Feldafing, Germany.

Meinzen-Dick, R. and Zwarteveen, M (1998). Gendered Participation in Water Management: Issues and Illustrations from Water User Associations in South Asia. In Merrey, D and Baviskar, S (eds). *Gender analysis and reform of irrigation management: concepts, cases and gaps in knowledge*, Proceedings of the Workshop on Gender and Water, 15-19 September 1997, Habarana, Sri Lanka. International Water Management Institute.

Meinzen-Dick, R., Brown, L. R., Feldstein, H. S. and Quisumbing, A. R. (1997). Gender, Property Rights and Natural Resources. *World Development* 25(8): 1303-15.

Mellor, J. W. (1976). *The new economics of growth: a strategy for India and the developing world*. Cornell University Press: Ithaca.

— (1999). Pro-poor growth. The relation between growth in agriculture and poverty reduction. Abt Associates Inc: Bethesda.

Mellor, J. W. and Desai, G. M. (1985). *Agricultural change and rural poverty: variations on a theme by Dharm Narain*. Published for IFPRI by John Hopkins University Press, Baltimore.

Mellor, J. W. and Moorti, T. V. (1971). Dilemma of state tubewells. *Economic and Political Weekly* 4.

Migot-Adholla, S., Hazell, P., Blarel, B. and Place, F. (1991). Indigenous land rights systems in sub-Saharan Africa. *World Bank Economic Review* 5: 155-75.

Milanovic, B, (1998). *Income, inequality and poverty during the transition from planned to market economy*. World Bank Regional and Sectoral Studies. World Bank: Washington DC.

Mingay, G. (1968). The agricultural revolution in English history: a reconsideration. In Minchinton, W. (ed.), *Essays in agrarian history*. David and Charles: Newton Abbott.

Mitra, A. (1978). *India's population: aspects of quality and control*. Family Planning Foundation (New Delhi) and Indian Council of Social Science Research (India).

Moffat, M. (1998). A gender analysis of community forestry and community leasehold forestry in Nepal with a macro-meso-micro framework. MA dissertation in Development Policy Analysis, Department of Economics and Social Studies, University of Manchester.

Mollinga, P. P. (1998). *On the waterfront: water distribution, technology and agrarian change in a South Indian canal irrigation system*. WOTRO: Wageningen.

Morduch, J. (1998). Does microfinance really help the poor? Unobserved heterogeneity and average impacts of credit in Bangladesh. Mimeo. Harvard University, Department of Economics and HIID: Cambridge, MA, USA.

— (1999). The microfinance promise. *Journal of Economic Literature* 37: 1569-614.

Morgan, P. (1993). Maintenance, the key to handpump survival. *Waterlines* 11(4): 2-4.

Moslehuddin, M., Kabir, M. and Bose, G. K. (1993). Rural markets in Bangladesh and the rural maintenance programme. *Economic Affairs* 38(3): 149-60.

Mosley, P. (1996). Bancosol, Bolivia. In Hulme, D. and Mosley, P. (eds) (1996). *Finance against poverty*. Routledge: London.

— (2000). *The performance of the research system and the African green revolution: maize, sorghum, cassava*. Sheffield University Department of Economics and Gatsby Charitable Foundation. Occasional Paper No. 2000-02.

Mrema, M. (1994). Tanzanian women and progress in 'Tuke' consumers' marketing cooperative. *PULA* 8(2): 18-36.

Mroz, T. A. and Popkin, B. M. (1995). Poverty and the Economic Transition in the Russian Federation. *Economic Development and Cultural Change* 44(1): 1-33.

Mudege, N. R. (1993). Handpump maintenance in Zimbabwe. *Waterlines* 11(4): 9-12.

Mukherjee, A. (1994). *Diversification of contracts in rural labour markets*. Discussion Paper Series No. 44. Institute for Economic Development, Boston University.

Muller, C. (1997). Transient, Seasonal and Chronic Poverty of Peasants: Evidence from Rwanda, Working Paper S/97-8. Centre for the Study of African Economies, Oxford.

Murray, W. (1997). Competitive global fruit export markets: Marketing intermediaries and impacts on small-scale growers in Chile. *Bulletin of Latin American Research* 16(1): 43-56.

Murthy, G. (1989). Needing long-term rural housing strategy. *Kurukshetra* 37(12).

Narain, D. and Roy, S. (1980). *Impact of irrigation and labour availability on multiple cropping: a case study of India*. Research Report No. 20. International Food Policy Research Unit: Washington DC.

Narayan, D., Chambers, R., Kaul Shah, M. and Petesch, P. (1999). *Global synthesis. Consultations with the poor*. Paper prepared for global synthesis workshop. 22-23 Sept. 1999. World Bank: Washington DC.

— (2000). *Crying out for change: Voices of the poor*. Volume II. World Bank: Washington DC.

Nathan, D. (2000). Timber in Meghalaya. *Economic and Political Weekly*, January 22: 182-86.

Nathan, D. and Kelkar, G. (1997). Collective villages in the Chinese market-I. *Economic and Political Weekly* 32:951-63. May 3-9.

Nathan, D. and Kumar, D. (2001). Sustainable community fisheries for poverty alleviation. In Kumar, D. (ed.), *Proceedings of NACA Workshop*. FAO: Rome (forthcoming).

Ncube, W., Stewart, J. F., Dengu-Zvobgo, K. C., Donzwa, B. R., Gwaunza, E. C., Kazembe, J. L. and Nzira, T. G. (1997). *Paradigms of exclusion: women's access to resources in Zimbabwe*. Women and Law in Southern Africa Research Trust: Zimbabwe.

Neitzert, M. (1994). A woman's place: household labour allocation in rural Kenya. *Canadian Journal of Development Studies* 15(3): 401-27.

Nelson, M., Dudal, R., Gregersen, H., Jodha, N., Nyamai, D., Groenewol, J., Torres, F. and Kassam, A. (1997). *Report of the study on CGIAR research priorities for marginal lands*. Consultative group on international agricultural research, Technical Advisory Committee Secretariat, Food and Agriculture Organisation: Rome.

Ninan, K. N. (1998). *An assessment of European-aided watershed development projects in India from the perspective of poverty reduction and the poor*. Centre for Development Research (Denmark). Copenhagen. CDR Working Papers 98.3.

Noronha, R. (1985). *A review of the literature on land tenure systems in Sub-Saharan Africa*. Discussion Paper ARU43. World Bank: Washington DC.

Nsabagasani, X. (1997). *Land privatisation, security of tenure and agricultural production: The Ugandan experience*. Working Paper No. 263. Institute of Social Studies, The Hague.

Nuffield Foundation (1999). *Genetically modified plants: The ethical and social issues*. Nuffield Council on Bioethics: London.

Nyonator, F. and Kutzin, J. (1999). Health for some? The effects of user fees in the Volta Region of Ghana. *Health Policy and Planning* 14(4).

Oberai, A. S. (ed.), (1988). *Land settlement policies and population redistribution in developing countries: achievements, problems and prospects*. Praeger: New York.

Odii, M. A. C. A. (1997). Land resource use efficiency of rural women farmers under alternative tenurial arrangements. *Journal of Rural Development and Administration* 29(1): 1-9.

OECD (1987). dataset. OECD: Paris

OECD/DAC (2000). International Development Satatistics 2000 edition. OECD: Paris

Oosterlee, L. (1988). *Marketing of export crops in tropical Africa: a comparative analysis of cooperative societies and private licensed buying agents in the Southwest Province, Cameroun*. State University of Utrecht Department of Geography of Developing Countries. Diskussiestukken 40.

Osmani, S. R. (2000). *Institutions for the poor*, Theme Paper prepared for IFAD's Rural Poverty Report 2001: the challenge of ending rural poverty.

Ostrom, E. (1990). *Governing the commons: The evolution of institutions for collective action*. Cambridge University Press: New York.

— (1994). *Neither market nor state: governance of common-pool resources in the twenty-first century*. International Food Policy Research Institute: Washington DC. Lecture Series No.2.

— (1999). *Self-governance and forest resources*. Occasional Paper 20. Centre for International Forestry Research: Indonesia.

Osunade, M. and Reij, C. (1996). 'Back to the grass strips': a history of soil conservation policies in Swaziland. In Reij C., Scoones, I. and Toulmin, C. (eds.) *Sustaining the soil: indigenous soil and water conservation in Africa*. Earthscan: London.

Otsuka, H. and Chuma, H. (1992). Land and labour contracts in agrarian economies: theories and facts. *Journal of Economic Literature*.

Otsuka, K. and Hayami, Y. (1988). Theories of share tenancy: a critical survey. *Economic Development and Cultural Change* 37: 31-68.

OXFAM/IDS (1999). *Liberalisation and poverty*. Final Report to DFID, August

Pal, D. P. and Mondal, S. K. (1994). The changing pattern of landholdings in rural India. *Economic Affairs* 39(1): 41-53.

Palamuleni, M. E. (1994). Mortality level, trends and differentials in Malawi. *Eastern and Southern African Geographic Journal* 5(1): 68-74.

Pallen, D. (1997). *Environmental source book for microfinance institutions*. Canadian International Development Agency, Asia Branch, Canada.

Pant, N. (1984). *Organisation, technology and performance of irrigation systems in Uttar Pradesh*. Giri Institute of Development Studies, B42, Nirala Nagar, Lucknow.

Parthasarthy, G. (1991). Lease market, poverty alleviation and policy options. *Economic and Political Weekly* 30 March: A31-8.

Pasha, S. A. (1992). CPRs and rural poor: a micro level analysis. In *Economic and Political Weekly*, 14 November.

Pathak, R., Ganpathy, K. and Sarma, Y. (1977). Shifts in pattern of asset-holdings of rural households, 1961-2 to 1971-2. *Economic and Political Weekly* 12(12).

Patrinos, H. A. and Psacharopoulos, G. (1993). The cost of being indigenous in Bolivia. *Bulletin of Latin American Research* 12: 293-309.

Payne, P. and Lipton, M. (1994). *How third world households adapt to dietary energy stress: The evidence and the issues.* Food Policy Review No. 2. International Food Policy Research Institute: Washington DC.

Pearson, S. R., Stryker, J. D., Humphreys, C. P. *et al.* (1981). *Rice in west Africa: Policy and economics.* Stanford.

Piggott, S. (1981). Early pre-history. In Thirsk, J. (ed.), *Agrarian history of England and Wales.* I.i, Prehistory. Cambridge University Press: Cambridge.

Pingali, P., Bigot, Y. and Binswanger, H. P. (1987). *Agricultural mechanization and the evolution of farming systems in Sub-Saharan Africa.* Johns Hopkins University Press for the World Bank: Baltimore, London.

Pinstrup-Anderson, P., Pandya-Lorch, R. and Rosegrant, M. W. (1999). *World food prospects: Critical issues for the early twenty-first century,* IFPRI Food Policy Report. International Food Policy Research Institute: Washington DC.

Place, F. and Hazell, P. (1993). Productivity effects of indigenous land tenure systems in Sub-Saharan Africa. *American Journal of Agricultural Economics* 75(1): 10-19.

Platteau, J.-P. (1992). *Formalization and privatization of land rights in sub-Saharan Africa: a critique of current orthodoxies and structural adjustment programmes.* London School of Economics: London. Suntory and Toyota Centres for Economics and Related Disciplines DP No. 34.

— (1993). *Economic theory of land rights as applied to sub-Saharan Africa: a critical assessment.* Department of Economic and Social Sciences, University of Namur.

— (1996). Physical infrastructure as a constraint on agricultural growth: the case of sub-Saharan Africa. *Oxford Development Studies* 24(3): 189-219.

Postel, S. (1992). *The last oasis: facing water scarcity.* Worldwatch Environmental Alert Series. Worldwatch Institute.

Prathapar, S. A. and Qureshi, A. S. (1999). *Mechanically reclaiming abandoned saline soils: a numerical evaluation.* International Water Management Institute: Colombo, Sri Lanka. IWMI Research Report 30.

Prescott, N. M. and Pradhan, M. (1997). World Bank: Washington D.C A poverty profile of Cambodia. World Bank Discussion Paper No. 373.

Pretty, J. N. (1996). Participation, learning and sustainability: emerging challenges for agricultural development. *Social Change* 26(1): 7-33.

— (2000). *Can sustainable agriculture feed Africa? New evidence on progress, processes and inputs.* Environment, Development and Sustainability, Special issue on sustainable agriculture.

Psacharopoulos, G. (1993). Ethnicity, education and earnings in Bolivia and Guatemala. *Comparative Education Review* 37: 9-20.

Psacharopoulos, G. and Patrinos, H. A. (1993). *Indigenous people and poverty in Latin America: an empirical analysis.* Latin America and the Caribbean Technical Department, Regional Studies Program Report No. 30. World Bank: Washington DC.

Quisumbing, A. (1994). *Gender differentials in agricultural productivity: a survey of empirical evidence.* Education and Social Policy Department Discussion Paper Series No. 36. World Bank: Washington DC.

Quisumbing, A. (1996). Male-female differences in agricultural productivity: A survey of empirical evidence. *World Development* 24: 1579-95.

Raczynski, D. (1991). *La ficha CAS y la focalizacion de los programmas sociales.* Corporacion de Investigaciounes Economicas para Latinoamerica, CIEPLAN: Santiago, Chile.

Radcliffe, S. A. (1990). Between health and labour market: the recruitment of peasant women in the Andes. *International Migration Review* 24(2): 229-49.

Rahman, A. (1992). The informal financial sector in Bangladesh: an appraisal of its role in development. *Development and Change* 23(1): 147-68.

Rajan, A. (1993). Mortality in India: 1970-85. *Demography India* 22(1): 91-109.

Randel, J., German, T. and Ewing, D. (2000). *The reality of aid 2000: an independent review of poverty reduction and development assistance.* Earthscan: London.

Ranger, T. and Werbner, R. P. (eds.) (1990). *Postcolonial identities in Africa.* International Centre for Contemporary Cultural Research. Zed Books: London.

Rao, C. H. H., Ray, S. K. and Subbarao, K. (1988). *Unstable agriculture and droughts: implications for policy.* Institute for Economic Growth: Delhi. Studies in Economic Development and Planning No. 47.

Rao, R. (1995). Goats and sheep: a vital factor in rural economy. *Kurukshetra* 43(4): 44.

Ravallion, M. (1991). *Quantifying the magnitude and severity of absolute poverty in the developing world in the mid-1980s.* World Bank: Washington DC. Policy, Research and External Affairs Working Papers No. 587, and Background paper for the 1990 World Development Report.

— (2000). On the urbanisation of poverty. Mimeo. World Bank: Washington DC.

Ravallion, M., Datt, G. and Chaudhuri, S. (1991). *Higher wages for relief work can make many of the poor worse off: recent evidence from Maharashtra's 'Employment Guarantee Scheme'.* Policy, Research and External Affairs Working Paper No. 568. World Bank: Washington DC.

Ravallion, M. and Jalan, J. (1996). *Transient poverty in rural China.* Policy Research Working Paper. World Bank: Washington DC.

Ravallion, M. and Sen, B. (1994). *How land-based targeting affects rural poverty.* Policy Research Working Paper No. 1270. World Bank: Washington DC.

Ravallion, M., van der Walle, D. and Gautam, M. (1995). Testing a social safety net. *Journal of Public Economics* 57(2): 175-99.

Ray, S. K. (1996). Land system and its reforms in India. *Indian Journal of Agricultural Economics* 52(1,2): 220-37.

Raza, M. and Ramachandran, H. (1990). *Schooling and rural transformation.* National Institute of Educational Planning and Administration: India.

Reardon, T. (1997). Using evidence of household income diversification to inform study of the rural nonfarm labour market in Africa. *World Development* 25(5): 735-47.

— (2000). The interface between the rapidly changing global agricultural economy and the small poor farmer: strategic implications for the CGIAR. Paper presented at the special TAC meeting on CGIAR vision and strategy, Jan., Rome.

Reardon, T. and Taylor, J. E. (1996). Agroclimatic shock, income inequality and poverty: evidence from Burkina Faso. *World Development* 24(4): 901-14.

Reardon, T., Taylor, J. E., Stamoulis, K., Lanjouw, P. and Balisacan, A. *et al.* (2000). Effects of nonfarm employment on rural income inequality in developing countries: an investment perspective. *Journal of Agricultural Economics* 52(2).

Reddy, S. and Vandemortele, J. (1996). *User financing of basic social services: a review of theoretical arguments and empirical evidence.* UNICEF Staff Working Papers, Evaluation, Policy and Planning Series. UNICEF: New York.

Reij *et al.* (1996). *Evolution et impacts des techniques de conservation des eaux et des sols.* Centre for Development Cooperation Services, Vrije Universiteit: Amsterdam.

Republic of Botswana (1975). Rural Income Distribution Survey.

Reynolds, J. (1992). *Handpumps: towards a sustainable technology: Research and Development during the Water and Sanitation Decade.* Water and Sanitation Report 5, UNDP-World Bank Water and Sanitation Program. World Bank: Washington DC.

Richards, P. (1985). *Indigenous agricultural revolution.* Hutchinson: London.

Riddell, R. C. and Robinson, M. (1995). *Non-governmental organisations and rural poverty alleviation.* Clarendon Press: Oxford.

Riedinger, J. (1993). Prospects for land reform in Nepal. *South Asia Bulletin.* 13(1,2): 23-34.

Riverson, J. D. N. and Carapetis, S. (1991). *Intermediate means of transport in Sub-Saharan Africa.* World Bank Technical Paper 161. World Bank: Washington DC.

Robb, C. M. (1999). *Directions in development: can the poor influence policy?: participatory poverty assessments in the developing world.* World Bank: Washington DC.

Robinson, M. S. (1996). Addressing some key questions on finance and poverty, *Journal of International Development,* 8, No. 2: 153-61.

Ronchi, L. (2000). *Fair trade in Costa Rica: An impact report.* University of Sussex: Brighton.

Rose, L. (1988). A woman is like a field: women's strategies for land access in Swaziland. In Davison, J. (ed.). *Agriculture, women and land: The African experience.* Westview Press: Boulder and London.

Rosegrant, M. W. (1995). *Dealing with water scarcity in the next century.* 2020 Brief, 21 June. International Food Policy Research Institute: Washington DC.

Rosegrant M. and Hazell, P. (1999). *Transforming the rural Asian economy: The unfinished revolution.* Oxford University Press for the Asian Development Bank: Hong Kong.

Rosegrant, M. W. and Perez, N. D. (1997). *Water resources development in Africa: a review and synthesis of issues, potentials, and strategies for the future.* EPTD Discussion Paper 28. International Food Policy Research Institute: Washington DC.

Rosenzweig, M. (1995). Why are there returns to schooling? *American Economic Review: Papers and Proceedings* 85: 153-8.

Rosenzweig, M. R. and Schultz, T. P. (1982). *Market opportunities, genetic endowments, and the intra-family distribution of resources: child survival in rural India.* Yale University: New Haven. Economic Growth Center Discussion Paper No. 347.

Roth, M. J. and Bruce, J. W. (1994). *Land tenure, agrarian structure, and comparative land use efficiency in Zimbabwe: options for land tenure reform and land redistribution.* Land Tenure Center, University of Wisconsin: Madison. Research Paper No. 117.

Rudel, T. K. and Richards, S. (1990). Urbanisation, roads and rural population change in the Ecuadorian Andes. *Studies in Comparative International Development* 25(3): 73-89.

Rukuni, M., Svendsen, M., Meinzen-Dick, R. with Makombe, G. (1994). *Irrigation performance in Zimbabwe.* Faculty of Agriculture, University of Zimbabwe, Harare.

Russell, S. and Gilson, L. (1997). User fee policies to promote health service access for the poor: a wolf in sheep's clothing? *International Journal of Health Planning and Management* 27(2): 359-79.

Ryan, J. G. and Ghodake, R. D. (1980). *Labour market behaviour in rural villages of South India: Effects of season, sex and socioeconomic status.* ICRISAT Economics Program Progress Report No. 15.

Sahn, D. E. and Alderman, H. (1988). The effects of human capital on wages, and the determinants of labour supply in a developing country. *Journal of Development Economics* 29(2): 157-83.

Sahn, D. E. and Arulpragasam, J. (1991). *Development through dualism? Land tenure, policy, and poverty in Malawi.* Cornell University: Ithaca, New York. Cornell Food and Nutrition Policy Program Working Paper No. 9.

Sahn, D. E., Stifel, D. and Younger, S. (1999). *Inter-temporal changes in welfare: preliminary results from nine African countries.* Cornell University, Ithaca, New York. Cornell Food and Nutrition Policy Program Working Paper No. 94.

Saito, K., Mekonnen, H. and Spurling, D. (1994). *Raising the productivity of women farmers in Sub-Saharan Africa.* World Bank: Washington DC. World Bank Discussion Paper No. 230.

Sanyal, S. K. (1976). A review of the conceptual framework of land holdings surveys. *Indian Journal of Agricultural Economics* 31: 2-10.

Sara, J. and Katz, T. (1997). *Making rural water supply sustainable: recommendations from a global study.* World Bank: Washington DC.

Sarin, M. and Singh, N. (2001). Analysis of Joint Forest Management in UP and Orissa. In Contreras, A. *et al.* (2001). *Creating space for local forest management*, CIFOR: Bogor (forthcoming).

Sarvekshana (1979). National sample survey organisation. Department of Statistics, Government of India.

Sarvekshana (1997). 21:3. National sample survey organisation. Department of Statistics, Government of India.

Sastry, N. (1997). What explains rural-urban differences in child mortality in Brazil? *Social Science and Medicine* 44(7): 989-1002.

Satya Sundaram, I. (1989). Improving rural housing. *Kurukshetra* 37(12).

Saxena, K. B. (1990). Access to land as an instrument of poverty alleviation. *Journal of Rural Development* 9(1).

Saxena, N. C. (1996). Forests under people's management in Orissa. *Social Change* 26(1): 68-83.

Schneider, G. and Sharma, M. (1999). Impact of finance on poverty reduction and social capital formation: a review and synthesis of empirical evidence. *Savings and Development* 23(1): 67-91.

Schultz, T. P. (1988). Education investments and returns. In Chenery, H. B. and Srinivasan, T. N. (eds), *Handbook of Development Economics* 1. North Holland: Amsterdam.

— (1999). *Women's role in the agricultural household: bargaining and human capital.* Economic Growth Center Discussion Paper 803. Yale University.

Schultz, T. P. and Tansel, A. (1997). Wage and labor supply effects of illness in Côte d'Ivoire and Ghana: instrumental variable estimates for days disabled. *Journal of Development Economics* 48: 1-36.

Schultz, T. W. (1964). *Transforming traditional agriculture.* Yale University.

— (1975). The uneven prospects for gains from agricultural research related to economic policy. Paper prepared for the conference on Resource Allocation and Productivity in International Agricultural Research, Airlie House, Virginia, January 26-29, 1975. International Maize and Wheat Improvement Center: Mexico.

SCN Special Commission (2000). *Fourth report on the world nutrition situation.* United Nations Administrative Committee on Co-ordination-Subcommittee on Nutrition.

Scott, C. D. (1999). Mixed fortunes: a study of poverty mobility among small farm households in Chile, 1968-86. Presented at IDS/IFPRI Workshop on Poverty Dynamics, April 1999. Institute of Development Studies, Brighton.

Scott, C. D. and Litchfield, J. A. (1994). *Inequality, mobility and determinants of income among the rural poor in Chile 1968-86.* London School of Economics, London. Suntory and Toyota Centres for Economics and Related Disciplines DP No. 35.

Seabright, P. (1997). Is cooperation habit forming? In Dasgupta, P. and Maler, K. G. (eds). *Environment and emerging development issues.* Clarendon Press: Oxford.

Sen, A. (1981). *Poverty and famines: an essay on entitlement and deprivation.* Oxford University Press: Oxford.

— (1990). Gender and cooperative conflicts. In Tinker, I. (ed.). *Persistent inequalities: women and world development.* Oxford University Press: New York.

Seyoum, S. (1992). *Economics of small ruminant meat production and consumption in Sub-Saharan Africa in small ruminant research and development in Africa.* Proceedings of the first biennial conference of the African Small Ruminant Research Network, ILRAD, Nairobi 10-14 Dec. 1990. International Livestock Centre for Africa, Nairobi, Kenya.

Shaffer, P. (1999). The poverty debate with application to the Republic of Guinea. PhD Thesis, Institute of Development Studies, Sussex.

Shah, A. (1997). Jurisdiction versus equity: tale of two villages. *Wastelands News*, February-April, 58-63.

Shah, T. and Raju, K. V. (1988). Working of groundwater markets in Andhra Pradesh and Gujerat: results of two village studies. *Economic and Political Weekly* 26 March: A23-8.

Shaka, J. M., Ngailo, J. A. and Wickama, J. M. (1996). How rice cultivation became an 'indigenous' farming practice in Maswa District, Tanzania. In Reij, C., Scoones, I. and Toulmin, C. (eds), *Sustaining the soil: indigenous soil and water conservation in Africa.* Earthscan Publications Ltd: London.

Shankar, K. (1981). *Working of tubewells in Phulpur Block.* GB Pant Social Science Institute, Allahabad. Project Report No. 3.

Shanmugaratham, N. (1996). Nationalisation, privatisation and the dilemmas of common property management in Western Rajasthan. *Journal of Development Studies* 33(2): 163-87.

Shari, I. (1992). National agricultural policy, rural poverty and income inequalities: a critical evaluation. *Malaysian Journal of Agricultural Economics* 9.

Sharma, R. and Poleman, T. T. (1994). *The new economics of India's green revolution: income and employment diffusion in Uttar Pradesh.* Vikas Publishing House: New Dehli.

Shearer, E., Lastarria-Cornhiel, S. and Mestah, D. (1991). *The reform of rural land markets in Latin America and the Caribbean: research, theory and policy implications.* Land Tenure Centre: University of Wisconsin, Madison. Paper No. 141.

Shetty, P. S. (1997). Obesity and physical activity. *Bulletin of the Nutritional Foundation of India.* 18(2).

Shiferaw, B. and Holden, S. T. (1997). *A farm household analysis of resource use and conservation decisions of smallholders: an application to highland farmers in Ethiopia.* Department of Economics and Social Sciences, Agricultural University of Norway. Discussion Paper D-03/1997.

Sidahmed, A. (2000). Rangeland development for the rural poor in developing countries: the experience of IFAD. In Scherr, S. and Yadav, S. Y. (ed.).

Simmons, N. (1981). *Principles of crop improvement.* Longmans: Harlow.

Singh, A. J. and Byerlee, D. (1990). Relative variability in wheat yields across countries and over time. *Journal of Agricultural Economics* 41(1): 21-32.

Singh, B. (1985). *Agrarian structure, technological change and poverty: microlevel evidence.* Agricole: Bombay.

Singh, G. (1995). An agroforestry practice for the development of salt land using prospis juliflora and leptochloa fusca. Agroforestry Systems, 29(1):61-75.

Singh, I. J. (1990). *The Great Ascent: the rural poor in South Asia.* Johns Hopkins University Press: Baltimore.

Sinha, S. (ed.) (1998). Micro-credit: Impact, Targeting and Sustainability, *IDS Bulletin*, Vol. 29, No. 4.

Sinha, S. and Lipton, M. (1999). Damaging fluctuations, risk and poverty: a review. Background paper for the World Development Report 2000/1. Poverty Research Unit at Sussex, October.

Siroki, S. and Siroki, S. K. (1993). Socio-economic profile of livestock owners: a case study. *Journal of Education and Social Change* 7.

Sjaastad, E. and Bromley, D. W. (1997). Indigenous land rights in Sub-Saharan Africa: Appropriation, Security and Investment Demand. *World Development* 25(4): 549-62.

Skoufias, E. (1993). Labour market opportunities and intrafamily time allocation in rural households in South Asia. *Journal of Development Economics* 40(2): 277-310.

Sperling, L. and Berkowitz, P. (1994). *Partners in selection: bean breeders and women bean experts in Uganda*, CGIAR Gender Program, Washington DC.

Spillman, W. J. (1919). The agricultural ladder. *American Economic Review.* Papers and proceedings 9: 170-9.

Srivastava, H. C. and Chaturvedi, M. K. (1989). *Dependency and common property resource of tribal and rural poor.* Commonwealth Publishers: New Delhi.

Stanfield, J. D. (1989). Agrarian reform in the Dominican Republic. In Thiesenhusen, W. (ed.), *Searching for agrarian reform in Latin America.* Unwin Hyman: Boston.

Stanfield, J. D., Lastarria-Cornhiel, S., Bruce, J. and Friedman, E. (1992). *Property rights in Albania's new private farm sector.* Land Tenure Center, University of Wisconsin: Madison. Paper No. 1496.

Stark, O. (1991). *Migration of labour.* Oxford: Blackwell.

Stockle, C. O. and Villar, J. M. (1993). Efficient use of water in irrigated agriculture and limitations to increasing water use efficiency. In Singh, S. D. (ed), *Arid land, irrigation and ecological management.* Scientific Publishers: Jodhpur.

Strasma, J. (1989). Unfinished business: consolidating land reform in El Salvador. In Thiesenhusen, W. (ed.), *Searching for agrarian reform in Latin America.* Unwin Hyman: Boston.

Strauss, J. and Thomas, D. (1995). *Health, nutrition, and economic development.* Labor and Population Program Working Paper Series 23, RAND, Santa Monica, CA.

Sudhardjo (1986). *The effect of iron intervention on work productivity of tea pickers.* Bogor Agricultural Unit: Indonesia.

Sultana, N., Nazli, H. and Malik, S. J. (1994). Determinants of female time allocation in selected districts of rural Pakistan. *Pakistan Development Review* 33(4): Pt.2, 1141-53.

Svedberg, P. (1989). Undernutrition in Africa: is there a sex bias? Mimeo. Stockholm Institute for International Economic Studies.

Swallow, B. M. and Bromley, D. (1994). Institutions, governance and incentives in common property regimes for African rangelands. *Environmental and Resource Economics.*

Swamy, D. S. (1988). Agricultural tenancy in the 1970s. *Indian Journal of Agricultural Economics* 43(4).

Tabbal, D., Lampayan, R. and Bhuiyan, S. I. (1992). *Water saving irrigation technique for rice.* Presented at the International Workshop on Soil and Water Engineering for Paddy Field Management, Agricultural Land and Water Development Program. Asian Institute of Technology, Bangkok, Thailand, January 28-30, 1992.

Tamang, H. D. and Dharam, K. C. (1995). *Innovation in primary school construction: community participation in Seti Zone, Nepal: a case study.* UNESCO Principal Regional Office for Asia and the Pacific: Bangkok.

Tang, S. Y. (1991). Institutional arrangements and the management of common pool resources. In *Public Administration Review* 51(2): 42-51.

— (1992). *Institutions and collective action: self-governance in irrigation.* Institute for Contemporary Studies Press: San Francisco.

Tapson, D. (1990). A socio-economic analysis of smallholder cattle producers in KwaZulu. Ph.D. thesis. Department of Business Economics, Vista University, Pretoria.

Taylor, C. E., Kielmann, A. A., de Sweemer, C., Uberoi, I. S., Takula, H. S. and Newman, C. G. (1978). The Narangwal project on interactions of nutrition and infections, 1. Project design and the effects upon growth. *Indian Journal of Medical Research* 68 (suppl).

Tendler, J. (1991). *New lessons from old projects: the dynamics of rural development in north-east Brazil.* Operations Evaluation Department, World Bank and Department of Urban Studies and Planning: Massachusetts Institute of Technology.

— (1997). *Good government in the tropics.* John Hopkins University Press: Baltimore.

Tendulkar, S and Jain, L. R. (1997). *Macroeconomic policies and poverty in India, 1966-67 to 1994-95.* International Labour Office: Geneva.

Thiesenhusen, W. C. and Melmed-Sanjak, J. (1990). Brazil's agrarian structure: changes from 1970 through 1980. *World Development* 18(3): 393-415.

Thiesenhusen, W. (ed.) (1989). *Searching for agrarian reform in Latin America.* Unwin Hyman: Boston.

Thobani, M. (1997). Formal water markets: why, when and how to introduce tradable water rights. *World Bank Research Observer* 12(2): 161-79.

Thomas, D. (1986). Can food shares be used as a welfare measure? Unpublished Ph.D. dissertation, Princeton University.

Thomas, D., Strauss, J. and Hendriques, M. (1991). How does mother's education affect child height. *Journal of Human Resources* 26: 183-211.

Thomas-Slayter, B. and Bhatt, N. (1994). Land, livestock and livelihoods: changing dynamics of gender, caste and ethnicity in a Nepalese village. *Human Ecology* 22(4): 462-94.

Thome, J. R. (1989). Law, conflict and change: Frei's law and Allende's agrarian reform. In Thiesenhusen, W. (ed.), *Searching for agrarian reform in Latin America.* Unwin Hyman: Boston.

Thorner, D. (1980). *The shaping of modern India.* Published for Sameeksha Trust by Allied Publishers Ltd.

Thrupp, L. A., Bergeron, G. and Waters, W. (1995). *Bittersweet harvests for global supermarkets: Challenges in Latin America's agricultural export boom.* World Resources Institute: Washington DC.

Tiffen, M., Mortimore, M. and Gichuki, F. (1994). *Population growth and environmental recovery: policy lessons from Kenya.* Sustainable Agriculture Programme, Gatekeeper series No. 45. International Institute for Environment and Development, London.

Turner, S. D. (1996). *Conservancies in Namibia: a model for successful common property resource management?* University of Namibia. Social Sciences Division Discussion Paper 13.

Turner, T. E., Kaara, W. M. and Brownhill, L. S. (1997). Social reconstruction in rural Africa: a gendered class analysis of women's resistance to export crop production in Kenya. *Canadian Journal of Development Studies* 18(2): 213-38.

Tyler, G. J., El-Ghonemy, R. and Yves, C. (1993). Alleviating rural poverty through agricultural growth. *Journal of Development Studies* 29(2): 358-64.

Udall, A. T. (1981). Transport improvements and rural outmigration in Colombia. *Economic Development and Cultural Change* 29: 613-29.

Udry, C. (1996). Gender, agricultural production and the theory of the household. *Journal of Political Economy* 104(5):1010-46.

UN Demographic Yearbooks 1979, 1985, 1996. United Nations Statistical Office.

UN (1991). *Barriers to access of rural women to land, livestock, other productive assets and credit in selected African countries.* United Nations Economic Commission for Africa: Addis Ababa.

— (1998). World urbanization prospects: The 1996 revision. Estimates and projections of urban and rural populations and of urban agglomerations. United Nations: New York.

— (1999). *World population prospects: the 1998 revision.* 1. United Nations: New York.

UNDP (1993). *Human development report 1993.* Oxford University Press: New York

— (2000). *Human development report 2000.* Oxford University Press: New York

UN/ECOSOC (1998). *World urbanisation prospects: the 1996 revision.* United Nations, population division: New York.

UNESCO Statistical yearbooks. United Nations Educational, Scientific and Cultural Organisation.

UNICEF (1995). WATSAN India 2000. United Nations Children's Fund.

— (1996). The state of the world's children. United Nations Children's Fund.

— (1999). The state of the world's children. United Nations Children's Fund.

UNICED (1992). Report of the United Nations conference on environment and development. 26 A/Conf.151/26. 12 August 1992.

USDA/ARS. (1993). USDA programs related to integrated pest management. USDA Program Aid 1506. Beltsville, MD: United States Department of Agriculture/ Agricultural Research Service. *Cambridge Journal of Economics* 11: 95-106.

van de Fliert, E., Pontius, J. and Ling, N.R. (1995). Searching for strategies to replicate a successful extension approach: training of IPM trainers in Indonesia. *European Journal of Agricultural Education and Extension* 1: 41-63.

van de Sand, K. (2000). The role of rural organisations in empowerment of the rural poor -- the experience of IFAD, Agriculture - Rural Development, 1:2000

van den Breemer, J. P. M., Drijver, C. A. and Venema, L. B. (1995). Local resource management in Africa. Study Group 'Environment and Development'. Wiley: Chichester.

van der Grift, E. (1991). Gender relations in traditional irrigation in Malolo, Tanzania. M.Sc. dissertation, Department of Irrigation and Soil and Water Conservation, Wageningen Agricultural University in collaboration with SNV Tanzania.

van Koppen, B. (1998). Water rights and poverty alleviation: inclusion and exclusion of resource-poor women and men as rights holders in externally supported irrigation development. In Merrey, D. and Baviskar, S. (eds), (1998). *Gender analysis and reform of irrigation management: concepts, cases and gaps in knowledge*, Proceedings of the Workshop on Gender and Water, 15-19 September 1997, Habarana, Sri Lanka. International Water Management Institute.

van Tuijl, W. (1993). *Improving water use in agriculture: experiences in the Middle East and North Africa.* World Bank: Washington DC. World Bank Technical Paper No. 201.

van Veen, T. W. S. (1997). *Integrated pest management: strategies and policies for effective, environmentally sustainable development.* World Bank: Washington DC. Studies and Monograph Series No. 13.

van Vilsteren, A. E. M. and Srkirin, S. (1987). *Computerised water allocation scheduling and monitoring in the Mae Klong irrigation scheme in Thailand.* 1B, question 40, reply 71. Transactions of the Thirteenth International Conference on Irrigation and Drainage, Rabat. ICID: New Delhi.

Varughese, G. (1998). Coping with changes in population and forest resource: institutional mediation in the middle hills of Nepal. In Gibson, C., McKean, M. A. and Ostrom, E. (1998) (eds). *Forest resources and institutions*, Forestry, trees and people programme, FAO: Rome. Working Paper 3.

Virk, D. S., Harris, D., Raghuwanshi, B., Roy, A., Sodhi, P. and Witcombe, J. (2000). A holistic approach to participatory crop improvement in wheat, presented at an International Symposium on *Participatory Plant Genetic Resource Enhancement: An Exchange of Experiences from South and South East Asia*, held at Pokhara, Nepal, 1-5 May 2000.

Visaria, P. (1980). *Poverty and unemployment in India: an analysis of recent evidence.* World Bank: Washington DC. World Bank Staff Working Paper No. 417.

Vogel, I. (2000). *Supermarkets.* Background note prepared for IFAD's Rural Poverty Report 2001: the challenge of ending rural poverty..

von Braun, J., Bayes, F. and Akhter, R. (1999). Village pay phones and poverty reduction. ZEF Discussion Papers on Development Policy No.18. Centre for Development Research, University of Berlin.

von Braun, J. and Kennedy, E. (1994) (eds). *Agricultural commercialization, economic development, and nutrition.* John Hopkins University Press for the International Food Policy Research Institute.

von Braun, J., Hotchkiss, D. and Immink, M. (1989a). *Nontraditional export crops in Guatemala: effects on production, income and nutrition.* International Food Policy Research Institute: Washington DC. Research Report No.73.

von Braun, J., Puetz, D. and Webb, P. (1989b). *Irrigation technology and commercialization of rice in the Gambia: effects on income and nutrition.* International Food Policy Research Institute: Washington DC. Research Report No. 75.

von Oppen, M., Njehia, B. K. and Ijaimi, A. (1997). The impact of market access on agricultural productivity: Lessons from India, Kenya and the Sudan. *Journal of International Development* 9(1): 117-31.

von Pischke, J. D. and Adams, D. W. (1992). Microenterprise credit programs: déjà vu. *World Development* 20(10): 1463-70.

Vosti, S., Reardon, T. and von Urff, W. (1991). *Agricultural Sustainability, Growth and Poverty Alleviation.* Food and Agriculture Development Centre, Feldafing.

Vyas, V. S. (1976). Structural change in agriculture and the small farm sector. *Economic and Political Weekly* 11: 1-2.

Wade, R. (1975). *Irrigation and income distribution: three papers.* Institute of Development Studies: Brighton. IDS Discussion Paper No. 85.

— (1982). Corruption where does the money go? *Economic and Political Weekly* 20 Oct: 1606.

— (1987). The management of common property resources: finding a co-operative advantage. *World Bank Research Observer* 2(2): 219-34.

— (1988). *Village republics: economic conditions for collective action in South India.* Cambridge University Press.

Walker, T. S. and Ryan, J. G. 1996. *Village and household economies in India's semi-arid tropics.* John Hopkins University Press: Baltimore.

White, H. (1996). How much aid is used for poverty reduction? *IDS bulletin* 27(1): 83-99.

White, I.. (1962). *Medieval technology and social change.* Oxford University Press: Oxford.

White, T. A. and Runge, C. F. (1995). The emergence and evolution of collective action: lessons from watershed management in Haiti. *World Development* 23(10): 1683-98.

Whitehead, A. (1990) Wives and mothers: female farmers in Africa. ILO World Employment Programme. Population and labour policies programme Working Paper No. 170. International Labour Organisation: Geneva.

WHO (1999). *World Health Report.* World Health Organisation: Geneva

Windle, J. and Cramb, R. A. (1997). Remoteness and rural development: economic impacts of rural roads on upland farmers in Sarawak, Malaysia. *Asia-Pacific Viewpoint* 38(1).

Winters, L. A. (1999). Trade policy and poverty. Background paper for World Development Report 2000.

— (2000). *Trade liberalisation and poverty.* University of Sussex: Brighton. Poverty Research Unit at Sussex Working Paper No. 7.

Witcombe, J. R. (2000). *Participatory varietal selection in high-potential production systems.* Proceedings of South Asian Conference on Participatory Plant Breeding and Plant Genetic Resource Management, 1-5 May 2000, Pokhara, Nepal.

Witcombe, J. R., Subedi, M. and Joshi, K. R. (2000a). *Towards a practical participatory plant breeding strategy in predominantly self-pollinated crops.* Proceedings of South Asian Conference on Participatory Plant Breeding and Plant Genetic Resource Management, 1-5 May 2000, Pokhara, Nepal.

Witcombe, J. R., Joshi, K. R., Rana, R. B. and Virk, D. S. (2000b). Broadening genetic diversity in high-potential production systems by participatory varietal selection. Euphytica special issue of participatory plant breeding, forthcoming.

Wittfogel, K. (1957). *Oriental despotism: a comparative study of total power.* Yale University Press: New Haven.

Wodon, Q. (1999). *Poverty and policy in Latin America and the Caribbean.* World Bank Discussion draft: Washington DC.

Wolff, P. and Stein, T. M. (1998). Water efficiency and conservation in agriculture-opportunities and limitations. *Agriculture and Rural Development* 2: 2-20.

Wolters, W. (1992). *Influences on the efficiency of irrigation water use.* International Institute for Land Reclamation and Improvement: Wageningen. Publication No. 51.

Wood, G. D. and Palmer-Jones, R. (1991). *The water sellers: a co-operative venture by the rural poor.* Intermediate Technology Publications.

World Bank (1989). India: Poverty, employment and social services. World Bank: Washington DC. Country Economic Memorandum, India Department. Report No. 7516-IN.

— (1990). *World development report 1990.* World Bank: Washington DC.

— (1991). *World development report 1991.* World Bank: Washington DC.

— (1992a). *World development report 1992.* World Bank: Washington DC.

— (1992b). *China: strategies for reducing poverty in the 1990s.* A World Bank Country Study. World Bank: Washington D.C.

— (1993). *Peru: poverty assessment and social policies and programs for the poor.* World Bank: Washington DC. Report No. 11191-PE.

— (1994a). *World development report 1994.* World Bank: Washington DC.

— (1994b). *Poverty in Colombia.* World Bank: Washington DC. Report No. 12673-CO.

— (1994c). *Honduras poverty assessment.* World Bank: Washington DC. Report No. 13317-HO.

— (1995a). *Rural women in the Sahel and their access to agricultural extensionsector study: overview of five country studies.* World Bank: Washington DC. Report No. 13532.

— (1995b). *Guatemala: an assessment of poverty.* World Bank: Washington DC. Report No. 12313-GU.

— (1995c). *Republic of Nicaragua: poverty assessment.* World Bank: Washington DC. Report No. 14038-NI Vols. I & II.

— (1995d). *The KyrgyzRepublic poverty assessment and income strategy.* World Bank: Washington DC.

— (1995e). *Ghana: poverty past, present and future.* World Bank: Washington DC. Report No. 14504-GH.

— (1995f). *The Philippines: a strategy to fight poverty.* World Bank: Washington DC. Report No. 14933-PH.

— (1995g). *Sri Lanka: poverty assessment.* World Bank: Washington DC. Report No. 13431-CE.

— (1995h). *Ecuador poverty assessment.* World Bank: Washington DC. Report No. 14533-EC.

— (1995i). *Pakistan poverty assessment.* World Bank: Washington DC. Report No. 14397-PAK.

— (1995j). *Kenya: poverty assessment.* World Bank: Washington DC. Report No. 13152-KE.

— (1995k). Chile: Estrategia para elevar la competitividad agricola y aliviar la pobreza rural. World Bank: Washington DC.

— (1996a). *Nigeria: poverty in the midst of plenty: the challenge of growth with inclusion: a World Bank poverty assessment.* World Bank: Washington DC. Report No. 14733-HO.

— (1996b). *Bangladesh rural finance.* World Bank: Washington DC. Report No. 15484-BD.

— (1996c). Bolivia: Poverty, equity and income. World Bank: Washington DC. Report No. 15272-BO.

— (1997). *World development report 1997.* World Bank: Washington DC.

— (1998a). *World development report 1998/1999.* Knowledge for development. Oxford University Press: New York.

— (1998b). *Nicaragua basic education project. Staff appraisal report.* Latin America and the Caribbean. Human and Social Development Group. In. Gaynor, C *Decentralisation of education. Teacher management.* Directions in development. World Bank: Washington DC.

— (1999a). Voices of the poor PREM 29 Sept 1999.

— (1999b). *World development indicators.* World Bank: Washington DC.

— (1999c). *Gender, growth and poverty reduction.* World Bank Technical Paper No. 428. World Bank: Washington DC.

— (2000a). *World development report 2000/2001.* World Bank: Washington DC.

— (2000b). *World development indicators 2000.* World Bank: Washington DC.

— (2000c). Voices of the poor. World Bank: Washington DC.

— (2000d). Cambodia: Discussion note on partnerships. Draft prepared for Consultative Group meeting May 2000.

— (2000e). Poverty status report for Sub-Saharan Africa. Special Programme Assistance for Africa. World Bank: Washington DC.

WHO (1999). *World health report.* World Health Organisation: Geneva.

World Resources Institute (1992). *Annual report of the state of the world's resources.*

World Water Council (2000). *A water secure world: vision for water, life and the environment.* World Water Vision Commission Report. World Water Council.

Xie, M., Küffner, U. and Le Moigne, G. (1993). *Using water efficiently: technological options.* World Bank: Washington DC. World Bank Technical Paper 205.

Yaqub, S. (2000). *Poverty dynamics in developing countries.* IDS: Brighton. Development Bibliography 16.

Ye, X., al-Babili, S., Kloeti, A., Jing Zhang, Lucca, P., Beyer, P. and Potrykus, I. (2000). Engineering the provitamin-A (beta-carotene). biosynthetic pathway into (carotenoid-free). rice endosperm. *Science* 287: 303-5.

Yoder, R. A. (1989). Are people willing and able to pay for health services? Social *Science and Medicine* 29(1): 35-44.

Young, A. (1998). *Land resources: now and for the future.* Cambridge University Press.

Yudelman, M. (1993). *Demand and supply of foodstuffs up to 2050 with special reference to irrigation.* International Irrigation Management Institute: Colombo, Sri Lanka. Report prepared for the International Irrigation Management Institute.

Yugandhar, K. and Iyer, G. (eds) (1993). *Land reforms in India. Volume 1, Bihar: institutional constraints.* Lal Bahadur Shastri National Academy of Administration. Sage: New Delhi.

Zaman, H., 1998, 'Can Mis-Targeting be justified? Insights from BRAC's micro-credit programme', IDS Bulletin, V. 29, No. 4: 59-65.

Zevallos, J. V. (1989). Agrarian reform and structural change: Ecuador since 1964. In Thiesenhusen, W. (ed.), *Searching for agrarian reform in Latin America.* Unwin Hyman: Boston.

Zimmerer, K. S. (1993). Soil erosion and labour shortages in the Andes with special reference to Bolivia, 1953-91: Implications for conservation-with-development. *World Development* 21(10): 1659-75.

Zwarteveen, M. Z. (1997). Water: from basic need to commodity: a discussion on gender and water rights in the context of irrigation. *World Development* 25(8): 1335-49.

Zwarteveen, M. and Neupane, N. (1995). Gender aspects of irrigation management: the Chhattis Mauja irrigation system in Nepal. *Asia-Pacific Journal of Rural Development* 5(1).

Acronyms and abbreviations

ADAB	Association of Development Agencies in Bangladesh
AP	Asia and the Pacific region of IFAD
CAM	Carte d'assurance Maladie
CAMPFIRE	Communal Areas Management Programme for Indigenous Resources
CBN	Cost-of-basic-need
CBRM	Community Based Resource Management
CE	Conveyance Efficiency
CEPAL	Economic Commission for Latin America and the Caribbean
CFM	Community Forest Management
CGIAR	Consultative Group on International Agricultural Development
CDF	Comprehensive Development Framework
CFC	Clorofluorocarbon
CIAT	International Centre for Tropical Agriculture
CIMMYT	International Centre for Maize and Wheat Improvement
CIS	Confederation of Independent States
CLUSA	Cooperative League of the USA
CONCRAB	Confederation of Agrarian Reform Cooperation in Brazil
CT	Conservation Tillage
DAC	Development Assistance Committee
DHS	Demographic and Health Survey
DRAW	Demand Responsive Approach to Water
DWACRA	Development of Women and Children in Rural Area
EEW	Economic Efficiency of Water
EGS	Employment Guarantee Scheme
ESA	East and Southern Africa region of IFAD
ESAF	Extended Structural Adjustment Facility
FAO	Food and Agriculture Organization of the United Nations
FE	Field Efficiency
FEE	Food for Education
FEM	Food Energy Method
FLO	Fair Trade Labelling Organization
FSM	Food-share Method
GDP	Gross Domestic Product
GM	Genetic Modification
GNP	Gross National Product
HCI	Head Count Index
HDI	Human Development Index
HIPC	Highly Indebted Poorest Countries
HIV/AIDS	Human Immunodeficiency Virus/ Acquired Immunodeficiency Syndrome
HPI	Human Poverty Index
HYV	High Yielding Variety
ICARDA	International Centre for Agricultural Research in the Dry Areas
ICRISAT	International Crop Research Institute for the Semi-Arid Tropics
IDA	International Development Association
IDS	Institute of Development Studies
IFAD	International Fund for Agricultural Development
IFPRI	International Food Policy Research Institute
IITA	International Institute of Tropical Agriculture
ILMT	Improved land Management Technology
IMT	Irrigation Management Transfer
IMF	International Monetary Fund
IPM	Integrated Pest Management
IRRI	International Rice Research Institute
JFM	Joint Farm Management
LAC	Latin America and the Caribbean region of IFAD
LSMS	Living Standards Measurement Study
MC	Marketing Cooperative
MFI	Microfinance Institutions
MKSS	Mazdoor Kishan Shakti Sangathan (Workers, Farmers Power Organization)
MST	Movimento des Trabalhadores Rurais Sema Terra
NARS	National Agricultural Research Centres
NABARD	National Bank for Agricultural and Rural Development
NENA	Near East and North Africa region of IFAD
NGO	Non Government Organizations
NTG	Non Target Group
OECD	Organisation of Economic Cooperation and Development
PGI	Poverty Gap Index
PIM	Participatory Irrigation Management
PPP	Purchasing Power Parity
PRGF	Poverty Reduction and Growth Facility
PRSP	Poverty Reduction Strategy Paper

REFLECT	Regenerated Freirean Literacy through Empowering Community Techniques		UNESCO	United Nations Educational, Scientific and Cultural Organization
RGE	Rural Group Enterprise		UNCED	United Nations Conference on Environment and Development
RNFS	Rural Non-farm Sector		UNICEF	United Nations Children's Fund
ROSCAS	Rotating Savings and Credit Associations		UP	Union Parishad
SEWA	Self Employed Women's Association		USD	United States Dollar
SMC	School Management Committee		USDA/ARS	United States Department of Agriculture/ Agricultural Research Survey
SSI/WC	Small Scale Irrigation/Water Control		VLOM	Village Level Operation and Maintenance
TFR	Total Fertility Rate		WARDA	West Africa's Rice Development
UCLA	University of California at Los Angeles		WCA	West and Central Africa region of IFAD
UNAIDS	Joint United Nations Programme on HIV/AIDS		WHO	World Health Organisation
UNDAF	United Nations Development Assistance Framework		WUA	Water Users' Association
UNDP	United Nations Development Programme		WUE	Water Use Efficiency
ECOSOC	Economic and Social Council			